The Big Tomorrow

Lary May

THE BIG TOMORROW

Hollywood and the Politics of the American Way

The University of Chicago Press • Chicago and London

LARY MAY teaches in the history and American Studies departments at the University of Minnesota. He is author of *Screening Out the Past: The Birth of Mass Culture and the Motion Picture Industry* (reprint, 1983) and editor of *Recasting America: Culture and Politics in the Age of Cold War* (1989), both published by the University of Chicago Press.

The University of Chicago Press, Chicago 60637
The University of Chicago Press, Ltd., London
© 2000 by The University of Chicago
All rights reserved. Published 2000
Printed in the United States of America
09 08 07 06 05 04 03 02 01 00   1 2 3 4 5

ISBN: 0-226-51162-6 (cloth)

Library of Congress Cataloging-in-Publication Data

May, Lary.
    The big tomorrow : Hollywood and the politics of the American way / Lary May.
       p.   cm.
    Includes bibliographical references and index.
    ISBN 0-226-51162-6 (cloth : alk.)
    1. Motion pictures—Social aspects—United States. 2. Motion pictures—Political aspects—United States. I. Title.

PN1995.9.S6M343   2000
302.23'45—dc21
                                                                                99-057265

For Jimmy, Norma, and Larry
Who Lived the Big Tomorrow

Contents

Illustrations

Acknowledgments

W ill Rogers loved to satirize promoters of the self-made man and lone pioneer as spinners of bogus ideas intended to deny our dependence on the labor of our friends and associates. In the process of writing this book, I have become acutely aware of the Cherokee comic's wisdom. This work simply could not have been completed without the support and cooperation of a larger scholarly and publishing community that bound us together in mutual interdependence.

My major debt begins with those who made the research possible. I wish to thank the staff and leaders of the American Studies program, the College of Liberal Arts, and the Graduate School of the University of Minnesota, who supplied support, a sabbatical, and released time to complete my investigation and writing. I also wish to thank the National Endowment for the Humanities and the University of Minnesota McKnight Fund for providing me with summer research grants.

All who do research recognize that our work could not be completed without the assistance of a number of institutions and their archivists. Linda Mehr, director of the Academy of Motion Picture Arts and Sciences Library, and her assistant Carol Cullen, Sam Gill of Special Collections, and Robert Cushman of Photographic Reproductions were especially helpful, along with their able staffs. Joseph H. Carter, the director of the Will Rogers Memorial Archive in Claremore, Oklahoma, and Patricia Lowe, its librarian/archivist, embody the spirit of Will Rogers, whose generosity and dedication to the public good were remarkable. I could not have written and illustrated the chapter on Will Rogers without their research facilities and their assistance. Charles Silver and Mary Corliss of the Museum of Modern Art Film Library provided valuable help. Kim Felner and Valerie Yaros of the Screen Actors Guild generously allowed me entry into the Guild's files in Hollywood. The chapter on the Guild could not have been written without their aid. I also wish to thank David Eldridge and the staff at the Dwight D. Eisenhower Library in Abilene, Kansas, for providing materials on the work of the Central Intelligence Agency in Hollywood.

Several graduate student research assistants provided invaluable aid. Stephen Lassonde provided major assistance in unraveling the contradictions between official attendance data and our findings from other sources concerning audiences from the twenties through World War II. Colette Hyman worked as a research assistant in the early stages of the project. Chris Lewis, Scott Zimmerman, Jonathan Munby, and Michael Willard traced the changing contours of narrative structures over time. Without their superb computer skills and keen eye for telling details, the measurement of plot data would have been impossible. Near the end, David Gray, Mary Rizzo, and Matt Becker provided invaluable editorial assistance.

A number of friends and colleagues have read some or all of the manuscript. At a critical stage David Noble and Carl Schorske alerted me to the major transformation in American culture and politics that unfolded after World War II. Since this shift in identity is one of the major themes of this book, their advice helped me to make sense of conflicting evidence that refused to fall into traditional conceptual categories. Jeffrey Brooks, Steven Ross, Harry Boyte, and Lynn Dumenil read the manuscript and helped me to see new lines of organization and conceptualization. I am also grateful for the encouragement and advice of John Wright, Riv-Ellen Prell, Reinhold Wagnleitner, George Lipsitz, Carol Miller, and the anonymous reviewers for the University of Chicago Press, who saved me from a number of errors and pointed to new lines of inquiry. Lastly, Lewis Erenberg, my close friend for over thirty years, read the manuscript with a keen eye and encouraged me when I needed it most. I will always remember and cherish his advice and companionship.

Douglas Mitchell of the University of Chicago Press has been a most supportive editor over the long process of developing and writing this book. I wish to thank him for many a good meal and keen advice all along the way. I wish also to thank Matt Howard, Robert Devens, and Leslie Keros of the Press. Richard Audet deserves special mention for being an imaginative and careful copyeditor.

A very different kind of acknowledgment is due to my children, who became adults over the ten years that I worked on this project. Michael May discussed the relation between politics and art and helped fix the computer when it seemed to me nothing but a ball of confusion. Daniel May avidly joined me in watching old movies late at night and then dealt with friends who thought he was crazy for watching such "ancient stuff." Sarah May came up with interesting ideas in her own inimitable way about popular art that made me rethink old films and stars in a fresh way.

Above all, I wish to thank my wife, colleague, and love, Elaine Tyler May. More than she would care to acknowledge, she heard my ideas, read rough drafts, and helped me overcome paralyzing roadblocks. I owe her far more than I can express. All I can say is that it has been a joy living with her and our children over the past three decades.

Prologue: Nothing Is More American

Nothing is more American than Hollywood. All agree on that. Yet what does it mean to be "American" in the twentieth century? To believe current politicians and commentators, the question is up for grabs. Over the last twenty years our elections and everyday life have been dominated by pundits automatically assuming that the mass media are somehow deeply involved in defining what it means to be a citizen, a good wife and mother, a model minority. During every election, politicians from Ronald Reagan to Bob Dole, from Dan Quayle to Bill Clinton, debate on the stump the merits of rap music, black "gangsta" films, and television shows that focus on sex and unmarried pregnancies such as the famous episode of *Murphy Brown*. Before the 1996 election Bob Dole told conservative Republicans, "We have reached the point where our popular culture threatens to undermine our character as a nation" with "nightmares of depravity."[1] Critics from both the left and right assert that in the past Hollywood promoted traditional values, in sharp contrast to the present. Yet if this were the case, why did guardians of official culture from the twenties through the fifties often launch militant censorship crusades, perceiving many Hollywood films as a threat to family values and Americanism itself? What is not at all clear is why the mass media should evoke such controversy. How does the nation's popular culture become enmeshed in debates over the meaning of good citizenship in terms of sex, race, and class? Clearly, all the fury is not simply about "entertainment." Something else is going on, something that connects Hollywood to political power, cultural authority, and the very meaning of national identity.[2]

The Big Tomorrow argues that the film industry from the thirties to the sixties already played an important role in reshaping nationalism and public life. When Franklin Roosevelt became president, the country was largely an isolationist nation rooted in values of an Anglo-Saxon America that had marginalized women, ethnic minorities, and people of color from public life. The next four decades witnessed the rise of the United States to world leadership and redefined the nation to include women and minorities as full participants. And yet by the 1950s, evidence of discontent emerged from women and minorities, reflecting a national promise that was unfulfilled. Most scholars associate the transformation from an exclusive, homogeneous society to a more tolerant and inclusive one with the 1960s. But *The Big Tomorrow* demonstrates that the transformation began in the 1930s, and that the 1950s represented a return to a more intolerant and monolithic national culture, spurred by World War II and the Cold War. The makers of film noir and youth culture movies reflected the tension and anxiety generated by this turnaround and created the outlines of a distinct postwar culture.

By exploring the relation of politics to struggles over popular values, this study reveals how the modern film industry has been a major institution for shaping nationalism. Over the last decade the issue of nationalism—that is, the values, norms, and beliefs that mold a diverse people into a nation—has occupied scholars in a variety of fields. Yet it has not been studied in the context of the film industry. Led by Benedict Anderson, scholars have shown that the print media and the popular arts can provide the basis upon which a people "imagine" their common identity. In the United States prior to the thirties the country in many ways was "insufficiently imagined." That is, it excluded from positive representation the immigrants from southern and eastern Europe, racial minorities, and the modern culture of the cities. In the thirties, popular films began to validate these groups and experiences. While racism and sexism persisted, of course, the subtle shift in portrayals of minorities and women signaled the displacement of the older ethos of Anglo-Saxon nationhood in favor of a new Americanism rooted in ethnic pluralism, abundance, and modern life.[3]

It was also not accidental that I first became aware of the magnitude of this transformation for our understanding of modern American culture and civic values when I started to investigate the roots of a unique development that baffled the rest of the world: Why was it that a former movie star, Ronald Reagan, had become president of the United States? Why did he gain success by reviving the Cold War and containing the counterculture and the politics of the sixties? I also thought that I knew the general outlines of the answer. In writing my first book, *Screening Out the Past: The Birth of Mass Culture and the Motion Picture Industry,* I found that the Anglo-Saxon middle class at the turn of the century mounted fierce "Progressive" politics to at once "break up" the trusts and save Victorian family life. Yet by the twenties, politicians and the motion picture industry validated both a new corporate order and a new consumer culture focused on the home. Here the vision of the frontier—the central myth of the nation—was to be found in "Hollywood," where freedom could be pursued in leisure and a moral revolution based on European standards of high art and white superiority.[4] When I looked at Ronald Reagan's rise, I assumed my research would show how Hollywood was aligned with business and political interests from the thirties to the sixties and that Ronald Reagan was a prodigy of that inheritance.

Yet once I began my research, these preconceptions began to crumble and a planned book focusing on Ronald Reagan dissolved into something much larger and more important than I could have anticipated. My reassessment began as I gained permission to enter the archives and files of the Screen Actors Guild where Reagan had first entered politics as president of the actors' union in the forties. Instead of finding a Guild geared simply to protecting actors' job security and advancing the craft, I found many letters, magazine articles, minutes, and speeches detailing the involvement of the actors in the political movements of the New Deal. I found reviews of the social impact of the "realistic" films in which Guild members performed. Crammed into the files were dozens of fliers and announcements of meetings where actors supported President Roosevelt, formed alliances with workers, and backed the efforts of Mexican farm laborers to organize in the San Joaquin Valley. At the same time, the "stars" used their celebrity status to promote Labor Day parades and the inclusion of women and minorities in public life.

From there I found that an early Guild member and the most popular star of the 1930s was Will Rogers, a Cherokee Indian who promoted on the radio and on screen a "republican" creed hostile to monopoly capitalism and class inequality. According to Rogers and many other Guild leaders and moviemakers, the dream of abundance that in the twenties had been framed in aristocratic trappings had now become linked to the American democratic promise.[5] Drawing on a creed that had dominated American life for over a century, moviemakers imagined America as a place where citizens engaged in self-governing and created a New World republic free of aristocracy and capitalist power. In the past, the promoters of abolitionism, Black Reconstruction, unionization, and populist movements had evoked that republican promise to demand control of their work and civic life. By the late nineteenth century, the older republican creed had become permeated with racism and hostility to the city. But many moviemakers modernized the vision of a producers' democracy to forge a New Deal culture and politics. Although they were not fully freed from the racist assumptions of their day, they opened the possibility for a more inclusive vision of pluralism and popularly based abundance for the nation.[6]

Thomas Hart Benton, the noted regionalist painter of the 1930s, captured this spirit in his painting *Hollywood,* which graces the cover of this book. A staunch supporter of the New Deal, Benton believed in the values of a producers' democracy and used his art to promote that promise. His painting depicts Hollywood not simply as a fantasy but as a place built by common workers who brought their skills together to make a collective work of art. In keeping with much of the work-centered art of the thirties, Benton's *Hollywood* takes the viewer behind the scenes to show how the image is created. Benton fuses a traditional realistic narrative to modernist forms and techniques. The painting shows multiple aspects of the moviemaking process, including makeup for the players, lighting for the sets, and the rolling cameras themselves. At the center stands a scantily-clad starlet, typical of Hollywood sex symbols. Yet her pose also evokes the image of Athena, goddess of liberty and wisdom, associated with republican ideals. The background includes a tower of smoke and fire, found in many Benton paintings, suggesting heat, light, creation, and destruction. This vision of a worker republic prevailed in the Screen Actors Guild as well as in many of the major films of the thirties.[7]

World War II and the Cold War brought a profound shift to this vision of American democracy. The call for wartime unity and postwar anticommunism generated a new politics in the movie industry as well as new types of films. Now the Guild and its stars aligned with conservative businessmen and politicians to create a new vision grounded in liberal capitalism and private consumerism. As I began to realize that a major change in American values emerged in the 1940s, I began to question everything I thought I knew about the contours of twentieth-century American culture.

Ever since the pioneering work of Warren Susman, historians have seen the vast importance of studying popular art as a measure of the values and sentiments informing society. Susman argued in two enormously influential essays that the sounds and images that permeated the mass media in the Depression promoted the values of small-town, Anglo-Saxon America. As such, the mass media provided a vision of security amid hard times and took the fans' attention away from labor-capital strife and gender and racial conflicts. Since that time, most film and cultural historians have echoed that argument.[8] Drawing on literary and cultural theories associated with Frankfurt School sociologists, French semiologists, and Gramscian concepts of hegemony, scholars argue that the mass media from the thirties through the fifties promoted a uniform narrative.[9] Besides reinforcing the power of the studios, moviemakers from the thirties through the fifties advanced the norms of white racism, liberal individualism, and futuristic dreams of consumerism that fortified conservative values and interests. Recently Lawrence Levine has argued effectively that although audiences in the thirties actively reinterpreted the mass media to suit their own purposes, the overall content of the Hollywood product remained conservative.[10]

What made this argument so convincing is that it appeared that popular art operated on the same tracks as the conservative impulses of New Deal politics. Whether the story has been told by New Left, liberal, or conservative historians, the New Deal is understood as saving rather than altering the capitalist system.[11] Yet as my research into the Screen Actors Guild records unfolded, I began to question these assumptions. As I thought about this puzzle, my investigation took a new turn when I recalled memories that I once had dismissed as having no bearing on my scholarship. During my youth in Los Angeles, my mother, like her mother before her, aspired to be a movie actress. In pursuit of that ambition, Norma moved in the fifties to New York City, hoping to gain experience on the Broadway stage. When I arrived in Manhattan in 1954 to join her, she had begun a long relationship with one of the most famous black stage and film comics of the day, James Cross. As the dancer, singer, and humorist of a well-known comedy duo, "Stump and Stumpy," he performed in both white and black nightclubs from Atlantic City to Las Vegas. I grew up in a world where whites and blacks interacted in a common public arena, where people like Dizzy Gillespie, Louis Armstrong, Lena Horne, Frank Sinatra, Joe E. Lewis, and Larry Storch were part of the community, and where virtually everyone had left-wing sympathies. As a young man, I became friends with Jerry Epstein, one of Charles Chaplin's closest associates. Jerry told me how Chaplin, America's most beloved clown, was driven from the country as an alleged communist because he supported radical politics and made films critical of established institutions. Jerry recounted how he had to go to the bank to remove Chaplin's money because they feared it would be confiscated by the state or by congressional committees.[12]

The materials I found in the Hollywood archives made me realize that my experiences in the fifties were not unique. The convergence of my research and my memories brought home the fact that anticommunism had succeeded all too well in making us forget that a non-Marxist republican radicalism was a powerful force in America before World War II. Fortunately, as I began to question the inherited wisdom, several books appeared that supported my interpretations. Work by the new labor and social historians, particularly Gary Gerstle, Lizabeth Cohen, and Alan Brinkley, revealed that the mass unions and populist movements of the thirties emerged as a result of their capacity to create cross-cultural coalitions.[13] At the same time, intellectual and cultural historians began to alter our understanding of the artists and writers of the era. They demonstrated that in the thirties there existed a competitive civic sphere in which regionalist painters, swing musicians, progressive historians, and popular artists expressed criticism of social injustice, capitalism, and racial exclusion. Michael Denning has recently argued that this creativity was linked to politics via the efforts of communists to create alliances with all progressive groups in the antifascist Popular Front, which formed after 1935.[14] Unlike Denning, who credits the rise of a new pluralistic nationalism to the Popular Front, I found that long before the Communist Party came to Hollywood, moviemakers popularized an inclusive republican creed hostile to exclusion and inequality. In this regard the artists of the Popular Front may have given depth to that radical élan, but they were not the initiators.

To illustrate the wide-ranging interplay between audience demand and the values informing the Hollywood product, this study is also guided by a different methodology from what currently guides cultural or film history. With the help of several research assistants, I have developed a systematic survey to trace the changing values among competing film narratives. To chart that conversion, a sample of film plots was drawn from the film industry's major trade journal, the *Motion Picture Herald*. Geared primarily to theater owners, it offered exhibitors a number of services, including weekly plot summaries of recent releases. These plot synopses included films geared for first-run distribution, called "A" films, and those exhibited as second or double features, called "B" films. We have selected for examination the plot summaries of the first and last films released in each month in even-numbered years from the teens to the fifties. By analyzing the plot formulas, it was possible to see how attitudes toward family life, gender and sexuality, cultural authority, wealth, big business, and race shifted in dialogue with the changing face of politics and power from the Depression to the Cold War.[15]

As I rummaged around in the film archives gathering all this material, I came across an intriguing document that seemed to encapsulate the themes of this book and prompted the title, *The Big Tomorrow*. In exploring the career of John Huston, I found that he made an independent film in 1949 about a revolution in Cuba that brought whites and minorities together in a common cause. Despite an epilogue quoting Thomas Jefferson that in the past as in the present "revolution against tyrants is obedience to God," critics condemned *We Were Strangers* as un-American. With the Cold War at high tide, the film soon faltered at the box office and disappeared. Yet an admirer wrote to Huston that the production should have been titled "The Big Tomorrow." For some characters in the film, the revolution succeeded, while for still others, it created tragedy and loss. As I explored the contours of the film industry, I began to realize that this title captured the essence of my story. "The Big Tomorrow" evokes a postwar future that represented triumph for some and defeat for others. As in Huston's film *We Were Strangers,* many artists and civic leaders in the 1930s promoted a vision of America that was inclusive of minorities and hostile to monopoly capitalism. Yet their great expectations were defeated by events. With the withering away of their civic idealism under the impact of anticommunism, they used their art to promote cultural innovations that set the stage for the upheavals of the 1960s.

PART ONE

The Modern Republic Comes of Age

Chapter 1

"My Ancestors Did Not Come Over on the Mayflower": Will Rogers and the Radicalism of Tradition

I used to wonder why it was that Will Rogers was the head man of all the public figures of the day. . . . Then one day, I realized what it was. If you took Will Rogers and pitched a dab of whiskers under his chin, put a red, white, and blue hat on his head, crammed his legs into star spangled pants, he'd be Uncle Sam. He was a symbol. He was more than a symbol. He was the bass drum.
—Clarence Kelland, novelist, 1935

Will's traits—visible in his writings as vividly today as when he set them to paper—are the unending virtues of the American Indian. Will Rogers introduced the world to this ethical view of life.
—W. W. Keeler, Principal Chief, Cherokee Nation, 1973

*O*n a hot summer day in the middle of August 1935, millions of Americans heard the tragic news that an airplane flying from Alaska to Moscow crashed, killing Will Rogers. Quickly, the death of a Cherokee cowboy who rose from the vaudeville stage to become the single most popular radio and film star of the Depression years took on dimensions that in retrospect seem hard to believe. In the nation's capital, the vice president adjourned Congress, and President Franklin Roosevelt sent a well-publicized letter to the comic's grieving family. Farther west, the governor of California proclaimed a day of mourning, flags in Los Angeles County flew at half-mast, and officials in Oklahoma offered the state capital as a place for the body of their native son to lie in state. Across the nation newspapers reported that bells rang in Rogers's honor in over a hundred cities, and nearly 100,000 people passed by his coffin at Forest Lawn Cemetery. The next day radio stations broadcast the memorial service from the Hollywood Bowl presided over by a Protestant minister, a Catholic priest, and a Yiddish performer singing a Hebrew mourning chant. Across town Mexican-American citizen groups placed a wreath on

Olvera Street saying "Nosotros Lamentamos la Muerte de Will Rogers," while in Watts an African-American fraternal group named the "Friends of Ethiopia" joined black performers from Rogers's films in holding a parade in the star's honor. Back in his hometown of Claremore, Oklahoma, the Cherokee Indians performed a death dance in memory of their fallen kinsman. Capturing the civic spirit that sparked officials to build state parks, local schools, and national monuments in Rogers's name, which dot the American landscape to this day, a reporter commented:

> the country loses a great political power with the death of Will Rogers. While he was in no sense a politician, he exercised an influence on public sentiment perhaps greater than political leaders. He was the most widely read humorist on and off the screen and one of the very few who made intelligent and frequent comments on public affairs and issues. His homely philosophy had a tremendous influence on the public mind. . . . He came nearer to probably expressing the thoughts of the average man than anyone in his line. Politicians and statesmen sought him out eagerly for his friendship and approval. . . . There were those who thought he would make a good President of the United States.[1]

To contemporaries, the reason why Rogers would make a "good President of the United States" was as clear as the smile on the comic's face. Evoking the central symbol of the nation's mythic identity, the West, he told listeners on his weekly radio show that it was "not the working classes that brought on the economic crisis, it was the big boys that thought the financial drunk was going to last forever, and over bought, over merged and over capitalized." Over the last few years, the "difference between our rich and poor grows greater every year. But the 'Big Men' tell us there is as much as we had and all that. . . . But what they don't tell us is that what's the matter with us is the unequal division of it. Our rich are getting richer all the time. No wonder that the good Lord said . . . 'how long has this thing been going on, this living on dog-eat-dog principles? We'll stop this thing right now and give the folks a chance to reorganize and redeem themselves.'"[2]

Redemption, however, was not to be found by turning to what he saw as the "cuckoo ideas" of Marxists or fascists, whose views echoed those of the "Ku Klux Klan" and "prison wardens." Rather, reorganization would emerge by renewing a republican critique of the monopoly capitalism that had pervaded national identity for over a hundred years. Evoking the traditional language of a "producers' democracy," he explained that since "there was not a millionaire in the country whose fortune did not come from the labor of others, we need to arrange it so that a man that wants work can get work, and give him a more equal division of the wealth the country produces." By the early years of the Depression, Rogers's impact on audiences was all too evident.

The sociologists Robert and Helen Merrell Lynd found in their *Middletown in Transition* that the businessmen in Muncie, Indiana, feared that Rogers's comments bred discontent among workers, and hoped broadcasters would remove the humorist from the radio. Writers in the *Wall Street Journal* and the *New York Times* condemned Rogers's criticism of business and Wall Street. Yet "Will" responded with a joke, noting "I have a different slant on things . . . for my ancestors did not come over on the Mayflower. They met the boat." Drawing on the myth of the West, he noted that

> I hope my Cherokee blood is not making me prejudiced, I want to be broad minded, but I am sure it was only the extreme generosity of the Indians that allowed the Pilgrims to land anywhere. Suppose we reverse the case. Do you reckon the Pilgrims would have ever let the Indians land? Yeah, what a chance, what a chance. The Pilgrims wouldn't even allow the Indians to live after the Indians went to the trouble of letting them land, of course, but they'd always pray. . . . You've never in your life seen a picture, I bet any one of you have never seen a picture of one of the old Pilgrims praying when he didn't have a gun right by the side of him. That was to see that he got what he was praying for.[3]

More than sixty years after these events, it seems almost impossible that a rope-twirling Cherokee Indian became the most popular figure of the Depression, calling for a redistribution of wealth and a counternarrative of nationality. The reason lies in the manner in which scholars have explored the relationship between politics, Will Rogers, and filmmaking. Not only is the New Deal considered a conservative movement and the popular arts of the era permeated with backward-looking images preserving the status quo,[4] but biographers and film scholars have seen Rogers as a "cracker barrel philosopher" who, like Hollywood moviemaking in general, "helped the nation's fundamental institutions escape unscathed by the attempts to keep alive the myth and proverbial fantasy of a mobile and classless society."[5] Presumably, Will Rogers's career illustrates the axiom that in the 1930s the cry was not so much for radical reform as for a restoration of the values of security and Anglo-Saxon Americanism.

Yet Rogers's capacity to combine left-wing populist rhetoric with calls for a redistribution of wealth to realize an inclusive Americanism suggests that these views have to be revised. This chapter demonstrates that the source of Rogers's great popularity was that he evoked a left-wing populism, what Craig Calhoun has called a "radicalism of tradition." In this mode radicalism finds its efforts to save traditional institutions undermined by an untrammeled market and exploitive power relations. Within this framework, Rogers embodied the central myth of the old producers' republic: the frontier where citizens created a republic free of aristocracy and monopoly. But where the producers' republic had been identified with Anglo-Saxon exclusion and deep hostility to urban peoples and morals, Rogers did the impossible. He drew on his Cherokee tradition to modernize the producers' democracy to include the city and the country—a process that identified the popular arts with stimulating rather than thwarting radical reform.[6]

The Crisis of Anglo-Saxon Americanism

What Rogers and millions of Americans faced in the early years of the Depression was the inability of earlier radical movements to create coalitions across groups to advance common class interests against big business. Due to that failure, the corporations and the Republican Party dominated the federal government after World War I. Policies that favored big business allowed concentrations of wealth to become far more unequal. Under these conditions, the population did not have the purchasing power to buy the goods flowing from mass production techniques. Buying on credit and speculation on the stock market postponed the coming crisis. But after the Crash of 1929, the gross national product fell more than one-third by 1932, prices were cut in half, and over 15 million people—25 percent of the labor force—were unemployed. Even for those employed, wages fell precipitously. Despite the disaster, official leaders, best exemplified by the Republican president Herbert Hoover, claimed over the next three years that prosperity was "just around the corner."[7]

Yet as the disaster spread, the corner failed to appear and a political reorientation slowly spread. Where voters in the most racially and ethnically divided society in the western world had been divided by cultural wars, the Democratic Party slowly began to forge a political realignment that brought together Anglo-Saxon farmers, immigrants, minorities, the reform-minded middle class, intellectuals, and southern segregationists. The coming to power in 1933 of President Franklin Roosevelt saw the creation of a New Deal administration that backed the labor movement and populist crusades. Many New Dealers and "progressive" Republicans saw that the key to prosperity lay in the promotion of mass consumption. The economic downturn in this analysis emerged because of the lack of purchasing power in a society where one-tenth of 1 percent of the population earned as much as the bottom 42 percent. This maldistribution made it impossible for people to buy the cars, appliances, and homes that flowed from industry. Social welfare and government spending served, in the minds of many New Dealers, to spur the rise in consumer demand by encouraging both policies to redistribute wealth and unions.[8]

Yet to gain a wide following for the political revolution and economic policies, it was also necessary to recast the meaning given to the new consumer culture. Instead of making it appear natural that the wealthy held power and most of the wealth, it was necessary to create a more democratic vision of affluence. Yet those who looked to the recent past for models had little to encourage them. Prior to the twentieth century, the homes, leisure, print media, theater, families, and institutions of middle-class and working-class people existed in entirely separate spheres. When combined with divisions of wealth, the cultural divisions—the bourgeoisie were predominately Anglo-Saxons, the workers were minorities—suggested that few common bonds existed. Yet as the new corporate economy solidified at the turn of the century, urban men and women turned to a new realm of freedom in mass entertainments that had their origins in the lower classes. Soon dance halls, amusement parks, and movies became linked with a revolution in morals that had its roots in urban immigrants and minorities. By the teens this urban market spurred labor unions to finance films dramatizing class conflict, women to patronize female stars who challenged sexual roles, and comics to express the rebellion of outsiders.[9]

The combined efforts of corporate reformers and ambitious showmen sanctioned the new popular art in accord with the standards of the middle class who looked to their fellow Anglo-Saxons, the wealthy industrialists, for their models of cultural authority. Out of those efforts a new frontier, that of Hollywood, emerged on the West Coast in the twenties. Over a hundred small firms engaged in film production prior to that time. Legitimizing the moral revolution in accord with the ethos of high art derived from Anglo-Saxon tastemakers, the major studios began to consolidate their power. Doing so, they used censorship to eliminate images of class conflict and challenges to traditional sexual and racial roles. By the late twenties film producers surrounded their product with a foreign imagery that served various purposes. At the point of reception, large theaters designed to resemble French, Italian, Spanish, and English palaces emulated the tastes of European aristocrats and the American rich. This not only removed the movies from their disreputable origins in the working class but isolated the revolution in manners from the myths and symbols of Americanism permeating public life and politics. The effect was to create a divided culture where official institutions remained isolated from the views of racial minorities and the desires focused within the new urban culture. The appeal of cultural mixing, ribald youth, and rebellious women was confined to private life, a process that served the interests of the corporate leaders.[10]

Yet at the same time moralists worried because moviemakers constantly pushed at the limits, spurring a series of troubling questions: What did it mean for the taste of the lower class to come into contact with high art? Would the lower class remain a crowd taking their cues from official tastemakers, or would they become a public making their own choices and launching a contest over language and symbols? The question was, who would speak in the name of the "people"? Such fears became a flood once the corporate order collapsed in the Depression years. Suddenly, the business order crumbled under the impact of the crisis. Studio profits now fell dramatically, and firms that borrowed from banks to build lavish theaters and monopolize stars faced bankruptcy.[11]

Meanwhile once-optimistic trade commentators turned into prophets of doom. One observed that "1932 was a trying year for the industry and its close found the fortunes of the business at their lowest ebb. The year marked the end of the so called era of extravagance. Unless the general economic situation takes a decided change for the better, the industry can hope for very little in the way of progress or of genuine prosperity." As business failures spread, *Film Daily* reported that the past year had "exploded the theory that the motion picture industry is depression proof." Between 1929 and 1932, the number of theaters in the country dropped from 22,000 to 12,480, a decline of 43 percent. Heavily mortgaged, over-seated film theaters closed their doors, and the average price of admissions declined from 36 to 24 cents. In addition, gross receipts fell from $90 million to below $60 million, a full 33 percent drop. It followed that trade journalists' optimism waned and with 1932 passing into history, a trade reporter wondered "whether the movie producers will ever again know the popularity" they experienced in the twenties.[12]

Slowly and unwillingly producers also came to realize that as the "golden era of extravagance" receded, they were "all out to sea" as to what would attract fans back to the movies. True, 50 percent of the lost profits could be explained by the economic crisis: The fans were simply unable to spend meager income on leisure. But what caused the other 50 percent? Industry leaders noted that stars of the silent-film era were making smooth transitions to the new sound productions. A year before, John Gilbert, Gloria Swanson, and Clara Bow made talking films that were successes at the box office. Only a year later, however, theater owners and critics determined that these stars were failures. Silent stars were linked to the tastes of "arty and aristocratic critics." Now the "international picture stars as known during the silent film days" and the "regal atmosphere" and "high hat" aura of film palaces turned the audiences away. Beset with troubles on all sides, industry leaders saw that styles derived from business "supermen" and "millionaires" lay in disrepute. Having sanctioned the movies with status symbols that looked to Europe and static historical models of public life and morals, producers found that audiences in the Great Depression had lost faith in the cultural authority of the wealthy in favor of the unmediated expressiveness unfolding in the mass arts of the large cities. With audiences rejecting the atmosphere of the "400" society families, a critic shrewdly observed that the motion picture "business had to be reincarnated. . . . Everyone knew it . . . but no one could predict what year."[13]

Nonetheless, by 1933 the industry not only began to recover but to expand beyond the markets and profits of the twenties.[14] Amid hard times the seeds of that reincarnation appeared evident. The producers catered to audiences' rejection of foreign formulas in favor of talking films that dramatized a counternarrative of "Americanism" emerging from the bottom rather than the top of the social order. In addition, instead of isolating the revolution in morals to the private domain, the carnival spirit of mass art and modern amusements entered the center, altering both in the process. Nowhere was that more clear than in the rise of Will Rogers from the urban world of vaudeville and the penny press to become the top male box-office attraction of the era. Known as the "Mark Twain of the Screen," Rogers exuded the aura of Huck Finn and the con men memorialized by Herman Melville in *The Confidence Man*. But where these comic figures had critiqued the official norms but remained outsiders, Rogers yoked the comic to the dramatic hero who combined work and play, high- and low-brow. Giving form to interpenetrating opposites, he did what was impossible: Root cultural and political reform in a renewal of traditional values.

"You Know I'm an Indian"

In trying to account for Rogers's enormous appeal in the thirties, writers have correctly seen that he embodied the key myth of the nation, the western cowboy. Yet they confront the fact that Rogers claimed to be an Indian only to dismiss it—he was not really an Indian, they argue, because he was only one-quarter Cherokee by "blood." Since he had more white than red ancestors, he embodied the model of the old Anglo-Saxon citizen. Embedded in this view are two highly misleading assumptions. One is that the determination of one's identity lies in biology: A person is inherently defined by race rather than culture. The other is that only one form of the West, that ideal symbol promoted by the Anglo-Saxons, defined the frontier experience. Here, so the story goes, the whites destroyed or assimilated the "savage" Indians to create in the New World a society grounded in white western civilization.

Neither of these binary views, however, can account for the appeal of Will Rogers, the distinctiveness of Indian life on the frontier, or what Rogers meant when he told his fans he has a "different slant on things . . . my ancestors did not come over on the Mayflower. They met the boat."[15] Behind that anecdote lay more than meets the eye. Will Rogers was born in Oolagah, the Indian territory of Oklahoma, in 1879. His parents, Clem and Mary Rogers, were mestizos, members of a class of American Indians who had intermarried with the Europeans. Living on a frontier borderland where three races had came into contact, the Cherokees had responded by undergoing a major revitalization movement that created one of the first multicultural republics in the New World.[16] In the eighteenth century the Cherokees had accepted the assistance of both George Washington and Thomas Jefferson to create a constitution modeled on that of the United States. Rogers, like his ancestors, evoked Washington and Jefferson as "founders" equally of their Cherokee nation. Furthermore, with the aid of New England missionaries, the Cherokees converted to Christianity and created a syllabary and printing press to forge a written language.[17]

By the early nineteenth century, one-third of the Cherokee population was the result of racial mixing, spurred by intermarriage among Indians, blacks, and whites. The Cherokees had shed their former hunting-based economy in favor of growing cash crops for the Atlantic marketplace and had adapted Indian slaveholding practices to include black bondage. Though many Cherokees grew rich off the exploitation of black labor, it was critical that they—unlike white southerners—

continued the Native American slaveholding tradition that allowed slaves to buy their freedom and intermarry.

At the same time, the Cherokees practiced a communal ethic in which they retained the Indian practice of holding land in common to ensure that the desire for profits did not overrun the public good. When a family or individual did not use land productively, it reverted back to the tribe and was given to another. Honor among the wealthy no doubt resided in their accumulation of goods, yet they also complemented their acquisitiveness with an honor code of "redistributive economics." Here prestige accrued to those who shared wealth with those whose labor made them rich. Furthermore, Cherokees differed from white middle-class Americans in their views of gender roles. While the women under most laws of the United States could not vote, hold office, or own property after marriage, Cherokee women participated in tribal councils of government and retained the fruits of their labor.[18]

In addition to building a society rooted in cross-cultural communication and exchange, Cherokees differed from Victorian Americans in their approach to the relation of art to public life and politics. At the most sacred event of the year, the Green Corn Ceremony, the Cherokees celebrated the processes of death and rebirth. As evidence of their traditional belief that a balance must inform all parts of life, the ritual leader was not a politician or priest. Rather, he was a comic trickster who used humor to address the issues of psychic fear and social disorder affecting his audience. Fusing the hero with the clown, the trickster, on the one hand, clearly subverted fixed beliefs and, on the other, spurred audiences to reshape the self and society. Using masks and masquerade, the Indian trickster destroyed notions of essential and eternal identities to create an ethos of movement and change at the heart of all things. For an audience confronted with disease or strife, the trickster, as the anthropologist Barbara Babcock explains, broke up "patterns of thought and tradition that hold us in bondage so that the established order is deformed, reformed and reformulated."[19]

If Rogers inherited the ethos of the trickster who fused humor with drama and politics, he also identified the frontier with the making of a mestizo republic rather than an Anglo-Saxon republic rooted in racial exclusion.[20] Symbolic of the hybridity at the center of Cherokee life, Rogers had two names, one derived from his own paternal Scotch Irish ancestors (who had intermarried with Indians), the other derived from a long line of maternal Indian grandparents. Similarly, young Will matured in the Indian territory known as Oklahoma. The county of his birth, the Cooweescoowee district, derived from the Indian name of

John Ross, the first president of the Cherokee nation. Ross, like the mestizos Clem and Mary Rogers, was a mixed-blood Cherokee.[21] In many ways the identification with a multicultural democracy also provided Rogers with a view of the West less as a place of individualism than as a place where freedom and community merged.

That frontier counternarrative also bred a different form of political identity than informed the host society. Take Rogers's opinion of Andrew Jackson. Jackson was revered by contemporary historians, ranging from Frederick Jackson Turner to Charles Beard, for expanding the white man's democracy into the West. But Will Rogers was "none too sweet on Old Andy," for he regarded him as the "great betrayer." At times the memory of Jackson would provoke Rogers into a highly emotional condemnation of "Andy" before a gathering of Cherokees. The reason for that animus was not too hard to find. In the early nineteenth century, Jackson removed Rogers's ancestors from their southeastern lands and forced them on a deadly winter march called the "Trail of Tears." During the trek from the East to Oklahoma, over one-third of the population died. Will Rogers's grandparents were among the "treaty party" that accepted the government's terms.

Still the memories of removal were so enduring that Rogers's father joined with over half of the Cherokee nation in fighting for the South in the Civil War. Their goal as Confederates was to attain independence from the federal government that had expropriated Cherokee lands and destroyed so many of their people.[22] Once the Union armies defeated the Confederacy, Clem Rogers proved a model for young Will of how tragedy stimulated one to refashion beliefs. Clem returned after the end of the Civil War to Oklahoma and participated in a Reconstruction that differed from that in the other southern states. Where the defeated southerners excluded and segregated their former slaves, Clem saw that the outcome of the Civil War provided a signal that a Cherokee republic had to recreate a balance in the universe. One path to balance lay in affirming African Americans' rights to the common land, to public schooling, and to full suffrage.

Once these reforms passed, Clem led a multiracial coalition composed of Indians, blacks, and whites and became one of the most prominent leaders in the Cherokee nation. With the support of voters composed of diverse groups, Clem served as a territorial judge and Cherokee senator who saved a young African American from a lynching. Not long after, Clem and Mary became known among blacks and Indians for "helping all people whether colored or white." Most important, they also led Cherokee resistance to the invasion of railroads and

Senator Clem Rogers of the Cooweescoowee district among the Cherokee delegation to negotiate the Dawes Act in 1896. Clem Rogers is in the back row, first on the left. The men in
their western-style attire reveal how Cherokees drew on western values and traditions to
suit their own purposes. (Courtesy Will Rogers Memorial Commission of Oklahoma)

white land hunters into the Indian territory. The heat of that battle saw
Clem write to the Cherokee president, asking "Are we powerless to
enforce our own laws? Are we to submit to such great wrongs by white
men not our citizens? . . . We are *fast, fast* drifting into the hands of
white men."

That drift led into further disaster. Clem served on the Cherokee
commission to resist the Dawes Act, a federal law that broke up the
Indians' land. After its passage Clem lost his land, but soon emerged
as a partner in an Indian bank and as a politician who supported the
populist movement associated with William Jennings Bryan in the
presidential election of 1896. The entry of Oklahoma into statehood
saw Clem resist other white efforts to curtail Cherokee political power.
Over the decades he grew wealthy by the standards of the territory;
indeed, some biographers have likened him to a Horatio Alger figure—
a self-made man on the far frontier. This was a half-truth, however, for
Clem operated in a different moral universe. When he died, the local

paper caught that difference. It described him as a Cherokee public man whose honor lay in service and practicing the code of redistributive economics:

> Clem Rogers was one of the most prominent citizens of the Cherokee people and was known far and wide as a philanthropic and public spirited citizen. . . . he resisted the federal government all his life, and every person in distress could find a ready helper in Clem Rogers. He amassed a fortune in his time, but a large portion of it had been devoted to charity when he died.[23]

Given this tradition, Clem hoped that his only son, Will, would also become a public man in Claremore. Yet in the wake of the havoc wreaked by the Dawes Act, Will Rogers left Oklahoma to seek employment in foreign lands. Most biographers perceive these wanderings as a reflection of his revolt from his father and, by implication, the old Cherokee past. Yet the evidence supports neither claim. Though there was tension between the two, Will repeatedly sent loving letters home to his father and family, returned home for family events, paid for the education of his relatives, and all his life sent money to his family to buy back the ranch lost with the passage of the Dawes Act. To top it off, these letters were not kept private but published in a newspaper geared to Cherokee public affairs. Clearly, young Will's departure was not a mark of rebellion or removal from the community.[24]

Something else was going on, namely, that after the loss of Cherokee independence, Will Rogers joined with other young Cherokees in a diasporic movement to find a new frontier where the Cherokee could relocate. How else can we explain the letters that he wrote from Latin America that indicate he was exploring for land that could sustain his people? In one letter he stated that "I am shoulder to shoulder with every nation on the globe for every ship brings four or five hundred people that are to live by their labor alone. You don't know how good your country is 'til you get away from it. Just tell all of those boys that want to come here to stay right where they are, that is good enough. I have given this place a trial and I know that it is no place for a man with small capital or none at all." Young Will perceived that Latin America would not be a good place to settle since the wealthy monopolized landholdings and exploited their immigrant and Indian laborers.

When his two sisters wrote that allotment in Oklahoma, the end of the communal land system, "was the order of the day for every body now," and when Cherokee leaders, including his father, failed in their effort to create the independent state of "Sequoia" in Oklahoma, Will adjusted to a lifelong commitment to a hyphenated or dual citizenship.

Writing to his "loving father," he explained that his travels had allowed him to come to terms with the land of his birth that had bred such tragedy. As he explained, "I was always proud in America to own that I am a Cherokee but I find on leaving that I am equally proud that I am an American. I have had arguments with every type of nationality of man under the sun in regard to the merits of our own people and country."[25]

Not long after, Rogers carried that debate concerning "the merits of our own people and country" into show business. At first he did not master his new vocation; on the contrary, it almost mastered him. During a stay in South Africa he moved from laboring as a cowboy to performing in touring Wild West shows that staged reenactments of westward expansion and white superiority that permeated the popular arts of the day. Typically, fans were entertained by dramatizations of the destruction of dangerous Indians by whites.[26] Back at Madison Square Garden in New York, entrepreneurs advertised Rogers as the "Cherokee Kid . . . a full-blooded Indian . . . his father is chief of the tribe."

The psychic effects of these descriptions were abundantly evident. Writing home, Will noted "I play the Indian and Negro parts," notably the black minstrel and the savage Indian stereotypes that whites used for over a century to justify colonization of non-Europeans.[27] And like other Indians asked to play these roles in Wild West shows, including Sitting Bull, Black Elk, and Geronimo, Will reflected on the psychic scars it inflected. He wrote that "I am living a lie," and now have "no mind of my own . . . for I am easily led . . . to God knows where." In these years he also composed sad songs derived from black ragtime and blues, evoking the alienation of minorities who confronted racism on multiple fronts. Once, for example, he tried to impress a young woman attending one of the Wild West performances in New York. He recalled that she was "strong for me . . . till she read in the program that I was an Indian . . . which she said went against her better nature." The same fears of miscegenation appear to have clouded Will's courtship of Betty Blake, his future wife. She was a wealthy, white Arkansas woman who wanted to live, as she wrote to Clem, like "white folks." Will, in turn, wrote that he knew her relationship with an "ignorant Indian cowboy" was a deep "slam on your society reputation."[28]

"A Civilization Without Satisfaction"

Soon, however, Rogers gained success on a new frontier of show business where he began to speak in his own western voice rather than

Will Rogers, "The Cherokee Kid," and his horse "Comanche" in between acts for the Wild West Show, about 1902. (Courtesy Will Rogers Memorial Commission of Oklahoma)

in the voice of those who had colonized the Cherokees. Little of the magnitude of this change is apparent unless we realize that mass culture was dramatically different in that era. At the local level, minorities retained their own language and oral traditions, but at the national level, subordinate groups had their views mediated through the perceptions of official leaders. In the context of, say, the Wild West shows, the whites were the citizens and heroes, while minorities were fools, dangerous villains, criminals, or fallen women.[29] As Rogers conformed to these views at the cost of "living a lie," he nevertheless began to find himself in a mass-art culture that brought together groups that had formerly been apart. On an urban frontier similar to the Cherokee West, he now gained popularity in vaudeville shows that appealed to a polyglot audience of immigrants, who, like Rogers, lived in an ambivalent relation to the dominant groups. Like the Indians, the immigrants had left their homelands and encountered exploitation as well as discrimination in the new industrial society.

Unlike the immigrants, Rogers had one existential advantage: He could claim to be more "American" than the Anglo-Saxons. Soon he emerged as the headliner comic at the Ziegfeld Follies, then on the local radio, and finally as a newspaper columnist for the *New York Times*. In this world of play and frolic, fans came to know him as a man who embodied a style of interpenetrating oppositions. On the one hand, he was a rope-twirling cowboy who was not too proud to say, "You know I'm an Indian, my parents are Cherokee." On the other, he was also a self-confessed "hick" who loved nightclubs, a good drink, sports, vaudeville, gambling, and urban restaurants. Crossing ethnic and racial barriers at ease, he appeared at a banquet to promote a labor union; the *Jewish Daily Forward* reported that Rogers learned just enough Yiddish to tell recent immigrants that he too was a "landsman" who just got off the boat from Russia.

Most important of all, unlike the educated men of the day, Rogers dealt with political affairs from the viewpoint of the "street." Saying exactly what "everybody thought," and speaking in a free-flowing stream of consciousness, he addressed listeners as if they were intimate friends, asking them to "see things from the other person's angle." Even as he noted that "all I know is what I read in the papers," he was a man in motion. After flying across the globe to "get the facts," unmediated by expert opinion, he had a "little anecdote" to explain the very purpose of his trips. On the frontier the white man always got lost. But Rogers's Indian ancestor had

> always looked back after he passed anything so he got a view of both sides. You see the white man just figures that all sides are the same. That's like a dumb guy with an argument. He don't think there's any other side, only his. That's what we commonly call politicians.[30]

Rogers's "serious streak," however, did not simply overturn the formal modes of authority or literary syntax. On the contrary, as one of his contemporaries saw it, he had "punctured by way of comedy the things that were the shibboleths of the Victorian era, the poses and pomposity, the slyness and the lies—all he had to do was to say what it was in simple words." Yet he did not simply satirize Victorian gentility, a common tactic. Seeing the world from a different angle, he

Left, Will Rogers on the New York City vaudeville circuit, about 1904. Notice the rope, the quizzical smile, the cowboy attire, and contrapposto stance that link Rogers's Cherokee humor to the classical wisdom of Europe, transposed to the popular arts of the mestizo United States. (Courtesy Will Rogers Memorial Commission of Oklahoma)

Below, Will Rogers and the belles of the Ziegfeld Follies, backstage in 1924. Here we see the Cherokee comic identified with the moral revolution of the "big city." (Courtesy Will Rogers Memorial Commission of Oklahoma) updated the élan of the Cherokee trickster, fusing it with a double-voice style of humor typical of minorities. As the black novelist Ralph Ellison noted, racial minorities are both insiders and outsiders. Their vision is thus double. Working within this dualistic mode, Rogers observed that our "fine leaders" advanced 100-percent Americanization efforts in schools and civic organizations, and promoted Prohibition and imperialist crusades to civilize the "heathens." But as he then meandered around the subject, Rogers also noted why it might be that "Mexico wasn't crazy for us, for we always had their good will and oil and coffee and minerals, at heart." He also saw that at home the rich built fine opera houses to educate the masses; however, the utilization of European high art as a model of emulation was simply a form of "artistic graft" that separated the rich from ordinary people. If Rogers was well aware of what the Italian social theorist Antonio Gramsci called "hegemony"—the use of prestige and status on the part of powerful groups to gain acquiescence to their rule—Rogers, like Gramsci, was also aware that this arrangement was not eternal but open to transformation from the bottom up.

Knowing that his audience had internalized standards promoted in lavish theater palaces and department stores, Rogers used his humor to present an alternative basis of authority. "Why just the other day," he noted, the banker and patron of the high arts J. P. Morgan had left on an ocean voyage to Europe, surrounded by so many guards that a bystander could not see him. "Still you will hear some bone head say that we have no classes in America." As for bankers and wealthy financiers, he wondered, "Why is it alright for these Wall Street boys to bet millions and make that bet affect the fellow plowing a field in Claremore, Oklahoma? . . . It does seem funny that these guys can sit here and produce nothing, ride in Fisher bodies and put a price on a whole year's labor." If this was an age when the rich advanced the "bogus idea" of the self-made man who owed nothing to the community, he answered his critics who pointed to the frontier as a model of ruggedness that

> We're always talking about pioneers and what good folks the pioneers were. Well I think if we just stopped and looked history in the face, the pioneer wasn't a thing in the world but a guy that wanted something for nothing. He was a guy that wanted to live off everything that nature had done. He wanted to cut down a tree that didn't cost any thing, but he never did plant one you know. He wanted to plow the land that should have been left to graze. He thought he was living off nature, but he was really living off future generations.[31]

At the core of Rogers's humorous critique of individualism and capitalism lay not just "Indian" values but the vision of the democratic republic in opposition to monopoly capitalism and acquisitive individualism. Yet because Rogers realized that the audience admired the rich, he saw that they had acquiesced in the creation of a "civilization without satisfaction," permeated with "more unhappiness than at any time in history." Commenting on a bankers' convention in the twenties, Rogers noted that though Secretary of Commerce Herbert Hoover spoke about American prosperity, if we "looked reality in the face," our "American Standard of Living" benefited "them that had more than the have-nots." Rogers related how large department stores loved to be magnanimous and create Mothers' Day to honor women. But this was a cruel joke since these firms failed to offer women well-paying jobs to buy goods for their families. Sentimental admiration for women was nothing without purchasing power: "No, Sir. [Women] want to know what kind of break they are going to get out of commerce and industry. If they have to make a living for their family, they want to know what kind of inducement the government is going to make to them for doing it."

Such sentiments did not remain isolated to the world of pure "entertainment." Repeatedly Rogers used his newspaper column and magazine articles in the twenties to enlarge on the implications of his jokes. Writing to Al Smith of New York, the Irish Catholic Democrat whom he supported for the presidency in 1928, Rogers noted that Smith represented "my kind of people . . . the underdog." Yet he used his double-voice style to show how the new consumer culture undermined the world of the underdog. Though he enjoyed a good time, and realized that the populace desired the same, Rogers also saw that the problem of the "great prosperity" was that the rich have the funds to go on European vacations and place a number of bathrooms in their homes. But the majority of the people lived below the poverty line where they could not "buy another loaf of bread."

Throughout Rogers drew on American traditions of a republic to provide an alternative to the ethos of liberal capitalism advanced by official leaders. Over and over he used that backward-looking myth not to promote, but to undermine, the status quo. Symbolic of his use of historical memories and myths to critique present inequalities, he asked what would the "Founding Fathers" think if they came back and saw the vast unemployment in the "land of the free." Similarly, what would happen if our "savior" Jesus Christ returned to the earth in modern times and preached the code of love thy neighbor? "Why he wouldn't last near as long as he did then, since our civilization has got past truth and poverty and renunciation and all that old junk. Throw those nuts in jail." Rogers also admired Gandhi's struggle in India against British rule. Yet noting that many saw Gandhi's pacifism as "out of date," he quickly switched gears and linked such "new" ideas to the reason why youth were so cynical, for

> it is not a bright future that we ask them to enter into. They feel that they are the ones to right it. We feel that we are the ones that lost it, and that we are the ones to find it. It's just a difference of opinion, it's not a difference of nature. . . . We look at it from the old days, they look at it from the now. We are looking in different directions. We can't help but look back, they can't help but look forward. But we are both standing on the same ground, and their feet is there as firmly as ours.[32]

"A Statesman in Love as in Politics"

The evocation of a common ground soon emerged from the margins to the center with the advent of the Great Crash in 1929. During the twenties Rogers operated largely in the local arena of New York City, catering to an audience composed of immigrants, their children, minorities, and middle-class patrons out for an adventure in slumming. Yet as the Depression struck, Hollywood producers found that films featuring Will Rogers were successful. Unlike other featured players created by the studios, Rogers's success emerged in direct proportion to film producers' ability to give a form and narrative structure to Rogers's well-known views.

In practice the transformation signaled a major change in mass culture. Prior to the thirties, moral reformers and Hollywood filmmakers uplifted the movies with Victorian standards of high art and Anglo-Saxon cultural mores. During the twenties Rogers had appeared in over forty silent films. None made him a significant box-office attraction, and several produced with his own money failed. At the time he noted, "I was about to quit pictures. Gosh it was awful." Producers believed that since Rogers could not talk in silent films, it was impossible "to put the best part of him on the screen." Yet there was more to it. The problem was that in his performances outside films, Rogers articulated his own views. In the film studios, however, Rogers found that performers had their views mediated by the perspective of Victorian tastemakers who divided "trivial" comedy from the world of "art." No wonder he complained in the twenties that his films were not a success because "[w]hen I go before the camera, that's not Will Rogers, it's the director acting through me."[33]

The coming of the Great Depression delegitimized the film formulas and stars popular in the twenties. In that vacuum, Rogers found that the new audience demand allowed him to do what was impossible, namely, to control his own work. With the large firms going into bankruptcy, innovative producers at Fox Studios found, as a trade reporter described it, that Will Rogers's ideas "were much better equipped to entertain the public than the ideas of the film salesmen," with the result that he had his "career under his own control." Meanwhile, producers hired directors and writers whose task was to transfer Rogers's well-known ideas into film form. The novelist Homer Croy recalled that he willingly had joined the "team" at Fox because Rogers "always reminded me of Judge Bishop, the circuit judge who provided the character about whom I wrote my Priest stories. . . . When he was on the bench he used the finest legal phraseology. But when he went politician, as he used to say, he talked exactly like the man in the street." To ensure that the view of the "street" prevailed, Rogers attended studio script conferences where his views prevailed. Afterwards he noted exactly why: "They were talking about a story, they said it had to be changed a lot, that the loss of a mortgage on the old farm was all out of date. They claimed that stories had to be made modern and up-to-date. I told 'em 'Say listen! There never was a time in our lives when foreclosing the mortgage on the farm was as timely as it is today. It comes as standard equipment on most homes and farms.'"

Once filming began, Rogers's influence over style and performance left its mark on all his talking films. The famed Irish Catholic director John Ford, who worked with him on three talking films, recalled that when Rogers did not like his lines he suggested that they must have been written by a wealthy "Oxford graduate." He would discard the scripts and "go away, muttering to himself, getting his lines ready, and when he came back, he'd make his speech in a typical Rogers fashion, which was far better than any writer could write for him. Because no writer could write for Will." An actor remembered that Rogers told him, "You see what I do is I write a great deal of the script myself. Sometimes I improvise . . . but go along with it. And then when I think I've said enough, I will stop, and then I'll poke you and then you talk." The result, according to still another, was that he "didn't stick to the script; he always improved upon it. And you know, you had to be ready for it; you just had to play with him, that's all. It fascinated me and I loved it and played right along with it . . . and I can guarantee that whatever he did was better, because it was strictly Will Rogers and that's what they wanted, and everybody loved it . . . He just wouldn't rehearse. No director could tell him how to do something, for he knew the how always." He was "full of idiosyncracies," but since that was the style that made profits, Rogers had the capacity to place "on the screen that within himself which he really was."[34]

Once films permeated with what Rogers "really was" reached the screen, they signaled a significant expansion in the national civic sphere to include group interests and desires that had formerly been excluded. The rebellious views of racial minorities, women, and youth had remained linked to comedy or deviancy in films of the twenties. But now producers found it highly profitable to advertise Will Rogers films as a reflection of his politics and memories. As such, the main character was the "champion of the underdog," the "warrior against injustice," "Mr. Be Yourself," the "Mark Twain of the Screen," a "Jeffersonian Democrat," and, after 1933, "The Number One New Dealer." But where the Jeffersonians excluded minorities and Mark Twain's characters in *Huckleberry Finn* and *Tom Sawyer* only remained youthful comics unable to change the adult world, Rogers emerged as a dramatic hero as well as the clown who articulated views he honed in other media. Hence, when the Rogers character in *So This Is London* (1930) explained to a government agent that as a Cherokee Indian he always wondered why the Pilgrims were ever allowed to land, the lines came from his newspaper column. When the hero in *Judge Priest* (1934) rescued a poor black worker from lynching, the event mirrored the actions of Will's father Clem in the old Cherokee territory. When lovers had to overcome class and ethnic prejudice to marry, this echoed Will's courtship of his wife Betty years earlier.[35]

Just as Rogers was the country boy in the city, so the "Rogers formula film" gave dramatic form to his view that in the modern age of the corporation and a consumerism stylized in accord with the status symbols of the rich, the people lived in a "civilization without satisfaction." Typically the stories focus on communal life in urban areas and small towns where businessmen and established leaders exercise hegemony. Over and over the stories echoed Rogers's perception that affluence and family values in middle-class life reinforce the power of the wealthy over the mind and material conditions. Emblematic of the ensuing malaise, Rogers's films repeatedly focus on two young lovers who represent different social classes and groups. Due to the racial and class divisions that permeate the culture and society, they cannot consummate their romance. Only by reshaping consciousness and by reforming the society can these lovers come together and herald the birth of a more just society.

Since it was "Citizen Rogers" who found a way to realize that dream, Hollywood producers advertised his screen character as "a statesman in love as in politics."[36] A classic example unfolded in *Handy Andy* (1934). Andy, played by Rogers, embodies the ideal citizen and "producer" immersed in the consumer ethos of the late twenties. Like the propertied middle class, Andy owns a small drug store in a midwestern city, and his wife, Lulabelle, looks to the wealthy to satisfy her desire for a moral revolution. In line with these norms, Lulabelle forbids her daughter to marry a youth from the lower class, and Andy follows the "good advice" of corporate leaders who explain that his small drugstore has "gone by the boards." So Andy sells his firm for stock, and uses the proceeds to go to New Orleans where he and his family can find freedom in refined leisure and play. To uplift their desire for play—which is associated with blacks and the lower classes—they turn to French aristocrats to teach them manners and find a suitable mate for their daughter.

The comedy, however, derives from the way these dreams lead to disaster. No longer in control of his work, Andy experiences boredom as Lulabelle finds her wishes manipulated by advertisers. To top it off, the chain store that had supplied the funds for the "good life" has gone broke. Lulabelle and Andy's response, however, is not to renew the norms of liberal capitalism or a privatized consumer ethos or to look fondly back to the static past. On the contrary, Lulabelle and Andy experience a major conversion that frees them from the symbols of authority promoted by the wealthy.

Realigning authority, they turn to the vernacular art of the lower class—the Cajun French, a group discriminated against in Louisiana—for a model of new vitality where diverse groups come together. The affirmation of that élan allows them to form a public coalition across groups. This alliance in turn allows them to displace the corrupt rich who have oppressed them. In the end, because the corporation that bought his store has failed, Andy can return home to regain control over his work and property. The happy ending shows that Lulabelle has shed Victorian domesticity for productive work outside the home. Andy and Lulabelle approve of their daughter's marriage to the poor boy she loves. The result forges bonds of reciprocity across the classes and community, dramatizing that Rogers is, indeed, a "statesman in love as in politics."[37]

At the core of this narrative is a pattern that informed over twenty-four of the "Rogers formula films." Though each had a different locale and story, the same conversion narrative occurs over and over. Whether that conversion emerged in *Ambassador Bill* (1931), *Young As You Feel* (1931), *Doctor Bull* (1933), *David Harum* (1934), or *Judge Priest* (1934), the characters speak for the ideologies vying for power in the local community. In this locale, Rogers played not only the comic but the hero who served variously as a judge, ambassador, doctor, store owner, and politician accountable to the community. Operating in an autonomous civil society, he also engaged in volunteer groups, the professions, family life, and religious groups. Yet the local elites, played by actors who resemble the Republican presidents Herbert Hoover and Warren J. Harding, threaten this world. They speak in formal English and explain that the "bank's interest is your interest," "business is business," and that a disciplined, "strict interpretation of the Constitution is best." Behind this rhetoric viewers see that the rich exclude poor whites and ethnic and racial groups; moreover, the drawing of social boundaries makes it impossible for romance to reach culmination among lovers from diverse groups.[38]

Yet it is more than simple prejudice that creates unhappiness, for exclusionary practices reinforce the exploitation and class power of the rich. Typically the wealthy, as in *The County Chairman* (1935), isolate their sons and daughters from lovers of "dubious inheritance," refusing to let romance unfold across class or ethnic barriers. In this film and many others, the wealthy all commit crimes, such as stealing funds for parks and poisoning the public reservoirs. They then blame disorder and crime on poor and marginal groups that have no one to champion their cause. To discover the truth, the Rogers character reveals that politics and cultural transformation are two sides of the same coin. For people to recognize and act against unjust power they have to be emancipated from their cultural dependence on the status symbols and prestige of the wealthy and their tastemakers. Though each film would differ in its emphasis, a realignment of authority sets the stage for forging alliances across groups. Only this shift makes it possible for people to rebuild the society.

Take one of Will Rogers's most popular films, *Ambassador Bill*. The story mirrors Rogers's trips abroad to investigate conditions in Russia, Asia, and Latin America. At the start "Bill" has been appointed by the president as an ambassador abroad. Soon he flies into a foreign land where a tyrant aided by a United States senator, Pillsbury (named for the rich Republican businessman from the state of Minnesota), represses a popular revolution. The tyrant advances the interests of a

Will Rogers and Fifi D'Orsay in *Young As You Feel* (1931). Well before the end of Prohibition, Will Rogers shows that a good drink and urban nightlife renew the personality. (Courtesy Will Rogers Memorial Commission of Oklahoma)

rich American businessman and then evokes aristocratic symbols to justify his rule. Ambassador Bill responds by teaching the people baseball, a popular sport where divided classes learn to cooperate as equals. When the economy falters, the oppressed people cooperate to make a successful revolution. Success yields a society where lovers from different groups can marry and the state promotes the public good rather than the selfish interests of any one class or interest.[39]

At the same time, *Ambassador Bill* is typical in that it links reform with the formation of a more holistic culture. An example of that cultural renewal informs *Young As You Feel*. Made in 1931, it charts the rebirth of a staid widower. At first the central character, played by Rogers, embodies the "old-fashioned ethic" of work and no play, a trait that has made him wealthy. In a home exemplifying European aristocratic models, he remains apart from his sons' youth culture of jazz and sports. The widower eventually comes into contact with a modern woman, who shows him how to drink and play, and he becomes a devotee of urban nightclubs. Dressed in dapper clothes, he shows his sons the foolishness of a life that isolates play from labor. His offspring, in turn, convert to the new ethos and combine the carnival ethos of youth with adulthood. Together father and sons expose businessmen who charge exorbitant prices for the status symbols of the rich. Liberated from false values, the renewed father tells his sons that "I learned a lesson. When I think back over the last ten years of my life, I wonder why the health department did not arrest you boys." One son asks why.

> Because it is against the law not to bury the dead, and I certainly was dead. Anybody is who lets life pass them by. . . . Age is just a word somebody invented for somebody who needed an alibi. I was 108 going on 35. Now I'm 51 going on 24. From now on I am going backward.[40]

The collapse of barriers also serves to reconstruct inherited sexual roles, using that transformation to include the vitality of the new woman in public life. *State Fair,* released in 1933, dramatizes the contours of that shift. Rogers plays a midwest farmer whose daughter is discontent. Envisaging her future life, she finds that her fiancé believes that in their home the "men will decide." Feeling despair, the bride-to-be goes to a state fair, where she comes in contact with the new woman of the city, who works and dresses in stylish clothes and dances to music played by African Americans. Here the heroine enters a world where blacks and whites interact in a world of carnival. With a Ferris wheel spinning in the sky—symbolic of her inner shift in values—the heroine falls in love with her opposite, a newspaperman who resembles the young Rogers. Like Will the news columnist of the thirties, the journalist admires the radical midwest farmers, whom he calls the "Bolsheviks of the corn belt." He also dislikes the Republican editors who employ him, and he believes in women's emancipation. Together they merge stark opposites—the city and country, the new moral revolution and politics. At the end the Will Rogers figure facilitates their union, creating a marriage that repairs the cultural divisions of the modern era and heralds a new American culture.[41]

The fusion of reform and moral revolution also yielded films that challenged the racial divisions that thwarted radical politics since the era of Black Reconstruction. On one level this may appear impossible, since Rogers's films often featured Stepin Fetchit and Bill "Bojangles" Robinson, black performers whom scholars have depicted as perpetuating minstrel images that demeaned African Americans.[42] Though this is undoubtedly true, what is also striking is the way Rogers's films undermined stereotypical goals and purposes, opening the way for alternative race relations. In *In Old Kentucky* (1935), for example, Rogers plays a poor farmer who resists the efforts of bankers to steal his farm. When the farmer is thrown in jail, his friend and hired worker, played by Bill Robinson, brings his friend burnt wood to blacken his face. With this mask the farmer tries to escape disguised as a black. On the way out of the jail, the sheriff mistakes him for an African American and says, "Boy, I heard you can dance. Start dancing." The white farmer, whom Bojangles has earlier taught to tap-dance like a black, shuffles his feet, claiming this is the way "white folks like it." No doubt white viewers had a laugh seeing Will Rogers recreate their old, demeaning racist stereotype. Yet the message was also twofold: Audiences saw their populist hero subjected to the same class injustice as that faced daily by blacks, showing beneath the humor that both poor whites and blacks were in the same boat and had to cooperate to gain social justice from corrupt businessmen and politicians.[43]

Still another film, *Judge Priest,* advanced the same message of bringing black energies and voices into public life. It begins in a southern court with a pompous prosecutor, who, again, looks and speaks like

Bill "Bojangles" Robinson teaches Will Rogers how to tap-dance in *In Old Kentucky* (1935). The hybrid hero engages in cross-cultural communication and exchange across racial barriers. (Courtesy Will Rogers Memorial Commission of Oklahoma)

Will Rogers and Bill "Bojangles" Robinson plot to escape from jail in *In Old Kentucky* (1935). Here blacks and whites cooperate to overcome oppression and to reform the community. (Courtesy Will Rogers Memorial Commission of Oklahoma)

the recently defeated President Hoover. The prosecutor tells an all-white jury that the black defendant, played by Stepin Fetchit, has stolen chickens. Such "tramps" have "no place" in "our" community, explains the lawyer. Fetchit falls asleep at the bench, seeming to verify the prosecutor's accusation. But Judge Priest, played by Rogers, reads the funny papers and tells jokes, while at the same time reminding the jurors that they too stole food from corrupt officers in the Civil War. This appeal to common oppression persuades the jury to let the black "criminal" go free. The scene fades to a lake where Fetchit shows the judge how to catch the "big fish." Later still, Priest saves Fetchit from lynching (a scene cut from the version shown in southern theaters), and Fetchit responds by articulating an African-American view of history. This happens when the judge asks Fetchit if he can play "Dixie." The black comic says no, but he loves to play "Marching Through Georgia," a song performed by General Sherman when he burned plantations and helped emancipate the slaves during the Civil War.[44]

Audiences got the message, but many did not like what they saw. A telling example occurred when a self-proclaimed "Southern Lady" wrote Rogers about his role in *Judge Priest*. She wrote that this film would "ruin you with the Southern people." The story, she noted, was "poor history" since it portrayed a southern woman entering public life aligned with African Americans. In the past as in the present, Negroes "kept their places as servants, always respectful and obedient, never appearing in public except in caps and aprons, the young women with clean dresses, the men wearing white coats all the time, keeping a respectful silence." Rogers replied by pointing out that he and his wife Betty were born "South" of the Mason-Dixon Line and his father fought in a Confederate regiment. Though he failed to mention that the white southerners also took Cherokee lands, and that Clem Rogers supported black citizenship, Rogers acknowledged that her view would make "poor drama" as well as "poor history," for it was a fantasy. Indeed, if one followed the "Southern Lady,"

> you couldn't have any villains, or mean parts, for they would have to be Northerners, for no Southerner would ever be mean or a villain, so you would have to bring in a couple of Yankees for those. I tried to get old Steppin' Fetchit to not speak in public, but we figured he wouldn't be understood anyhow, so we just let it go ahead, and that, I know, was a breach of the old South etiquette.[45]

Beneath this dialogue lies the heart of the matter. Though the twenty-four Rogers formula films differed in setting and emphasis, they served to realign the basis of cultural authority in the community. Over and over the main characters initially affirm the hegemonic values of the corporate order, of static gender and racial roles, and of separation of the classes. Within this new order arising from the 1890s through the early thirties, businessmen make liberal capitalism, a hierarchical consumer ethos, and unequal sharing of wealth appear natural and good. Yet as these norms lead to disaster, the characters shed loyalty to the wealthy to reconstruct public life and Americanism itself. Undergoing a bottom-up conversion narrative, they align with the lower class to create a civic arena that begins to include women, minorities, and youth. The cross-cultural communication and exchange shatter the divisions between work and play to create a more inclusive public life—symbolized in the finale where romance and marriage now occur across classes and ethnic groups.

Will Rogers and His Public

The exchange with the "Southern Lady" revealed that a contest over traditional values lay at the center of the Will Rogers formula film.

How did Rogers's films affect audiences and politics? These questions connect with some of the most critical issues informing the study of popular art and politics: the relation between the ideas of artists and civic leaders and their respective audiences. Though the problem can never fully be resolved, it is important to realize that some of the basic assumptions we take to the study of politics can help resolve this issue. One assumes that Theodore Roosevelt or Woodrow Wilson gained office because their personalities and views converged with the beliefs of the majority of voters. A similar assumption can also help clarify the relation between film personalities and their audiences. Commenting on critics who complained that film stars made too much money, Rogers noted that writers rarely ask if the major banker or businessman who heads a corporation is overpaid. But in comparing a banker with a film star's worth, there was no contest:

> Is there any way [of] checking up on a bank president or vice president to see what he can actually by his own efforts draw into the bank? Is there any other business you can think of outside of stage or screen where they know exactly how good you are to them in dollars and cents? Greta Garbo don't get that dough because she is a long tall Swede; she drags it into a box office and they know just how much she dragged in. . . . So they are all worth what they can get, and they can get only what they can draw.[46]

It was also abundantly clear that in making this observation Rogers had his own career in mind. Where in the silent films of the twenties, his appeal to producers was minimal, the thirties were different. Symbolic of that shift, a journalist saw that *The County Chairman* gained success in direct proportion to its capacity to provide a dramatic "opportunity for Mr. Rogers to give his views on politics and numerous chances to comment on public affairs and the progress of science, making it possible for him to reach his public with a direction that was not at all possible through subtitles." Another saw that *David Harum* "packed them in" at the box office because the main hero "was a replica of Rogers' personality . . . an asset that should be exploited to the limit."[47] A theater owner wrote to a major trade journal that in his southern mining town it was impossible "to keep the fans away . . . all we have to do is advertise Rogers and they flock out to see him. . . . He speaks the language these boys that toil under the ground like to hear. I could sell them a Rogers picture every month."[48] A theater owner in Chicago similarly named a modern movie house the "Will Rogers" and featured a mural of Rogers on horseback with the legend,

"There is only one thing wrong with the world today . . . selfishness." Still another observed that Rogers's films drew fans because his "philosophy of fellowship and good faith . . . offered an antidote to what today passes for business success." Indicative of that appeal, a New York critic saw that Rogers's characters possessed a "curious national quality. He gives the impression that somehow the country is filled with such sages, shrewd yet gentle. He is what Americans think other Americans are like."[49]

What made this "Americanism" so popular, however, was that it gave form to the contours of an unprecedented mass art. Rogers recognized that transformation when he noted that in the early Depression years "everything is changing. People are taking their comedians seriously and their politicians as a joke, when it used to be vice versa." Rogers meant that in the past filmmakers validated a static Victorian artistic canon that pervaded nineteenth-century art geared for educated Anglo-Saxon readers. The frontier stories of James Fenimore Cooper and the detective tales of Arthur Conan Doyle were part of middle-class leisure pursuits separate from those of the lower orders. By contrast, the ribald comics and criminals that graced the lowbrow stage were seen as racially marked, childlike, and irrational. Rogers's films broke down these divisions, creating a hero who gave form and meaning to mass art that crossed groups and barriers. In the process the hybrid hero was less the embodiment of universal norms and more an American character capable of reinventing the self.

To heighten the aura of change, Rogers's most innovative film directors, ranging from Henry King to John Ford, utilized a visual style that evoked a world where metamorphosis of the self and society operated as two sides of the same coin. The Rogers hero was both outsider and insider. On the one hand, he held power in the institutions of law, the state, and the professions, and, on the other, he played the comic who undermined official norms. Rooted in the vernacular, the Rogers hero operated in a world where the soundtrack played folk and popular songs, while the dialogue revealed the ethnic and class roots of the main characters. The wealthy spoke in the language of the educated, while Rogers used the language and dialects of the folk. And as the Rogers family embarked on trips—a common motif in film after film—they encountered new people that compelled them to alter their inherited beliefs. Commenting on the way Rogers's performance style evoked comic and dramatic opposites in constant dialogue and change, Frank Borzage, the director of Rogers's first talking film, observed that his fans simply forget he is a comedian. This quality was apparent in scenes where he was called upon to portray the simple, human emotions that touch the very soul of mankind. The sincerity and conviction with which he did them was what might be expected of a great tragedian.[50]

At the same time these converging trends—films that evoked his Cherokee memories, the hybrid comic hero, the movement and metamorphosis—created a vision of America as a place that was mass culture writ large, as an entity constantly reinventing itself in accord with the inclusion of new peoples and experiences. Nowhere was that narrative more evident than in one of Rogers's last and most revealing films, *Steamboat 'Round the Bend.* Directed in 1935 by John Ford, the son of an Irish Catholic immigrant, and produced by William Fox, the son of Jewish immigrants, the story takes place in a landscape evocative of the myth of the nation: the frontier and the Mississippi River. Here Rogers plays Dr. John Pearly, the owner of a broken-down steamboat, who incarnates the Anglo-Saxon capitalist whose rugged individualism creates chaos. His reckless ways have destroyed his steamboat, and his racism leads him to forbid the marriage of his nephew to a "new woman" of the "swamp people" (a clear reference to the Seminole Indians, Rogers's neighbors in his youth). Yet when his family falls apart, and Dr. John learns that the young woman has tried to save the nephew from a corrupt judge who intends to send the youth to jail for a crime he did not commit, John realizes that she is a virtuous woman.

Shortly thereafter, John undergoes a conversion. Symbolic of his change of mind, Dr. John renames his steamboat the "Claremore Queen," evoking the name of Rogers's birthplace in the Oklahoma Indian territory. Reflective of that mestizo republic, John also teaches the young woman how to engineer the boat and makes a black, played by Stepin Fetchit, his first mate, and an old New England temperance crusader (similar to preachers who converted his own ancestors) his second mate. Individuals from different lands and places engage in collective work to restore the boat. Together they sail downriver where John and his crew perform a wedding for the mixed couple in a jail cell. Black prisoners whom John calls "brothers" sing spirituals to unite lovers across different groups. Geared to realizing that dream of romance in the real world, the crew sails south to gather new evidence to nail the true killer.

On the way the world becomes a borderland that mirrors the mestizo West of Rogers's Cherokee traditions rather than the Anglo-Saxon West permeating mainstream myths. When the polyglot crew comes to

Will Rogers as Dr. John Pearly teaches "Fleety Belle," played by Anne Shirley, how to navigate the "Claremore Queen" in *Steamboat 'Round the Bend* (1935). Rogers portrayed a hero who facilitates the empowerment of women in public life. (Courtesy Will Rogers Memorial Commission of Oklahoma)

the northern side of the water, Dr. John takes on the role of the trickster or "shape-shifter." Turning a wax figure of England's King George into President George Washington, the crew gains favor with northerners. When they reach the southern side of the river, a wax figure of Gen. Ulysses S. Grant becomes Robert E. Lee, and Stepin Fetchit becomes Jonah the biblical prophet. Between shows the crew gathers evidence to free John's nephew. To take their new proof to the governor, they fire up the engines with liquor, which John calls "The Daughters of Pocahontas Medicine Brew" (named after a women's group among the Cherokees). Merging art and life, John proudly says that this brew has been "in my family for generations." Next, a workforce composed of a woman, blacks, and New Englanders win a steamboat race sponsored by towns along the Mississippi River. In that contest, the "Claremore Queen" earns not only first place but a large sum of money. After conquering a self-made man of the "old school," the victors arrive at the statehouse where they present evidence that saves the youth. Soon they share the fruits of victory: Fetchit takes the trophy, the lovers acquire money for their family, and Dr. John sails upriver

Will Rogers holds a bottle of the "Pocahontas Medicine Brew" that "has been in my family for generations" in *Steamboat 'Round the Bend* (1935). This is one example of Rogers's capacity to interject Cherokee traditions into his film roles. (Courtesy Will Rogers Memorial Commission of Oklahoma)

on the "Claremore Queen," where like the reborn Cherokee, the boat provides a model of common enterprise for all.[51]

"The Number One New Dealer"

Once viewers came out of the theater, they could also turn on their radios and hear Rogers juxtapose democratic renewal against the failure of liberal capitalism to fulfill its promise. Rogers's radicalism of tradition took a different tone from the two major ideologies competing for loyalty in the thirties. The ethos of fascism embodied in films like Leni Riefenstahl's *Triumph of the Will* celebrates heroic military leaders who cleanse the nation of racial impurities and restore military authority from the top down. Initially Rogers had admired Mussolini, whom he saw as an Italian socialist. But, like many others, Rogers changed his mind when Italy invaded Ethiopia. Similarly, on a tour of Russia in the twenties he had written sympathetically of the Bolshevik revolt that overthrew the aristocratic exploiters who ruled under the czar. Nonetheless, Rogers also understood that state efforts to create new collective farms were destroying religion and private property, leading to a new top-down tyranny. As he saw it, the state in the Soviet Union "owns everything . . . a little like bankers here."[52]

Beyond this stab at bankers lies the core of the matter. Far from promoting a backward creed that would support the status quo, films created in accord with Rogers's own Cherokee values advanced a modernized republican ethos where citizens' cooperative work rebuilds the community and saves the promise of democracy. In *Steamboat 'Round the Bend,* the multicultural crew that rebuilds the "Claremore Queen" features new groups entering public life via a collective effort generated from the bottom up. Nor was this idea isolated to the screen alone. Early in the Depression Rogers supported President Roosevelt's move toward isolationism. Like other reformers, he feared that internationalism had allowed business to work in a global economy free of homegrown domestic controls. Able to operate independently, big business had advanced colonial projects in Latin America and Asia and created an unstable economy. Concentrating on reform at home, Rogers told fans of his radio show that the Republican Party had become like a "pioneer that could not change with civilization."[53] Soon he became identified with alternative politics as civic leaders—who realized Rogers's impact on public life and values—asked him to fly to the Mississippi Delta, Latin America, and the Southwest to aid flood and earthquake victims. Speaking before a series of black churches, Mexican-American relief groups, and Jewish Anti-Defamation League meetings, he asked individuals to cooperate in common public work to save their communities.

So popular were these efforts that politicians sought out Rogers's approval and endorsement, and Democratic Party leaders asked him to run for the Senate from the state of California.[54] Though he refused the latter offer, he supported the socialist writer Upton Sinclair in his bid to become the governor of California, believing that Sinclair might truly "make a good President of the United States."[55] Rogers similarly advocated fresh policies to restructure wealth. Commenting on Louisiana senator Huey Long's plan to "share the wealth," Rogers told millions of his radio listeners that "I kind of work with Huey. He's my inside man in there [the Congress] and I make the balls and let him throw 'em. See? But I really believe this scheme ought to get somewhere." He explained further that "this is becoming the richest and poorest country in the world. Why? Why, on account of an unequal distribution of money." When commentators in the *Wall Street Journal* and *New York Times* complained of his "un-American" ideas, Rogers

Will Rogers launching the presidential campaign of Franklin Roosevelt at the Democratic National Convention in 1932. From left to right: Franklin Roosevelt, James Roosevelt, Senator William McAdoo, James Farley, and Will Rogers. (Courtesy Will Rogers Memorial Commission of Oklahoma)

responded that there was truly a "whole lot of hollering going on among the rich and the near rich. . . . We are living in a great time."[56]

Once the New Deal came to power in 1933, the good times got better. After campaigning for Roosevelt in the election, Rogers used his radio show to advance New Deal policies. So significant was that advocacy that Roosevelt's campaign manager James Farley said that the president responded favorably when the comedian in his "own clever way" conveyed the president's program to millions. In fact, there was no doubt that the president "appreciated" it,[57] and not merely as a nice sentiment. By 1933, commentators referred to Rogers as the "Number One New Dealer." On the radio he mixed humorous advice on health and good food with words of support for "Franklin's" effort to pass social security, to levy high income taxes on the rich, and to provide jobs through public works. In the world of foreign affairs, Rogers was also one of the first to recognize the rise of the fascist threats. He demanded that the country begin to rearm, noting that the invasion of China revealed the price one paid for not possessing a "gun" to defeat the tyrants expanding across Asia and Africa.[58]

Though bankers did not care for his calls to reshape the basis of wealth and power, it was clear that Rogers's coworkers and his public did. A young fellow actor, Joel McCrea, explained, "We stood in awe of him and knew what he stood for. . . . [He] had an influence on every thing he touched. He brought glory to it. The behavior on the set was improved, the attitude towards America, the attitude towards Jews, the attitude towards colored people, he could do all that by his example." A cameraman recalled that when Rogers went on location, civic groups tried to "prevail upon him to speak before their organizations." And even though the cameraman was a devout Republican and "Will and I didn't agree politically, there was much about the man that you had to admire, that you unconsciously tried to emulate his thinking." Others saw that Rogers truly liked to make money and cut the best deal, but close friends said that he was also the "most generous man [they] ever knew." He sent checks to poor actors "as if they were relatives," and when a film finished ahead of schedule, he paid laborers for the time they missed and invited the crew to his home for a party.[59]

When the guests arrived at his estate in the Santa Monica hills, they entered a home that represented a vastly altered approach to consum-

Interior of Will Rogers's ranch in the Santa Monica hills. In this vision of the western style, Indian and western traditions mix, exactly like Rogers's Cherokee ancestors. (Courtesy Will Rogers Memorial Commission of Oklahoma)

Exterior of Will Rogers's ranch in the Santa Monica hills. Rogers's home popularized an American style of consumerism that mixed work and play. (Courtesy Will Rogers Memorial Commission of Oklahoma)

erism and abundance than that prevailing in the lives of the stars of the twenties. Formerly Hollywood stars stylized their homes in accord with European aristocratic modes. But Rogers's home was a western-style ranch house, rooted in the vernacular of a multicultural people. A wooden exterior had no references to high art, and Will and Betty furnished the interior with Indian paintings and rugs draped over plain wooden chairs and tables. The upstairs bedroom contained a picture of Chief Sequoia, the mixed-blood Cherokee who developed the syllabary for Rogers's ancestors. Outside, horses carried the brand of his father's ranch in Oolagah, Oklahoma. Down the hill, Rogers built a polo field where he brought earthiness to a sport identified with kings. A friend noted that Rogers played polo "in a different manner" from all the others. "He'd start yelling, slapping the horse with his hat and riding like a Comanche." Once the game ended, the guests often moved inside for a party. There Rogers was known to praise his coworkers, especially the unappreciated artists of color who helped make his films successful. To show his gratitude, he named hills after Stepin Fetchit and praised the work of another African American, Bill "Bojangles" Robinson. Years later, Robinson told a reporter, "I don't know anybody else as high as him who would have said that. He put me in fifteen or sixteen scenes in [a] picture that weren't written for me. He wouldn't let them hide my face."[60]

"History Ain't Necessarily the Truth"

At this point we can begin to answer the questions with which we began: How did Rogers gain fame by promoting a redistribution of wealth and power to save the core of the American republic? And why has that memory been forgotten? Evidence of his vast impact arose after the airplane crash in 1935 that killed Rogers and his friend Wiley Post. At a time when many equated Americanism with Anglo-Saxon superiority and liberal capitalism, Rogers had drawn on his Cherokee roots and communal memories to popularize a more inclusive and radical vision of nationality. Indicative of that public élan, those who gathered at his funeral included Anglo-Saxons, Catholics, Jews, blacks, Mexicans, and Rogers's fellow Native Americans. Reporters eulogized the man they called a "living Uncle Sam" and recalled his generosity to "all in need." Little wonder that when the nation mobilized to fight World War II, the government commissioned battleships in Rogers's name, and public opinion polls found that he was still the most popular film star of the day. In this context, the folk singer Woody Guthrie told audiences that the two greatest men in history had been "Jesus Christ and Will Rogers."

Ironically, the impact of World War II and then the Cold War began the process of distorting Rogers's memory that has lasted to this day. Government leaders christened battleships, national and local monuments, highways, parks, and schools in Rogers's name, all the way from the Capitol Rotunda in Washington, D.C., to a public park in the black area of Watts, California. The most enduring monument emerged when Betty Rogers put into practice her husband's Cherokee traditions of redistributive economics. Along a beach that has many areas removed from public access due to ownership by wealthy homeowners, Mrs. Rogers gave a large tract of land to the state for public use. She also donated their Santa Monica ranch to the people of California as

The USS *Will Rogers* moving out to sea in World War II. Here we see the way that the state drew on Will Rogers's memory to justify the battle against fascism. (Courtesy Will Rogers Memorial Commission of Oklahoma)

a public park.[61] Yet these parks and monuments failed in many ways to offer future generations any sense of why an entertainer had risen to be arguably the most noted public man of the day.

With the exceptions of the Oklahoma State Historical Society and the Rogers Memorial in Claremore, Oklahoma, Rogers's deep Cherokee roots were ignored along with his call to redistribute wealth to save the producers' democracy. Rather, once Rogers was no longer around to speak for himself, those who served as the butt of his criticism proved the most influential in defining his memory for future generations. This process began in 1935 when former President Herbert Hoover memorialized Rogers as a "splendid American who sprang from the soil recently won in the westward march of civilization." Hoover's fellow Republican in Hollywood, Cecil B. De Mille, furthered the distortion when he told audiences that Will Rogers symbolized a "frontier spirit that gave the nation Abraham Lincoln, Andrew Jackson and General Custer, a spirit that stirred the cauldron of the frontier that was boiling to smelt and bring forth the American character as we know it today."

The pinnacle of this historical amnesia centered on the "Shrine of the Sun," located at the base of the Rocky Mountains in the town of Colorado Springs. Built to memorialize Rogers's name, the Colorado shrine was constructed by a wealthy businessman. Inside the tower, viewers saw paintings and murals that linked Rogers's life to the "winning of the west." Visitors entered a large room decorated with paintings that portrayed soldiers killing Indians, police suppressing striking miners, and industrialists creating factories to become wealthy. These historical triumphs culminated in a new world of leisure, symbolized by the Broadmoor Hotel, a resort situated near the shrine and built by the same local industrialist. Embodying the consumer culture of the new West, the Broadmoor artwork featured wealthy Caucasians dining, dancing, and engaging in sports. While enjoying the pleasures of modern life, visitors were encouraged by the resort's brochure to see that progress led to the "white man's playground" of Broadmoor.[62]

One might expect more from scholars, but a recent biographer, for example, concludes his investigation by telling us why Will Rogers's memory and appeal no longer attract audiences: Since Rogers never really "questioned the basic beliefs of his audience," his humor remains inapplicable to the profound complexities of the world after Pearl Harbor.[63] This compels one to recall Rogers's view that "history ain't necessarily the truth, only something that somebody wrote down." A more telling explanation might have allowed that the call for unity in World War II and postwar anticommunism made Rogers's ideas seem "un-American." Under the impact of the Cold War at home, the popular arts and scholarly discourse became not more complicated but more simple and distorted when assessing past "complexities."

Contrary to the large-scale whitewashing of his image, the historical evidence compels us to recognize that Will Rogers rose to become the most popular artist of his day precisely because he was nothing like the image that has emerged since his death. A more relevant question to ask is not why the arts of the Great Depression were so conservative and innocent, but why they were so radical. It is not enough to answer that economic hardship fueled resistance. Long before the New Deal came to power or the Communist Party formed in the film capital, Will Rogers gained success in all the mass media of the day. When we ask why this was so it is necessary to see that he participated in a major cultural realignment that preceded the rise of insurgent politics.

To gain perspective, it is well to remember that though economic depressions in the past bred mass movements of protest, such movements had not been able to succeed due to the power mobilized against

SHRINE OF THE SUN

— on —

Cheyenne Mountain, Colorado Springs, Colo.

A Memorial to WILL ROGERS

America's best loved citizen, by his devoted
friend, Spencer Penrose.

The Shrine of the Sun, dedicated to Will Rogers in Colorado
Springs, Colorado. Here a wealthy industrialist appropriated Rogers's memory to celebrate what the comic satirized all his life: a
business system that colonized and exploited nonwhite people and
workers to advance the "Manifest Destiny" of the Anglo-Saxon
West. (Courtesy Will Rogers Memorial Commission of
Oklahoma)

them as well as the cultural and racial divisions within their own ranks. At the local level workers had created communal civic spheres, but at the national level the Anglo-Saxon middle class excluded them and mediated their views through their own stereotypes. In this way the national "imaginary community" excluded the lower class. However, in the twentieth century a mass art arose that held the potential to forge a common basis of communication. That great potential failed in the twenties because a mass culture that encompassed the diverse groups within society gained its legitimacy solely in Anglo-Saxon terms. That is, state leaders and show people of immigrant stock uplifted mass entertainment with older Victorian standards of morality. The institutions of the mass arts and the new consumer culture were thus informed with the status symbols of the rich—a process that perpetuated the view that an "American" public life found its roots in European norms of Anglo-Saxon civilization.

The coming of the Depression, however, delegitimized official values. In that vacuum, views and voices that had been repressed and marginalized in the national civic sphere entered the center and altered both. It was in this context that a Cherokee Indian, Will Rogers, gained control of his work in Hollywood. Drawing on a Native American tradition of the trickster, Rogers interjected into the national civic sphere memories of a mestizo republic, of a community of redistributive economics, and of women's and racial minorities' inclusion in communal life. Equally important, this was seen as an oppositional vision that appealed to the minorities of the city and the poor of the countryside, for it appeared to be a more "American" vision than that promoted by Anglo-Saxon tastemakers. As Rogers gained success, his Hollywood films and radio shows promoted a major realignment of cultural authority from the top to the bottom of society. The mass arts now provided what was missing in the past: a free space that promoted images and voices of cultural communication and radical reform.

By giving expression to what remained inexpressible, Will Rogers dramatized the modernization of an inclusive republican creed in which the citizens cooperated to realize dreams of abundance and pluralism. Indicative of the way he blurred art and politics, when Rogers appeared before Congress to promote flood relief in the Mississippi Delta, he told the lawmakers that "regardless of what you say, when anything is put before the people and they know there is a need for it, they are for it every time."[64] By forging an Americanism composed of interpenetrating opposites, Rogers had merged the utopian desires of mass art with politics. And because he did what had seemed impossible, when the Cherokee trickster died on that hot summer day in 1935, he was mourned by myriad racial and ethnic groups with all the pomp and ceremony of a fallen statesman, one who many believed might have become a "future President of the United States."

Rogers's unprecedented success signaled that mass art generated a competitive civic sphere of art and politics.[65] If Rogers set the tone for an alternative Americanism in the popular arts of the Depression era, was he the exception or the rule? To that issue we turn our attention in the next chapter.

Chapter 2

The Recreation of America: Hybrid Moviemakers and the Multicultural Republic

American popular culture is the only culture that has been created and accepted by a multiethnic population. Within its own boundaries the U.S. is already a world culture. To the extent that popular culture has been exported from anywhere it has come to America in the physical embodiment of the immigrant masses. . . . American films created a whole new artistic expression that imitated nothing which had existed in previous artistic achievements.
  —Shuichi Kato, one of Japan's leading social critics, July 1987

The thirties, though they had their own load of sentimentality, were the hardest headed period of American movies, and their plainness of style, with its absence of "cultural overtones," has never got its due aesthetically.
  —Pauline Kael, *The Citizen Kane Book*, 1971

Will Rogers often remarked that he neither was self-made nor acted alone: He participated in a wide upheaval in American culture. Yet how did that upheaval inform moviemaking as a whole in the New Deal era? One way to answer that question is to listen to the recollections of another famed artist who came to prominence in the thirties: Orson Welles, the boy wonder and creator of the work that has been acknowledged as the greatest film ever made in the United States, *Citizen Kane* (1941). As he looked back, Welles proudly traced his ancestry to a family whose members fought in the Civil War. Committed to making a republic free of slavery and aristocracy, they hoped to create a democracy where the people controlled their work and participated in civic affairs. By the twentieth century his grandparents backed Theodore Roosevelt's efforts to master big business and order industrial society.

Yet the reform-minded Progressives disdained alignments with immigrants and racial minorities. Instead, they aligned themselves with corporate leaders to pass immigrant restriction and the new southern segregation laws. Welles believed that out of their efforts to save Anglo-Saxon civilization, they became trapped in what they had disdained: the corporate order. Out of that impasse Welles's relatives began to emulate the status symbols of the rich and European high art. Soon his aunts got into the "imitation place business" and decorated their lavish homes with historical styles of a bygone time, a process that had the great advantage of elevating white western culture above the vernacular arts of immigrant workers and minorities.

Young Welles, however, matured at a time when many intellectuals and artists launched a quest for an alternative. Describing his childhood as a "lost paradise," he evoked the imagery of the Edenic West that lay at the heart of the nineteenth-century republic, a vision undermined by the new era of industrialism and his family's emulation of the wealthy. To recover that dream Welles turned to radio and movies as a modern form of "education . . . to dramatize the art of imparting knowledge" so that "people will listen to what I have to say politically." Breaking away from the elevated white culture of his ancestors, he joined the Federal Theatre Arts Projects to produce a "Harlemized and gangsterized" version of *Macbeth*. Late in the Depression he gained control over his work in the Hollywood studios to create a "cinema" that "should always be the discovery of something . . . revealing the sort of vertigo, unceasing lack of stability, that melange of movement and tension that is our universe." The result yielded *Citizen Kane,* a film that Welles saw as a tragedy about our big "business plutocrats . . . who believed that money had automatically conferred stature to a man. Kane is a man who truly belongs to his time."

Welles, like Will Rogers, combined moviemaking with promotion of radical politics. Working as a newsman, he wrote that in the modern world citizens had renewed the faith that "America . . . is an adventure . . . a new world that for the races of man was a new place, a new beginning." Only now we must realize that "race hate is a disease." Racism formerly had aligned whites with those big business "marauders" who had "greed for all things possessed by the people." These forces together led to the "oppression of the Indians, Blacks, Hispanics and Asians." But Welles retained faith that the New Deal of President Roosevelt and the battle against fascism in World War II made it possible that "America can write her name across the centuries . . . if we the people—brown and black and white and red—rise to the great occasions of our brotherhood." Carrying that élan into politics, he backed the "wonderfully encouraging" rise of unions, the New Deal, civil rights, and the Popular Front. But when conservatives called him a "communist," Welles noted that "the idea of interdependency ante-dates Karl Marx." Evoking the American radical ethos—the "splen-dour of our republic"—he explained that

> I believe—and this has very much to do with my notion of free-dom—I believe I owe the very profit I make to the people I make it from. . . . If this is radicalism . . . it comes automatically to most of us in show business, it being generally agreed that any public man owes his position to the public. . . . A free man owes to the world's slaves all that he can do for them . . . free them.[1]

Welles's effort to modernize republican traditions at odds with mo-nopoly capitalism and inequality suggests that Will Rogers was not alone. No doubt backward-looking images and demeaning racial prej-udice informed moviemaking and politics.[2] Nonetheless, views that as-sert that a monolithic, Anglo-Saxon Americanism pervaded popular art and politics cannot account for Welles's view that the film capital provided a site for creating a discourse of nationality and public life. Yet why did this occur and what implications did it have for movie-making and politics? How was it possible that the young Welles saw that Hollywood moviemaking provided a site for modernizing the "splendour of our republic"?[3]

The Margins Talk Back

To answer these questions, it is important to realize that unlike earlier forms of mass amusements, the film industry provided the means for immigrants to alter the American values that had been promoted by elite tastemakers for over a hundred years. In the teens, small studios aligned with labor unions created films promoting labor-capital con-flict, and the industry as a whole allowed non-Anglo-Saxons to alter the contours of traditional American myths and symbols.[4] No doubt the most visible example of that transformation was the rise of Holly-wood, where outsiders appeared to dominate the production of movie images. In reaction, state leaders spurred film producers to enact cen-sorship that eliminated overt images of class conflict and defiance of moral codes. The result was that moviemakers contained the moral revolution within standards promoted by the rich. Still, even as this legitimated a new mass consumer culture, moralists were also alarmed that "no American born actors or directors have a prominent part" in Hollywood studios. It was pointed out that the "majority of American movie picture producers are of foreign birth" and over 425 foreign-born directors and players "comprise the leaders of the profession."[5]

No doubt the most visible example of this trend were the founders of the film studios that dominated the scene. Generally, these producers represented first- and second-generation immigrants from eastern and southern Europe. Seven of the eight founders of the studios descended from either Jewish immigrants or their children. Coming from outside the old forms of power, they exemplified what Max Weber aptly called "pariah capitalists." That is, they seized chances in marginal trades shunned by members of the host society. It was these marginal endeavors that served them well as producers. At a time when movies generated a revolution in morals that was feared by defenders of the old order, the Jews had experience in Europe and the United States with marginal trades, ranging from clothing to furs and jewels, where the key to success was the tapping of consumer tastes.[6] Commenting on the way these skills overlapped with catering to audience tastes, the screenwriter Dudley Nichols told readers:

> Do not think for a moment that these skillful men who run the production machines do not have their great abilities and worries and perplexities. They have probably the most abominable task in modern industry: they must attempt to produce a standard product where the elements of production are human ideas and feelings and personalities, those most fluid, intangible, nonstandard, inconsistent things. They must envy the motor car manufacturer who can design ten standard models each year and then watch over the blueprints and the office records. Or steel industrialists with their tangible goods.[7]

The Jews were so successful because they supplanted the original Anglo-Saxon producers and hundreds of independents by making films that catered to audiences' ambivalent approach to the new urban culture of the twenties. A clue to their success was supplied by the sociologist Thorstein Veblen. Asking why Jews were so often at the center of twentieth-century innovations, he argued that Jews were marginal in a cultural sense. For innovators, however, that was an asset rather than a liability. Never fully integrated into the host society, they possessed a dual consciousness. Ostracized by the host society, they had lived as outsiders. As such they could question the norms promoted by the official tastemakers.[8] In the United States as in Europe the Jews also emerged as middlemen and women adroit at devising means of communicating and selling across groups. Having experience on the margins, they could be critical of all closed systems of national blood purity, while advancing visions of a more open life. To the early studio founder Carl Laemmle and the producer Sam Spiegel, the movies provided a way to forge a multicultural public, for as Laemmle observed, "Regardless of creed, color, race or nationality, everyone in the universe understands the stories that are told by Universal pictures."[9]

While Jewish immigrants possessed traditions that made it possible for them to innovate with cultural forms, they also possessed a tradition that placed them at odds with the restrained work ethic and family life promoted by the Anglo-Saxon middle class. Like other ethnic and racial minorities, the Jewish immigrants from eastern Europe possessed a rich life of festivals permeated with humor, exuberant music, and dances. Within their communities there was no concept of the protected, pure woman who remained outside the economy and shunned sexual pleasure. The Jewish immigrants did not sanction premarital sex, but eroticism within marriage was encouraged. When couples found that they were incompatible, divorce was permitted. Unlike the gender divisions of Victorian culture, Jewish women played a major role within the economy. Within Jewish life the enjoyment of material goods—when one could afford it—was not a sin but a part of life's pleasures.[10]

During the twenties, Jewish producers' status as marginal businessmen and cultural brokers made it possible for them to cater to the moral revolution associated with the rise of mass art. The key to their success lay in generating films that sanctioned the new consumer culture and the revolution in morals within the highbrow "foreign" models of aristocracy. Yet they also constantly pushed at the limits. Our own plot samples derived from the industry's major trade journal revealed the contours of that duality. In the teens and twenties producers dignified the moral revolution within the standards of the Anglo-Saxon middle class. More than 60 percent of the characters had roots in small towns and rural areas as well as the milieu of the older professional and small propertied middle classes (see appendix 2, figs. 3, 31). The trend found its best illustration in the films of Cecil B. De Mille. Whether in *The Affairs of Anatol* (1921) or *The Ten Commandments* (1923), the lures of the new urban culture endangered the protagonists, symbolized by their fall into the hands of Asian femme fatales or the decadence of mass amusements and the excesses of affluence. The main characters find salvation only by redeeming the moral revolution and consumer desires with refined norms (appendix 2, fig. 12).[11]

The advent of the Depression, however, collapsed the old barriers and allowed the lures of mass culture to move from the private to the public domain, altering both in the process. It began when producers found that audiences now had a mind of their own. Watching that change unfold, a *Variety* reporter noted that "general conditions no longer make theatre patronizing a matter of after dinner routine. The patrons go to pictures these days because there's something specific they want to see. Every thing else gets the go-by."[12] Searching for an explanation for this shift, reporters found that the patrons no longer admired studio formulas derived from "high brow standards." Young people who "cared not a hoot about tradition" showed their displeasure at one local theater by throwing objects at the screen until the projectionist showed a film that they approved. Observers told film producers that the "imitation of successful pictures was passe," for "times were eliminating class distinctions so far as the industry is concerned."[13]

This elimination of "class distinctions" manifests a major realignment of cultural authority. No longer could high art contain the revolution in morals and visions of cross-cultural communication in a realm separate from public life. In the new "catch as catch can" atmosphere, a critic saw that "the industry is finally admitting that its only collateral is the barometer of motion picture mindedness."[14] Those who continued in the old ways got the message as the once invincible studios lost profits and filed for bankruptcy, while firms that tapped the "new audience" generated an upheaval in the structure of Hollywood. Suddenly the assumption that large studios could monopolize production, ward off newcomers, and generate predictable profits gave way before audiences who had a mind of their own.

A classic example of the transformation unfolding in the wake of the "new audience" is the career of William Fox. Early in the Depression Fox provided the socialist author Upton Sinclair with an in-depth interview. Like other Jewish film producers, Fox's parents came to this country to escape pogroms in eastern Europe. Fox had joined the Socialist Party in New York City to attain higher wages and a new world for the workers. Seeing opportunity in the marginal world of mass entertainment that was shunned by official culture, he entered the world of movies "when it was little above the crude burlesque stage, which was alright for men, but not for an audience made up of men and women too." Soon he grew inspired by the "idea of putting entertainment and relaxation within the reach of all." To legitimize the new entertainment, Fox surrounded movies with wealthy status symbols and style.

The advent of the Crash sent Fox's company into bankruptcy and forced him to rethink the contours of his product. At his nadir, he contemplated a way to merge his early socialist values with movie-making. Ruminating out loud, he told Sinclair that "I distinctly remember, capital claiming that labor was destroying the nation by its attempts to reduce hours and gain higher wages . . . which should be the aim of this great republic." Formerly his movies and lavish theater palaces had spurred the worker to "discover all the modern conveniences we have in this nation. . . . Once he has that he feels he is in heaven."[15] After his bankruptcy, a disaster he blamed on bankers and his inability to gauge shifts in audience taste, Fox saw that in the future producers had to find profits by creating films that combined consumption with reformist themes—a process that led Fox Studios to experiment and succeed with the Will Rogers formula film.

Fox, however, was not alone. From the late twenties to early thirties several fresh companies—Warner Brothers, Disney, Columbia, Radio Corporation of America—moved from marginal status to that of majors. Unlike the established firms, they were not encumbered either with heavily mortgaged movie houses or silent stars with expensive contracts.[16] Capitalizing on the new sound technology, they hired journalists and writers from New York City, spurring a major turnover in industry personnel. It also appears that they aimed their products more to the vernacular tastes of the lower classes. Illustrating that market segmentation, pollsters found that stars contracted to studios that dominated production in the past—for example, Metro-Goldwyn-Mayer and Paramount—appealed to audiences centered in the upper-income groups. But the newer firms, such as Warner Brothers, featured stars that appealed predominately to lower-income audiences.[17]

To top it off, the major studios' monopolistic control was also challenged by the rise of independent studios, which found their markets among marginal groups. Where in the twenties, fifty-one small firms catered primarily to rural markets, the ranks of the independents rose to ninety-two between 1929 and 1934. These new firms turned over more than 90 percent in every five-year period, but the number of films the small firms made almost equaled that of the majors in any year. In 1932, 1936, and 1938, their film production actually surpassed that of all the majors combined (appendix 2, figs. 5, 6, 7).[18] The independents also had a competitive advantage since they had no high-priced theaters or stars nor did they have to submit their product to the industrywide censorship boards, since the large firms excluded most small independents from the Hays Commission and its censorship panel.

The creation of a competitive product by the smaller companies also supplied thousands of independent theaters with films that appealed to their patrons' desire for productions featuring both stories and stars derived from the stage. Reporters saw that as the "indies" expanded, the major studios "recognized against their will that stage talent in its various departments is now essential . . . and that is the reason the independent producer is in such a good spot. . . . Independent theatres are hungry for good pictures." The "indies" also catered to the vast expansion in the new decade of over a thousand German, Yiddish, Spanish, and black theaters. In contrast to the audiences for mainstream studio products, these patrons wanted films in foreign languages or productions that dealt with their social and class interests. With directors like Oscar Micheaux and Edgar Ulmer making independent black as well as Yiddish-language films, trade reporters observed that the "exhibition of foreign language talkers, in their native tongue, has crystallized as an important part of the film business."[19]

Just as the independents and innovative studios catered to a "new audience" arising outside mainstream institutions, they also created a symbiotic interchange with the large studios in making a different type of film. Increasingly, artists who made it in the world of the "indies" took their inspirations to the larger studios. Central to that alteration was the creation of a new type of production, the "talkie" film that interjected into the national civic sphere the voice and views of formerly silenced groups. In some ways the disruption created by sound seems unlikely, since scholars have taught us, as Warren Susman explained, that "sound helped mold uniform national responses; it helped create or reinforce uniform national values and beliefs in a way that no previous medium had been able to do." As Susman observed, a standardized film could mold language and promote the tastes of the educated. Yet this was far more the case in the twenties than the thirties. In the silent era dialogue and plots emerged with written subtitles composed in accord with the standards of official tastemakers.[20]

The advent of sound, however, generated films that officials saw as capable of reversing the basis of cultural authority from the top to the lower classes. Nowhere was that fear more evident than in moralists' comments concerning *The Jazz Singer* in 1927–28.[21] In contrast to other early feature-length talkies, where heroes spoke in highbrow "Broadway English," this Warner Brothers' film focused on what one critic saw as the "low group tastes of the masses of people, reproducing for them their own language with appropriate profane, suggestive and . . . obscene decorations that have delighted the 'groundlings' from Shakespeare's time."[22]

The story featured the famed vaudeville performer Al Jolson as Jakie

Rabinowitz, a Jewish boy who sings and dances to music derived from African-American jazz. His father—a cantor in the synagogue—despises his son's "nigger music" and wants him to take his place as cantor. The father has assimilated in part to Anglo-Saxon Americanism, symbolized by a Thomas Cole painting, of the Hudson River school, that hangs prominently in the family living room. Unwilling to reject his black-inspired music and wishing to become "American" in his own way, Jakie leaves home and performs in lowbrow nightclubs. For over three-quarters of the film Jakie defies racial norms by singing and dancing to African-American songs without a black mask, yet this rebellion is eventually contained. To please his dying father, Jakie sings the traditional Kol Nidre on Yom Kippur in the synagogue. Shortly thereafter he gains success on the Broadway stage; conforming to conventional standards, he sings in blackface and succeeds by succumbing to the highbrow standards of the wealthy.[23]

Nonetheless, the film generated an enormous controversy that centered on the power of talking films to undermine normative racial and class conventions. The author of the play, Samson Raphaelson, wrote that Jakie turned to black music to explore the dynamic and "vital chaos of America's soul. I find no more adequate [language] than jazz. . . . It is a prayer, distorted, sick, unconscious of its destination. The singer of jazz is what Matthew Arnold said of the Jew, 'lost between two worlds: one dead, the other powerless to be born.'" Many feared what that power might mean. D. W. Griffith, the director whose *Birth of a Nation* linked racial superiority to the redemption of Anglo-Saxon America, refused to make the film because of its "racial themes." Furthermore, Jakie's story failed to draw audiences in small towns and rural areas populated by Anglo-Saxons.[24] In the city, moral guardians condemned the film's focus on "degenerate, black young Hebrews" whose celebration of "jazz" served as the means to undermine the "immortal decencies of human life." In sharp contrast, black journalists noted that in Harlem "sobs were heard all over the theatre" because of Jolson's "sympathetic portrayal of Negro life," while the *Amsterdam News* observed that "every colored performer is proud" of Al Jolson for making "one of the greatest films ever produced." Trying to explain why the first "talkie" succeeded among immigrant and working-class audiences, a trade reporter noted that when Jolson spoke, urban audiences responded

> as though to wine. It was an epochal moment. They could not get over it—he had spoken to them from the screen! It was a little strange too; for there had been much Vitaphone speech before, in

many of the shorts. But this coming from a picture that the crowd was interested in, a picture which swayed their emotions, that they for a moment were *living* with the players, struck deeply home.[25]

Once the Depression hit, the power of talkies to strike "deeply home" continued as producers created films that utilized sound to create characters who challenged inherited visions of art and civilization. An indication of that change was described by a writer of Jewish-American stock, who noted that when he first came to Hollywood in the twenties he had to conform to studio rules. But with the advent of sound, "producers let us have our head [saying] 'I didn't hire you to write what other people write. . . . I want you to write what you really feel like writing.'" His response was to make talkies that rejected the "bloody revolting English of the Broadway stage," drawing instead on the dialects of the "street" to formulate a "literate dialogue for ordinary people." Similarly, W. R. Burnett, a newspaperman and son of an Ohio politician, recalled that when he wrote the gangster novel and then script for *Little Caesar*, he discarded "literary English . . . I dumped all that out. I just threw it away. It was a revolt in the name of a language based on the way the American people spoke." Another writer saw that the key to success was to write dialogue that evoked the way real people spoke, giving it the "Woolworth touch." Furthermore, Edna Ferber, the writer of novels and plays that became the films *Cimarron* (1931), *Dinner at Eight* (1933), and *Showboat* (1936), regarded her work as part of an intellectual revolt against the educated who looked to Europe for models of emulation. Her motto was that

> it's time we stop imitating. It's time we denied this libel that we're crude, unformed and undeveloped. Let us write in the American fashion about America. Let's paint in the American fashion from American subjects. . . . Why do we imitate when we can create?[26]

It was not accidental that the emphasis of sound to evoke the vernacular speech of the people also brought to the fore moviemakers who drew on their immigrant pasts to reshape the nation's myths. Film industry personnel turned over by more than half from 1929 to 1935.[27] In this context, directors such as John Ford (Irish Catholic), William Wyler (Alsatian Jew), Busby Berkeley (eastern European Jew), Frank Capra (Italian American), Mervyn LeRoy (eastern European Jew), Edgar Ulmer (German Jew), William Dieterle (German Jew), and Lewis Milestone (Russian Jew) moved from a marginal status in the world of the silent film to the center of the world of the talkies. The success of their films not only allowed them to gain control over production in the studios, but they worked with set companies of actors, crew members, and even writers. Scenarists ranging from Dudley Nichols to Ben Hecht, Robert Riskin to Lester Cole, John Huston to W. R. Burnett and Billy Wilder accordingly found freedom in working with one major director. On the way they carried into movies the public views they developed in the tabloid press, the ethnic stage, and the avant-garde world of New York, Chicago, and Los Angeles.[28]

The Return of the Repressed

So what were the themes of the new talking films? To answer this question it is necessary to realize that trade reporters clearly saw that "subjects which would have been a failure in the past were successes today." Current writers and directors saw the key to success was "less art for more box office." By returning to the industry's roots in the lowbrow "nickelodeon" élan, the new films were, as one producer noted, "cut from the cloth the times provide." The success of one of the new upstarts, Warner Brothers, lay in providing films that were "timely, topical, but not typical."[29]

Along with the shift to "realism" there also occurred a major transformation in cultural authority. From the twenties to the thirties our plot samples showed that the number of characters who dealt with a world out of control increased from 10 to over 50 percent. Businessmen cast as villains similarly rose from 5 to over 20 percent, while the rich portrayed as morally evil or a social danger accelerated the most of all, from 5 to over 60 percent from 1929 to 1940 (see appendix 2, figs. 1, 2, 22). If this revealed that filmmakers had become more critical of established values, protagonists who met death and defeat increased from zero to over 10 percent through the early thirties (appendix 2, fig. 21).

This alteration in authority had two major themes: the way in which adherence to mainstream values of success and the home created the disasters of the age, and the eruption from below of characters who rebelled against their former status and position as racialized and gendered inferiors. These two themes—the fall of the old order and the rise of marginal characters—ran parallel to each other. One theme revolved around the way patriotism and individualism created not progress but war and economic chaos. *Cavalcade* (1933), for example, won the Academy Award for best picture by charting the history of a British family. Emblematic of the glories of Anglo-Saxon civilization, the central characters raise children who advance the English empire around the world, but all their sons are killed in World War I. In the aftermath the couple sit in their home as the viewers see workers in revolt, punctuated by the heroine's statement that "something has gone out of us." The scene cuts to a nightclub where a young woman, the offspring of the working classes, sings the "Twentieth Century Blues" to Duke Ellington's black jazz band, evoking a new world where mass art carries themes of vitality and tragedy.

The traditions of the older generation also reveal that patriotism is a sham in the Academy-Award-winning best picture of 1930, *All Quiet on the Western Front.* Directed by Lewis Milestone, a young immigrant Jew from Russia, this adaptation of Erich Maria Remarque's antiwar novel focused on German youth who believed in the patriotic call to war in 1914. But as Milestone noted, the aim was to have "new ideas . . . build up in the consciousness" of the audience. Reversing normal narrative strategies, he took the youth into battle at the start of the film; the action "wanes emotionally," but "ideas wax intellectually." That is, the youth realize that rich financiers and their patriotic leaders have created death, leaving the new generation angry and antagonistic toward their elders' civilization.[30]

Characters in some of the most popular films of the early thirties learn that their personal success and individualism have created not progress, but decline. In *Little Caesar* (1930), *I Am a Fugitive from a Chain Gang* (1932), *An American Tragedy* (1931), *Frankenstein* (1931), *Dracula* (1931), *The Invisible Man* (1933), or *King Kong* (1933), the story focuses on self-made men whose pursuit of gain generates the "lost paradise" of the national promise. Cast as the heroes of the age— soldiers, inventors, explorers, bankers, businessmen, and journalists— these heroes' values lead to destruction. In the *The Invisible Man* and *Frankenstein*, inventors' quests to master nature disrupt the bonds between man and the earth. Commenting on Dr. Frankenstein, a trade reporter saw that "his experiments carry him along until he is obsessed with the unholy desire to create life in his own image. But he fails to reckon with God." Similarly, the white explorers in *King Kong* (reminiscent of slave traders in the nineteenth century) take a giant ape from his jungle home. When they display Kong in chains to New York City audiences, the ape breaks his chains and flees. As the director focuses audience sympathy on the victimized ape, he dies at the top of the Empire State Building.[31]

What made these films so "realistic" was that they collapsed the boundaries between popular drama and the stories of chaos and disruption that permeated the newspapers. In order to link these fictions

The great ape in *King Kong* (1933), transported from Africa and chained like a crucified Christ before the altar of commercial spectacle in New York City. Here the monster, victimized and exploited by scientists and businessmen, is more sympathetic than his captors. (Courtesy Academy of Motion Picture Arts and Sciences)

with public events, the new talking films often opened with a panoramic shot of an urban skyline, usually that of New York City. Derived from magazines and advertisements, the skyline image grounded the story less in the myths of the old agrarian countryside than in the modern world of "today." Repeatedly newspaper headlines drove the plot forward and served to root the characters' private lives in historical events and the news, a practice similar to the innovations pioneered by John Dos Passos in his 1936 novel, *The Big Money.*

Trade critics noted that the new icons and stories made moviemaking a form of journalistic muckraking and exposé, a practice that collapsed the barriers between the newspapers' public sphere and the entertainment provided by the movies. Commenting on why films of this journalistic "ilk" and "topicality" had gained popularity, one trade critic noted these works took the viewers "behind the newspaper headlines, behind the scenes of industry and politics." Film productions such as *Washington Show* (1932) revealed the "grip" of "'big business' . . . on the government of this country" and the "ways in which it makes its power work to insure the accomplishment of its own purposes and the defeat of the will of the people." Screenwriter Dudley Nichols noted that "for good or ill" mass entertainment matched the Greek stage of antiquity. Now artists sought to

> deepen our understanding of ourselves and society so that movie making was a tremendous educative force. What we see enacted we unconsciously relate to our immediate problems and draw practical conclusions. . . . Our exposure to the theatre is either helping us to resolve our own conflicts and the conflicts of society by making us understand them, or it is engendering more conflicts.[32]

Intimately linked to this effort to "resolve our own conflicts . . . by making us understand them," the new films also interjected into the public domain formerly silenced groups and repressed wishes. Moralists criticized these new films and called for censorship, but nothing could thwart the popularity in the early Depression years of gangsters, ribald ethnic comics, and fallen women. In the past, the middle class saw criminals as the exemplars of racial minorities and deviants who disrupted modern life. But the Italian or Irish criminal in *Scarface* (1932), *Public Enemy* (1931), and *Little Caesar* reversed the formula.[33] As one critic noted, the treatment of crime as "picture material has now changed radically." Formerly the "criminal characters were infected with desires for coin and for bloody spoils," but the hoodlum featured in the talking films "thirsts primarily for power." W. R. Burnett, the author of *Little Caesar*, explained that the reason why his work was a "smack in the face . . . was the fact that it was the world seen completely through the eyes of a gangster. . . . It had never been done before then. You had crime stories but always seen through the eyes of society. The criminal was just some son-of-a-bitch who'd killed somebody and then they got 'em. I treated them as human beings. Well, what else are they?" Burnett observed that in contrast to the moral deviant of the past, the modern gangster was a sympathetic "Gutter Macbeth."

The distinctiveness of the cinematic gangster thus was his capacity to shift the audience's moral viewpoint. That is, he met defeat because he was the victim of official leaders and institutions' false values. At first he rebelled due to the discrimination and exploitation confronted by immigrant workers. As Burnett saw it, if you have "this type of society, you will get this type of man." Ethnic youths facing poverty and a world that excludes them turn to crime to gain money and power. Reinventing themselves with new clothes, cars, and "fast" women, much as Rico Bandello becomes famous in all the newspapers as "Little Caesar," they utilize consumer goods to serve their own purposes. Yet the attainment of the American dream also means that they emulate the laissez-faire capitalist ethos of the robber barons of industry, a flaw that leads to their downfall. To Edward G. Robinson, the son of Jewish immigrants and the star of *Little Caesar,* these films were a modern Americanized version of a

> Greek tragedy. Inherent in it was the drama of the humblest, the most despised, seeking to break his way out of the anonymity of ignorance, toward a goal in which he would be not one of many men, but a man on his own. I even spilled out some of my own longings that were parallel. While Rico's goals were immoral and anti-social, we had this in common . . . somehow we would be different, above, higher.[34]

The urge to be "different, above, higher," and a "man on his own" identified the gangster not only with revolt against class exploitation but with revolt against the stereotypes that linked the racially marked outsider with passivity before the forces of history dominated by the Anglo-Saxons. The Fu Manchu film series, for example, featured an Asian businessman whose family was destroyed in the Boxer Rebellion. To seek revenge on white colonists, he reinvents himself as an Asiatic gangster. Along similar lines, *The Emperor Jones* (1933) featured a poor southern black who rejects his subordinate status. Derived from a play by Eugene O'Neill, the film featured the black activist Paul Robeson as Brutus Jones. Initially Brutus lives in the segregated South and sings in the local church, but, like many other blacks, he moves North for freedom from segregation. On the way the soundtrack punctuates his travels with the black blues songs "Let Me Fly," "The St. Louis Blues," and "I'm Travelling." Brutus finds employment as a Pullman porter, where a white businessman teaches him how to exploit and cheat others. After killing a man, Brutus works on a chain gang, only to escape to a Caribbean island. There he overthrows rulers who have exploited and degraded him. But as he transforms his identity and gains power over both whites and blacks, he emulates the gangster tactics of whites. When his black subjects revolt, Brutus dies in a jungle dreaming of his youth in an organic African-American community. Noting the larger message of the film, DuBose Heyward commented that in altering O'Neill's play for the screen,

Rico Bandello, played by Edward G. Robinson, the poor Italian making good as *Little Caesar* (1930). Crime provides the money to buy fine suits and thereby transform the self. The composition, as directed by Mervyn LeRoy, exemplifies the popularization of cubistic techniques, with multiple focal points of interest, and a vision of modern life as a series of surfaces that ask the audience to choose between viewpoints. (Courtesy Academy of Motion Picture Arts and Sciences)

> I added the character of the earlier Jones, as I had imagined it, and by throwing this character into contact with the disintegrating power of our white civilization, I broke Jones down from the rather simple Southern Negro to the shrewd, grafting Negro of the play. I enjoyed making him a black counterpart to our own big business pirate.[35]

Films featuring the rebellious outsider shattered stereotypes in what many saw as truly the most sacred realm of all—that of gender. The gangster rebel was in fact often accompanied by his female counterpart, the fallen woman. By the early thirties films like *Rain* (1932), *Blonde Venus* (1932), *Imitation of Life* (1934), *Anna Christie* (1930), *Ann Vickers* (1933), *Back Street* (1932), *Of Human Bondage* (1934), *Red Dust* (1932), and *Dinner at Eight* (1933) were condemned and criticized by moral guardians for undermining the female identity as mother and wife. Trying to account for the popularity of the fallen woman genre, a reporter in *Variety* explained, "Audiences' unexpected

Paul Robeson in *The Emperor Jones* (1933). Jones, a formerly subservient black, has become the ruler of a Caribbean island, turning the tables on his oppressor, the white man to the right. Like the white ethnic gangster, Jones transforms himself and beats western rules and businessmen at their own game, signaling the entry of blacks into the public arena. (Courtesy Academy of Motion Picture Arts and Sciences)

refusal to accept talking pap, their sudden discrimination, wrought an upheaval in the ranks of the silent goddesses. Routed by their helplessness before the mike, little by little they began to disappear, leaving only the girls who kept their brains hidden . . . to move to the center stage." Increasingly "flappers" of the twenties—heroines who linked sex to "girlishness"—gave way to females who exuded "some intelligence behind the performance. Contrary to earlier trends, The Great God Public, formerly considered a Puritan censor, voiced its approval with admission fees that fully endorsed heroines of easy virtue." The result:

> No longer does the beautiful but dumb girl intrigue when it comes to placing the admission price on the line. There has got to be some intelligence behind the personal performance because now they talk.[36]

Each woman of "easy virtue" used sex and glamour either to manipulate men or cross official racial and gender barriers. Instead of uplifting consumer pleasure in the private domain, the heroines entered public life where they took delight in the clothes, cars, and penthouses of the city. Unlike the foreign "vamps," these were American women who sold their bodies to gain material success. In the 1932 film *Call Her Savage,* the white heroine, played by Clara Bow, grows discontent with Anglo-Saxon men and marries an Indian. Similarly, the devoted wife in *Blonde Venus,* played by Marlene Dietrich, leaves her husband and sings hot blues songs like "Hot Voodoo" in nightclubs. Fleeing her husband, she lives with blacks in vice districts, wears a man's suit, and earns her own money. In sum, she has taken on masculine qualities and crossed racial barriers in order to reconstruct the coordinates of female identity.[37]

The assault on convention also gained popular currency in ribald comedy that gave voice to the humor and language of working-class minorities. Here again the innovation on traditional forms was all-pervasive. Over and over the films of W. C. Fields, the Marx Brothers, and Mae West broke from the forms that had pervaded earlier vaudeville and popular entertainments. It had once been necessary for comedians to perform under a minstrel mask. Not only did this degrade blacks, but it linked rebellion against official work, sex, and class roles with African Americans. In a society where work required repression of instincts, a minstrel show allowed whites to put on a black mask and express whites' repressed desires for play and for crossing sexual boundaries. Yet at all times the performer identified the disruptive desires with nonwhites. At the end, the white performer took off the burnt cork and emerged as a dignified Caucasian family and working man. Black minstrelsy thus allowed whites to release their hidden desires without guilt and to degrade nonwhites.[38]

Yet the importance of comedy in the early talking films was that it allowed ethnic comics to validate the desires of whites, once linked to blacks alone, for a different self and society. As these comics shed the minstrel mask, the challenge to racial stereotypes happened on two clear levels. This is exemplified by the rise to success of the black comic Stepin Fetchit. On some levels Fetchit seems to perpetuate the old minstrel stereotype without alteration, yet it is also important to realize that Fetchit was not a white, but a black artist who utilized the old imagery to suit his own purposes. In so doing he was also well prepared. Fetchit honed his art on the black vaudeville stage where his comic style showed black audiences how to exploit demeaning stereotypes to manipulate the oppressor. Symbolic of that subversive style, he told reporters in a slow drawl that his real name derived from Toussaint L'Ouverture, a Haitian revolutionary. Once in the film capital, he established a black utopia called "Harlemwood" where blacks would

Marlene Dietrich as the fallen woman in Josef von Sternberg's *Blonde Venus* (1932). Dietrich embodies the capacity of the fallen woman to transgress barriers. Not only does she live in a black neighborhood but she takes on masculine power, symbolized by wearing a man's suit. (Courtesy Academy of Motion Picture Arts and Sciences)

never have to work for whites. Likewise he hired box seats at the Hollywood Bowl for friends to enjoy the art of black composers and to demonstrate to whites that blacks appreciated high art. Transferred onto the screen, this subversive mode meant that in films like *Stand Up and Cheer* (1934), Fetchit assumed at first the image of the lazy black but then at the end led a parade to advance the New Deal government hated by the characters who speak for big businessmen.[39]

The undermining of minstrel stereotypes was not confined to blacks. The most famed comics of the early thirties, the Marx Brothers, Will Rogers, W. C. Fields, Charles Chaplin, and Mae West, came to the

Stepin Fetchit in *Stand Up and Cheer* (1934). In the final scene of a musical that celebrates the coming of the New Deal, Fetchit assumes the aura of the leader of the Pullman Car Porters, who announces a new day. (Courtesy Academy of Motion Picture Arts and Sciences)

movies from the urban vaudeville stage.[40] Where in the past vaudeville comics used the black mask to distance the humor that subverted established values, these new comics presented that rebellious stance as part of the white self. Over and over Fields gloried in the cliche of the dumb and lazy Irishman's proclivity to drink and use wordplay to overturn convention. The Marx Brothers similarly exuded the aura of the cliched stingy Jew or the foolish Italian, only to turn the image against their oppressors. Accordingly, Fields in *The Bank Dick* (1940) and the Marx Brothers in *A Night at the Opera* (1935) humorously attacked the pretensions of the rich and status symbols. In a similar vein Mae West celebrated the image of the fallen woman who was not ashamed of her desire for plenty of sex. *I'm No Angel* (1933) portrayed her as "more savage than the savages," a woman who reversed roles by telling a young lady that "marriage is nothing more than contracted prostitution. I believe in a single standard for men and women."[41]

Just beneath the surface of this comic mode can also be found a critique of the new consumer culture. Nowhere was that more evident than in the work of Charles Chaplin. In *City Lights* (1931), for example, Chaplin began his story at the unveiling of a patriotic monument. Chaplin's tramp sleeps at the base and catches his pants on the sword held by one of the classic figures of freedom. Once the police eject the tramp, the scene suggests that public life and "liberty" are the preserve of the rich and their middle-class followers. Moving down the road, the tramp saves a banker who wants to commit suicide because life, so the viewer assumes, is meaningless. Soon the tramp and the rich man share the promise of equality in a night of cabaret hopping. Though they live the promise of democracy in amusements, the daylight world sees realities of power descend. Once the sun comes up, the rich man rejects the tramp as an inferior. The final indignity now occurs: In their nightly frolics, the rich man had given the tramp money to pay for a blind girl's operation, but when the banker awakens he has the tramp jailed for stealing. Years later the tramp returns to encounter the girl whose sight has been restored. To disabuse her of the notion that a rich man saved her, he touches her hands. As she recognizes the truth, their eyes meet and she "sees" at last where true virtue lies: among the poor rather than the rich bankers and industrialists.[42]

Fundamental to these converging trends—the rise of the social problem, gangster, fallen woman, and ribald comic films—is a major transformation in mass art. This shift generated renewed cries for stiffer censorship guidelines than those promoted by the official industry regulatory body, the Hays Commission. During the twenties, pro-

Charles Chaplin portrays the tramp evicted from civic rituals in *City Lights* (1931). This opening scene reveals that the rituals of Americanism exclude the poor, dramatizing that the ideals of democracy remain reserved for those with middle-class status. (Courtesy Academy of Motion Picture Arts and Sciences)

ducers and ethnic artists had promoted a consumer ethos that preserved Victorian standards and Anglo-Saxon civilization. The Crash saw audiences rejecting the formulas of the twenties. In that vacuum, new producers and independents made sound films that realigned authority from the top to the bottom of society. Increasingly, artists of immigrant stock inverted racial and ethnic stereotypes to give voice to subordinate groups. But that strategy also yielded a sharp and ambivalent duality at the core of the early talking films. On the positive side, rebellious gangsters and fallen women made it possible for marginalized characters to take images that had been rejected by officials and reshape them for their own ends. No longer were they passive recipients of cultural imagery, but men and women of passion who reinvented their identities as modern men and women of desire and instinct. The negative side of this strategy was that it left the established opinion makers with the full power of description. The rebels might wear a pejorative slur with pride, but they still remained caught in the constructions of their oppressors. Since they were unable to alter established social roles, at the end of the film the outsiders adapted to conventional family values, "hit the road," met death, or were incarcerated.

One might think that such endings satisfied the censors, but there was far more to it. It is worth noting that in recalling the process of writing scripts, John Huston claimed that in the thirties and forties "no picture of mine was ever really damaged by the censors in any form. There was usually a way around them."[43] Yet the ethic that rebels and bandits had to pay for their sins was not simply a formula imposed by external censors. Folk songs, for example, emerged out of a long tradition of oral culture that existed outside the control of moral guardians and commercial pressures. Over and over popular songs such as "Tom Dooley" and "Stagger Lee" and "Frankie and Johnny" evoked the glamour of men and women whose defiance of social convention led to defeat and destruction. These widely held beliefs emanated less from official leaders than the popular consciousness of the people themselves. The problem was that in defining modernity, the quest was conducted in the guise of inappropriate inherited forms. That is, all moviemakers had inherited the strictures of the Victorian artistic canon that defined that a dramatic hero was to be Anglo-Saxon, while criminals, clowns, and fallen women exhibited the qualities of lasciviousness and disorder. It followed that to bring outsiders' desires into the center one had to reimagine an artistic language for what did not exist: a self and nationality that brought artistic and social opposites into an interpenetrating whole altering each other.[44]

The Art of Interpenetrating Opposites

To open the possibility of an alternative public life and culture, filmmakers and audiences had to reimagine the canon and bring together all that Victorians tore apart. Gradually films that collapsed the Victorian hierarchy altered the ideal self and national identity—a trend that set the stage for a new star system and film formula. One of the most significant trendsetters appeared in the form of the Academy-Award-winning film for 1931, *Cimarron,* based on Edna Ferber's novel. In a society in which nationality came to focus on the image of the "West," it was not accidental that the film charted a contest between two competing visions of the frontier for the modern era. The first vision of the frontier was promoted by the family of the heroine Sabra. Believers in Anglo-Saxon superiority, they resist her romance and marriage with Yancey Cravet, a man with a "cimarron" or dark complexion that suggests he is an Indian. Yet the two marry and move to Oklahoma, where Yancey, who owns a newspaper and embodies the second vision of the frontier, defends the rights of fallen women, Jews, a poor black, and Indians.

At first Sabra condemns her husband's actions, enforcing the code of racial purity and Victorian norms of her past. However, when Yancey leaves for another frontier adventure, his wife undergoes a conversion. Taking over Yancey's newspaper, she defends Indians from capitalists and exploiters. Due to her efforts, she becomes a senator from Oklahoma. Combining masculine with feminine traits, she blesses her own white son's marriage to an Indian. At the end, set in 1929, Sabra appears at a banquet in Washington, D.C., attended by officials from across the land. There she introduces to the guests her mixed-blood grandchildren. Her speech suggests that marriage across the races, coupled with the capacity of women to reinvent themselves, provides a vision of reform and nationality for the twentieth century.[45] Edna Ferber—the daughter of Jewish immigrants in the Midwest— explained that films like *Cimarron* undermined Anglo-Saxon visions to reveal the truth about the nation and its peoples. That is, the

> United States seems to be the Jews among the nations. It is resourceful, adaptable, maligned, envied and feared . . . its peoples are travellers and wanderers by nature, moving, shifting, restless.[46]

Once the image of a dynamic democratic republic gained success in *Cimarron,* it also paved the way for films that celebrated the reshaping of cultural authorities from the top to the bottom of society. One of the most important alterations could be found in the meanings given to the consumer culture. The Academy-Award-winning film of 1932, *Grand Hotel,* for example, unfolded in the modern city of Berlin. Initially the camera takes the viewers into a modernist hotel. As the camera sweeps up the lobby, it stops at a nightclub named the "Café American," where jazz music can be heard. Inside the lobby we meet characters who speak for the ideological conflicts of the day. Baron von Preysing has gained success as a manufacturer and buys aristocratic symbols to advance his prestige. Preysing clearly exploits Mr. Kringelein, a poor clerk who has saved up his meager "slave wages," and a secretary who supplements meager wages by serving as her employer's mistress.

Just as a society rooted in liberal capitalism evokes the ethos of consumerism and its wealthy status symbols in order to solidify the new order, Kringelein and the secretary are initially awed by the power and social prestige of industrialists. But they both learn from an aristocrat, a member of a dying class embodying grace and generosity, that they must resist the greedy ways of the monopolists. Learning to laugh and use humor to undermine the wealthy, the duo refuse Preysing's offer of more money to cover up a murder that he has committed. Instead the two outsiders learn to cooperate to have the industrialist jailed. With their new confidence they learn from the aristocrat how to win at gambling. In the end, the liberated clerk and mistress now leave the Grand Hotel as masters of their fate. On the way they show that collective action can realize dreams of freedom, a more egalitarian-based abundance, and modern sexual relations.[47]

By shedding their psychic dependence on the wealthy, these new heroes and heroines embody the ethos of interpenetrating opposites in that they combine the shrewdness of the fallen woman, the comic, and the gangster with the heroic citizen. That conversion narrative in other films also provides a model for overcoming the cultural barriers that prevent the population from cooperating in order to advance their common interests. Take the most successful commercial film of 1933, *42nd Street*. The music incarnates the show-within-a-show musical, which takes viewers backstage to watch artists and commoners work to create a new culture that earns success and public approval. The narrative of fall and rebirth also echoes one of the most pervasive themes of the Depression era, providing a model of redemption amid hard times.

The means to renewal centers on the symbol of "42nd Street" as the embodiment of the dreams of mass culture. The film opens as the camera glides over New York City, moving down to the main thoroughfare of Manhattan that links the world of the wealthy East Side with the world of the working class on the West Side. The bonds holding both worlds together exist in the appeal of the new mass art and consumerism. Yet as the story opens we meet Julian Marsh, a showman who symbolizes the contradictions that have led to the Depression. He has speculated and lost on the stock market. Though in poor physical health, Marsh decides to make a new type of "show." Initially he encourages a female star to sell her body to a monopoly capitalist who will finance the new endeavor. Meanwhile, the chorus girls sell *their* bodies, and a cast composed of diverse ethnic comics and dancers cannot get along. Emblematic of the whole, the selfish star breaks her leg, and the financier threatens to withdraw his money.

Yet in response to this fall from grace, the characters are reborn by recreating the basis of American culture itself. The disaster spurs

Marsh to turn to outsiders for assistance. So he asks a new dancer, Peggy Sawyer (played by Ruby Keeler), to replace the stricken star. That choice is not accidental. At a time when cultural wars pitted rural areas against the modern city, Peggy comes from a small western town but combines the ethos of the frontier with urban wisdom. Having learned from the fallen women, the ethnic comics, and gangsters how to "make it" in the city, she becomes a composite heroine who inspires the divided group to cooperate. Incarnating a new spirit of interpenetrating opposites, she engages in vernacular dance and jazz derived not from the upper orders but from the "street." At the end the diverse cast sings "42nd Street" while the camera pans down the avenue. As the audience voices its approval, we see that on the street all races and ethnic groups dance and mingle. In the foreground the heroine tap-dances, and a skyline filled with towering buildings evokes the city culture. Now Peggy sings to the audience:

> Take your dancing feet down to 42nd Street
> Where the underworld meets the elite
> Little nifties from the fifties, innocent and sweet
> Shady ladies from the eighties who are indiscreet
> They're side by side and glorified
> On naughty, bawdy 42nd Street[48]

The protagonists of the show-within-a-show musical have done the impossible. Instead of undermining society, a moral revolution and a popular art engendered by blacks and the lower classes provide a new cross-cultural exchange. By the mid-forties that fusion bred formula films in which the hybrid heroes and heroines gave birth to a new man and woman. Take the case of the "Thin Man" series. Derived from a famed detective novel by Dashiell Hammett, the series focused on a playboy citizen and his urbane wife. Unlike the older detective Sherlock Holmes, Nick Charles has little interest in remaining aloof from nightclubs, ribald comedy, and gangsters. On the contrary, Nick and his beautiful young wife Nora are "comedians of no mean ability." Nick stylizes himself as a gigolo who is an "amusing drunk, a smart wisecracker" but "a very devoted husband and detective." Nick and Nora enjoy what her wealthy relatives disdain—drink and nightclubs—and together they exude an identity that defies older gender roles. As the heroine enters public life to master criminals, and the hero lives off his spouse's earnings, the writers who forged their dialogue decided "all of our characters were homosexuals." Similarly critics saw that the "Thin Man" films, by mixing male and female traits, "amal-

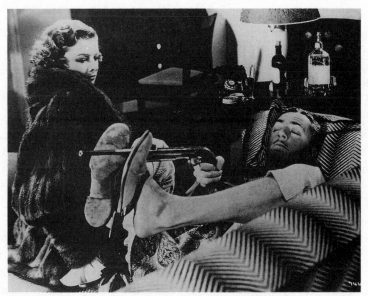

Myrna Loy and William Powell portray Nora and Nick Charles in *The Thin Man* (1934). After a night on the town, the married detectives playfully plot their next move. Nick wields a town gun, and liquor bottles from the previous night remind the audience that the couple enjoys liquor and city life. But Nick and Nora also advance family and civic values by taking aim on corrupt businessmen and politicians. (Courtesy Academy of Motion Picture Arts and Sciences)

gamated two modes" of art that were formerly apart with the result that

> seldom do pictures so effectively combine so many different forms of entertainment normally appealing to so many different classes of patrons. . . . basically it's straight hokum that grabs the masses. Paradoxically it's a smart sophisticated production for the class crowd. Here's mystery and melodrama with all the thrill and suspense of the hollowed penny dreadfuls; comedy in which there is a laugh in almost every line of dialogue, action and situations. . . . The mystery is solved by a retired detective who drinks and plays around with his wealthy wife and a dog that can't be bothered by detecting.[49]

Other hybrid characters break down cultural barriers that had thwarted cooperation among groups from different regions. The "Hardy Family" films showed that the new culture would not undermine but renew home and public life. Each film in the series focuses on Judge Hardy and his family in Idaho. Symbolic of the western small-town myth, the judge incarnates the ethos of the virtuous citizen.

Whether fighting monopolists aligned to corrupt politicians at home or in Washington, D.C., the judge cooperates with youthful offspring who embody the élan of the modern age, especially his son Andy, played by Mickey Rooney. Together adults as well as adolescents cooperate to reform and renew the community.[50]

Each of these fresh narratives features a story of fall and rebirth that generates an alternative mode of perceiving the self and society. Whether we consider the Thin Man or Hardy Family series, the Rogers formula films, the show-within-a-show musicals, or *Cimarron,* these films show the main characters initially adhering to the values promoted by the wealthy and established leaders. Yet they soon find that the old faith has led to disaster in the forms of poverty and public chaos. To explain social disorder, the wealthy villains blame crime and disorder on the poor or aliens. Yet as the hero or other main characters learn the truth, they undergo a conversion experience. Overcoming the fall, they are reborn by cooperating with former outsiders to save traditional family and communal life. Their efforts yield a just society and a more inclusive and better tomorrow.

Directors complemented the conversion story with a visual style that emphasized that the world, like the self, was not fixed or static but in metamorphosis. To convey visual forms that evoked these sensations in the audience, the major directors of the day—Busby Berkeley, Lewis Milestone, King Vidor, Edmund Goulding, Frank Capra, John Ford, and Orson Welles—developed an art form that restructured the inherited studio practices of the twenties. King Vidor explained that he wanted to "get away from all those old ways of doing things. . . . When I arrived in Hollywood, there was a sort of unreality about a film, a falseness. The acting was overdone. The make-ups were overdone. . . . Acting had no connection with reality."[51] To him the films of Cecil B. De Mille and D. W. Griffith conveyed a static Victorian worldview. The camera remained outside the frame, and subtitles written in accord with proper English interpreted the action in accord with the views of official tastemakers. Films constructed around such rules told the viewer that the story conveyed eternal morals. Since there existed only one truth for the audiences, the composition emphasized one focal point, while makeup and lighting ensured that the blonde hero or heroine embodied the ideals of civilization that would eventually triumph over the villains. Within this visual universe villains possessed dark complexions and clothes, linking them to the outsiders in an Anglo-Saxon world.[52]

In reworking these cinematic practices, directors incorporated into the movies some of the central principles associated with modernism, in which the world was seen not as something known but something to be discovered and reinvented. To shatter the older viewpoints, the directors often had their players shed makeup that demarcated the white characters from the dark villains. Frank Capra noted that by photographing a player devoid of makeup the audience saw the "secret beauty" contained in the lowly and despised.[53] Capra and others also used a mobile camera to enter inside the frame to create a story where the characters engaged in a process of discovery rather than reinforcing known truths. One of the earliest examples of that ethos arose in Milestone's *All Quiet on the Western Front*. At the start the viewer sees a large door that looks exactly like a proscenium arch in the theater. If this suggested that the audience was to sit on the outside and watch eternal illusions unfold on the screen, its expectations were undermined as the door opens and the camera moves inside, down the halls, and up stairs to start the search for the truth beneath "illusions" promoted by the official leaders of Kaiser Germany.[54]

The viewers encountered a world where they looked beneath the surface to see the interconnection among apparently isolated events and material things. A society where white and black, men and women, work and play were seen as diametrically opposed gave way to an interdependency. To convey that relational view directors like John Ford often moved the camera from one object to another, avoiding cuts that divided characters and objects from each other. Ford similarly transferred into movies some of the principles of modern art, particularly multiple spaces and scenes photographed within a flat picture plane that suggested that the world was less a transparent set of truths than a work of art made by human effort. His designers conveyed this holistic view with compositions where several spaces overlapped in one multiple image. Unlike in the past, no single focal point or authority figure dominated. Busby Berkeley's musical numbers in *42nd Street,* for example, often have dancers interacting in concentric and asymmetrical circles and layers. The visual effect provided a communal dynamism where change and movement brought things together in a mutual reinforcement of renewal and vitality. Working in a similar vein, Welles and Capra used overlapping dialogue from one scene to the next to reveal their connectedness. Edmund Goulding, the director of *Grand Hotel,* often used a moving camera to focus on one character seated in the foreground, another in a middle ground, and still another in the background. As the parts interacted, the viewers saw action unfolding on several layers at once. In Goulding's own description:

> I tried to make the camera as much like a human being as possible. . . . It sees and hears of its own accord. This is the manner in which we introduce the various centrals in the story. We stealthily happen upon them in the life of the cosmopolitan hotel in which the story unfolds.[55]

The total effect of these innovations—the multiple views, the moving camera, the overlapping dialogue, the elimination of makeup—made it possible for the audience to become active rather than passive spectators. Critics saw that in many ways this placed into popular currency the principles of cubism, for the director asked the viewers to experience the world from many different perspectives—only here the subject matter focused on living characters making choices in the modern world. The directors of thirties films utilized montage principles similar to those of cubism as well. Scenes in a Will Rogers film directed by John Ford or Busby Berkeley's dance scenes in *42nd Street* showed several objects at once in simultaneous images. To Frank Capra, having all parts of the set "equally lighted [in] the back, middle and foreground" meant that all the characters "get equal billing." Orson Welles similarly observed that in *Citizen Kane* "I find it marvellous that the public may choose with its eyes what it wants to see in a shot." William Wyler, in turn, noted that by creating scenes with multiple layers, one "shot" made it possible

> to have background and foreground action. . . . I can have action and reaction in the same shot, without having to cut back and forth from the individual cuts of the characters. This makes for smooth continuity, an almost effortless flow of the scene, for much more interesting composition in each shot and lets the spectator look from one to the other character at his own will, do his own cutting.[56]

At the same time the moving camera, the multiple layers, and minimal makeup undermined fixity, it promoted an aesthetic rooted in discovery and reinvention. Several forms and icons furthered that dynamic vision. One of the most common was for directors to use mirrors and windows to reflect the main characters' images. Standing before a mirror, gangsters in *Little Caesar* or *The Emperor Jones* put on new modern clothes, signaling their capacity to reinvent their self-presentation. Or the camera might follow characters on trips where they learn from fresh experiences and new people, or the camera could enter behind the scenes to find out how men really made and produced the material world. The new investigative style, noted one critic in describing *42nd Street*, allowed one to understand that "the most exciting point of the play, and . . . continuously exciting, is that the spectator is taken into the theatre where he watches the construction—and the attendant heartaches and headaches of a musical comedy. That building of a play keeps the tune talkie alive." Noting the way these new techniques altered cinematic aesthetics from the late twenties to the thirties, Lewis Milestone observed that

> before the film had been like the stage. . . . the camera was in the position of the audience and photographed everything from the same position. We learned how to use the camera from the point of view of the actor. We built our sets differently. We could not just move on one wall, but all of them. We could shoot from any one position and follow the actor around.[57]

Composite Personalities and Interdependent Publics

If the camera followed the actor around in multiple spaces to convey imagery of movement and change, the most prominent films also gave rise to a new, hybrid personality that restored the star system shaken by the Depression. Grounded in a world of change and flux, these new personalities combined formerly dualistic opposites: the comic fool and the dramatic hero. Where the hero had embodied the values of the Anglo-Saxon citizen and the fool the impulses of rebellious youth or minorities, now these opposites fused. Commenting on the reason why this new mode fit audience taste in the Depression, the director Frank Capra explained that comedy was an essential, for the "man in the street has had so many dogmas crammed down his throat that he is prepared to revolt against current underestimation of his intelligence. He's fed up." According to Capra, current politics, Prohibition, patriotism, big business, and high-powered advertising were all subjects "ripe for ridicule." Comedy also allowed one to imagine not just "what exists" but "the way things should be." Norman Krasna, a writer who was a "big fella for the underdog," noted that comic heroes allowed one a "protest against the existing system and it's all in the framework of comedy." Still another writer, Alan Scott, saw that his goal was to make an "American" character and art that "combined all that anyone knew of the stage, burlesque, black comedy routines—refurbished for legitimate actors and actresses."[58]

Central to the style of characters who brought these influences together was that they exuded an aura of what the critic Gilbert Seldes called the "metropolitan type." Unlike in the past, "the influence of the gangster film has worked through the whole business of making pictures, so that in nearly every picture the adult and intelligent observer catches a glimpse of its factual rudeness; in nearly every one there is a character who drastically or sourly says what human beings really think, or mocks at heroics, or deflates pretensions." This shift in style gave birth to stars like William Powell. When he arrived in Hollywood, his dark, swarthy looks decreed that producers cast him as a gangster. Yet by the thirties these same swarthy looks made Powell an ideal hero for the role of Nick Charles in *The Thin Man.* Along similar lines, the most popular male star of the day was Clark Gable. Initially Gable's dark features meant that he played gangsters, one appropriately named "Blackie" in *Manhattan Melodrama* (1934). Yet two years later trade reporters observed that a "cinema upstart stole the crown that rested on the heads of established knockouts." Becoming the top male player of the era, Gable carried the aura of a "patent-leather-haired, swarthy-skinned, glint-eyed racketeer." Only now he brought that élan to a comic hero in Capra's *It Happened One Night* (1934), to the dark, romantic gunrunner in *Gone with the Wind* (1939), and to the rebellious officer in *Mutiny on the Bounty* (1935). At the same time, James Cagney, Humphrey Bogart, James Garfield, Paul Muni, Spencer Tracy, and Edward G. Robinson incarnated what Robert Sklar has called the ethos of "city boys," who merged their tough-guy gangster style with roles as citizens who served a public good.[59]

A similar combination of opposites characterized the major female stars as well. Myrna Loy, who played Nick Charles's wife Nora in the "Thin Man" series, noted that prior to the thirties she "played orientals"—characters who in those days were invariably "wicked ladies"—in films like the Fu Manchu series because "I with my slanty eyes and my sense of humour—which was unforgivable in a woman—seemed to fit into the category of 'doubtful ladies.'"[60] Loy, however, gained greater success as the "dream wife of a million men" by combining the aura of "doubtful ladies" with the dignity of Nora Charles, a good wife, mother, and public citizen. Other female stars followed suit as Joan Crawford, Carole Lombard, and Bette Davis combined the aura of the "bad girl" with the spunk of the empowered woman. Furthermore, Vivien Leigh as Scarlett O'Hara in *Gone with the Wind* and Claudette Colbert in *Imitation of Life* (1934) shed the refined image of protected sweetheart in favor of the shrewd businesswomen who beat men at their own game. Summarizing these trends, Carole Lombard wrote that she "lived by a man's code."[61]

The ethos of interpenetrating opposites also permeated genres and formula films associated with traditional American myths. The major cowboy stars after Will Rogers's death were Gene Autry and Roy Rogers. Both incorporated the values of a rugged cowboy with the expressiveness of the urban singer of swing ballads. Along the same lines, the major child players of the era, Shirley Temple and Deanna Durbin, incorporated youthful spontaneity with the adult wisdom to help save rather than undermine family life. *Little Miss Broadway* (1938), for example, features Shirley as a young girl who confronts bankers and staid rich matrons when they attempt to evict poor showmen from their homes. In response she mobilizes diverse peoples to overcome the power of these corrupt businessmen and society matrons. Walt Disney's cartoon characters, as Steven Watts has shown, combined animal traits with human sentiments and beliefs. The Soviet filmmaker, Sergei Eisenstein, saw that Disney's cartoon characters were popular because they evoked a vision of wholeness to counter the deep fragmentations of the modern world. In this vein he noted:

> For those . . . whose lives are divided up into little squares like a chess board . . . that divide up the soul's feelings, thoughts . . . Disney's films blaze with color. Like the patterns in the clothes of people who have been deprived of the colours in nature. That's why the imagination in them is limitless, for Disney's films are a revolt against partitioning and legislating, against spiritual stagnation and greyness.[62]

The political message flowing from these innovations was also not too hard to find. By incorporating into the self the desires of outsiders, whether they be gangsters, fallen women, ribald comics, or cartoon animals, the new citizen carried into the civic sphere the capacity to cooperate with outsiders to reinvent oneself and society. Nowhere was this more in evidence than in the populist trilogy of Frank Capra, an artist deeply committed to the ideal of the composite personality and film formula. In *Mr. Deeds Goes to Town* (1936), *Mr. Smith Goes to Washington* (1939), and *Meet John Doe* (1941), Capra and writers like Robert Riskin created conversion narratives that focused on competing views of cultural authority. Traditional authority resided in the official leaders and the monopoly capitalists who were his villains. The villains' view of life was complete and closed to new ideas. They manipulate the mass media to gain power over the people and turn to force and power—embodied in their assistants—to impose on the central hero demands to do their bidding.

Typically the environment of the rich reflects the imposition of the power of aristocratic lords and monopolists on the dreams of the old republic. As such the rich threaten to destroy the democracy and im-

Frank Capra's *Mr. Smith Goes to Washington* (1939). A corrupt businessman, played by Edward Arnold, teaches a new senator, played by James Stewart, how to serve the interests of monopoly capitalists. (Courtesy Academy of Motion Picture Arts and Sciences)

pose the values of the "Old World" on citizens dedicated to the public good. The Capra hero thus embodies the ethos of the producers' democracy that is in danger, while the Capra heroine initially works as a reporter or political aide for the rich. Once the hero and heroine meet, they engage in humor, song, and urban nightlife. Slowly they shed their psychic dependency and find in each other what they lack to make themselves complete. Armed with a code that combines both tough realism and idealism, they undergo a conversion experience. Modernizing republican ideals, they align with the lower classes to launch a collective battle for justice as well as a more holistic life. Watching this contest unfold in *Meet John Doe,* a critic saw that

> the text—and it is all entertainment, not screen editorial—is right
> down the broad highway of human concern. And through the
> compelling human equation runs a patriotic strain which relies
> on no flag waving, no stilted eloquence, but is all the more stir-
> ring because it leaps from the heart of almost inarticulate folk to

confront injustice, oppression, and selfish aggrandizement every-where around the world.[63]

Importantly Capra and others evoked the myths of American tradi-tions, but did so as a means to critique and alter the present. With names like Jefferson Smith and Long John Willoughby, Capra's heroes embodied the recovery of the traditional republic and democratic com-munity. Much as in the Will Rogers vehicles, the vision of the past in films of this period suggests an alternative American ethos. Take *Stagecoach,* made in 1939 by John Ford. The western charts the jour-ney of a stagecoach across the Southwest. Inside the coach are an outlaw, a fallen woman, a southern gambler, a drunken Irishman, a re-fined Victorian "lady," and a banker who evokes the image of Herbert Hoover and the corrupt financiers of the day. Under the threat of In-dian attack, they expel the banker and learn how to forge a public life where opposites cooperate. Similarly, Ford's *How Green Was My Valley* (1941) showed how rich capitalists exploit poor miners. In response the commoners form a union to advance their class interests. The So-viet director Sergei Eisenstein observed that Ford's *Young Mr. Lincoln* (1939) portrayed a Lincoln who came directly from the "womb of pop-ular and national spirit," of the "progressive tradition of America" that is struggling to restore "harmony" to a fragmented world. Even apparently escapist films turned to an alternative past as a model for public life and republican renewal. *The Wizard of Oz* (1939), for ex-ample, originated as a populist novel depicting the farmers' uprising in the 1890s. Transferred into the Great Depression, the novel gener-ated a film that charted the actions of a young girl, Dorothy, and fanci-ful characters who learn through doing that they are not inferior, and that they can trust their resources to achieve common goals and suc-cess through collective effort.[64]

Within these productions, the music often reinforced the theme that American folk culture and modern culture operated on the same tracks. During the thirties, for example, swing bands played at inter-missions in urban theaters. An audience could see bands like Benny Goodman's that featured white and black musicians performing to-gether, then see a main feature like *How Green Was My Valley* and *Young Mr. Lincoln* that featured the songs of workers and the folk, a process that would inspire Eisenstein to note that Ford's Lincoln was "half Rabelais and half Michelangelo." Similarly, Paul Robeson sang "Old Man River" in *Showboat* (1936), and the Caucasian heroine did a "sand dance" accompanied by blacks playing music on the Mississippi River. Together these images gave dignity to the music of slaves and suggested that America was rooted in cross-cultural exchange. To immigrants who had been discriminated against, and seen as not "yet white" by official leaders, the effect of talking films was evident. In the twenties minorities had reinterpreted the silent films to suit their own interests.[65] In the thirties there was a much closer relation between working-class spectators and what appeared on the screen. Commenting on that shift, the *Jewish Daily Forward* noted that though silent films encouraged immigrants to model themselves on "Anglo-Saxon austerity," sound films encouraged working-class immigrants to learn that "an accent instead of impoverishing a personality, lends interest to it . . . [making] accents . . . into an asset."[66]

The advent of sound film generated a competitive discourse of pluralism as the heart of the national tradition. Yet what about nonwhites? Were they included as well? There is no doubt that many films perpetuated racial stereotypes. While negative images continued, it was also true that in the thirties the racism permeating mainstream culture began to decline and formerly ostracized groups and characters gained dignity. Classic examples of the more complicated portrayal of racial minorities are the Charlie Chan films. Though the series perpetuated many traditional white stereotypes of Asians, the central character, played by Warner Oland, a Finnish actor with Asian features, often turned these views upside down. In the twenties Oland had played the evil Asian gangster, Fu Manchu.[67] Yet as that genre faded in the early thirties, he gained success as the detective Charlie Chan who combined gangster qualities with that of the dedicated detective who served the public good.

Throughout Chan reversed many of the conventional stereotypes that whites had used to subordinate and demean Asians. To begin with, he was a family man with a wife and three sons, all played by Asians. He also appealed to urban whites as well as what reporters called the "oriental trade" at home and in the Far East. At a time when whites forbade Asian immigrants to attain citizenship, and states on the West Coast forbade the Japanese to hold land, Chan was the skilled "urbane oriental who took delight in unravelling the most complicated crime mysteries." A critic said of *Charlie Chan at the Race Track* (1936) that Chan may have "the help of Inspector Fifer of the Scotland Yard and Inspector Flannery of New York. But as far as helping they're a couple of stooges . . . baffled by foolish facts which cannot fool Chan." Moreover, Chan emerged as a "witty philosopher" and hero who also delighted in modern consumer goods such as flashy cars, good wine, and nightclubs. Like Nick Charles, Charlie Chan was "full of wise-

Charlie Chan in Paris (1935). Charlie Chan, the dignified Asian detective, demonstrates that nonwhite races can be wiser than European Americans. (Courtesy Academy of Motion Picture Arts and Sciences)

cracks." He solved crimes that "baffled others," the result being that the Charlie Chan films celebrated Asians as skilled men and women who aided whites and the victims of crime.[68]

A similar alteration informed the portrayal of blacks as well. Though a self-directed detective failed to emerge in the guise of an African American in mainstream Hollywood films, a more inclusive vision of blacks did receive representation. No doubt films like *Gone with the Wind* continued to perpetuate demeaning images. A sample of plot descriptions, gathered by Thomas Cripps from trade journals, shows that during the 1920s black performers were cast in the traditional role of servants in 80 percent of all films; however, during the thirties that number fell to 40 percent.[69] Similarly, our plot samples show that racial minorities cast in favorable roles rose from 4 to about 15 percent from the twenties to late thirties (appendix 2, fig. 19).

Black journalists also perceived that a more dignified black portrayal of African Americans graced the Hollywood screen. Even though they wanted to see blacks in more positive roles, they praised players like Paul Robeson, Bill "Bojangles" Robinson, Rex Ingram, Lena Horne, Hattie McDaniel, and Louise Beavers, who now attained major billing and success in Hollywood films.[70] Rex Ingram told a re-

Rex Ingram as "De Lawd" in *The Green Pastures* (1936). This film gave a sympathetic and dignified presentation of black spirituality and faith. (Courtesy Academy of Motion Picture Arts and Sciences)

porter that things indeed had changed. Where in the twenties Hollywood producers cast him as either a "Nubian slave" or a subordinate servant, he now found more positive roles, playing God himself in films like *The Green Pastures* (1936).[71] Similarly, in the adaptation of Edna Ferber's *Showboat*, Paul Robeson sang "Ol' Man River" to give voice to the reality of blacks' exploitation by whites. As Robeson sang "[we] tote that bale, get a little drunk and land in jail," the lyrics and montage reveal that African Americans have made the South rich but remain racially oppressed.[72]

If major films portrayed minorities in a more positive light, some of the most prominent also challenged the foundation of white superiority: the enforcement in a majority of states of miscegenation laws that outlawed intermarriage between whites and racial minorities. In many ways these select films resemble the beginnings of what literary scholars and students of new nationalities call "foundational myths." That is, stories that focus on unions of lovers of different regions and races often provide models for overcoming divisions that thwart the making of new "imaginary communities." *Cimarron,* for example, portrayed lovers whose romance and marriage created new bonds across the races, foreshadowing the birth of a multicultural America.[73]

This was not an isolated occurrence. *Showboat* as well as Will Rogers's *Steamboat 'Round the Bend* (1935) challenged miscegenation codes. The Academy-Award-winning film of 1935, *Mutiny on the Bounty,* continued that trend by focusing on the adventures of a British ship manned by a tyrannical captain who disdains nonwhites, whom he exploits with shrewd business practices. But when the crew meets South Sea islanders who believe in cooperation and love across the races, the white subordinates revolt and intermarry with the nonwhite islanders, all of whom were played by Polynesian actresses. *Juarez* (1939) told the story of a mixed-blood Indian who defeats an army of French imperialists. Not only does Juarez find inspiration in the ideals of Abraham Lincoln, but to make a republic he foresees that land has to be redistributed so citizens can attain both political and economic independence. Similarly, Frank Capra's *The Bitter Tea of General Yen* (1933) depicted a white woman who falls in love with an Asian. The star of the film, Barbara Stanwyck, recalled that "the women's clubs came out very strongly against it, because the white woman was in love with a yellow man and kissed his hand. So what! I was so shocked [by the reaction]. I accepted it and believed in it, and loved it."[74]

By the end of the decade films that evoked the élan of the composite protagonist gave visibility to the possibility of a more pluralistic and just republic. Our plot samples reveal that this was not an isolated occurrence. As criticism of business and the rich ranged from 25 to 60 percent in plot samples, characters who engaged in a conversion narrative that shifted loyalty from the upper to lower classes occurred in over 25 percent of all plots (appendix 2, fig. 8). Similarly, the lures of mass culture—nightclubs, dance halls, jazz, the new woman, and "youth"—altered as well. In the twenties, mass art was seen as dangerous in well over 50 percent of all films, implying that the characters' desire for a new life should incorporate the status symbols of the wealthy (appendix 2, fig. 23). But fears of mass art—with its links to the expressive culture of blacks and immigrants—receded to almost zero in the thirties. In sharp contrast, the lures of mass art emerged as a force for personal and social renewal. With that change, protagonists linked to the old middle class dropped to less than 40 percent, and a new man and woman came clearly into prominence (appendix 2, fig. 3). Rooted in the new "trades of the city," the new man and woman

Love and marriage occurring between the races in *Mutiny on the Bounty* (1935). The first mate Christian, played by Clark Gable, and an island woman, played by a Polynesian actress, Movita, marry—a prime example of the breakdown of racial barriers in some of the major films of the thirties. (Courtesy Academy of Motion Picture Arts and Sciences)

appeared as urban singers, dancers, comics, radio announcers, sportsmen and women, pilots, and nightclub performers. Along with this shift the new man and woman were disproportionately found in films in which the heroes engaged in social reform, a category that fluctuated from a low of 10 percent to about 25 percent of film plots from the mid-twenties to the late thirties (appendix 2, fig. 4).

"Our Collective Unconscious" or the Audience Takes Command

By the late thirties it was clear that moviemakers were not adapting, as Neal Gabler has told us, to every "old bromide" of society. Instead, major films and Jewish producers displaced an Anglo-Saxon Americanism with an alternative, pluralistic vision. As is so often the case in the study of the popular arts, the question arises: How did the audiences respond to these themes? What was the relation between film content and audience belief and public values? Though a definitive answer is impossible, one thing is clear. Producers' awareness of audience demand spurred them to make productions dramatically different from the formulas of the twenties and to give directors and performers such as Frank Capra, Will Rogers, John Ford, and Orson Welles control over their work in the studios.

The audience had become less of a passive "crowd" than a "public" that made their own choices. A telling testimony to that shift informed the recollections of the screenwriter Lester Cole. Early in the thirties, Cole participated in creating Hollywood guilds that drew on a republican critique of capitalism to mobilize unions. Meanwhile, Cole and his friend Nathanael West—soon to be the famed writer of *The Day of the Locust* (1939)—created scripts based on current news. One featured a lawyer who sides with striking workers. In *The President's Mystery* (1936) Cole recalled that he combined love with "mystery, romance and a generous dash of Roosevelt propaganda." At first Republic studios refused to release the film because it was too radical. Yet when President Roosevelt won reelection in 1936, the producers released it to the tune of great profits. Summarizing the lessons learned from these events, Cole saw that

> certain producers began to see profit in film topics other than sheer escape and inane fantasy. Even though the ideas expressed and social realities depicted caused them some extreme uneasiness, the magnetism of the new fields of profits conquered such misgivings. To show poverty, joblessness and hunger not only awakened the consciousness of millions who saw themselves represented realistically on the screen, but aroused their consciousness and stimulated what was most dreaded by the producers who made the films—a sense of dignity of the common man and woman, their courage and their strength to fight back.[75]

Besides the convergence between market demand and the making of more socially conscious films, popular values did take a leftward swing. As our plot samples recorded hostility to the old order and to business coupled with reformist themes, pollsters found that over 63 percent of the public expressed great fears of unemployment and wished for more security in their lives. At the same time over 65 percent felt that big businessmen and elites had too much power, and that sharp inequalities of wealth were undemocratic. They had not, however, lost faith in the possibility of progressive reform. When asked what class they came from, 88 percent responded they emanated from the solid middle class. When asked about their hopes for the country, the majority had faith in the glories of American democracy and a tomorrow where technology and science created abundance. Most thought that Franklin Roosevelt and the New Deal offered hope for realizing these goals, a faith that was strongest among those under thirty-five years of age and those situated in the middle and working classes—the groups most drawn to the movies.[76]

At the grassroots it appeared that moviemakers' capacity to give form to these beliefs had an impact on political attitudes. The novelist John Clellon Holmes recalled that movies provided him and his friends with "our collective unconscious. I for one still associate certain films with the dawning of certain ideas." Sound made Hollywood films a "universal part of puberty" that generated a "heightening of psychological involvement so pervasive that the gulf between the audience and the image was all but obliterated." In his neighborhood "an entire generation went to the movies two or three times a week." Holmes recalled that it would be "difficult to calculate the number of hours that people of my age spent talking about movies in those years." When he saw *All Quiet on the Western Front* in 1930, or went to a Marx Brothers or W. C. Fields comedy, he learned that the "pompous" world of adults was a fraud, but he went back home "renewed by [the] knowledge that the bores could be foiled by cagey irrationality." By watching films like *Meet John Doe*, Holmes also learned that big business could be a fraud. In fact, when he became involved in "party politics," the memory of this Capra production "and others like it" had an "influence on my decisions and aversions which is incalculable." Movies during the thirties thus provided "a continuation of our schooling by another means," teaching that war and big business constituted the "siren call of the devil."[77]

Just as it appeared that many in the audience altered their political values watching major films, so the critics and the artists themselves saw moviemaking as part of creating an alternative public life. A writer in Tennessee observed after watching *All Quiet on the Western Front* that "this is the first time that those who fought the war with only bonds and thrift stamps have ever been shown what the real thing is." The real thing inspired veterans in Los Angeles to charge the screen to aid the hero under siege. Lewis Milestone, the director, noted, "that's how close we came to the truth of the thing." In San Francisco the film sparked a critic to note that the same work "should run until every man, woman and child . . . has seen it, then shown periodically to the maturing generations." So powerfully did the theme strike home that the main actor, Lew Ayres, wrote to Milestone that almost "everyone in the large cast . . . were deeply impressed by their involvement in a significant work . . . that had overtones of a critique upon worldwide nationalism and imperialism." In fact, "my own youthful involvement in a project of this kind was bound to have a formative effect." It led to a conversion to pacifism, a commitment that continued into World War II.[78]

At this point one can also see why Orson Welles recalled that Hollywood provided a site to advance a shift in symbols, racial norms, and politics that would renew the "democratic republic." Public opinion polls, memoirs, audience response, and alterations in narratives showed that even before the New Deal came to power in 1933, many moviemakers created a language for what did not yet exist: a pluralistic producers' democracy rooted in hostility to what President Roosevelt called the new "money changers" and "feudal lords" of industry. Indicative of that political drift, progressive civic associations created a series of film study guides that provided questions to stimulate students to see the civic implications of each story. The guide for John Ford's *How Green Was My Valley* observed that the film "shows admirably the beginnings of the labour movement." Another pamphlet noted that *Fury* (1936), a film about lynching, focused on a white victim. But the story nevertheless helped to promote the national antilynching legislation to protect African Americans. Still another focused on a Hardy Family production that featured the judge protecting an ostracized citizen. To have students think about the story's larger implications, the writer asked, "What if the man had been a Negro, or foreign born? . . . Can you think of any instance where your standing in the community is likely to affect the quality of justice which will be meted out?"[79]

Besides the study guides and their encouragement of discussion about the "quality of justice" meted out in the community, Hollywood producers directly combined the élan of the new art with social reform. Such a merger surfaced in the organization of Hollywood unions as well as Will Rogers's radio programs. In public rituals that impulse came inescapably into view with the Roosevelt victory in 1932. The southern California organizers of Roosevelt's campaign came from the Warner Brothers studio. Once Roosevelt won the presidency, Jack Warner organized a streamlined train to participate in the inaugural of the "New Deal Chief." Accordingly, the "42nd Street Special" stopped in major cities to announce the arrival of the "Better Times Special" linking the film *42nd Street* with a "New Deal in entertainment." Citizens groups and Mayor Curley met the train and its stars

Warner Brothers' "42nd Street Special" on the way to President Roosevelt's first inaugural. (Courtesy Academy of Motion Picture Arts and Sciences)

in Boston, while reporters interviewed the stars, taking care to feature players from the local area. On several occasions, newsmen observed with surprise that the actresses dressed like "men" and enjoyed performing the roles of the "bad girls" in order to let loose their "inhibitions." The actors similarly enjoyed playing gangster roles rather than the "colorless" leading men. Along the way commentators saw that the train embodied the spirit of an alternative public, rising from the ashes of hard times. If we "needed," explained one observer, "to be sold on ourselves" the train with its silver Pullman cars and modern interiors did the trick. The Hollywood stars captured the attention of fans precisely because in days of deflated hopes,

> we Americans must find some hat rack to which we can hang our national affection. At this moment celebrities are the number one vote getter. To be sure we haven't much choice. What with Big Business hiding its naughty face in the drawer and society turning out to be a boring lead-headed princess, there is nothing left for us to idealize except the clan of pretty boys and girls who live on the rhinestone shore of Hollywood.[80]

The heart of the matter lay beyond the lure of the "rhinestone shore of Hollywood." With official institutions in disarray, the train and the film signaled the incorporation of politics and the popular arts into remaking the nation. At a time when established institutions continued to exclude racial minorities and women, a new mass culture arose that evoked dreams of a more inclusive and modern culture. In response moviemakers who themselves were often minorities, immigrants, or the children of immigrants rejected European status symbols and turned to the lower classes and vernacular arts for inspiration for a new public life. On the screen, films evoked the vision of a modernized republic, rooted in citizen action, pluralism, and dreams of contemporary morals and abundance. While the process of cultural and social reform had only begun, there was no doubt that feature films now brought to the fore composite heroes and heroines who combined instinctual vitality with the art of interpenetrating opposites. Exactly how this affected theaters and audiences at the grassroots is the subject of our next chapter.

Chapter 3
Utopia on Main Street: Modern Theaters and the "New" Audiences

When our society was established this "natural" process of Americanization continued in its own unobserved fashion defying the social and
political assumptions of our political leaders and tastemakers alike.
This . . . was the vernacular process, in the days when our leaders still
looked to England and the Continent for their standards of taste, the
vernacular stream of our culture was creating itself out of whatever elements it found useful, including the Americanized culture of the slaves.
So in this sense the culture of the United States has always been more
democratic and American than the social and political institutions in
which it was emerging.

—Ralph Ellison, *Going to the Territory,* 1986

A certain type of life has inspired the modern world. It is our life, but
it is particularly America's. And our life is the motion picture. There is
a natural affinity between modernist art and the photoplay theater
which it would seem the architect and the exhibitor cannot ignore.

—George Schultz, "Modernistic Art: Its Significance
to America and the Photoplay" (1928)

Three years into the Great Depression, Terry Ramsaye, editor of
the *Motion Picture Herald,* wrote an editorial entitled "The New
Deal—Superman and Today." Many readers must have thought
the world had turned upside down. For years reformers attacked the
movie industry for incarnating the dangers of city life. Yet with the
"42nd Street Special" moving across the nation for the inaugural of
Franklin Roosevelt, and Will Rogers's films and radio shows rendering
a Cherokee Indian the "Number One New Dealer," the editor of the
industry's major journal saw that the time had come to make grassroots movie theaters a model of civic renewal. From the editorial pul-
pit, Ramsaye explained why. Hollywood producers in the twenties emulated monopolists whose grandiose speculations brought the stock
market crash. Symbolic of those false values, large studios and theater
owners built lavish, sumptuous theaters that identified abundance

with the standards of the rich who looked to Europe for models of social hierarchy. Within structures that emulated the historical styles of an older age, it appeared natural that wealth and power were unequal. Yet after three years of Depression, Ramsaye exhorted theater owners to design a modern theater "more a part of the town and less something imposed by the outside Supermen," for

> the fated Ides of March have come and Caesar is dead. A new order came to Rome when the Dictator fell at the foot of Pompey's statue that day. And on this anniversary . . . we marked the death of a recent race of dictators, the supermen of oft-acclaimed bubble-based genius of the era which today litters the path of progress with the debris and the empty leaseholds of their tinsel glory. So a new order comes to America, to industry and the motion pictures.[1]

Among all the visionaries of the Great Depression Ramsaye had the good fortune to see his prophecy come true. In the twenties, no downtown section of a major city could claim to be up-to-date unless it was graced with a historically styled picture palace. Even the names—the Regal, the Tivoli, the Egyptian—recalled times and places removed from everyday life. Yet starting in the thirties, exhibitors converted the large, ornamented cathedrals of the movies, with seating capacities of 1,500 to 3,000, to smaller, 600-seat structures with interiors of steel, glass, concrete, and formica. Inside, the designs and murals merged into dynamic streamlined forms of functional simplicity. To the trade journalists this was a theater to match the new talking films, which rooted characters and audiences in the vernacular art of a diverse people.

No doubt the advent of the New Deal provided what journalists called a "godsend" for the spread of the new style. The fresh administration of Franklin Roosevelt created the conditions that encouraged the spread of modernist theater. Having formed a coalition that included immigrants and their children, racial minorities, workers, and the reform-minded middle class, Roosevelt struck down Prohibition, releasing the hold of the old Anglo-Saxon middle class on defining the populace's amusements. Next he signed the New Deal Housing Act, which made capital available for theater owners to redesign in the modern mode. When coupled with public works projects that put money in the hands of the people, architects observed that "in designing and building theaters in various communities, the day of the garish, ornate, nonfunctional elements which marked, even marred the theaters of the past is gone forever."[2]

The rise of the modern style was not simply a change in models, geared to stimulating demand. In response to hard times, the modern movie house evoked the ideals of a modern pluralistic producers' democracy, which mirrored the themes that appeared on the screen. At a theater named for Will Rogers, built in the heart of a working-class area of Chicago, the streamlined style heralded a merger of the star's appeal with that of the movie house. On the inside, regionalist-styled murals depicted Will Rogers on horseback, with the legend, "My ancestors didn't come over in the Mayflower—they met the Boat." As theaters in a similar style spread, the modernist design soon swept others aside, so that by the second half of the decade film exhibitors imitated it as unthinkingly as they had the earlier and far more lavish "atmospherics." Yet the wholesale adoption of the modern design was more than the rejection of a stale commodity for a fresh look. Underlying the promotion of the modern aesthetic, in the view of critics and architects, was the creation of a democratic public space that had shed the past in favor of a new "Americanism."[3]

Can this be true? What is this new national vision and how did it come to theaters, heralding a vast expansion in moviemaking? Generally we have learned that attendance at the movies declined in the thirties, and that audiences remained passive "spectators" who had little inclination and power to become agents who influenced mass-produced sounds and images. Yet wherever Terry Ramsaye traveled after 1933—to Italian and Jewish neighborhoods in the Bronx, to small Anglo-Saxon towns in the Midwest, to the Spanish villas in Santa Fe—he praised the rise of modern theaters, which spearheaded a vast audience expansion and created a new "mass culture" in touch with the republican values of a virtuous people. Yet why did the modern theater become identified with civic renewal and an alternative public space? Was this new design promoted by big business to advance its interests and values as the national norm?[3] Why did the modern theater spread to a mass audience in the United States but not in Europe?

"A Trick Stopped Working"

To answer these questions it is critical to realize that the origins of this change do not lie, as one might expect, in the thirties, but in the Crash of 1929 when journalists saw that the "trick" embodied in the old lavish movie house "stopped working." To many critics and modern architects the lavish movie theater expressed the false front of civilization in the twenties. The pervasive corruption and hollowness of the current

The Will Rogers Theater in Chicago, built in 1935. The machine aesthetic, with its flowing modern lines, creates a dynamic movement to echo the busy street. Located in a working-class area of Chicago, the Will Rogers exemplified the penetration of modern consumer styles in local areas. (Courtesy Chicago Historical Society)

corporate order and morality were screened behind the historical fa-cades. To these critics, the Gothic, baroque, Renaissance, and classical theaters emulated the European styles prevalent in the museums, homes, and theaters patronized by the rich. Architects working in the cathedral mode evoked historical styles that concealed the identity of modern life behind images of a bygone time that had no relevance to modern desires or needs. Or in a kinder mode, critics would argue that, much like architects in all fields, the theater designers had not found a stylis-tic expression to give form to modern experience and moviegoing.[4]

Ramsaye and other critics also saw that these theaters served to rein-force the cultural authority of the wealthy. In so doing the movie pal-aces had evocative names, such as the Paramount, the Majestic, and the Capitol in New York City and Brooklyn. Modeled on the palaces of aristocrats, these theaters contained flowing stairs, ornate mirrors, lavish lobbies, and gilt-laden auditoriums. Inside, these auditoriums divided the high-paying from low-paying customers in boxes, balcon-ies, and loges that mirrored divisions of the larger social order.[5] At the

Regionalist-style mural in the Will Rogers Theater in Chicago. Notice the inscription to the left—"My Ancestors didn't come over in the Mayflower—they met the Boat"—and the mixture of cowboy and Indian motifs. The condemnation of the elite Mayflower crowd links the star and the modern theater with popular non-Anglo-Saxon values. (Courtesy Chicago Historical Society, Russell Philips, photographer)

Capitol or Paramount in New York or at the Uptown in Chicago, fans entered a world that was modeled on the wealthy legitimate theaters or the homes of the rich who lived in Newport or on Fifth Avenue. Here the "average" citizen escaped the "cares of the day" to partake in the refinements of the new abundant economy. As one commentator saw it,

> the wealth of our country has permitted the erection of costly buildings for the service of our communities. Tacitly we recognize that the old order has changed, that the palace of the aristocracy is now the playhouse of democracy. Where royalty deemed it as its own particular right to revel in the created beauty of artists and craftsmen, the democracy is now privileged to enjoy its creation for its hours of leisure.[6]

Throughout the twenties official tastemakers perceived that the movies served the enlightened function of bringing highbrow art and civilization within the reach of the masses. Yet amid that process, they also worried and wrung their hands for it appeared that theatrical designs catering to the tastes of the lower classes could get out of control.

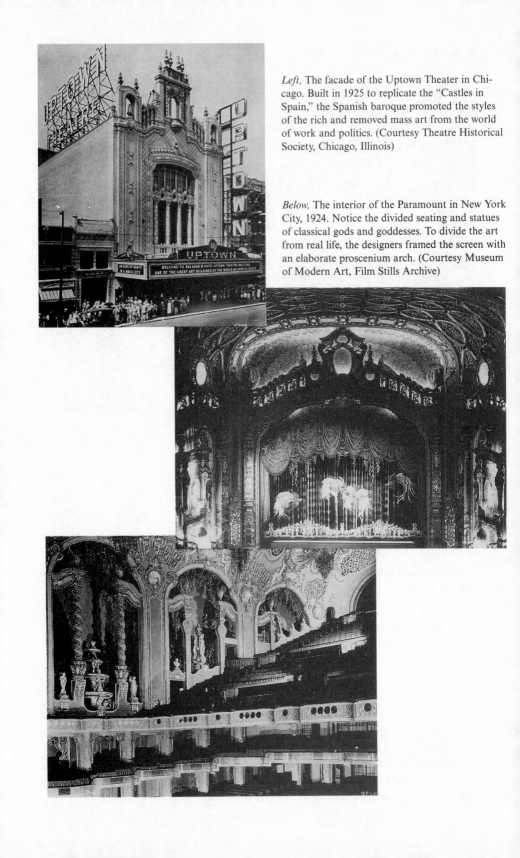

Left, The facade of the Uptown Theater in Chicago. Built in 1925 to replicate the "Castles in Spain," the Spanish baroque promoted the styles of the rich and removed mass art from the world of work and politics. (Courtesy Theatre Historical Society, Chicago, Illinois)

Below, The interior of the Paramount in New York City, 1924. Notice the divided seating and statues of classical gods and goddesses. To divide the art from real life, the designers framed the screen with an elaborate proscenium arch. (Courtesy Museum of Modern Art, Film Stills Archive)

The reason was not hard to find. Formerly, official institutions of the middle class excluded the images and desires of workers. Producers and exhibitors, however, now had no choice but to cater to lowbrow taste in order to garner profits. To attract this audience, theater designs underwent a major alteration from the bottom up. A well-trained architect, for example, believed that a "temple to art" had to be removed from the commerce and chaos of the street. Symbolic of the elevated ideal, theatrical box offices were removed from the "street." In addition, theatrical architects muted advertisements and had entrances for different classes.

Designers of the lavish movie houses were of course emulating highbrow theater design, but the demands of commerce began to undercut their desire to uphold refined standards. Catering to a mass rather than select market, theater owners placed the box office directly on the sidewalk and used "garish" electronic billboards to attract viewers from blocks down the thoroughfare. To create a democratic aura they also furnished one entrance for all groups and even built theaters in accord with Asian and Islamic forms rather than western classical models. Grauman's Chinese in Los Angeles evoked "fantasy" removed from the "daily round" of work and civic life. At the Capitol in New York, the architect Thomas Lamb found that a mass audience associated some areas of the building with second-class status. As Lamb made the balcony seating equal in rank to the ground-floor lobby, William Fox explained the reasons why one had to defy established designs. As he explained to a reporter,

> movies breathe the spirit on which the country was founded, freedom and equality. In the motion picture theater there are no separations of classes. Everyone enters the same way. There is no side door thrust upon those who sit in the less expensive seats. There is always something abhorrent in different entrances to theaters. . . . in the movies the rich rub elbows with the poor and that is the way it should be. The motion picture is a distinctly American institution.[7]

If the quest for "freedom and equality" generated alterations in conventional playhouse design, the defenders of "standards" perceived that mass art threatened Anglo-Saxon visions of public space. In response Thomas Talmadge, a famous architect of the classical European tradition, called for an intensification of the effort to uplift the cinema. Writing in a major journal, he wrote that it was now necessary to "divorce the motion picture from vaudeville and jazz . . . [so that] it will take its place among the educational and moral forces in the country." Talmadge also criticized the "garish design" of the movie palaces

The Grauman's Chinese in Hollywood. Built in 1927, the Chinese exemplified the pinnacle of the exotic, non-European style that horrified architectural critics in the twenties. (Courtesy Museum of Modern Art, Film Stills Archive)

Interior of the Grauman's Chinese, 1927. (Courtesy Museum of Modern Art, Film Stills Archive)

drawn from foreign exotic locales. Instead, he pointed to the classical forms of New England as a means to evoke an Anglo-Saxon style for the new art. The major designers of theater palaces, however, complained that the "fickle" tastes of the patrons "forced" their choices. Confessing that they were "guilty" of building in a "vulgar" mode, they also noted that the "average picture house exhibited a jazzy interior" for the "motion picture is an expression . . . for the masses." One theater owner chimed in to comment that

> our operations will be different from the ordinary chain stores or other lines of business in so far as we are selling an intangible something which we call entertainment. We appeal wholly to the people in their moments of relaxation and we have no gauges, no standards as to whether this food or that food will produce certain results. We appeal wholly to the imagination and that provides interesting material to work with.[8]

Behind this is more than meets the eye. Prior to the rise of mass art, buildings had often manifested different styles for different classes, mirroring the cultural hierarchy of the large cities. The new mass art, however, drew different groups together. To give form and refinement to that process, designers turned to the historical styles of the past, but they fashioned a cloak that did not fit. In response to market demand, architects began to democratize the inherited theater style, undermining the norms of western civilization. So popular was that shift that even during the Depression audiences continued to patronize the movie houses in record numbers. Yet hardly had the 1932 season begun than theater owners found that patrons no longer wished to be seen in movie palaces and instead were patronizing neighborhood theaters located predominantly in working-class areas.

Given the Crash, producers realized that the "golden era of extravagance" was gone, and they were "all out to sea" on what would attract the fans. Executives naturally asked managers of their theater palaces what caused fans to stop coming. Soon they discovered that half of lost profits clearly resulted from the economic effects of the Depression. But what caused the other half? Owners noted that the tastes promoted by "arty and aristocratic critics" had failed. With the "international picture stars as known during the silent film days . . . failing," the "high hat" environment of the film palace also turned fans away. Since the paying customers lost faith that they could be "millionaires," they rejected an atmosphere modeled on the homes of the "400" society leaders. Little wonder that journalists observed that the motion picture business had to be recreated in a mode "more in touch with the times."[9]

"A Natural Affinity": Modernism and the Democratization of Public Space

Soon the trade commentators began to ask what form of theater would embody this "reincarnation." Everyone realized that this was no joking matter, for theater construction represented a much larger investment than the production of a particular film. Soon contenders for styles in "touch" with "today's" audiences began to fill the pages of the major trade journals. Out of that effort now emerged three competitive schools. Though we have often been told that modernism in the United States, unlike in Europe, was devoid of political meanings or ideology, this was definitely not the case with the three modern designs that competed for attention in the realm of film exhibition.[10]

All the contenders agreed on one thing: The symbols represented in the lavish theater palaces indicated a failed capitalist order. All understood that if their designs gained prominence, the movies would expand into new markets and regions, end the decline in profits and audiences, and point the way to a better tomorrow. One of the first to link modernism to the utopian visions that each school held in common was Paul Frankl. In his book, *Machine-Made Leisure* (1932), Frankl wrote that exotic structures like the movie palaces at the Roxy and Capitol symbolized social disease. Yet these "faults" of design were tokens of a larger crisis in the relation of technology to the new consumer culture. Frankl saw that the "machine" yielded a vast increase in goods. But in a society where big businessmen monopolized wealth, the populace could not purchase the goods, with the result that the economy collapsed. As an antidote Frankl argued that the Great Depression served as punishment for a people who had turned away from a producers' democracy to a consumerism "degenerate in its oriental power." Seeking to create a model of abundance, one where the populace had a right to more money and purchasing power, he now evoked the traditional family values that informed the Victorian era: "Man had a romance with the machine, but she had turned into a tyrannical mistress. . . . Can she ever be turned into a willing wife?" Despite the assertion of male dominance and the use of racial language to express his fears of debilitating leisure, Frankl's analysis of the larger economic crisis and its solution was a correct one. To create a democratic model of abundance, he saw that policy was not enough: At the grassroots people's approach to consumerism had to alter dramatically. It was thus necessary to create buildings that undermined the linkage of consumerism to social and cultural hierarchies of the past, for

> we must master the machine as the instrument for the creation of
> a new leisure. In so doing we are recreating our own values. We

are establishing an end for which it is desirable to work, providing of course that we may utilize leisure as a method of educating and developing the race. . . . if the machine can be mobilized toward the realization of that happy state, toward the creation of a really good life, its tortuous and tragic history will fully be justified and leisure will once more be a blessing and not a curse.[11]

Soon the trade journals were filled with architects taking up their pens to create a style that would make the machine a "blessing and not a curse." Among the mix, three competing designs promised to overcome the "tragic" history of the new consumer culture. The first was the playful International style of modernism emanating from France and Germany. At Berlin's Kermode or at the Parisian Gaumont, the designers created a lavish world for audiences who wished to "live happier lives." In expensive shopping areas and the International World's Fairs in the United States and Europe, art-deco theaters merged modernism with the older status symbols of the wealthy.[12] Within the United States this new form appeared in the late twenties at the Pickwick and Aurora theaters in the Chicago suburbs. These theaters failed, however, to capture a mass market, despite the best efforts of their promoters.

Why? An answer to this question unfolded with the construction of the International Music Hall in New York City in 1933. At the top of Times Square, the Music Hall composed part of a complex of office buildings sponsored by John D. Rockefeller, Jr., the son of the richest man in the nation.[13] By the late twenties young Rockefeller sponsored buildings that gave monumental form to the images of public renewal guided by enlightened businessmen and expert technicians. In this vein Rockefeller Center displayed the sleek art-deco style derived from Europe. Publicists saw that Rockefeller Center incarnated the American "Taj Mahal" that would ban "ignorance and illiteracy." Firmly believing that a building was a monument that linked individuals to the ideals of civilization, Raymond Hood, the chief architect of the Center, ensured that the friezes, sculptures, and murals provided a "powerful influence for good" conveyed in a structure where all its parts told an "understandable story." As Hartley Alexander, a philosophy professor at Columbia University, saw it, the structure provided a "City on a Hill," that evoked

> the first clear expression in our economic life of a new social ideal. That is, of human welfare and happiness centering on the work that we do, and not on some incidental wage: if a whole population, such as Rockefeller City will possess, can be lifted into a finer life in their working and leisure hours, then the economic democracy of America will have begun its answer to the Bolshe-

Left, Pickwick Theater, Park Ridge, Illinois, 1929. Typical of the playful, French-derived art-deco style that merged modernist motifs to the monumental structures of the theater palace. (Courtesy Theatre Historical Society, Chicago, Illinois)

Below, Interior of the Paramount in Aurora, Illinois, opened in 1931. The art-deco styles merged to the old cathedral style, complete with murals portraying images of a bygone time. (Courtesy Theatre Historical Society, Chicago, Illinois)

vik challenge. In all of these phases, then, Rockefeller City is a builder's enterprise, and it is appropriate to announce its theme as Homo Faber, Man the Builder.[14]

To designers who aimed to answer the "Bolshevik challenge" the modern theater expressed the elite version of the republican creed. The murals and the friezes praised "Man the Builder." But the theatrical buildings remained separate from worlds of work. Expressing the Enlightenment ideal that art was a handmaiden to the serious business of politics and science, the International Music Hall stood apart from the buildings devoted to business. Yet on opening night, Will Hays told the well-heeled audience that the "International Music Hall" restored "faith in America's indomitableness and fearlessness."

Given such hopes, journalists had to report the next day that the "International Music Hall" was a "colossal bust," a gravesite for America's folly rather than fearlessness. In fact, S. L. "Roxy" Rothafel—the former operator of several lavish theater palaces—had met his "Waterloo." When the critics tried to determine why, they discovered that despite its modern frame the Music Hall was the theater palace in a new dress. The lavish lobby and gigantic staircases still evoked grandeur. The auditorium seated over 6,000 while the murals presented images of Greek myths, which the average customer could not begin to understand. Conspicuously missing from the murals and friezes were images of the common people whose labor had built the Music Hall. To top it off, for the opening night show Roxy refused to screen talkies since he hated the dialects heard in gangster and social problem films. Instead he presented a stage show narrated by what critics described as "God Almighty Himself," unfolding in "one long multiplication table." Over the next few weeks, the high admission price turned fans away, and the board of directors fired the great "Roxy." At the nadir, Roxy told the eager press:

> I'll be back in April, after a trip South, and go to work and settle all this stuff that is going around about me. Oh, I've heard all the things they've been saying. They're all wolves, this Broadway crowd. They're glad when somebody who has always stood for something in the theater stubs his toe. . . . I'm sick of it. These sophisticated, worldly wise, narrow faced, star-eyed low life that hang around Broadway! I used to walk down Broadway in the old days. Now I never walk there when I can help myself. I feel like I ought to go home and take a bath when I do. The whole street exists by shots in the arm of excitement and filthy scandals and rumors.[15]

Behind this bitter wailing lay a clear message. Though the International Music Hall would change its name to Radio City and arise once again as a tourist attraction after World War II, it never became a trendsetter in the thirties. The lesson, as trade journalists noted, was as clear as the blazing lights on the marquee. Modernism draped in the cathedral mode, complete with hierarchical seating and highbrow murals, would "not cut the mustard." In the wake of the disaster, trade journalists saw that audiences wanted a change, but neither the Music Hall nor the International style fit the bill. In that vacuum competitors naturally came to the fore, eager to promote alternative utopias.

One of the contenders derived from the European avant garde unfolding under the constructivist banner in the Soviet Union and the Bauhaus in Germany. At the Bauhaus architects such as Walter Gropius and Eric Mendelsohn "got their chance," in the words of a contemporary critic, when the "red flag was a sign for a cultural revolution." In designing movie houses as agents of socialist education and revolt, architects rejected the playfulness of art deco, which they identified as "bourgeois" culture in a new form. Instead, they created a functionalist film theater stripped of all national and historical symbols. The seating was no longer divided by status, and the plain auditorium encouraged the audience to see film not so much as entertainment than as a means to teach principles of class struggle.[16]

Transferred into the United States, functionalist design found a limited market in urban areas identified with the avant-garde artist. A well-publicized example emerged at the Film Guild Cinema in New York City's Greenwich Village. Designed by the Austrian functionalist Frederick Kiesler, it specialized in showing experimental films far from "Broadway palaces." Kiesler stripped the movie house of references to European high art and symbols evocative of American nationality. In keeping with the principles of modern science, the structure displayed the steel, wood, and glass of the modern age and shed hierarchical settings in favor of an auditorium where all sat at the very same level. Kiesler also eliminated the proscenium arch that had separated the film from the life of the audience. To merge art with experience, the narrow auditorium resembled a camera lens. Describing the effect, a critic told his reader to "picture yourself a dwarf inside a camera, for that is indeed what the auditorium of this theater surely resembles." Images appeared on walls, "lending atmosphere to the piece that is played on the main screen." So that "if 'Jeanne D'Arc' showed the heroine burned at the stake the screen on the left or right side of the auditorium could be bathed in the flames, immersing the viewers inside the action."[17]

The fate of the functionalist moderne resembled that of the playful art deco at Rockefeller Center. Both failed to attract mass audiences. In the wake of the functionalist failure, others found success with designs that did the impossible: combine the ethos of play with the functionalist ethos of work. Robert Boller, one of the central promoters of the new design, believed that the architect had to reject the "working class architecture" as well as the new "European modernism," which is "an imported idea with no relation to our daily life or habits." By way of sharp contrast, he saw that the path to the future lay in the past achievements pioneered by architects of the Chicago School. The work of Louis Sullivan, Frank Lloyd Wright, and John Root contained a radical message in an American frame. Indicative of that ethos, Wright noted that the wealthy built grandiose homes modeled on European aristocratic styles, but the modern architect must create buildings that revived the spirit of the producers whose labor built the society. The Chicago School had failed to find a mass audience for its work at the turn of the century. But a commentator promoting the Chicago School as the model for movie theaters wrote as early as 1928 that

> nothing can be better than experimentation if it is not aimless. But it must be towards the expression of the Twentieth Century in the United States and not in terms of Chinese pagodas, Greek temples, Roman amphitheaters, Moorish palaces and Gothic cathedrals. We are going to see motion picture theaters conceived and staged for a democratic republic. We have a civilization of our own [not] yet realized in the fine arts, but even in its partial manifestations more our own than anything the world has yet seen.[18]

Yet what would a modernist theater reflective of the forms and styles of the Chicago School look like? Soon an answer to this question pervaded the "Better Theaters" section of a major trade journal. Among the trendsetters none was more influential or creative than Ben Schlanger. Born in New York City where he had attended Columbia University, Schlanger, like many of the film producers, descended from Jewish immigrants. Initially he gained notice as one of the major critics of theater palaces as well as the International Music Hall. In response he offered a viable alternative. Over and over he meticulously diagrammed "changes in theater planning factors," contrasting the "old with the new."

At the center of Schlanger's principles lay a fusion that the Marxist and corporate designers saw as opposites. If Raymond Hood separated the Music Hall from labor, and Bauhaus architects used the theater for education, Schlanger created a synthesis. Over and over he argued that fans rejected the old lavish movie houses for their "pretentious-

CHANGES IN THEATRE PLANNING FACTORS

(A) THE OLD	(B) THE NEW
1. Expensive land.	1. Less expensive land.
2. Excessive costly and useless cubic contents of structure.	2. Minimum useful cubic contents of structure, also reducing amount of mechanical heat and ventilation.
3. Costly special structural framing due to excessive spans and large balcony overhangs.	3. Simplified and economical structural framing, using standard structural shapes.
4. Costly overornamentation, affording poor aesthetic environment, besides being disturbing to restful screen exhibition.	4. Simplicity in decoration, accented by effective lighting complementing the screen performance.
5. Poor vision of screen due to seating arrangement inherited from the stage theatre form. (Seats placed too much to one side of or too high above screen and full view of screen prevented by preceding heads.)	5. Full vision of screen highly improved by placing seats within physical areas best adapted for screen vision. (The valuable area charts and the Parabolic Reversed
6. Lack of bodily and ocular comfort due to seating positions in poor relation to position of screen and inadequate study of physical comfort in chair design.	6. Scientifically fixed angles and placing of seats, as provided for in Parabolic Reverse Floor design, as well as scientifically designed chair.
7. Different admission prices for different portions of theatre (necessary only because of inferior seat locations common in most existing theatres).	7. Single admission price possible, all seats having practically the same degree of desirability in well designed structural form.
8. High admission prices.	8. Reduced admission prices.
9. Excessive walking and stair climbing to seats.	9. Minimum of effort expended in reaching seats.
10. Costly stage construction and rigging (in most cases never made use of).	10. Complete elimination of all traces and influences of a stage.
11. Elaborate equipment, costly draperies and other furnishings.	11. Simplified equipment and elimination of dust-collecting draperies.
12. Ornamental proscenium frame, hangover from stage theatre. (Poor transition from audience to screen.)	12. Elimination of obvious proscenium frame. Side walls of auditorium made to blend towards screen.
13. Faulty screen masking and poor screen lighting.	13. Recessed screen masking, eliminating fuzzy and moving edges of picture. More scientific study of screen lighting.
14. Poor shape and size of present screen.	14. Much study is yet needed along these lines. (This is the producer's problem.)
15. Excessive projection angles, causing distorted images on screen. This is due to poor locations of booth caused by unadaptable form of stage theatre.	15. Diminished projection angles, made possible by scientific study of motion picture theatre form.
16. Poor acoustical quality due to makeshift acoustical correction and unscientific study of theatre form.	16. Exacting acoustical quality. Obtaining proper response to broad range of frequencies.
17. Costly film booking.	17. Greater film buying power for small exhibitor.
18. Theatre construction by speculative builder insufficiently interested in functioning of theatre.	18. Low construction costs, enabling exhibitor to build for himself, assuring proper function of theatre.
19. Maximum expenditure for advertising exploitation and house staff.	19. Minimum advertising for neighborhood house and minimum staff required.

Ben Schlanger's chart comparing the faults of the palatial theater with the advantages of the "new" modern theater. The two sides of the chart list the economic and cultural advantages of shifting from the European style to the American machine style. *Motion Picture Herald,* November 19, 1932.

ness." They were "fancy fakers" whose false fronts "hid the faults of design." The over-ornamented theaters failed because they were "intended to create a sumptuous feeling and to intrigue the beholder with their glittering cornices, their excess ornamentation. . . . It is assumed that these places will be patronized irrespective of the quality of performance given in them." But it was clear that the time had come when a "trick stops working."[19]

Repelled by the "tricks" of the past, Schlanger promoted forms that gave structure to an art different from anything that the world had seen. As he saw it, the modern movie house provided not simply education, as advocated by Marxist designers, nor was it geared only for play, as promoted by the International Music Hall architects who looked to France for their models. Rather, the modern movie house combined entertainment with functionalism, creating a merger of interpenetrating opposites. True, the modern theater must be efficient, attractive, cheaper, and smaller to suit "today's" audiences. It must also provide the setting for talking rather than silent films. Yet Schlanger's aim was not simply to minimize costs in hard times. If that solely had been the case, it would have been practical to retain the small-scale historical designs, but "wired" for sound films. He astutely saw that the values manifest in the structure of the palaces turned people away. Evoking republican language, he indicated that the theater palace mirrored the tastes of nonproducers who exploited others. Deluxe theaters promoted waste and "fantasy." Inside, their mysterious illumination and eclectic styles distracted attention from the screen, creating a theater that diminished the impact of the screen and the unique experience of moviegoing.

To Schlanger, the answer was obvious. All the "garish" lobbies, staircases, ornamented walls, fluted columns, soaring pilasters, and arches must be "slaughtered." To keep the focus on the films and to encourage community and intimacy, the seating capacity would be trimmed to 500 to 800 seats, as compared to the 1,500 to 3,000 seats of the movie palaces. Similarly, the old marquee, lobby, and auditorium no longer would remain separate but would be collapsed into a dynamic whole, displaying the beauty of modern technology: steel, Formica, chrome, and glass. Throughout the structure, colored lights remained hidden behind walls, exuding tints that blended white with gray, brown, and beige into a dynamic, flowing whole. The light frames and the geometric and circular shapes of the walls and the fixtures linked the theater to principles of technology and work. Chrome rails guided the patrons from one area to the next, while the interior and the exterior walls blended into each other. In addition, rounded corners evoked flowing forms that broke down the divisions between the street and the interior.[20]

The liberation of design would also allow people to reimagine the relation between consumerism and democracy. To Schlanger the organization of designs around a horizontal rather than a vertical axis symbolized this cultural shift. In the old theater palace, he and others argued, vertical forms worked in tandem with a seating pattern that situated patrons according to their ability to pay: The boxes and loges were for the wealthy, the balconies for the cheap seats. The upward thrust of the whole coalesced with the creation of vertical pilasters, towering ceilings, and ornamented columns that carried the eye upward toward the high-priced seats occupied by the upper classes. Turning one's eye to the stage, one also saw a large proscenium arch. Like a painting frame, the proscenium separated the viewers from the art, making them spectators who accepted the moral lessons unfolding in a world of "illusion."[21]

Yet for Schlanger the goal of the modern theater was to do what was seen as impossible in modern architectural practice: to break down the division between work and play, entertainment and public life. Indeed, this merger was one of the great functional goals that the architect strove to create in making a building constructed solely for the modern art of the "movies." To engage the audience in the screen fare there had to be a "gradual simplification and omission of forms" from the back to the front of the auditorium, "making it possible for the new theater to have a horizontal direction that fastened the viewers' eyes on the screen." At one of his first buildings, the Thalia Theater in New York City, Schlanger incorporated these principles within a noted innovation, "a parabolic reverse floor design." Within the Thalia box seats disappeared, along with the proscenium arch. Seating descended from the rear as the separate side and middle sections were "slaughtered." The result was that viewers looked down a slight incline devoid of all interruptions from the back to the front of the auditorium.

The modern theater operated on principles similar to some of the main artistic innovations of the day. Inside the compact theater the viewer was part of a group, but experienced a heightening of individuality while watching the screen. Just as films featuring Will Rogers celebrated the making of a more vital life and community, the swing music and regionalist paintings of the era also evoked a group composed of creative individuals, all in a process of dynamic movement and propulsion toward the future.[22]

Working in a similar if different artistic framework, Schlanger saw that the parabolic design ensured that the theater seating would simultaneously revolve around democratic principles while uniform sight lines and the elliptically shaped auditorium broke down space between the stage and the audience. To heighten the impact of the film, Schlanger enlarged the screen and blended it into the surrounding walls. Commenting on the purpose of these innovations, he explained that

> it is this transition which should allow the viewer to feel as little consciousness of the surrounding walls and the ceiling as possible, so that he can completely envelop himself in that which he is viewing. This portion of the auditorium should be flexible . . . its form should be changeable and its lighting effects varied to suit the tempo of that which is being presented.[23]

Soon these varied innovations—the elimination of historical symbols, egalitarian seating, flowing design, the removal of the proscenium arch, the interjection of the screen into the audience space—appeared at movie houses like the Lake Theater outside Chicago. Watching the designs spread, architects like Paul Frankl and Robert Boller saw in them the renewal of American national identity. Boller, for example, noted that the modern theater was truly "American" because it asked the same price for all seats, and everyone sat on the same level. In an era when major politicians from Huey Long to Franklin Roosevelt condemned the "money changers" whose waste disrupted the potential of industry to create abundance for all, Boller saw that the modern theater revealed that the machine society could yield a world of affluence and security. Where the old cathedral style democratized the status symbols of a business system, the modern theater showed that technology could be made to serve the public good. The modern thus presented a cultural critique of the old order as well as a model for the future. Little wonder that a promoter of the new style argued that modernism pointed to a new day, for

> America is free from the influence of a dying royal conservatism and bureaucracy which in Europe still crush the vitality of the living with the dead weight of history and tradition. American life belongs to the future. America has the means, the opportunity; has she the spiritual endowment comparable to the Greeks two and a half millennia ago? It lies with America to allow the great promise to perish or mature.[24]

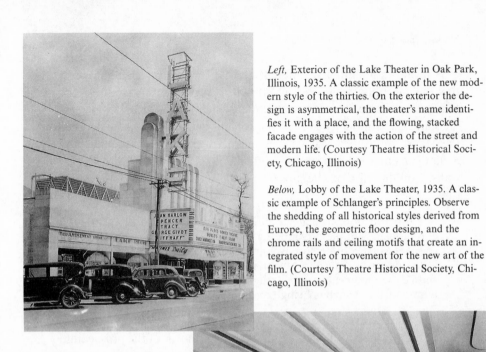

Left, Exterior of the Lake Theater in Oak Park, Illinois, 1935. A classic example of the new modern style of the thirties. On the exterior the design is asymmetrical, the theater's name identifies it with a place, and the flowing, stacked facade engages with the action of the street and modern life. (Courtesy Theatre Historical Society, Chicago, Illinois)

Below, Lobby of the Lake Theater, 1935. A classic example of Schlanger's principles. Observe the shedding of all historical styles derived from Europe, the geometric floor design, and the chrome rails and ceiling motifs that create an integrated style of movement for the new art of the film. (Courtesy Theatre Historical Society, Chicago, Illinois)

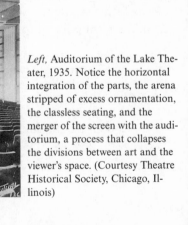

Left, Auditorium of the Lake Theater, 1935. Notice the horizontal integration of the parts, the arena stripped of excess ornamentation, the classless seating, and the merger of the screen with the auditorium, a process that collapses the divisions between art and the viewer's space. (Courtesy Theatre Historical Society, Chicago, Illinois)

"The Big City Comes to the Little Town"

What was the impact of modern design where it most counted—among movie audiences? In the trade journals it was clear by the mid-thirties that the new machine style provided the universal ideal for architects. The relationship of modern theaters and the advent of sound films to audience expansion has been overlooked in part because the statistics investigators utilized to measure attendance over time are grossly inaccurate. According to the figures compiled by the Hays Commission, which provided the basis for the census bureau calculations, attendance peaked at over 110 million weekly in 1929, plummeted in 1931–1939 to 60 million, and rose only to 80 million during World War II. Overall these data reinforce statistics that the number of theaters in the country fell from 23,000 in 1929 to 19,032 in 1939. Together this evidence has led scholars to conclude that film markets diminished by more than 25 percent over the same period.[25]

Yet even at the time journalists often questioned the accuracy of the figures emanating from the Hays Commission. They correctly noted that the census figures came from an industry trade association that refused to reveal the methods it used to gather the data or to open its books to independent investigators. And for good reason: The Hays Commission had an interest in distorting the data. To gain loans from bankers and creditors during the twenties, the film industry had inflated attendance figures to enhance its credit rating. Years later the novelist Harold Robbins, who at the time served as the vice president of Universal Pictures, admitted, "I was adroit at budgets, cost analysis and telling lies to bankers. I used to think the budgets that I had to write were more part of fiction than anything that I have written since." The accuracy of Robbins's recollection was confirmed in 1940 when a Gallup Poll, based on data gathered a year earlier, created a sensation in the trade press. Using more accurate data and methods, it revealed that instead of producers' official count of 80 million tickets sold weekly in 1939, the true number was only 54 million. Industry figures had overestimated attendance by 25 million people weekly, indicating that the figures derived from the Hays Commission were indeed highly misleading and unreliable (appendix 2, figs. 25, 30).[26]

Fortunately, a more accurate method of calculation demonstrates that contemporaries' impression that the movies gained great profits in the Depression was not far off the mark. According to statistical research derived from government tax receipts based on tickets sold from 1920 to 1945, it is possible to see that audiences expanded enormously amid hard times. By dividing the total receipts by the average admission prices listed in the *Motion Picture Herald,* one finds that the figures correlate exactly to the findings of the Gallup Poll published in 1940. Spread over the entire decade, these figures show that weekly attendance in 1929 was not 110 million, but only 37.6 million: The Hays Commission had inflated the figures for bankers and government agencies by 300 percent. Over the next two years gross receipts did indeed fall, because in the hope of gaining larger audiences, theater owners had ensured that ticket prices declined even faster than deflation. These recalculations reveal that from 1930 to 1932 total admissions did not decline but rose from 37.6 to 45.1 million weekly. Though nothing could stave off the fall in numbers in 1933, patronage rose again to 54.6 million weekly by 1940. Attendance accelerated again to over 70 million weekly by 1945, a growth beyond that of the twenties (appendix 2, figs. 26, 27).[27]

The evidence reveals that over the entire fifteen-year period attendance underwent an unprecedented expansion of about 100 percent from the thirties through World War II. So who made up this audience, why did it expand, and what did these changes mean for the manner in which scholars view the "studio system"?[28] To begin with, when the studios collapsed in the Depression and a flood of independents entered the market, reporters discovered an unpredictable "new audience." These patrons rejected studio products and demanded "new subjects," such as the show-within-a-show musicals, the Will Rogers formula films, the Thin Man and Hardy Family series, and the gangster and fallen women stories. As a trade reporter observed, a "rise in patronage for the talking pictures is not based merely upon the awakening of interest on the part of regular patrons; the new subjects are bringing in a following to which the silent picture did not have an appeal. The increased patronage is due to a new audience—an audience which for the first time has become included within the pictures' sphere of influence."[29]

Reporters suggested that as the "new audience" spread, it compelled not only the alteration of theater design and film plots, but the creation of films oriented toward a new national marketplace. It is true that the beginnings of a mass culture were discernible in the twenties; the Hays Commission recognized that movies differed from novels, the stage, and early vaudeville by uniting the classes and the sexes for the first time within a common public. But this mass art remained largely city-based. Conspicuously underrepresented in producers' calculations were the rural areas and small towns populated largely by Anglo-

Saxons—regions that composed about half the population. Independent companies appealed to the rural market, making films that often had different endings than those made for urbanites. Even then, the rural exhibition sites were not film theaters but were more likely to be the local store or auditorium that showed movies only on weekends. To top it off, local leaders often enforced Prohibition and Sunday closing laws so that filmgoing occurred only on Friday and Saturday nights.

By 1933 President Roosevelt ended Prohibition, and restrictions on urban amusements in rural areas began to evaporate. Symbolic of that change was the rise in film attendance and in the number of theaters constructed in the hinterland. Though because of hard times theaters declined between 1929 and 1933 from 18,000 to 12,000, after 1933 markets expanded dramatically and theaters opened at a rate of about 1,000 yearly, with modern theaters constructed at a rate of over 500 annually. The total number of theaters never surpassed that of the twenties, but attendance increased due to high turnover, much lower prices, and expansion into hitherto closed markets. In the rural areas, the end of Prohibition allowed moviegoing on Sunday in southern and northern small towns. In the city of Atlanta, the number of movie houses increased after 1933 by 39 percent, and in the state of Georgia as a whole by over 25 percent. Westward, both Portland and the state of Oregon experienced a 33 percent rise, while in both Los Angeles and California the number of movie houses increased 10 percent. In these states seats per capita rose as well (appendix 2, fig. 29). Lastly, in population centers that had once limited showings to one or two days a week, theaters now operated six or seven days a week from midday into the night. With rural fans attending movies in accelerating numbers, a sociologist found that

> the Little Towner no longer need glance enviously in the direction of the Big Citian because the talking picture has supplied the Big City to the Little Town. Our Little Town is in touch with the world and hears it speaking and sees the world in action.[30]

Equally important, urban exhibitors gathered larger audiences than in the twenties. One stimulus came from the lower prices. A reporter wrote of one southern city, Charlotte, North Carolina, "where 25-cent theaters are now playing at 10 cents admission, business is reported good and many of the 10-cent houses declare that persons who never had attended picture theaters before are among their patrons." Up north nickelodeons had originally spread in working-class areas, where over two-thirds of the people were first- or second-generation immigrants from eastern and southern Europe. Producers had expanded on that audience by building luxury theaters in either downtown or suburban areas, aiming their product at the tastes of the middle class. However, as the economic crisis spurred patrons to reject the movie cathedrals, the rise of modern theaters converged with increased expansion of attendance in lower-income neighborhoods.

By the mid-thirties the nation's first mass culture had become a reality. Formerly closed rural areas in the South and North came into the fold, and moviegoing became more ingrained among workers and lower middle-class residents in the large cities. Once there had been no one standard at the movies for the poor and the affluent. In the past, moral reformers condemned the lowbrow theaters in the immigrant and working-class areas, and during the twenties the construction of the lavish theater palaces was confined to the affluent suburbs and downtown sections. But in the thirties the modern style found its way into all parts of the city, promoting a democratic ethos of abundance across classes.[31] Nor was this expansion confined to white immigrants and the Anglo-Saxon middle classes. At a time when talking films featured minorities in more positive roles, and gangster films gave voice to the underclass, market expansion occurred among minority groups as well.

The trade press observed that filmgoing spread in Los Angeles where Mexican Americans now flocked to the movies.[32] Mexican-American men modeled their style and demeanor on the cinematic gangsters who, like them, spoke in a vernacular dialect, while Latino women modeled their dress and appearance on stars like Greta Garbo. Together films and the urban experience served to create the outlines of a hyphenated culture. In Minneapolis and St. Paul, Minnesota, the theaters in working-class areas had been modest and nondescript in the twenties, but in the thirties the modern style disproportionately appeared in areas inhabited by workers (appendix 2, figs. 27, 28). "First-class" theaters no longer remained the prerogative of the suburbs or downtown theaters. Although segregation of minorities still remained the norm, 800 theaters catering to African Americans opened across the country, featuring the new black films and on-stage appearances by swing bands like those of Count Basie and Duke Ellington, suggesting that despite continuing discrimination, the modernist dream cut across all classes and races.[33]

In retrospect, it is clear that the expansion of markets and the rise of the modern theater formed a uniquely American pattern. In a society whose groups had been divided by region, class, and culture, the spread of modern theaters and radio signaled the creation of common ties across the nation. Both at the local and national level the radio audience expanded from less than 25 to over 90 percent of the public from the twenties through the thirties, and brought the views and voices of immigrants and workers into the public domain. Together, the expansion of theaters and broadcasting indicated that audiences were not contracting but spending more on entertainment.[34]

When compared to other societies, the uniqueness of this change comes into high relief. In the United States the market was much larger than in the other industrialized western countries. Where theaters in the United States increased from 21,000 to 28,000 from the late twenties to the early thirties, the number in Germany rose from 2,826 to 5,000, and in France from 1,500 to 3,000. The total population of Germany and France almost equaled that of the United States, but America contained 20,000 more movie houses than the two combined.

The filmgoing audience in the United States encompassed groups otherwise divided vertically by class as well as horizontally by region. By way of contrast, European film industries often geared their products to a segmented market. In Germany, for example, major companies in the twenties produced films for the working class while others made movies only for the bourgeoisie. Though studios in the United States also catered to specialized markets, it was common for the most popular films to target and attract diverse groups.

More strikingly, modern theater design never gained popularity in Europe equal to that of the United States. Lavish art-deco theaters had catered to select audiences in such large cities as Paris, Berlin, and London, but they never penetrated the European countryside; in a similar vein, functionalist designs emerged among avant-garde and specialized audiences in Germany and Russia. Nowhere did either modernist form gain a mass audience across regions and groups. In many ways the streamlined American mode popularized modernism for the first time at a mass level in any country.[35]

The reason for this distinctiveness was not hard to find: The totalitarian regimes emerging in Europe actively repressed modern art. Under the Stalinist regime in Russia and the fascist regimes in Franco's Spain and Hitler's Germany, the totalitarian leaders used the mass media to preserve national racial and gender norms. In these countries filmmakers created narratives to affirm rather than undermine established traditions and domestic values. Both fascists and Russian communists outlawed modern art in the thirties, perceiving that its forms and content posed a challenge to a unified public.[36]

By way of contrast audiences in America operated in an open marketplace where the New Deal state promoted modernism through the Federal Arts Projects as well as in state funding via the New Deal Housing Act. A more significant difference was the way in which the Great Depression turned fans away from the values and institutions promoted by big business, whose legitimacy was now in question. In this crisis, critics and liberal commentators alike saw that the now-alienating theater palaces symbolized the waste and chaos of the order dominated by the power and tastes of the wealthy. With the capacity to choose buttressed by the state's support of independent theater owners, audiences rejected the lavish theaters and the stars and film formulas of the twenties. Instead, they supported modern theaters that incarnated in steel and technology republican values inherently at odds with the old order.

Little wonder that contemporaries believed during the thirties that the film industry enjoyed a "golden age." Amid a high sea of adversity, it expanded its audience far beyond the numbers of the previous decade and far beyond the audiences of film industries in any other nation. Yet why did this occur? Why would entertainment geared toward play and mass art gain such success? Why were conditions so much different than in Europe? The issue clearly can never fully be resolved, but the parameters of the problem can at least be outlined. Any argument that the modern theater style was imposed on the populace by studio or corporate leaders cannot be sustained. Exhibitors believed that their material interests lay in promoting the cathedral-style theaters, since they had already invested heavily in them. Nor was the new theater style initially promoted by the large studios or by theater owners; indeed, Ben Schlanger emerged from outside the mainstream, and it was the independent theater owners rather than the large chain theaters who first innovated and popularized the new style.

Audiences responded throughout. Instead of exhibiting a narrow psychology based on scarcity, the audiences of the thirties patronized modern movie houses and their promising dreams of abundance. A causal explanation that seeks to explain this phenomenon as a manifestation of corporate hegemony, escapism, or universal trends spanning modern nations is insufficient. Though an alternative hypothesis can only be offered in a tentative form, attendance seemingly rose in response to sound films, efficiency, and lower costs of admission. A more important factor, however, was the modern mode's answer to the crisis of public life affecting American identity in the modern era.

To gain perspective it is well to remember that most of the European nations industrialized within the context of a highly centralized state and structured hierarchies. In the United States the pattern was different. Here the national vision was of a producers' democracy where citizens could find freedom on an open frontier that offered release from aristocracy and monopoly capitalism. The rise of a structured corporate order, however, generated severe class and racial conflict. Because the populace failed to unite across racial and cultural barriers, the corporate order gained power. Both in films and in reality, the rise of the new economy undercut control over work and public life, creating a deep sense of anxiety.

Amid this crisis, urbanites responded by searching to find a new realm of freedom in mass amusements. In the twenties Mary Pickford, Douglas Fairbanks, Charles Chaplin, and Clara Bow had experimented with jazz music and dress styles drawn from immigrants, blacks, and other minorities. Due to fears that the new mass art threatened Anglo-Saxon manhood and family life, ambitious moviemakers ensured that the possibilities for a new life remained focused on a privatized leisure realm, elevated by European styles of high art at the movie cathedral. The result was that the moral revolution of the modern era was identified with "foreign styles" removed from public affairs and the nation's symbols, creating the basis for the "cultural wars" that pitted rural small towns against the new immigrant populations of the big city.

The legacy was a mass culture legitimized by theaters influenced by foreign modes that isolated play from work. In this vein the new consumer culture did not erode but reinforced the cultural authority of the wealthy. The Great Crash had discredited that effort and inspired a modern theater style that combined private and public spheres into a vital synthesis. The designs of the new architects fused the appeal of the moral revolution, cross-cultural mingling, and dreams of prosperity with traditional public values, altering both in the process. Even before the New Deal came to power, the popularity of the modern theater signaled that the democratic possibility of mass art had moved into the civic arena as a force for democratic renewal.

Nowhere was that combination of modern and traditional values more evident than in the shift in names that surrounded the rise of the modern movie house. During the twenties the theaters listed in trade journals had names that linked the movie house to a romantic world removed from public life and work. Lavish theaters had exotic names like the Granada (a Moslem capital in southern Spain), the Tivoli (a medieval town in Italy), the Rialto (an island in Venice), the Arcadia (a pastoral utopia in Greece), the Alhambra (a palace in medieval Spain), and, of course, the Palace and the Capitol and the Paramount. By the thirties, however, the allure of the popular arts reinvigorated communal and patriotic loyalties. Increasingly, exotic names declined in favor of theaters called the Roosevelt, the Lincoln, the Pocahontas, the Washington, the Will Rogers, the Liberty, the Colonial, the Varsity, the Oak, the Lake, or simply the People's Community Theater.

Unlike the old motion picture cathedrals, these modern movie houses were closely identified with Americanizing popular art and renewing civic life, a combination that spurred the opening of these theaters throughout the nation. The difference from the past could not have been more stark. Moralists in the twenties had strove to keep the appeal of mass art, with its lures of cross-cultural mingling and modern morals, separate from the world of power and politics. Yet on the walls and the facades of the newly recreated modern theaters in the cities and countryside, one could find images that evoked the labor of those who had built the nation. Merging popular art to the republican tradition, murals emulated regionalist styles promoted by painters like Thomas Hart Benton. To root the style in the local community, theater architects in the Southwest incorporated materials drawn from desert sand and stone. In New England, modernists mixed a machine aesthetic with bricks and wood drawn from the forests. The Newsreel theaters and the Trans Lux chain in New York City featured murals celebrating people whose skills and trades built the metropolis.[37]

Images that gave representation to minorities and formerly ostracized immigrants also graced many northern theaters. Murals at the Trans Lux depicted whites and racial minorities working and playing in the city, while at the Newsreel theaters the murals and friezes featured documentary moviemaking in racially diverse neighborhoods. A modernist theater situated at the port of Duluth, Minnesota, displayed murals portraying immigrant dockworkers building ships to sail down the Great Lakes. Downstate in Minnesota, modern theaters in New Ulm and Minneapolis portrayed German, French, and English explorers encountering the natives of the New World. To the west, the owner of a modern theater in Colorado Springs, Colorado, named it the Ute after a local Indian tribe. On the inside he placed murals that featured the productive activities of the natives. In another southwest locale,

Interior of the Ute Theater in Colorado Springs, Colorado. A model for blending local building materials and the modern style, coupled to murals displaying the history of the local Indian tribes. *Motion Picture Herald,* April 3, 1936.

Robert Boller saw the modern theater as a site of cross-regional and cultural exchange:

> Lloyd Moylan of the Taos artists' colony, situated a few miles from the city of Sante Fe, was brought to Kansas City by the lessees of the theater to paint the murals. The huge painting on one side of the auditorium depicts a scene on the Trail, showing a Prairie Schooner en route. On the opposite wall the scene is of a young adventurer serenading his light o'love before the campfire, surrounded by mule drivers, cooks and hangers-on who helped blaze the trail to the West.[38]

The evocation of the producers' democracy also signaled that the vernacular arts linked the modern theater to civic renewal. In sharp contrast to the twenties when reformers saw popular art as dangerous, the modern theater provided a site where hitherto outlawed working-class behavior entered and altered the coordinates of public life. Among the most dramatic examples of this trend were bank nights and amateur hours. Through the thirties these games spread to almost every theater in the land. Early in the decade, however, the local police closed theaters engaging in "give away games," since they violated local laws against public gambling, an activity that had been made illegal to control workers' lowbrow amusements. Once Prohibition ended, theater owners found ways to combine formerly outlawed pleasures with appeals to a "family audience." At Saturday matinees managers created games where they auctioned off household items, ranging from dishes to clothes. Commenting on the appeal of these events for fans who never went to the movies in the past, a theater owner remarked that the "average wage earner will go to the theater once a week . . . and he will take his entire family with him. His wife . . . may also attend a Wednesday matinee or a Saturday children's matinee as well."

Along the same lines the owner of a streamlined theater in New Ulm, Minnesota, appealed to his German-American patrons with amateur hours featuring the local talent, who imitated their favorite stars and performed popular songs. Such a movie house and its entertainment, advertised by the theater owner as a "family theater," were typical of the new ambience. In New York City, the comic Larry Storch, the son of Jewish immigrants from eastern Europe, as a young man played amateur-night contests at movie houses. He soon found that when he performed at houses patronized by distinct ethnic groups he won the amateur-hour contest by perfecting the sound and dialect of the fans' favorite players, such as James Cagney, the favorite of the Irish, or Edward G. Robinson and Eddie Cantor, the favorite of Jewish audiences. In black Philadelphia, the comic James Cross, who later formed part of the comedy team of Stump and Stumpy, got his start imitating white and black film stars for local audiences, selecting screen idols according to local taste.[39]

As bank nights and amateur hours linked national filmgoing to local audience amusements, the movie houses of the thirties also provided a site for civic events as well, ranging from high school graduations and charity functions to civic club and political gatherings. In the early years of the Depression, theater owners in New York provided food for the needy at Christmas time, linking the movies to community relief. By 1932, moreover, Hollywood Boulevard had become the site of a Christmas Day event, which featured film stars in an annual parade. Theater owners and civic leaders lined the streets of "tinseltown" with neon-lighted Christmas trees, while cars paraded down the avenue, known as "Santa Claus Lane."

The most dramatic indication of the fusion of modern popular art to local traditions and civic life were the film premieres that spread across the nation. In the twenties, the opening of a major film occurred solely in large cities, particularly New York City or Los Angeles. But by the late thirties producers linked movie art with national life in a threefold way. First, they began to eliminate advertisements for products in local theaters, since public opinion was unfavorable to big business.[40] Second, they opened key films in the locales where they were set: Hence *Santa Fe Trail* (1940) premiered in Santa Fe, New Mexico; *Dodge City* (1939) opened in Dodge City, Kansas; *Brigham Young* (1940) in Salt Lake City, Utah; *Gone with the Wind* (1939) in Atlanta, Georgia; and *Boys Town* (1938) in Omaha, Nebraska. Lastly, producers gained the cooperation of mayors and governors, who proclaimed holidays for the film openings. Amid hard times these premieres often promoted political causes advanced by labor and New Deal radicals. Take the premiere of *How Green Was My Valley* in 1941. At a time when the United Mine Workers was led by the Welsh immigrant John L. Lewis, John Ford's film told the story of Welsh workers striving to form a labor union. To link the story to local events, the production premiered in the mining town of Wilkes-Barre, Pennsylvania, populated in part by the Welsh and the site of United Mine Workers activity through the thirties.[41]

The Irony of Success: The Modern Movie House Goes to War

The onset of World War II saw Hollywood producers joining the struggle against the fascists to create a more just world. With the threat of Japan and Germany building from 1939 to 1941, President Roosevelt began to call for rearmament. During this "defense" period the *Motion Picture Herald* announced the making of "43 Features and Short Subjects on America from the Studios"; these plans resulted from State Department pressures and were a "direct outgrowth of the international situation and its effects on the country." In this same spirit, a theater owner in Minneapolis built the modernistic Uptown Theater in 1940, whose exterior featured a relief of athletes, soldiers, and aviators mobilized to defeat the foreign enemy.[42]

A relief on the outside of the Uptown Theater in Minneapolis. Built in 1940, the stone re-lief reveals the transformation of the producer tradition to the ideal of the citizen as sol-dier and aviator on the eve of World War II. Photo by Stephen Lassonde, 1986.

The combination of wartime élan and the new Americanism came to a head at a premiere in South Bend, Indiana. There Warner Broth-ers held a gala in 1940 to open *Knute Rockne, All American,* featuring a future president of the United States, Ronald Reagan. Drawing on the central myths of the Great Depression, the film tells the story of the Notre Dame football coach. Coming to the United States as an immigrant Norwegian, Rockne applies machine-like science to foot-ball, molding a team composed of immigrants into a winning enter-prise. Evoking the theme of fall and rebirth, the team's star player, George Gipp, dies, but the coach arouses his "boys" from defeat to "win one for the Gipper." After Notre Dame triumphs, the coach tells a congressional committee investigating the evil effects of sports that football provides an arena to revive the spirit of manhood that won the West, created solid families, and defeated the enemies of democracy.[43]

To reinforce that theme, the governors of Indiana and bordering states proclaimed the premiere a state holiday. Echoing the *42nd Street* tour, Warner Brothers enlisted a train, christened the "Knute Rockne Special," to travel from Hollywood to Indiana. Once arriving in South Bend, the stars joined a parade with ex-Notre Dame football players and Mrs. Rockne. At the cemetery they placed a wreath on the old coach's grave, while Kate Smith sang her trademark "God Bless America," written by the Jewish composer Irving Berlin, on national radio. At the banquet that followed, the Irish Catholic actor who played Coach Rockne, Pat O'Brien, declared that he idolized the Catholic university Notre Dame and its famed coach as a model for a pluralistic country composed of formerly marginalized Irish Catholics.

A reporter from the *South Bend Tribune* also took note that the other featured player, Ronald Reagan, invited his own Irish Catholic father and New Deal loyalist to the event. As Reagan spoke, his majestic voice "sent a hush through the crowd with the descriptions of his emo-

The concluding scene of *Knute Rockne, All American* (1940). Here Coach Rockne, played by Pat O'Brien, tells Congress that football fosters the type of manhood that will help defend the nation in time of war. (Courtesy Museum of Modern Art, Film Stills Archive)

tions as he played the immortal George Gipp." To ensure that no one missed the larger significance of these events, a studio executive appeared on the scene. Signaling the merging of public life and the new media, the executive was also the son of President Roosevelt. Young Roosevelt stood up and read a message from his father. The president's remarks praised Knute Rockne and, as if taking a note from the script itself, he told the attendees:

> We can draw deep inspiration from the ideals which he exemplified in his life and work, and from those ideals gather wisdom for our guidance in this anxious hour when the national defense has become our paramount political concern. Our need today is for men strong in body, strong in soul and strong in faith in the democratic way of life. In brief, for men who hold to the ideals which Knute Rockne held. I salute the memory of a great figure in our American life.[44]

What made the president's letter so telling was that the film and the new-style modern theater in which it premiered both embodied a dramatic reshaping of an American culture in the midst of the Depression. When the economic crisis struck, modernist critics saw that the motion picture cathedral embodied the bankruptcy of the old order. If the old tastemakers saw the United States as an Anglo-Saxon nation rooted in the ideals of Europe, the modernists noted that these ideals were now embodied in the empty status symbols and pretentious waste of the lavish theater palace. The new architects, led by Ben Schlanger, envisaged the modern theater as a utopian critique of the old order and a renewal of the republican commonwealth. Collapsing the barrier between play and work, it provided a model of cohesion and dynamic movement in which the egalitarian seating, the regionalist murals, and asymmetrical design pointed to the spirit of the New Deal that informed the work of Will Rogers and other moviemakers through the Depression era.

Above all, this modern style appeared to be distinct to the United States. Unlike totalitarian states, where the old historical model suggested that traditional social arrangements ruled, the modern style brought new groups and desires into the public arena. Built through the support of the New Deal Housing acts, the new movie houses heralded a vast expansion into hitherto excluded audiences. By the late thirties, the smooth, slick, glimmering lines of the modern dominated the Main Streets of hundreds of small towns and cities, and the lighted marquees beckoned passers-by with a reformulation of the American dream. Because that dream included consumption and civic renewal, a Hollywood producer was able to tell a congressional committee in 1939 that with war clouds spreading, "This industry has stood for a lot. By that I mean it has been the American Way of life."

Yet the war brought a paradox. A people fighting in the name of renewed republican dreams would find that the call for national unity legitimized the new corporate order focused on a private life of mass consumption rather than people's control over work and public affairs. How and why the war would reshape politics and moviemaking in Hollywood provides the subject of the next two chapters.

PART TWO

The American Way and Its Discontent

Chapter 4

The Birth of the White Consumer Democracy: Hollywood and the World War II Conversion Narrative

The principal battleground of this war is not the South Pacific. It is not the Middle East. It is not England or Norway, or the Russian Steppes. It is American opinion.

—Archibald MacLeish, future director
of the Office of War Information, 1941

Few wars in our history have altered the United States as much as World War II. The attack on Pearl Harbor brought a formerly isolationist nation onto the global stage as a world power. Against the backdrop of the Depression, defense spending created full employment, ensuring that among all the combatants the United States experienced unprecedented prosperity in a time of war. To assist in the war effort, the government mobilized the film industry, complete with its thousands of theaters and expanding audiences. Yet as moviemakers equated the war with fulfilling the promises of abundance and pluralism informing the arts of the Depression, Hollywood filmmakers altered the coordinates of that inheritance. Instead of class conflict and moral experimentation, the American Way focused on the rise of a consumer democracy that reinforced a classless society and introduced the dream of the white "pin-up girl" who channeled her wishes for liberation into the privatized suburban home.

Among the many who created the wartime American Way, it was clear that their efforts ironically bred a wartime victory culture undergirded with a new sense of anxiety and loss. A striking testimony to that paradox emerged in the autobiography of a major screenwriter, Philip Dunne. In *Take Two: A Life in the Movies and Politics,* Dunne told readers that though he had proudly created films that inspired the populace to win the war, he also felt responsible for having created during the war a vision of innocence in which criticism of the home front was seen as subversive and unpatriotic. To Dunne this altered the meaning of democracy and the direction of his career. Trying to explain why, he noted that after attending Harvard and working as a reporter on the *New York World,* he came to Hollywood where he collaborated with fellow screenwriter Dudley Nichols to form the Southern California Labor's Non-Partisan League with the Congress of Industrial Organizations (CIO).

Besides advancing the cause of labor and participating in the antifascist crusade, Dunne noted that the League's "greatest achievement" was to provide "movie stars to grace political functions" and build on "foundations laid by the socialist Upton Sinclair a few years earlier and transform the California Democratic Party into a fundamentally liberal organization." Throughout Dunne saw that his radicalism derived less from Karl Marx than the traditional republicanism of Thomas Jefferson and that of his own father, Finley Peter Dunne, who had created the newspaper character of "Mr. Dooley" as a vehicle to satirize public life. Carrying his politics into his own work, Dunne wrote the screenplay for *How Green Was My Valley* (1941) to dramatize the formation of unions. Dunne believed that through screen images he could reach public minds that were "otherwise unreachable." The power to mold public opinion on the screen was "a headier wine than either money or fame."

Once the war came, Dunne accurately saw that Hollywood politics and moviemaking refocused the meaning of democracy. Instead of struggling against injustice at home, artists depicted the United States as an innocent society that needed to be defended from foreign monopolists and tyrants. Film heroes and heroines now adapted to large organizations and accepted corporations as the "arsenal of democracy." With men and women losing control over work and public life, hostility to capitalism and foreign policy initiatives was deemed unpatriotic.

Though Dunne created films in line with the new consensus, he recognized that freedom was now found less in work than in a new consumer democracy focused on the suburban home and classless ideals. Looking back, Dunne noted that this twofold reconfiguration—the making of a homogeneous public life and a privatized ideal of consumerism—set the tone of the postwar era. Reflecting on his participation in this transformation, Dunne wrote:

> In the field of politics the greatest regret of my life is that I failed to foresee the ultimate perversion of the Messianic theory of American foreign policy we liberals so avidly endorsed in the 1930's and 1940's. It was so very clear to us then. We saw a Manichean world, a conflict between light and darkness. . . . It was our

mission, as we saw it to remake the world in our own liberal image. Vietnam was the bastard child of the messianic mission on which we as a nation embarked forty years ago. None of us who first proclaimed that crusade can escape our share of the unhappy consequences.[1]

Dunne's memoir posits a very different way of envisioning the impact of World War II on postwar politics and culture. Over the past two decades historians have shown that World War II promoted the interests of the new corporate order and set the stage for the affluent society of the Cold War era. There arose after a decade of strife and deprivation a class consensus and a consumer society that were promoted to the world as the "American Way." Scholars usually see these trends as a logical development from the politics and popular dreams promoted by leaders and artists in the New Deal era.[2] Yet the purpose of this chapter is to show that during the war years grassroots reform and class conflict came to be stigmatized as unpatriotic, with the result that a republican nationalism that pervaded the nation for a hundred years was delegitimized. In its place freedom was identified less with public life and an autonomous civic sphere than with a consumer culture identified with the rise of the "white suburban home" undergirded by anxiety.

Monopolizing the Public Sphere

To understand the transformation in American culture unfolding during World War II, it is important to realize that the call for unity generated a battle against the radical republican tradition that had pervaded national life ever since the early nineteenth century. After a decade of grassroots radicalism, ranging from unions to populist movements in the Midwest, South, and West, President Roosevelt announced that Dr. New Deal was being replaced by "Dr. Win the War." On the home front the major parties, including the Communists, agreed to postpone labor-capital conflict.[3] To back a popular war, labor leaders and big business agreed with government to arbitrate strikes, create price controls, and legitimize the spread of patriotic unions.

The film industry not only conformed to these strictures, but promoted films that gave meaning and purpose to the war. The unique status of the United States among all the allies heightened Hollywood's significance. Unlike the other nations, the United States remained isolated from the fighting and bombing. In these circumstances, leaders called on the Hollywood film industry to bring home the images of war to inspire the populace to support total mobilization. The central agency for coordinating this effort was the Office of War Information (OWI), which was guided by liberal, interventionist New Dealers who understood that the movies provided a mechanism to spur home-front morale. As the head of the OWI observed after Pearl Harbor, the "easiest way to inject propaganda ideas into most people's minds, is to let it go in through the medium of an entertainment picture when they do not realize they are being propagandized."[4]

Under the shadow of war, Hollywood recast national goals and purpose to satisfy the hopes that had emerged in the popular arts and politics of the New Deal years. The outlines of that shift emerged in the Manual for the Motion Picture Industry produced by the OWI. Written for all moviemakers creating films to promote the war, the manual noted that this conflict had to be portrayed as different from World War I. Where the battle against the Kaiser generated an Americanism rooted in Anglo-Saxon superiority, World War II was a crusade to defeat the "brutality, cruelty, treachery and cynicism" of the enemy.[5] Hitler and Mussolini thus embodied the tyranny of "Caesar and Pharaoh" that immigrants had left the Old World to escape. Victory would eliminate all "forms of racial discrimination or religious intolerance, for special privileges for any of our citizens are manifestations of fascism and should be exposed as such." The nation embodied a new "melting pot" of "many races and creeds that showed that people can live together in freedom and progress." To attain victory, the people must put aside "national, class or race war," opening the way for the country's fighting men to create a "new world free of fear and want" for the "common man."[6]

Disagreements would surface between the OWI and producers concerning how best to dramatize a society free of "want" and "race war," but it was clear that moviemakers proved willing allies. To begin with, the Depression was now a thing of the past: Hollywood profits had risen by a third and the audience had expanded by 20 percent. Since most studio heads descended from Jewish immigrants, the war against Nazi racism gained their support. Well before the attack on Pearl Harbor, Warner Brothers made *Confessions of a Nazi Spy* (1939) as a response to the murder of Joe Kauffmann, the studio's emissary in Berlin, because he was a Jew.[7] Similarly, film stars who had supported New Deal causes—James Cagney, Pat O'Brien, Edward G. Robinson, Myrna Loy, Carole Lombard, Bette Davis, Paul Robeson, Rex Ingram, Lena Horne, and John Garfield—participated in government-sponsored "Victory Parades," and screenwriters moved to Washington, D.C., to produce films that fused "characterization and the world struggle against fascism."[8] At the grassroots theater owners sold war bonds, generating over 20 percent of all bond sales. Linking the war to the people's heroes and heroines, the Department of Defense built ships named after the Cherokee Indian Will Rogers and Carole Lombard, while Lena Horne christened a Navy destroyer named for the black scientist, George Washington Carver.[9]

Many left-wing artists also envisaged the war as a chance to fulfill their reformist visions on a global scale. John Garfield, Lena Horne, Duke Ellington, and the black heavyweight boxing champion Joe Louis entertained the troops training to defeat the fascists. Bette Davis, known for her portrayals of rebellious women, challenged Army segregation and told news reporters that such stereotypes as Aunt Jemima and the comic butler Rochester had to give way to more dignified portrayals of blacks.[10] Similarly, the Jewish-American scenarist John Bright, author of *Public Enemy,* and the director Orson Welles, maker of *Citizen Kane,* joined forces to protect Mexican-American youths who were falsely accused by Los Angeles police in the Sleepy Lagoon murder. To justify the larger implications of these efforts, Welles became during the war a columnist for *Free World Magazine* where he wrote:

> Our Republican splendor in this new age will shine by its own virtues, not by contrasting it with tyranny abroad. . . . Much is against us on the records: we oppressed the Indian, we stole the Black Man from his home and held him in bondage. And the fragrance of American freedom rose over the stench of butchery. If the conquerors and the slavers left us a mad strain of hate . . . we've told our children this was hate from the old world, that in our climate this finally must perish.[11]

Writers on the left also saw the war as generating a restoration of faith and "manhood" against the defeats and humiliations of the Depression. According to Robert Rossen, the new chairman of a Hollywood writers' mobilization association, film narratives now expressed a "New Day." Those like himself who descended from immigrants and workers saw that after World War I and the corrupt twenties, "All our heroes had feet of clay and if they did not they weren't worth writing about." The Depression films had showed "corrupt, evil forces . . . crushing men and women." But the war turned all that around, revealing that the "people would win despite any conditions." In contrast to the dismal past, today the "average man sees and feels the difference between this and the last war." The "dark days are over," giving rise to a new character "who no longer despairs but has found dignity and a 'cause' worth dying for."[12]

The dream of renewed manhood paradoxically sanctioned the pluralistic inheritance of the thirties and identified the class conflict associated with that ethos as subversive and "un-American." Wartime show-within-a-show musicals like *This Is the Army* (1943), *Star Spangled Rhythm* (1942), and *Yankee Doodle Dandy* (1942) linked popular music to voluntary enthusiasm for the war. *This Is the Army* featured the black hero Joe Louis, while *Stormy Weather* (1943) featured Bill Robinson, Louis Armstrong, and Lena Horne. *A Walk in the Sun* (1945), written by Robert Rossen, depicted southerners and the children of the new immigrants defeating the Nazis, while *The Fighting Sullivans* (1944) dramatized the fate of an Irish Catholic family whose five sons die in battle against the Japanese. Similarly, eastern European laborers and factory owners voluntarily put aside class conflict in *Pittsburgh* (1942) and *An American Romance* (1944). Above all, American heroes in *Air Force* (1943), *Back to Bataan* (1945), *The Fighting 69th* (1940), and *Sahara* (1943) dramatized the formula of the "ethnic platoon" where blacks, Texans, Jews, and Italians cooperate to defeat the enemy. Similarly, *Lifeboat* (1944) spurred the black press to note that the black actor Canada Lee's disarming of a Nazi "did wonders for the morale of the Negro GIs who talked about it for days. To them it was the symbol of changing times, of acceptance, of full integration into the pattern of American life."[13]

Despite these gains, this pluralism bore a striking resemblance to the older ethos of assimilation defined by Anglo-Saxon opinion makers. True, members of formerly ostracized racial and ethnic groups gained acceptance, but historical memories and identities that collided with wartime nationalism had to be shed. Instead of finding their roots in the local community or an autonomous civic sphere, wartime heroes gave their loyalty to large "savior institutions" linked to the state or defense industries. To ensure unity, the OWI told moviemakers that those who "believe in the rightness of our cause" can no longer focus "attention on the chinks in our allies' armor." This type of criticism must be forbidden because that is precisely "what our enemies might wish. Perhaps it is unrealistic but it is going to be confusing to audiences."[14] Producers similarly labeled Lew Ayres, the actor who converted to pacifism after starring in *All Quiet on the Western Front,* a "disgrace to the industry" when he enlisted as a medic rather than a combat soldier. The president of MGM said, "As far as I am concerned . . . Lew Ayres is washed up with us since he washed himself up with

The new pluralistic American identity symbolized by the World War II "ethnic platoon" in *Bataan* (1943). Note the presence of racial minorities: an African American, fifth from left, and a Mexican American, sixth from left. (Courtesy Academy of Motion Picture Arts and Sciences)

the public." The FBI found it necessary to launch an investigation of Orson Welles since he engaged in radical causes and made *Citizen Kane,* a production critical of the newspaper magnate William Randolph Hearst. The FBI likewise labeled Philip Dunne a "communist" because he wrote the pro-union film *How Green Was My Valley* and supported progressive causes. Since he could not receive a security clearance to work with the director John Ford, now an admiral in the Navy, Dunne wrote:

> The hurt and the humiliation were not so easily exorcised. Apparently the only way citizens can be sure of remaining "clean" in the eyes of their own government is to abstain entirely from any political activity . . . abdicate their responsibilities as citizens in a democracy, and that is one of the worst crimes committed in the name of "security."[15]

Such crimes did not stop with the pre-production process. Frank Capra sought to re-release the 1937 film *Lost Horizon* during the war. In the thirties Capra had used the film in part to criticize imperialism in the Far East, but now the OWI cut a speech where the hero asks a British leader, "Did you say we saved ninety white people? Good. Hooray for us. Did you say we left ten thousand natives down there to be annihilated? No. No, you wouldn't say that. They don't count." Yet in the war years Capra dismissed writers from his own government-sponsored *Why We Fight* series (1942–1945) when the House Un-American Activities Committee (HUAC) investigated them for writing scripts that depicted the Japanese not as racial villains but as people who became imperialistic due to their unresolved class conflicts.[16]

Capra was not alone in encountering government censorship and subversion of wartime productions. The director John Huston found that his documentaries, *The Battle of San Pietro* (1945) and *Let There Be Light* (1946), were unacceptable to the Army because one portrayed men slaughtered by inept officers and the other showed that shell-shocked veterans were driven insane by combat. Yet not only government-sponsored documentaries drew the censors' attention. OWI officials considered *Mr. Skeffington* (1944), a film that dealt with anti-Semitism, "gravely detrimental . . . the Jewish question is presented in such a way to give credence to the Nazi contention that discrimination for which Americans condemn the fascists, is an integral part of American democracy."[17]

If censors believed that films critical of domestic life had to be eliminated, the war also created the conditions in which the large studios found it opportune to pay attention to their demands. Formerly movie-makers operated in a highly competitive public sphere open to the views and interests of marginal groups. A wide variety of independent films, some using foreign languages and experimental forms, appealed to diverse audiences. It was these independents who often pioneered gangster, fallen woman, social problem, and horror genres. So profitable were these productions that between one-third and one-half of all films made in the thirties came from independents. Yet during the war years the large studios gained the status of an "essential war industry," which allowed them access to raw film stock. When the smaller firms failed to attain that access, the number of independents declined from ninety-two in 1939 to fifteen in 1944. The result was that the large firms gained a monopoly, and foreign and independent films declined from half of all film production in 1939 to less than a fourth in 1944. Or to put it another way, independent productions decreased from 379 to 172 films, a decrease of more than 50 percent over five years.[18]

The decline of the independent film companies coincided with a closure of the public space between government censorship and the studios. No doubt censorship existed during the thirties, but the industry operated in a relatively autonomous manner and policed its own product through the Hays Commission.[19] When the OWI entered the equation, and the ranks of independents that skirted even industry censorship guidelines declined, the space between the state and the film industry collapsed. It was not just a matter of OWI influence. Rather, voluntary wartime cooperation by moviemakers with the OWI short-circuited the possibilities for dissenting views to gain visibility. As one director noted, "our primary responsibility was not to the box office, nor to our paychecks. It was a special responsibility . . . to the men who wore the uniform."[20] John Huston saw the film industry functioning in the war as the "conscience of our people," showing with a "blinding flash of truth" that we could overcome "race prejudice." Robert Andrews, the writer of *Bataan* (1943), saw the war as an extension of his career as a journalist who covered Chicago gang killings. The purpose at that time was to "wake the good citizens to what they were up against. That's all I'm trying to do today. . . . And I am determined to write a picture so shocking that people would say to themselves, if this is what our men have to stand up to, we've got a job to do." Though the effect made audiences "depressed," they "find [themselves] getting angry—angry that such things are being done to us."[21]

Transferred to the screen, the revolt against things "done to us" yielded a shift in the nature of cinematic visual style. In the thirties, such directors as Michael Curtiz, Lewis Milestone, John Ford, Frank Capra, and William Wyler popularized a dialogic cinema where the moving camera described a world where different viewpoints appeared as within a cubist painting. To convey this multiplicity, directors often ensured that the foreground, background, and middle ground were lit equally, while the horizontal rather than vertical planes predominated to place characters in spatial relations of equality. These multiple spaces shown in simultaneous and receding forms allowed different views and voices to appear, enlisting viewers to choose between them.[22] In addition, a camera that moved inside the frame and compositions photographed at a diagonal angle often emphasized a world where movement rather than stasis predominated and things appeared to be interconnected.

But the war gave rise to dramas that pitted unquestioned good against evil, ensuring that a dialogical perception gave way to a fixed and monolithic mode of perceiving the world. Indicative of this sharply divided worldview, one writer noted "No longer is it necessary [to] cloak the more serious thoughts and aspects behind a melodramatic yarn or sugar coat the message. . . . Terms such as 'fascists' and 'appeasers' can be used without offense."[23] To convey that worldview, multiple viewpoints that asked the viewers to choose between different voices and views necessarily receded. In their place balanced compositions came to the foreground, and the camera focused on one point. Directors ensured that viewers understood who was to be admired and who disdained through the utilization of sacred and fixed symbols of authority. The action might focus on preachers evoking the cause of the allies, while patriotic music, religious symbols, voice-over narrators, and maps told viewers exactly how to think about the action, giving a monolithic direction to their thoughts.[24]

Deradicalizing American Myths and Symbols

While wartime movies emphasized monolithic visual perceptions, and censors eliminated images that subverted state and business leaders, a central plot device—the conversion narrative—reversed the basis of cultural authority from the bottom to the top of society. In the thirties, the conversion narrative portrayed characters shedding dependency on the values promoted by the rich in favor of those of the "people" or the lower class. That transformation served to align the middle class with the lower class and revitalize America's traditional identity as a republic. But now films like *Casablanca,* the Academy-Award-winning film for best picture of 1943, portrayed the tragic consequences that flowed from having to convert to war: It meant the end of the republican dream where citizens controlled work and enjoyed a more inclusive and experimental culture and family life.[25]

Scripted by writers committed to New Deal reform, the movie opens with a montage of voices and maps that evoke images of a republic besieged. Refugees from Nazism seek to escape through Casablanca in North Africa. The moving camera stops on the frieze of a court-house where the democratic ideals of the French republic, "liberté, egalité and fraternité," grace the exterior.[26] The camera then comes to focus on a hero who embodies the American side of that republican code. Operating in an autonomous civic sphere, Rick Blaine, played by Humphrey Bogart, is the ideal of the hero who came of age in the

New Deal era. Merging cultural and social reform, he controls his property, "Rick's Café Americain," a nightclub where diverse peoples mingle in a pluralistic community and jazz music permeates the atmosphere, enacting dreams of a vernacular art and a more vital life. Rick also facilitates the escape of Jews from the Nazis, pays his employees high wages, and evokes the ideal of reciprocity across classes and isolation from Europe's quarrels that threaten to entrap the New World citizen.

In a scene that demonstrates Rick's merging of the modernized republican ideal of racial pluralism and resistance to the domestic oppressors of the New Deal era, he responds to a fellow nightclub owner's offer to "buy Sam," Rick's African-American piano player. Harking back to the producers' democracy of the abolitionist crusade, Rick says, "I don't buy or sell human beings." The audience also learns that Sam and Rick are friends who have forged ties across the races. Not only do they confide in each other, but Sam owns 25 percent of the Café Americain and has helped Rick escape from Nazis who "blacklisted" him and then put a "price on his head" since he ran guns to Ethiopia and Spain in support of African and Spanish citizens' battles to defeat fascist imperialism.

Above all, Rick couples the ideals of the producers' democracy with dreams of a more vital life, symbolized by his love affair with Ilsa, played by Ingrid Bergman.[27] When she appears on the scene and asks Sam to play "As Time Goes By," we learn that Ilsa and Rick were lovers in Paris, symbol of modern culture for a generation of Americans. Their love affair combined visions of a more passionate life with a commitment to social and cultural reform. Yet Rick believes that his lover deserted him, for when the Nazis invaded Paris, Ilsa disappeared. Amid his despair, Ilsa explains that their love had unfolded only when she believed her resistance-fighter husband, Victor Laszlo, had died in a Nazi concentration camp. When she discovered that he was still alive, she had to desert Rick to help Laszlo fight the Nazis.[28]

With Rick's faith restored that their love and mutual ideals had not been betrayed, he now acts again to fight tyranny and end his and, by extension, the nation's isolation from the fight. Yet that choice is seen as a tragic one, evoking a sense of the blues, which is associated more with black than white Americans, and is signaled by the haunting theme song "As Time Goes By," played at the piano by Sam. With blues music filling key scenes, Rick prepares for war by selling the Café Americain, symbolic of mass amusements rooted in the lower-class vernacular sensibility and of his autonomy. Knowing the full cost of

Casablanca (1943). Romantic dreams and the World War II conversion narrative: Sam plays "As Time Goes By" as Rick and Ilsa have to shed their dreams and conform to the demands of war. (Courtesy Academy of Motion Picture Arts and Sciences)

his conversion narrative, Rick tells Ilsa they must shed their dreams of merging politics with a new culture and integrated selves.

Explaining why the new woman must return in wartime to the traditional family, Rick explains that "inside of us we both know you belong to Victor, you're part of his work, the thing that keeps him going. . . . I have a job to do, too. Where I'm going you can't follow. . . . I'm no good at being noble, but it doesn't take much to see that the problems of three little people don't amount to a hill of beans in this crazy world. Someday you'll understand that." When Ilsa asks what about "us," Rick explains that she must help her husband and restore traditional sexual roles. That is, to create the cohesion necessary for war, Ilsa has to channel her allure into the home. Laszlo reinforces their choice by saying to Rick, "Welcome back to the fight. This time I know our side will win."

The lovers acknowledge their commitments to the war, and musical motifs fill the soundtrack with triumphant music of the French anthem the "Marseillaise," but the optimism is undercut by dark visuals, for Rick has to give up his dream of independence and a more vital life. As the camera penetrates through the night fog to show a sad Ilsa and Rick saying goodbye, Rick joins what he has disdained: a military organization grounded in hierarchy that has undercut his autonomy and personal freedom. To convey the ambiguity of that choice, Rick and the Vichy police chief (played by Claude Rains) move to the beat of the "Marseillaise." The dark scene, however, undercuts the music by evoking a deep undertone of loss beneath their commitment to the "good war."[29]

Within *Casablanca* are a series of narrative patterns that would recur in one form or another in the major films of the war: the need to shed oppositional values in favor of commitment to hierarchical institutions dedicated to saving the world. In film after film this choice converges with a deep undertone of rupture that the directors and writers try to overcome with a patriotic and optimistic commitment to defeating the enemy. On the home front American myths and symbols are deradicalized. Within the mainstream conversion narrative, subversive values belong to characters' earlier rejected selves. To shed guilt and prove one's patriotism, close friends and compatriots—whose beliefs mirror the protagonist's earlier loyalties—have to be destroyed.

Precisely because the need to convert the home front was so critical, the war in Hollywood films often takes place stateside as part of the quest to destroy "subversives." Take the case of *The Fighting 69th* (1940). Significantly, it featured the Irish Catholic actor, James Cagney, playing a role that evoked memories of his famous gangster rebel in *Public Enemy*. Drafted into the Army in World War I, the protagonist hates officers and subverts their power. Yet when his class and ethnic antagonism leads to the death of fellow soldiers, the antihero becomes a patriot by killing the Germans who attack the army he once disdained. Along similar lines, *Air Force* (1943) features a bomber crew flying to the Hawaiian Islands. On board are an Anglo-Saxon officer, a Jewish sergeant, and a Polish-American working-class tail gunner, Winocki, played by one of the classic "city boys," John Garfield. Like many an ethnic working-class man in the thirties, Winocki hates the Yankee commander, who he believes discriminated against him and denied him access to pilot training. Yet when the Japanese attack Pearl Harbor, this class antagonism dissipates in response to the need for unity. When Winocki turns his energies to killing "Japs," the screenwriter noted that he "has found something real to direct his embittered feeling against and his eyes grow hard." Similarly, in *Lucky Jordan* (1942) a gangster works to avoid the draft and makes money by stealing military secrets that he sells to criminals and German spies. Yet he ultimately shifts loyalties and violently destroys his former criminal friends, seeing them as tools of the enemy.[30]

Along with shedding class and ethnic identities, any earlier admiration for left-wing causes and the autonomy of minorities was seen as a tool of the enemy. *Americans All* (1941), a documentary made with the assistance of Louis Adamic, a promoter of minorities' inclusion in national life, opens with a narrator explaining that the country is proud of its racial and ethnic groups. The narrator warns, however, that Americans of Japanese, Italian, and German descent use the foreign language press and radio stations to support the goals of the enemy. The subversive threat most applies to black workers who participate in communist-led parades. Only when minorities turn over their former friends as subversives do unity and true Americanism predominate.[31] *Across the Pacific* (1942) advances a similar point. At the end Japanese plantation laborers revolt against white owners. Yet instead of portraying the laborers in valiant rebellion against oppressive plantation owners, the strikers' class antagonism aligns them to the Japanese army, which wants to build airfields to attack the American Canal Zone.

Besides condemning class conflict, moviemakers portrayed those who continued to advance left-wing populist causes as deadly traitors. In this vein, *Keeper of the Flame* (1942) tells the story of a reporter, played by Spencer Tracy, who deeply admires a public figure modeled on Huey Long and Charles Lindbergh. The reporter undergoes a conversion experience when he discovers that his populist hero, now dead, was really a Nazi agent. To dupe the people and aid the enemy, he had preached isolationism and attacked corporations. In *Mission to Moscow* (1943) isolationist traditions again aid the cause of Hitler. At the end an isolationist midwestern senator tells Congress, "And I say, gentlemen, not only can we do business with Hitler but we can make a nice profit doing so. . . . It's going to be Hitler's Europe and I say, what of it?" To top it off, any alternative sexuality was also seen as aiding the enemy. *The House on 92nd Street* (1945) depicts Nazi spies who steal secrets for a superweapon—one that resembles the atomic bomb. At the end they are revealed not only as traitors but as transvestites whose deviancy aids the enemy.[32]

All of these films depend upon linking subversive tendencies to protagonists' earlier beliefs and loyalties. But once they discover the folly of their pasts, the protagonists prove their patriotism by destroying those who represent parts of their early selves. Take the case of anti-imperialist values. In the thirties, Will Rogers criticized the colonization of nonwhite peoples as a product of American capitalist expansion. Similarly, films such as *All Quiet on the Western Front, Juarez, Ambassador Bill,* and *Mutiny on the Bounty* yoked European and American expansion to the exploitation of nonwhite people. Along the

same lines Progressive historians like Charles and Mary Beard promoted isolationism as the means to prevent big business from advancing its class interests and power around the globe.

Now moviemakers equated the war with the liberation of colonial
peoples and a holy cause to free the world. Yet if this were the case,
how would one convert pacifists and anti-imperialists? One answer to
the problem can be found in *Sergeant York* (1941). Using World War
I as a metaphor for current events, the story charts the story of Al-
vin C. York, a Tennessee farmer. In the first part of the film York op-
poses large farmers who have monopolized land and converts to pacifism. But when the war comes, York goes to a mountain where he
converts to a new patriotic cause. Seeing in the war a means to advance
the cause of liberty, he, in one critic's words, "sets aside his religious
scruples against killing for what he felt was the better good of his country and the lasting benefit of mankind." At the end York emerges as
the most decorated soldier in the war, and the government supplies
him with farmland. After the film's release, veterans groups feted its
star, Gary Cooper, who won the best actor Oscar for the role, while
President Roosevelt invited the real Sergeant York to the White House.
The War Department noted that during the next few weeks it experienced a boom in enlistments.[33]

In other films the war promises to free people from colonial oppression around the globe. *Back to Bataan,* for example, takes place in the
Philippines prior to the Japanese invasion. The enemy radio informs
the natives that the Japanese have come to liberate them from the im-
perial United States. A U.S. officer, played by John Wayne, mobilizes
the natives' resistance. The Japanese radio station asks the Filipinos
why they are not joining with Asians to expel white imperialists. That
question haunts the mind of the grandson of a Philippine patriot who
had fought against American invaders in the 1890s. The grandson has
resisted colonial power; moreover, his lover joins with the Japanese,
serving as the radio announcer who calls on the Filipinos to side
against John Wayne's troops. Once the Filipino patriots witness Japanese atrocities, however, they convert and join the American military
to expel tyrants.[34]

By the third year of the United States' involvement in the war, Hollywood films equated the war effort with a transformation in national
identity itself. Take the case of *The White Cliffs of Dover* (1944). It
portrays a young American woman and her father who, while traveling
by ship to England in 1914, express their disdain for the Old World
where the people are not truly citizens but subjects of the upper classes.

President Roosevelt welcomes the real Sergeant York, third from right, after a White House showing of *Sergeant York* (1941). (Courtesy Academy of Motion Picture Arts and Sciences)

When England goes to war, however, they realize that they must alter their views and join ranks with England to save Anglo-Saxon "civilization." In a similar vein, *Mrs. Miniver* (1942) focuses on a man who despises English aristocrats as decadent and lazy nonproducers. Yet when the war arrives, he marries an upper-class woman, and the final scene shows him, his wife, and his mother-in-law listening to a sermon that equates the war with a Holy Crusade to save Christianity from barbarians.[35]

More important, the conversion of American identity meant that the protagonists' attitudes toward race and the lures of mass culture had to undergo a dramatic alteration. Nowhere was that more evident than in the documentary *December 7th* (1943). Made in cooperation with the Navy by director John Ford and cameraman Gregg Toland, the story focuses on none other than "Uncle Sam" himself. Played by Walter Huston, known for his performance as Abraham Lincoln, Uncle Sam arrives in the Hawaiian Islands for vacation in December 1941.[36] At first Sam tolerates labor strikes and the Japanese Americans. Yet his conscience troubles him, for he knows that the hyphenated Japanese and their unregulated amusements breed subversion.

Mrs. Miniver (1942). In a church bombed by the Nazis, the minister proclaims that this is a war to "save civilization." Lovers from two formerly warring classes sit in the first row and convert to the demand for consensus. (Courtesy Academy of Motion Picture Arts and Sciences)

Why? Slowly the audience is shown that the Japanese Americans have bilingual schools and a Shinto religion, loyalties that attach them to the foreign emperor. Next viewers see that the Japanese spy on American ships, and Asian women use their sexual allure in nightclubs and bars to gain secrets from American sailors. These activities make it possible for the Japanese to attack the Pearl Harbor naval base, leading to disaster and defeat.

Drawing on the themes of fall and rebirth familiar in Depression-era filmmaking, the film shows men dying and battleships sinking. Uncle Sam undergoes massive guilt, leading to a conversion experience that yields a new America capable of defeating enemies within and without. Never recognizing that the United States' own involvement in imperialist competition with the Japanese and its colonial exploitation of Hawaii may have led to the war, Sam decrees that citizens can still be Asian racially, but must now become "One Hundred Percent American" culturally. The Japanese Americans shed their bilingualism and their Shinto faith, and bring unregulated amusements under patriotic guidelines. Now a unified nation emerges where immigrants look to white culture for a model of civilization. At the end they—"Americans all"—build the ships that will avenge Pearl Harbor and create on the home front a society devoid of racial and class difference.

The conversion narrative that dramatized such a dramatic rupture from older beliefs and values was not simply confined to the most prominent war films. On the contrary, a major alteration in popular values also took place. Calculations derived from our plot samples show that American myths were systematically reconfigured in World War II. With the enemy seen as outside rather than inside, the conversion narrative gave rise to a new vision of a classless society. In the thirties, stories wherein characters shed loyalty to the rich in favor of alliances with the lower class or oppositional identities informed more than 20 percent of all films in our samples. During the war this trend receded to zero, while over 30 percent of the plots dramatized characters shedding their earlier oppositional class identity in favor of loyalty to official institutions (appendix 2, figs. 8, 9). Protagonists left behind participation in an autonomous civic sphere in favor of wartime identities as "patriotic heroes" who served in "savior institutions" such as the Federal Bureau of Investigation, the military, and defense industries (appendix 2, figs. 8, 9). At the same time, the portrayal of subversives on the home front increased from less than 3 percent in 1940 to 20 percent by 1945. All in all, the conversion and subversion narratives acted as two sides of the same coin, informing over 50 percent of all films made in World War II (appendix 2, figs. 9, 10, 11).

The wartime conversion narrative ran parallel with the rise of a new cultural and class consensus. Portrayals of the rich as morally dangerous, for example, had informed over 50 percent of all films in the thirties; during wartime, however, such portrayals declined to 20 percent (appendix 2, fig. 1). Similarly, plots featuring big businessmen as villains had occurred in 20 percent of all Depression-era films, but declined to zero in the war (fig. 2). Fears of capitalism still remained; as noted, over 20 percent of films portrayed the wealthy as dangerous, and the spies in films such as *Keeper of the Flame* were aligned with corrupt businessmen. Still a pervasive trend was for patriotic businessmen and reformers to gain prominence in institutions that promised to save the nation; similarly, portrayals of minorities who helped to advance the cause also increased during the war era. All in all, these trends reinforced the view that formerly alienated groups had united behind the patriotic cause (fig. 19).

"Uncle Sugar" and the Taming of Mass Culture

Running parallel with the decline of class and racial conflict, the wartime consensus reoriented democratic dreams and values from the public to the private realm of consumerism. This was not an easy task; during the thirties mass art and the consumer culture had been the focal point of a moral revolution contrary to the values promoted by official leaders. To answer this challenge, moviemaking in the war operated on two distinct tracks. Films such as *December 7th* demonstrated that mass amusements that did not serve patriotic ends, such as nightclubs and dance halls, could serve as places where dangerous women aided the enemy. Thus in the war the institutions of mass art had to serve the cause of unity. Indicative of that change, themes linking popular art to social renewal declined from 30 percent of all Depression-era films to 10 percent during the war years (appendix 2, fig. 12). In this context, the most popular comic director of the war years, Preston Sturges, would satirize society in *The Great McGinty* (1940), *Christmas in July* (1940), *The Palm Beach Story* (1942), and *Hail the Conquering Hero* (1944); however, in each film comic heroes might personally resist wartime mores but no longer alter the society itself.[37]

If the lures of mass consumption and the popular arts could not challenge society, they could become the locus of a new dream of private freedom. Nowhere was the taming of mass culture more evident than in the films of the singer Bing Crosby and the comic Bob Hope—the two most popular stars of the war years. Crosby helped identify the consumer culture with preserving rather than undermining social order and the home. In *Going My Way* (1944), for example, Crosby plays a reformed Broadway jazz singer and ladies' man who becomes the hip priest Father O'Malley. He is assigned to work in a parish where an all-too-strict prelate has alienated youth and an exemplar of the new woman by condemning play and modern mores. As a result, the boys have become juvenile delinquents and the girls turn to jazz singing and, potentially, prostitution.

Father O'Malley brings order by creating a leisure world that promotes patriotism and religion in a new form. The priest teaches one jazz singer to "sing with your voice rather than your hips," so she can eliminate sensuality and bodily impulses from her music and dance; he too sings with the softness of a "crooner" who subdues jazz beats in favor of smooth, melodic harmonies. The priest organizes the boys into a multiracial choir and writes a song that becomes a popular hit, thereby rescuing the church from threatened bankruptcy. Finally, the female jazz singer sheds the aura of the loose woman and marries a banker's son before he departs to fight in the war. In the end O'Malley has shown how mass art restores savior institutions, the home, and the self.[38]

Besides showing how official institutions provided the foundation for the wartime consumer culture, Crosby's films also dramatized how loss of control in the workplace required American myths of democracy to focus on the static, privatized suburban home. A striking example of that transformation can be found in *Holiday Inn* (1942) where Crosby portrays a reformed Broadway singer and ladies' man. Growing weary with the "rat race" of public life, he persuades a young female singer to join in his quest to discover a preservation of American myths in the country. To recover tradition in a chaotic world, he buys a farm outside the city but soon finds that farmwork is laborious. He instead converts the farm into a "Holiday Inn" with a new swimming pool, tennis courts, and a nightclub review, complete with a black maid, minstrel show, and patriotic pictures of wartime heroes. All in all, this suburban dream links "victory" to a consumer culture that preserves traditional white values of home and democracy.[39]

The domestication of popular art also generated a deep discontent that could only be answered by identifying freedom with a consumer democracy separated from work and public life. The Crosby hero has subdued the potentially disruptive values of mass art—the new woman and youth—in a consumer dream paradise removed from work. The conflicted psyche emerging from that tension received its best representation in the successful "road films" that Crosby made with Bob Hope, his fellow major box-office attraction of the forties. In these films the two stars are doubles of each other, representing the division of the desires associated with comedy from the business of work and citizenship associated with the serious hero. Significantly, the formula of the road films centers on two "buddies" who cannot find satisfaction in a society that has become too organized and puritanical, rendering them discontent and anxious.

Whether at work or leisure, the youthful passions of the id (represented by Hope) and the social duties of adults and the superego (represented by Crosby) cannot merge or find satisfaction. In films like *The Road to Singapore* (1940), *The Road to Zanzibar* (1941), and *The Road to Morocco* (1942), the "boys" hit the road, going to exotic foreign lands looking for a new frontier. Yet these exotic places less resemble real foreign locales than a simulacrum. That is, they are closer to artistic recreations of the real thing, foreshadowing escapist leisure realms of the postwar era, especially Disneyland and Las Vegas hotels. In these artistic fairylands, the boys hope to find a restoration of pleasure and play before the Fall.[40]

In each film, however, this quest for wholeness divides the public realm of pluralism from a white private realm. The separation starts as the boys' youthful quest becomes a nightmare in which their search for pleasure and play destroys their willpower, trapping them in the pleasures of "nonwhites." Losing their power to resist these pleasures, they then become subject to murder and degradation by nonwhite races. In film after film, natives capture the white adventurers and threaten to kill them. Or the "boys" darken their faces and put on a new minstrel-type mask that threatens to turn them into nonwhites who fail to advance progress and civilization. The moral is all too clear. In a society that defines cohesion around the norms of white western civilization, the characters have once again revived the old minstrel fear, namely, that too much play and pleasure will make white men blacks. Accordingly, Hope and Crosby fall into the hands of black savages. The other danger is that they have been weakened by the allures of native young women whose dark skin creates sexual desires that undermine "duty."

One solution to this danger is to channel one's dark desires toward the ideal of the consumer home and erotic, but whitened, women. Around that formula the happy ending revolves. By winning the erotic woman, who they find is really "white," and returning home to "civilization" after having conquered the dark savages, the boys find freedom in the consumer culture removed from work. The Crosby character now reasserts his adult responsibility and subordinates his desires for youthful play—embodied in Hope—and sex—embodied in the exotic women—within the spheres of domesticity and leisure.

It would be possible to dismiss these film formulas as simply a fantasy if Crosby and Hope had not gained success by showing how a

Above, Bob Hope and Bing Crosby captured by natives in *The Road to Zanzibar* (1941). Here whites' quest for pleasure and play weakens willpower, leading to entrapment in the decadence and terrors associated with nonwhites. (Courtesy Academy of Motion Picture Arts and Sciences)

Left, Bing Crosby dancing with a native woman in *The Road to Singapore* (1940). Crosby puts on blackface to indulge in pleasure. When he takes off the mask, he conforms to the demands of white civilization. (Courtesy Academy of Motion Picture Arts and Sciences) cinematic dream could become both state policy and war goals. Throughout the war years, for example, Bob Hope was the single most popular entertainer of the American troops, whether one considers his enormously popular radio show, his syndicated news column, or his tours for the War Department to all parts of the globe. Hope's comic routines rested on his well-honed persona as the "perpetual juvenile" who always felt like a "jerk." Confronted by a world of chaos and large organizations, he played the constantly beleaguered everyman caught in forces beyond his control. Hope clearly recognized that this persona had great appeal for enlisted men. For their enemy, as he saw it, was "never just the Germans or Japanese" but "boredom, mud, officers and abstinence" and the all-pervasive fear that men at war were "aging fast." To recover their dreams of youth, Hope evoked comedy to say the unspeakable and offer an acceptable answer.[41]

If under the mask of good humor Hope unleashed a "barrage of irreverence against the brass, bureaucrats and the FBI," he also offered leaders a map to satisfy these rebellious ideas. The answer was found in reorienting democratic wishes. Emblematic of that change, he told audiences on the home front that the soldiers "can't talk about much except Uncle Sugar"—a dream of "America" as a "Shangri La" of consumer goods. Soldiers attending his shows wrote that they dearly "loved" Hope in part because he "spoke our language" and in part because he brought that new dream to life in the person of a young and beautiful singer of swing ballads, Frances Langford. When Langford followed Hope on stage and sang "You Made Me Love You," "Green Eyes," and "I'm in the Mood for Love," men yelled, "You have come to the right place, baby." It was at such times, wrote one soldier, that the men's thoughts turned to "wives and sweethearts" at home. Amid the wartime "threshing machine of chaos," Langford reminded them that intimate emotions still meant "something." In that vein, Hope explained that

> no matter what the politicians or the commentators or the war-mongers said, no matter who was charged with the blame for the war, it was apparent to me that [the soldiers] were fighting for only one thing—the right to get back to their families where they belong.[42]

The task of Hope's partner Bing Crosby was to show how that new ideal of "home" could be realized within the new corporate order. In the Hollywood fan magazines of the day, for example, the old nemeses of the industry, Catholic priests aligned with the Legion of Decency,

Bob Hope performing before American troops in New Caledonia, about 1943. The woman at his side is the singer and soldiers' "pin-up girl" Frances Langford. (Courtesy Academy of Motion Picture Arts and Sciences)

wrote articles praising Crosby as the new man of the future. They praised Crosby because he never supported unions nor did he play gangsters—the sort of role that producers had presumably imposed on Irish Catholics. By way of contrast, reporters described Crosby as leaving behind the "glittering night life of New York." In creating a new image of the star, Crosby lived in a suburban home with his wife, an ex-chorus girl, and four children. Writers saw that he valued the home as a place to be "relaxed" and "placid," removing domesticity from the stress of the world.

Unlike his former wild days, Crosby's leisure consisted of "golf" and smoking a pipe—symbols of the gentrified man of refinement. At the same time he transposed jazz into the soft tones of the "crooner" who eliminated "jarring transitions" from the black-derived music. At a time when the "voices of dictators turned men into wild animals," Crosby's recordings of "White Christmas," "God Bless America," and

"Silent Night" provided a vision of "happiness when the world needs it most, for the most popular film star of the day relaxes, eases tension, mends bruised hearts and promises peace, restored homes . . . and happier life to come."[43]

"Pin-Up Girls" and the "White" Consumer Democracy

Intimately related to Crosby's capacity to mend "bruised hearts" and restore homes for a "happier life to come" was the alteration in the nature of women's identity. In films like *Holiday Inn* and the Hope and Crosby road films, the "pin-up girl"—the erotic woman whose pictures graced the barracks—embodied the new democracy and leisure to be found on the home front.[44] Films such as *Hollywood Canteen, Casablanca, Lifeboat, Saboteur, Back to Bataan, The White Cliffs of Dover, Gilda,* and *Across the Pacific* featured the emancipated woman who had evoked such attention and fear in Hollywood films of the twenties and thirties. Whether portrayed by Betty Grable, June Allyson, Joan Crawford, Bette Davis, or Rita Hayworth, the presence of empowered women increased in the plot samples for the war years from 20 to over 30 percent, frequently appearing as defense workers, military nurses, government agents, and reporters (appendix 2, fig. 13). Only now she worked less for her own pleasure or to pursue a career than to help win the war and satisfy men's desires for stability and personal fulfillment on the home front.[45]

During the war years a new category appears in our plot samples. True, the ideal of the empowered woman continued, but moviemakers complemented it with images of a new woman who identified her personal goals with realizing the dream of "patriotic domesticity," a formula that increased from zero in 1940 to over 35 percent of all plots by 1948 (appendix 2, fig. 13). In *Hollywood Canteen* (1944), for example, two soldiers return home. Weary of war, they worry that their great struggle has been for nothing. But they find young lovers who fulfill their vision of the dream wife, complete with a white picket fence and ranch home in suburbia.[46]

When one asks why moviemakers thought that women would make this choice, the answer came front and center to millions of theaters across the land in the most popular female melodrama of the war, *Since You Went Away* (1944). The film opens with a prologue stating that it charts the story of that "unconquerable fortress, the American Home." The guardian of that fortress is a young wife and mother played by Claudette Colbert, who had gained fame as a heroine who rebelled from her father, hit the road, and married a roustabout news-man in Frank Capra's *It Happened One Night* (1934). Even though *Since You Went Away* references Colbert's previous role, she has trans-formed herself into a guardian of "American" tradition. As Anne Hil-ton, the wife of a soldier who has gone to war, she now controls her attraction to a young naval officer who wants to take her dancing. She tells a friend who goes to nightclubs that as a wife and mother she feels guilty for not doing more: "I have a husband who went off to fight for this home and for me. I have children who showed courage and intelligence while their mother lived in a dream world. Well, believe me, I've come out of it. I want to do something more."

To alleviate her guilt and do "more," Anne works in a defense plant. There a refugee tells her that she provides a model of "America," sym-bolized in a long, lingering shot of the Statue of Liberty. The finale shows Anne sitting alone in her home before a window on Christmas Eve as she reads a letter from the War Department, informing her that her husband is returning. The scene captures the abstract nature of her commitment. Though the audience never sees her husband, Anne protects and guards the home while her husband suffers. She has lei-sure and consumer goods, but her part of the new patriotic bargain is to channel her life goals and sexuality into preserving what men desire most of all: a supportive woman who will preserve the ideals of democ-racy not at work, but in the suburban domestic ideal. So as the white snow falls outside upon a picket fence, an epilogue explains, "BE OF GOOD COURAGE AND HE SHALL STRENGTHEN YOUR HEART ALL YE THAT TRUST IN THE LORD."[47]

The pervasive aura of whiteness and the identification of home with religious symbols signal that the domestic ideal preserves Victorianism with a modern, white face. Ironically, wartime films celebrated racial pluralism in public life, but when they looked toward the home to pre-serve democracy, domesticity and the new consumer dream came to focus on the "white" woman. No doubt this reflected long-standing prohibitions of mixed-race romance and marriage that had never been supplanted in the New Deal era, particularly in the segregated South. Yet this tendency appears to have intensified with the rise of the con-sumer democracy of the war years. That is, as men feared that they were becoming cogs in a machine, and as the lures of consumerism and the new woman threatened to undermine willpower, these trends aroused fears, as in the Hope and Crosby road films, that white males were becoming like blacks: dependent and subordinate. To preserve the ideal of autonomy, men looked to the home as the one remaining realm of freedom left.

Domesticity and the pin-up girl had to be stripped of all reminders that consumption and sex created "black desires" that undermined manhood, a process that gave birth to a home and a consumer culture that restored the Victorian gender roles and the coordinates of white civilization. As a result, the pin-up had above all to cleanse her body and behavior of images that whites had traditionally associated with minorities. The most striking example of that metamorphosis occurred in the career of the female star who was perhaps the most popular pin-up of the war. Rita Hayworth embodied in her films like *Gilda* (1946) and *Blood and Sand* (1941) the "bombshell" who, like gunpowder, could destroy men's will. So pervasive was the identification of Hayworth with destructive power that her picture adorned an atomic bomb that was used in a test to annihilate an island in the South Pacific.

With her body arousing such desire and fear, it was not too surprising that she had to be domesticated and tamed. Nor was it accidental that in Rita's case, this meant overcoming her identity as a member of the darker, nonwhite race. Unlike the other pin-ups of the war, Rita Hayworth was not fully white. Born into a Spanish family of vaudeville entertainers, Rita (born Margarita) Cansino appeared in Charlie Chan films as a dark, full-bodied Latin American heroine. However, she met and married a former used car salesman "on the make." Acutely aware that a young woman who wanted to be a success in Hollywood had to "have a new front," much like an automobile in a showroom, Edward Judson remade his wife into an image of white beauty for wartime consumption.

The first step was to change her name from Cansino to the anglicized Hayworth, evocative of the agrarian dreams of hay and rural life that men longed to find when they returned from war. Next Judson dyed her hair strawberry blonde and had her face altered with the expert skills of plastic surgeons. Finally, Judson provided Hayworth with the proper elocution lessons necessary to destroy all traces of her Spanish accent. To complete the circle, photographers created publicity images that dramatized the meaning of these changes. Over and over they portrayed Hayworth in the agrarian hay of the countryside or standing in patriotic bathing suits. Having linked sexuality to patriotism, Hayworth also had a child. Now the studio portrayed her as the ideal of the good, erotic wife who incarnated the ideal of patriotic domesticity, raising her family in the new suburbs.[48]

Rita Cansino as a native woman in *Charlie Chan in Egypt* (1935). This is Rita Hayworth prior to her conforming to the look of the white pin-up girl of World War II. Notice that her body is heavier, her skin darker, and her nose larger. Her clothes also embody the "exotic" nonwhite woman, in this case an Egyptian. (Courtesy Academy of Motion Picture Arts and Sciences)

So pervasive was the identification of domesticity with white ideals that even the single exception proved the rule. During the war, the most popular black female star was Lena Horne. Writers saw that she broke new ground by shedding what critics called the "Sambo" or "Mammy" images of African Americans. Gaining success as a singer in swing bands, which performed the "American" music of the era, Horne, like many in the jazz world, engaged in left-wing politics that brought whites and blacks together. She also served on the board of the Screen Actors Guild and toured soldiers' camps for the War Department. There she protested the segregation of black troops and walked out of one performance when officers allowed German prisoners to see her show but forbade the attendance of black soldiers. Amid these conflicts, she listened when the head of Metro-Goldwyn-Mayer explained that Hollywood producers were "interested in doing something with a black person different than Tarzan pictures, for good social reasons." Several films later, writers noted that Horne "ain't no . . . Aunt Jemima or Uncle Tom." Walter White, the leader of the National Association for the Advancement of Colored People, saw her as a model for her race. During the war, she became the "pin-up," the "girl back home

Rita Hayworth as the whitened, anglicized pin-up girl in World War II. To lose her Latin looks, her body has become thinner, her nose smaller, and her skin whitened by overhead lights. To signal her new American "white" identity, she wears a red, white, and blue swimsuit, and alters her name to "Hayworth," suggesting the American rural landscape rather than the urban landscape of "decadent" pleasure and desire. (Courtesy Academy of Motion Picture Arts and Sciences)

Rita Hayworth with her first child, about 1946. As an ideal suburban mother, the pin-up has focused her dreams of moral emancipation on domesticity. (Courtesy Academy of Motion Picture Arts and Sciences)

. . . to 800,000 Negro soldiers . . . who have named their planes, their jeeps and their daughters after her." Still, she could not play parts that would bring her into physical contact with white men, for producers feared miscegenation prohibitions. Later she recalled that this experience left her traumatized:

> They said at the time I got the job at MGM in 1943 that they were going to prove through me that we're all alike. They made me up and down, they decided the way they thought I should look. They decided how a Negro should look . . . they tried to make me look as close to white as possible. And they still proceeded to allow white women to play parts that black women looking like me might have played. And this went on and on, it never stopped . . . what they did was name me in all releases as the sepia Hedy Lamaar. . . . Why wasn't she advertised as the white Lena Horne?[49]

The Inheritance: Audiences and the Age of Anxiety

At this point it should be clear why the screenwriter Philip Dunne believed that the consumer democracy and global mission that emerged in World War II had reoriented the progressive political tradition and Americanism he helped construct in the New Deal era. The battle against the fascists not only generated the call for unity at home; it identified affluence with the "American Way." It was now the obligation of government and politicians to make real on the home front the consumer dreams instilled in those who had fought and won the war. If these expectations informed films during the war years, they corresponded to a realignment of the popular values of the audiences as well.

Indicative of that reorientation, pollsters found that during the thirties only 26 percent of their respondents approved of involvement in foreign affairs. Yet as in *Casablanca* and other wartime films, a commitment to internationalism unfolded in the forties. By 1945 fully 81 percent of respondents supported the United Nations and America's global commitments.[50] Along with validations of internationalism, attitudes toward big business and labor unions altered as well. A poll conducted by *Fortune* magazine in 1942 found that only 40 percent of the public opposed socialism, and well over 25 percent supported it, while 35 percent said they had an open mind. In other words, over 60 percent of the population saw the possibility of socialism as the "American Way." Other pollsters showed that majorities also supported the insurgent labor union movement. But by the late forties criticism of business slowly waned, and fewer than 15 percent now wanted to "move in the direction of socialism." In fact 65 percent wanted to move in the opposite direction, with the result that hostility to big business and support for unions receded dramatically.[51]

Even allowing for the distinct possibility that many of these respondents had only the vaguest notion of what socialism meant, it was a very remarkable alteration. Yet it was no more remarkable than the change in family life and moviegoing. As recent historians have shown, the commitment to suburban domestic life and the baby boom surfaced first in World War II and accelerated after 1945.[52] A series of interviews compiled by the historian Studs Terkel revealed that the movies deeply influenced women's commitment to a home life permeated with patriotic messages. One respondent saw that the war brought women out of the home and into the workplace; in fact, it was "just marvelous" that women took factory jobs that had formerly been closed to them. But, she added, "even here we were sold a bill of goods," for in films as on the radio "they were hammering away that the woman who went to work did it to help her man, and when he came back, she cheerfully leaped into the home." Another woman war worker saw that mobilization put "excitement in the air" for it offered her freedom from the parental home. She accepted employment for the first time at high wages, and used the money to engage in public amusements where she met "hundreds of men." But her family insisted that she get married. The movies reinforced the message, for "the central theme was girl meets soldier and after a weekend of acquaintance they get married and overcome their difficulties." Still another recalled that *The White Cliffs of Dover* convinced her to marry a soldier long before she was ready. Looking back, she recalled that the idea that "women married soldiers and sent them overseas happy was hammered at us. We had plays on the radio, short stories in magazines, and the movies, which had a tremendous influence in our lives."[53]

On the screen as in real life, moreover, the "tremendous" allure of the suburban home lay in its racial boundaries. Take the case of an Italian American interviewed by Terkel. Paul Pisciano recalled that he grew up in the working-class areas of Chicago. His parents and grandparents felt a "transient sense of our place here." They were hyphenated people who retained their Italian language as a mark of identity, and supported the cause of labor and making a more tolerant society. Not only did his grandmother serve as a union organizer, but Pisciano and his friends looked to the movies and sports for an alternative vision of America. "You go to the movies every week, right? . . . You grow up you're gonna be King Kong." Like all his friends he also "thought the black boxer Joe Louis was wonderful. He was such a champion. Nobody was gonna ruffle Joe Louis." While before the war Italian Americans may have seen themselves in the same boat as blacks, Pearl Harbor changed all that. Suddenly "you enlisted into the Marines, or go into the Navy." Afterwards, "all the guys" became "right wing" and stopped teaching their kids Italian. Instead, the "guys were talking about the niggers, I gotta move out my kids." So they moved out to the suburbs where they united with others in their "anti-black sentiments," a process that "obliterated our culture, and made us American," which "ain't no fun."[54]

In the postwar suburbs this turn to family life and the ideals of a white culture also altered the nature of moviegoing itself. As in a Hope and Crosby road film, theaters took on the aura of a leisured exoticism, a simulacrum removed from public life and the concerns of works common at the movie houses of the thirties. Theaters of the war and immediate postwar years kept the modern style. Only in Long Beach, California, or in Miami, Florida, did designers shed the streamlined look for the flowing, organic forms of art nouveau. On the outside names like "Holiday" and "Crest" linked moviegoing to a vacationland and the aura of a future Las Vegas hotel. Now interiors featured "fanciful" forms, fluted columns, and "warm colored" pastels complemented by plastic plants and elaborate women's cosmetic rooms that added "beauty" to everyday life. The wall murals in turn discarded the images of work and historical subjects that informed the regionalist mode in favor of images of birds, fish, and plants. Finally, as the new abstract expressionist styles associated with the work of Jackson Pollock and Mark Rothko arose, similar images graced the new theaters, appealing to audiences' desire for what reporters saw as "psychic" sensations and playful fantasies.[55]

Meanwhile the turn to private sensations gave rise to an unprecedented type of film exhibition site: the postwar drive-in. Formerly architects like Ben Schlanger cultivated designs that heightened the unique experience of moviegoing. But now audiences at the suburban drive-ins drove miles to sit in theaters where they endured rain, poor sound, and distorted screen images in order to watch films inside the privacy of their cars. Showmen now identified the drive-in with a family paradise, complete with a "picnic atmosphere" filled with playgrounds, gymnastic equipment, and tables where children played while their parents watched the movie. As drive-ins increased from five in 1939 to sixty by 1945 to 500 by 1947 and 1,500 by 1949, observers found that over 55 percent of the cars contained groups who went to

Drive-in theater in upstate New York, about 1960. Notice the rise of a moviegoing environment of privacy, far from the world of the city streets. (Courtesy Museum of Modern Art, Film Stills Archive)

the movies for a "family outing, a sort of holiday" removed from the city and the cares of the day.[56]

The explanation for this new audience was not just the population's move to the suburbs but the identification of freedom with family life. Yet moviemakers whose consciousness was formed by the expectations of the thirties began to feel that this world harbored an anxiety that had no name. Take the case of the most popular filmmaker of the late thirties, Frank Capra.[57] His populist heroes had struggled against the moneyed interests and validated the promise of a new culture. During the war he served as an Army officer and was assigned to make a series of documentaries, called *Why We Fight.* Along the way he fired writers accused by the FBI of subversion. Even though he too would find in the Cold War that his own security clearance and passport were taken away because he was suspected of being a radical, Capra made films such as *State of the Union* (1948) to celebrate corporate liberals as the engines of postwar reform. Here his heroines were no longer career women but good wives and mothers concentrating on the suburban home.

Even though after the war he evoked some of his earlier themes in *It's a Wonderful Life* (1946), Capra's hero was saved less by mobilizing the people than by turning to an angel for salvation. Still, even an angel could not save Capra at the box office. One of his coworkers explained the reason why the most popular filmmaker of the late Depression now failed: Once "he got into this government stuff, it gave him a new sense of values, and then he was dead. He was working with the people who were the heavies in his own pictures, and it turned him completely around. From that point on, in trying to develop scripts, he developed nonsense." In a moment of rare insight in the postwar era, Capra concurred, noting that after the war "I lived under the Judas curse . . . that I had ratted and sold out." And then his creativity dried up, for

> once you get cold feet, once your daring stops, then you worry a little bit. And when you worry about a decision, then you're not going to make the proper films any more. That is I couldn't. And I think that was the start. When I sold out for money, which is something I had always been against anyhow, and for security, I think my conscience told me that I had it. Really. There wasn't any more of that paladin out there in front fighting for lost causes.[58]

The dream also appears to have gone stale for many female stars who identified their lives and screen images with that of the pin-up and her dream of domestic bliss. Take the case of June Allyson. Called the "number one pin-up" and female "box office champion" of the war, producers billed her as "America's Sweetheart," the "girl the soldiers most want to marry." It was not hard to see why: Allyson exuded the aura of a honey blonde who was "girlish and laughs a lot." In order to maintain the image of the white pin-up, she was "compulsively clean," took three baths a day, and wanted only "one thing in life," to get married and to have a house full of children. Not long after, "Juney" got her wish. Over the next few years the new Mrs. Dick Powell wrote magazine articles telling wives that the key to a happy home was to subordinate the self and "never" to "dominate" their husbands. Yet by the fifties "Juney" confessed to having affairs with other men and drinking heavily in order to escape a husband who wanted to "control all things." Powell "made all her decisions" and wrapped her in a "cotton mist all my adult life." After Powell's death, she was confined to a psychiatric clinic for depression. Trying to explain why, Allyson told interviewers that in the ideal suburban home "I remained all my life a little girl" who "had no idea who I was."[59]

Among racial minorities who were excluded from the suburban dream and the affluence they had done so much to create, a postwar sense of disappointment and anger grew even more intense. Lena Horne, for example, was one performer well placed to know this frustration. She engaged in union activities and civil rights causes and was dedicated to ideals of pluralism, wearing both a Star of David and a St. Christopher medal around her neck. With the coming of the Cold War, she proved her patriotism by condemning an older ally, Paul Robeson—the famed black performer—as well as Barney Josephson, the owner of a left-wing nightclub, Café Society. In the wake of these events, a writer in *Esquire* noted that Horne "provided so far one of the success stories of racial adaptation to a changing world" because she could also compete "on an Aryan level."

Nonetheless, when Horne defied the racial code by marrying a white musician, she kept their marriage a secret by living in Paris while continuing to make a living as a jazz singer and actress. By the mid-fifties, she and her husband returned home and bought a house in Nichols Canyon in Los Angeles, where white neighbors petitioned their removal. Horne's husband bought a shotgun to protect them from harassment. Similarly, when Horne appeared in Las Vegas, her black musicians could not enter the hotel's front doors and her mulatto children could not swim in the pool. Horne later recalled that she even socked a white customer in a nightclub who shouted racial slurs. Recalling these events, she noted that

> it was a stifling experience. I lived kind of suspended in the atmosphere somewhere. I wasn't grounded in my own patch of dirt and neither on theirs. . . . [Feeling] rebellious against the white mold they tried to put me in made me create a kind of mold that nothing could get to. I was ice, so that nothing could touch me. . . . I didn't want what they had and I was also on account of this image removed from my own people. I just fell asleep.[60]

The tragedy of falling "asleep" in the immediate postwar period was that the anxieties expressed by June Allyson and Lena Horne remained on the level of private life, rarely entering the public sphere. During the war patriotism became synonymous with the avoidance of class or cultural conflict as well as the making of a new American Way of consensus. As the new corporations gained legitimacy, a consumer democracy emerged as a means to contain and privatize youthful urges for rebellion and discontent. On the screen as in political rhetoric, this new American Way centered on the home and white women. Removed from public life, the domestic realm offered a vision of freedom and affluence to counter discontent at work and social chaos.

The new consumer democracy accompanied a major shift in political and national identity. What made it so persuasive was that during World War II the population had voluntarily acquiesced in putting aside the visions of a modernized republic. Yet, as Dunne saw in his autobiography, *Take Two,* it took state repression in the Cold War to institutionalize what he saw as the "unfortunate consequences" of the new American Way forged in battle against the fascists. How that happened and what consequences it had for nationality, politics, and moviemaking provides the subject of the next chapter, which focuses on the Hollywood Red Scare.

Chapter 5

Movie Star Politics: Hollywood and the Making of Cold War Americanism

> If ever humankind and geography have been brought together under the most propitious circumstances, it is here in the United States of America. One feels almost that the kindly Providence which contrived this miracle is watching . . . to see how the epic test of man's capacity for grandeur is working out. Can man, thus richly dowered with all the prerequisites of greatness, live up to his magnificent opportunity? Can we temper his spirit and lift his mind to new and unprecedented levels?
> —Eric Johnston, *America Unlimited,* 1944

> Really and truly, the triumph of McCarthyism was, in effect, the cutting off of a generalized social movement that began before the war. . . . The picking on the Hollywood people . . . received a lot of attention because everybody knew who the stars were. What I'm trying to say is that you're not dealing with an isolated event, but the focus of such a national event as it happened in Hollywood.
> —Abraham Polonsky, blacklisted film director, 1970

I n the last year of World War II, the future head of the Motion Picture Producers' Association, Eric Johnston, wrote a front-page article for the Screen Actors Guild Magazine bearing the auspicious title, "Utopia Is Production." In this essay and a best-selling book, *America Unlimited,* Johnston fused practical politics with the rhetoric of a puritan jeremiad, calling on the American people to shed the sin of class conflict for the promise of a "utopia of production" and moral rebirth. Looking back to the twenties and the hardships of the Depression, Johnston saw that America had been in declension. Prior to that time, the people created an exceptional nation free of European exploitation and disorder. Yet the moral experimentation of the twenties and the Depression had given rise to the "nightmare of class rhetoric" and "crackpots" who ruled the day. The enemy attacked a morally divided country at Pearl Harbor. World War II, however, saw the people put aside class conflict and moral degeneracy, achieving victory over fascism. It followed that to avoid returning to the former "dark days," the populace must continue the politics of consensus and moral rebirth. By thwarting communism, the miracle of economic growth would provide prosperity and a moral domestic life. To lead the people to that utopia, Johnston saw that Hollywood had a great role to play, for

> it is no exaggeration to say that the modern motion picture indus-try sets the styles for half the world. There is not one of us who isn't aware that the motion picture industry is the most powerful medium for the influencing of people that man has ever built. . . . We can set new styles of living and the doctrine of production must be made completely popular.[1]

Eric Johnston was part of a generation of policymakers who, recent historians have shown, looked to World War II for a model of "produc-tion" to reshape the domestic and international economy in the Cold War era. What has not been considered is how these policies converged with an equally important transformation of the "imaginary commu-nity" or national identity that informed the popular arts and Holly-wood moviemaking.[2] Johnston, for example, promoted the ideology of class consensus and the ideal of the private home centered on con-sumer dreams that defined both postwar politics and culture. We nor-mally assume that the new ethos of liberal capitalism and a homoge-nous consumer culture flowed naturally without a major break from the values informing politics and popular art of the Great Depression.[3] In his efforts to transform Hollywood, however, Johnston saw that the consensus was not something inherited from the past but something that had to be created at the dawn of the Cold War era. He also saw that this would not be an easy task.

Johnston, a successful businessman in Seattle, Washington, became president of the United States Chamber of Commerce in 1941. From there he became President Roosevelt's business adviser to the Soviet Union in World War II. To Johnston the war demonstrated that a new order was possible. Where laissez-faire capitalism had created chaos and disaster, and militant labor bred class conflict, he saw that the people had now accepted the welfare state and "patriotic unions." As the center of mass communications, Hollywood provided the place to popularize these new ideals. The people of the world, noted Johnston, knew little about American leaders or policies, but they loved Holly-wood film stars. "We must strive constantly to utilize all the other tools of mass communications to tell the democracy story. Because motion pictures are my business I naturally think of them in this connection too. . . . In some areas they are the last link which the people share with America."[4] Johnston called on Hollywood labor leaders to purge the film capital of "American proponents" of "European" ideologies.[5]

Yet Johnston was acutely aware that all was not well in paradise.[6] A wave of strikes erupted over the nation that Johnston saw as a "test of our faith—in God, faith in mankind and faith in our institutions." Faced with the threat of the Soviet Union and class conflict, Johnston saw that we are "fighting . . . to protect the spiritual and ethical ideals which have guided mankind for over a thousand years." By winning the war at home, the populace would realize the "nation is only the sum total of its families. . . . The fascist-minded under various labels . . . the pathetic and despicable stooges for foreign dictatorships— all of them are excrescences. As long as the American body politic retains its democratic health, it can resist them as readily as the human body resists germs. Such minor successes as these people have scored in recent years were symptoms of our social and political ills and will be wiped out in the period of restored vitality which we have now entered."[7]

Unfortunately, Johnston saw the "American Century" endangered. Merging their celebrity with radical politics, stars like Charles Chaplin and Katharine Hepburn mobilized to support the militant Conference of Studio Unions (CSU). Together they endorsed the national strike wave and the doctrine of the "Century of the Common Man" advanced by Franklin Roosevelt's former vice president Henry Wallace. Strikers evoked the memory of Roosevelt and their service in war to justify their cause. Outside the studio gates the strike leader Herbert Sorrell, an ex-boxer, organized picket lines. The allied unions hosted benefit performances featuring Paul Robeson and John Garfield on behalf of the strikers. Defying the ideal of the privatized woman, one striking female came to Sorrell's aid in a confrontation outside the Warner Brothers studio, explaining "Gee, honey, don't cry. We'll give them hell before we're through."[8]

Johnston's response came sure and swift. Besides cooperating with Congress to investigate the communist inclinations of the union leaders, he told screenwriters in 1946: "We'll have no more *Grapes of Wrath,* we'll have no more *Tobacco Road*s, we'll have no more films that deal with the seamy side of American life. We'll have no more films that treat the banker as a villain."[9] Accordingly Johnston cooperated with the State Department in the creation of film attachés in foreign countries, ensuring that unacceptable films no longer received an export license. At the same time he worked with the Defense Department to ban the reissue of the antiwar classic, *All Quiet on the Western Front.* At a time when the United States was mobilizing to defeat the Soviets, a trade reporter observed that the "Pentagon wants to ban this reissue of antiwar propaganda since it is damaging to the current war

The boxer and populist turned labor agitator Herbert Sorrell exhorting the Congress of Studio Unions strikers outside the gates of Warner Brothers in 1946. (Courtesy Academy of Motion Picture Arts and Sciences)

effort." The trade press also condemned the Soviets' showing of a pirated version of Frank Capra's *Mr. Smith Goes to Washington.* Since Capra's hero condemned senators aligned with big business, the film damaged the nation's image abroad. Similarly the Hollywood press condemned Norwegian theater owners who rejected a revised version of John Ford's classic film *The Grapes of Wrath*

> because the American distributors insisted that the audience be told the conditions depicted are not normal at the opening . . . and that the show close with a statement that conditions recorded had been improved after being brought to the attention of the authorities.[10]

Johnston sponsored films and articles that promoted the benefits of the American Way. Nowhere was that convergence of interest more evident than when Bob Hope put aside humor and picked up his pen to write in a national magazine that "Tomorrow Is a New Day." Where formerly "Uncle Sam" stood for a nation rooted in a republic of producers, Hope spoke of the country as an "Uncle Sugar" who sup-

Strikers outside the gates of Metro-Goldwyn-Mayer Studios in 1946. Notice the signs demanding their jobs back to honor their wartime service and the promises of President Roosevelt. (Courtesy Academy of Motion Picture Arts and Sciences)

ported the Marshall Plan because this is "a wonderful Shangri La we are living in here. And we should share it with the Europeans before other forces move in and make them our enemies." Outlining why the country now presented a world model, Hope argued that "we" were a pluralistic society different from Europe because a Welsh immigrant like himself could succeed and enjoy the fruits of a consumer democracy. In "no other land," Hope explained, "is there such a high value placed on amusement and entertainment. Americans spend more time and money on it than other people, and generally feel rewarded because it's not a privilege or honor; it's part of their national heritage." In the United States, moreover, the populace did not dissipate their "lucky fortunes on meaningless trivialities," but focused their material plenty on "the American tradition of raising a family," exemplified by a photo of Hope, his wife, and children in their suburban home, far from the diverse city.[11]

Given Johnston's business interests, it was understandable that he sided with the film producers against the strikers and that he supported Hope's praise of the Marshall Plan. Yet it is not clear why he equated the Cold War with reshaping politics and moviemaking. In analyzing the Red Scare, scholars have assumed that the hysteria surrounding anticommunism expressed the paranoid side of a necessary effort to thwart Stalin and spies in the United States. Nevertheless the McCarthy era had little impact on political values or film content, the argument goes, since they had always been grounded in myths of liberal individualism and class consensus.[12] My purpose in this chapter is to offer a threefold corrective to these views. First, I will show that in the thirties Hollywood stars blended their screen images with the promotion of radical politics and a modernized republican creed. Second, as World War II generated a class consensus on the screen and in Hollywood politics, many saw their radical past as un-American. The rise of strikes spurred leaders like Eric Johnston and Ronald Reagan to identify anticommunist crusading with the legitimation of a new Americanism rooted in big business, class consensus, and consumer democracy. Lastly, this effort did transform the content of filmmaking, creating the basis for a new Cold War culture and ideology.[13]

The "Nightmare" of Class Conflict

Taking Eric Johnston's promotion of a "utopia of production" to the Screen Actors Guild as a starting point, it is important to realize that his perception that a "nightmare of class conflict" had informed Hollywood in the thirties was not far-fetched. Like other corporations, the film industry had generated radical unions as well as productions that promoted the cause of labor.[14] Yet businessmen stymied these developments until the Depression when a mass union movement spread in Hollywood. By the late thirties all the major artists organized into directors, writers, and actors guilds. By the mid-thirties the film capital vote for President Franklin Roosevelt had been well over 80 percent, making Hollywood solid New Deal territory.

The reason for union interest was not hard to find. When the Depression struck, most of the studios faltered. Producers cut salaries to save on costs, with the result that unemployment spread. In response, the studio employees organized unions. By the presidential election year of 1936, all employees had engaged in union activity and voted overwhelmingly for the New Deal. This support made Hollywood a bastion for progressive causes and the reforms promoted by President Roosevelt. Within the next decade, the film industry that laborers failed to organize in the twenties had become fully unionized from top to bottom. By bringing workers and the bourgeoisie into a broad-based labor movement, Hollywood was far ahead of workers' efforts in the other industries across the land. Hollywood was not only one of the most unionized industries in the nation, but one of the prime examples that in the thirties organizing and voting by class had entered into the heart of the two-party system.

At the forefront of union organizing stood the most popular figures in the nation: the new Hollywood stars. Mobilized into the Screen Actors Guild (SAG), their leaders, activist members, and board of directors included the major box-office attractions of the day. The earliest members included Will Rogers, Eddie Cantor, Joan Crawford, John Garfield, Jane Wyman, James Cagney, and Robert Montgomery as well as black artists such as Lena Horne and Rex Ingram. By 1933 the Actors Guild had created a charter, and after a threat of strikes gained a contract from the studios in 1937. The contractual agreement guaranteed minimum wages and better working conditions. Once their union formed, several stars, like Bette Davis, used the Guild's arbitration rules to demand greater control over their choice of roles in the studio system, and by 1940 almost 50 percent of the players had joined the Guild, creating an alliance internally across classes. On the verge of World War II, the Actors Guild composed well over 25 percent of all the employees in a labor force that fluctuated from 26,000 to 34,000 a year. Because the Guild included the featured players who guaranteed producers' profits, it controlled the most important ingredient of production, with the result that the Actors Guild became the most important and visible Hollywood union.[15]

The Guild restructured labor-capital relations in the film industry. In the twenties studio leaders had thwarted unionization by aligning with the International Alliance of Theatrical Stage Employees (IA). The alliance emerged from the American Federation of Labor (AFL), where Samuel Gompers organized skilled workers in bureaucratic groups removed from immigrant and racial minorities. Within Hollywood the IA worked in conjunction with gangsters, who received payoffs from the producers to stop mass labor organizing. Yet as the artists organized, they eventually aligned with the rising Conference of Studio Unions (CSU). Together they helped jail corrupt studio leaders and their hoodlum allies. The result was that the Guild participated in a national labor movement that increased membership from 8 percent of the national workforce in 1929 to 45 percent in 1945 and reshaped mass industries.[16]

The leader of the CSU, Herbert Sorrell, embodied the populist spirit animating New Deal radicalism. He joined with his "good friend John L. Lewis" of the Congress of Industrial Organizations and with a Catholic priest, Father Dunne, to promote left-wing causes. Sorrell was a charismatic speaker who linked unionization to saving American republican traditions. Born to a "deeply religious" Anglo-Saxon Protestant family and committed to the old roustabout élan of the Midwest plains, he gained fame as a boxer, then turned to painting film sets. By the mid-thirties Sorrell shed the disdain he once had for Jews and blacks, and organized studio employees, including white-collar workers. Sorrell was also acutely aware that low wages provided opportunities for powerful men to sexually exploit their female workers. Along these lines, Sorrell recounted that a major producer hated the idea of organizing white-collar workers in his studio. Why? The producer told Sorrell that since he took his secretary to "bed twice a week" and paid her well for her sexual services, a union might raise wages and end the secretary's dependence on the money the producer paid for sex. Little wonder that when the producers labeled Sorrell a communist, he answered:

> No true Communist can be a successful labor leader, because Communists thrive on poor working conditions. . . . A successful labor leader betters those conditions . . . and when it becomes too much better, the working class don't look to Communists any more. They come clear over to the other side. Thus the true Communist don't want to see the workers progress too much, because they lose their right to teach 'em how Communism is the only source of betterment and progress. In this respect, a Communist does absolutely no good for the union in the long run.[17]

The leadership of the various Hollywood guilds backed Sorrell against these charges, if for no other reason than their own promotion of class conflict and social justice was not far from communist thought. While a small contingent of communists could be found in all the unions, a host of issues united them in the thirties. Like the leaders of the guilds, Marxists believed that capitalism undermined the economy and prevented people from controlling their work. After 1935 communists as well as guild leaders evoked American patriotism to unite people in a common effort to promote their class interests. Indicative of that alliance, when businessmen and conservative politicians tried to deport Harry Bridges, the leader of the longshoremen's union, for his communist beliefs, the guild leaders protested. The board of directors of the Actors Guild supported Bridges because he had prevented strikebreakers from entering location sets and because the Guild believed in the cause of class

> solidarity . . . regardless of the immediate advantages. In the long run the slogan "one for all, all for one" is the proper guide for union action. Following this line of action [Bridges and his union] have built one of the strongest labor organizations in America. They have eradicated gangster control, raised wages, shortened hours and elevated the spirit of their men not only by educating them into the important role they are playing in their locality but making them conscious of their duty to aid American labor in its progressive march.[18]

Naturally commentators asked why the most well-paid employees in the film industry would find it their "duty to aid American labor in its progressive march." A study funded by the Carnegie Foundation found that the Actors Guild included unskilled extras with no speaking lines in films, as well as more than fifty-four artists who made well over $100,000 a year. Fewer than 10 percent of the entire Guild membership came from worker or farmer backgrounds; 80 percent came from families of urban merchants or tradespeople. If the membership came from the solid bourgeoisie, they emanated as well from the city at a time when less than 50 percent of the total population lived in urban areas. Most had finished high school and half had attended universities. Reflecting the high turnover of studio personnel (60 percent annually in the early years of the Depression), the majority had recently come to Hollywood and most were young people, under the age of thirty-five. An editorial in the screen actors' magazine noted that the Guild had created "something new in America, a pioneer organization of professional people. Its birth and steady growth make one of the most significant labor developments of the last ten years."[19]

Explanations for that development were that the stars joined the union movement simply to protect their high salaries or that this radicalism emerged from the Communist Party. But neither view explains why the various unions organized five years before the Communist Party came to Hollywood, or why long after their salaries rose, the stars supported the labor movement. No, something else was going on, and that something emerged when an Actors Guild publication featured an article entitled, "Are We Really Laborers?" Anyone who answered in the negative did not understand the new age. In the nineteenth century, the citizenry found freedom from European tyranny by moving to an open frontier, but that "safety valve" no longer existed and corporate leaders like the film producers "corresponding in a sense to the hereditary feudal lords, grew steadily in number and more concentrated." One could find success in large organizations during the twenties and find freedom in leisure stylized in accord with the tastes of the rich. But when the Great Crash came, monopolists fired employees, subjected them to the "tyranny" of foremen, and paid workers less for more labor.[20]

What made this so demeaning was that the stars and creative personnel operated in a special relation to production. It was this special relation, moreover, that spurred their radicalism. Unlike factory laborers, the work of the creative artists remained plainly in view on the screen. But once producers had made money off their images and work, they then fired them during the Depression. To recover control over their labor, the stars no longer could look solely to the private realm for happiness. In the films of Will Rogers and Frank Capra or the new show-within-a-show musicals, the modern characters realigned cultural authority from the top to the bottom of society. Carrying that theme into real life, the new stars formed unions when the studios profited from their creative skills without providing proper remuneration or respect. Their complaints echoed the republican themes that informed many of their most famous film roles.

Merging art and life, Rogers, Eddie Cantor, James Cagney, and Robert Montgomery condemned "economic royalists" whose "oppressive corporate practices" demanded a new "Declaration of Independence" to emancipate the modern "slave class." In 1933, Cantor, acting in his capacity as president of the Actors Guild, wrote President Roosevelt that Guild members proudly acted as "patriotic Americans" fighting the "financial pirates" who advanced "oppressive measures in their race for power." The loyal members found it impossible to join the producers' union, the Academy of Motion Pictures. Why? The Academy stood idly by while the producers exploited performers. Class harmony was impossible, for when the "millennium comes the lion may lie down with the lamb, but in the present the Guild thinks it indiscreet of the lamb, to lie down with the lion."

Above all, the Actors Guild updated the republican tradition to include women and minorities. This was no small thing, for both unions and populism had faltered on the incapacity of whites to organize across race and class. Central to that division was the code that required Caucasian males to protect white women as symbols of racial and class purity, wholly separate from the workplace. In the twenties racism intensified as stars and films, most notably those of Cecil B.

De Mille, forged a consumer culture ennobled with the ethos of white civilization and family life removed from the moral dangers of the diverse working classes.[21]

By the thirties, however, the collapse of the economy persuaded Guild members to bring women into a more inclusive public domain. More than one-quarter of the members were foreign-born, and about the same percentage descended from recent immigrants. By the late thirties and war years, blacks and women served in leadership positions on the board, making the Guild a symbol of the arrival of outsiders into public life. Similarly, the Guild newsletter condemned the Ku Klux Klan, explaining, "scratch an anti-Semite, anti-Catholic or anti-Negro [and] you will find an enemy of labor." In contract negotiations, moreover, union leaders argued that if producers recognized the Actors Guild, they would insure that groups like the Ritz Brothers, a zany comedy team noted for lateness, would now "show up on time."[22]

From these innovations, the Guild drew on stars' appeal to advance social reform in highly visible public arenas. In much the same way that Will Rogers's films and radio shows often mixed humor with calls for the redistribution of wealth, and the modern theaters promoted egalitarian dreams of abundance, the Guild linked the stars' appeal to New Deal causes. Advertisements frequently appeared in Guild publications stressing that higher wages and "union label buying" created the purchasing power to allow common people to attain a modicum of affluence. Guild publications similarly promoted consumer boycotts against businesses that prohibited the unionization of farm laborers and the unskilled. To spread the word, the stars also performed at World's Fairs and on labor radio shows. They also attended events at the White House to support Roosevelt. After one such visit, the Guild organized a "Film Stars Frolic" where leaders auctioned off a hat donated by President Roosevelt to build an actors' retirement home. Similarly, actors and actresses joined with the other Hollywood unions to sponsor beauty contests to choose the "Queen of the Picket Lines," while the labor press published many waiters' accounts of what their favorite stars ate at the new restaurants. All in all, union leader Sorrell envisaged the strikes organized at the Disney studio as ensuring that our "happy bunch of kids" could "dress like the stars." To top it off, Robert Montgomery, the president of the Actors Guild, wrote members under the byline of his newborn son:

> Since my advent into this world at Cedars of Lebanon Hospital, I have in my small way done a certain amount of work which may be of interest to you. I have organized the children of the nursery

"It's the Keystone to Recovery," an editorial cartoon in the labor press equating union demands for higher wages with stimulating market demand and restoring full production.

into the Junior Guild and we have now picket lines outside the door bearing placards "Cedars of Lebanon nurses are unfair to union babies." You may be interested to learn that we discovered a child who claimed to be a producer in the motion picture business. We took care of him![23]

At the center of Guild activities lay a major reorientation of cultural and racial authority. The place where this emerged most dramatically was at Labor Day parades. Since the twenties, Labor Day parades had been dormant, but by 1937 Guild publications promoted the event coupled with large pictures of Franklin Roosevelt, who was "loved by

The Film Stars Frolic of 1933. A promotional advertisement in the Guild magazine, *Screen Actor,* exemplifying the fusion of the stars' appeal to unionization in the Depression.

labor for the enemies he has made." On the "big day," the press recorded that the film stars were "going the very limit to contribute all the fanfare of show business at [their] command." Once the march began, the press reported that the Actors Guild "stole the show." Cars carrying current and future Guild presidents, Robert Montgomery, Edward Arnold, and "Brother" Eddie Cantor, rode at the front, followed by floats of bathing beauties, cowboy and Indian rider groups, and a veterans division accompanied by swing music. As the polyglot membership marched down the main thoroughfares, participants dressed in native garb, representing eastern Europe, the South Seas, Africa, the East Indies, and China, came into full view. On the side, an actor dressed as Abraham Lincoln proclaimed that producers should receive the fruits of their labor, while Popeye and the Keystone Cops chased away union "scabs." At the conclusion, the mayor of Los Angeles led a crowd of "300,000 strong" in singing the "Star Spangled Banner," spurring journalists to observe that the marchers felt "irresistibly headed for victory over the forces that have so long blocked the way."[24]

At this point one can see that when Eric Johnston looked back to the thirties, he was accurate in stating that Hollywood provided an example of New Dealers' proclivity to advance "nightmares of class

The Actors Guild leaders in the 1937 Labor Day parade in Los Angeles. From left to right: Chester Morris, Robert Montgomery, Lucille Gleason, Boris Karloff, and Charles King.

The Labor Day parade of 1937 in Los Angeles. Preceded by the car carrying the Guild leaders and floats representing diverse racial and national groups, the veterans division linked unions with American patriotism and the renewal of the producers' democracy.

conflict." With big business delegitimized, Hollywood artists had not only placed on the screen characters who equated social reform with realizing a consumer culture and republican aspirations, but brought that endeavor directly into grassroots politics. The Actors Guild promoted unionization that included the new woman, racial groups, and moral experimentation yoked to the class and public interests of the bourgeoisie and the workers. Having reshaped the traditional "American" republican creed, the film capital was fully unionized from top to bottom.

Young Man Reagan and the Rise of Unpatriotic Class Conflict

With the coming of World War II, many of the dreams associated with New Deal politics and popular art came to realization. The war restored prosperity and created full employment. After the attack on Pearl Harbor, Hollywood union leaders cooperated with producers and government to end class conflict. The Screen Actors Guild celebrated the stars who enlisted in the Army and Navy, while other stars

such as Bob Hope and Bing Crosby entertained the troops in all theaters of the war. Linking "victory" to attaining a consumer democracy,
advertisements in the Guild's publications highlighted nightclubs and
scantily clad chorus girls attired like Uncle Sam. Indicative of the
awareness of industry leaders that their dreams had spread worldwide,
one illustration in a Guild publication showed a world map with a
caption explaining that a "public once limited to the physical capacity
of a single theater has expanded through film and radio to global pro-
portions."

Though Guild leaders promoted the call for unity, the class-based
insurgency of the New Deal years did not die. In fact, it erupted across
the nation and within the Screen Actors Guild. It began as businessmen and labor leaders grew prosperous while government price controls kept workers' wages low. Guild leaders lobbied to have the stars'
salaries increased but neglected to include those for the extras. The
most unskilled of the acting profession responded by creating an alliance with Herbert Sorrell of the CSU to attain a "better deal." Quickly
labor conflict erupted, but now Guild leaders labeled the strikers traitors and formed a "patriotic extras" union. Amid the battle, Jack
Dales, the Guild's executive secretary, recognized that on the part of
the dissident extras "there was a quite understandable feeling that we
had our heads in the sand, that we did not really understand their
problems . . . and we viewed them as a bunch of malcontents who really didn't have a stake in the business." Soon Kenneth Thomson, a
Guild officer, lost his temper and nearly had a fistfight with CSU leaders in court and wrote to the Guild's board that the extras represented
a "Frankenstein monster" that could in time "destroy us."

The "monster" did not destroy the Guild but did spur a realignment
of power as the Guild joined with producers and its old nemesis, the
IA, to contain disruption from below. Under the leadership of Roy
Brewer, the IA claimed to be free of gangster control. It not only supported the Guild's patriotic extras, but banned members of the CSU
from film sets. This bargain culminated when Brewer and a delegation
of producers asked the Guild board to support a lockout of the "dissi-
dents" led by Sorrell, who promoted class conflict. Though the board
asserted its neutrality, the minutes of that secret meeting show that the
Guild leaders knew it would be "hard to refuse" in light of the IA's
own "unsolicited support in the extras' dispute."[25]

With class conflict erupting inside the industry and the Guild in time
of war, it was not accidental that Guild leaders began to listen with an

attentive ear to the writings and speeches of the new president of the Producers' Association, Eric Johnston. Like Henry Luce, who envisaged that the wartime economy set the stage for the "American Century," Johnston believed that labor-capital cooperation provided a model for reconstructing the world after a Depression and two world wars. He prophesied as early as 1944 that a commitment to military defense and worldwide economic arrangements would create a "utopia" of production that would enable the United States to destroy the threat of global communism.

Most Hollywood Guild and union leaders had, of course, traditionally turned a deaf ear to businessmen who regarded radicalism as a communist plot. Yet as class conflict erupted inside Guild ranks and across the land, Johnston's rhetoric proved attractive. His anticommunism was different from earlier varieties in that it was not a negative but a positive doctrine. It helped explain labor discord as the act of foreign agents and promised that a campaign to end discord and defend the free world from communism would provide a new purpose and identity for the nation—that is, Johnston identified anticommunism with a renewal of the nation's manifest destiny.[26]

Heady stuff indeed. But to achieve this consensus, one must make converts. Heads might have to roll, and many would have to perceive that their former beliefs had led to actions that thwarted American renewal and progress. To put it another way, Johnston's rhetoric spurred a battle over the meaning of national myths and symbols. Was the recent past a mistake or the road map to the future? There can also be no doubt that Johnston's most influential convert was the president of the postwar Guild and the future president of the United States, Ronald Reagan. In many ways Reagan was a prime candidate for conversion to Johnston's viewpoint because he too had concluded that the wartime economy and consensus heralded a better day.

Born and raised in the Midwest, Reagan descended from an Anglo Protestant mother and an Irish Catholic father whose small business failed in the economic crisis. Jack Reagan went on relief and became an avid New Dealer, and his son came to Hollywood where he too joined Progressive causes and worked as a contract player in the most pro-Roosevelt studio, Warner Brothers. Yet he also carried to his work and politics the views of a new generation whose most formative experiences lay outside Depression-era radicalism. He had spent the worst parts of the Depression years in high school and in college, removed from the hardship of his father's home. Young Reagan's arrival in Hollywood in 1937 meant that he had missed the unionizing drives; he joined the union only when closed shop agreements made membership mandatory for all who wished to find work.

The war years also demonstrated that Reagan, part Irish Catholic, could become fully Americanized and achieve success and fame. Indicative of his material success, when he and his wife Jane Wyman divorced in 1948, he had accumulated two ranch-style homes, two Cadillac cars, and five insurance policies. The war also made it possible for Guild leaders to appoint, rather than elect, Reagan to Guild offices where he slowly advanced to the presidency.[27] On the way up, he served as liaison between the Guild and the FBI in an effort to require Guild members to prove their citizenship. In doing so, he expressed the ethos of working-class patriotism that informed many in the union movement in the war. Similar to most Guild leaders, he remained silent in the face of the internment of Japanese Americans, which provided an apt signal that in time of war unity demanded limitations on pluralism and toleration.[28]

Informed by his Guild activities, these years provided the context in which Reagan began to see that class unity against an external enemy provided the bonds for a new consensus. The most useful evidence of that belief comes not so much from his writings, which were few, but from his role in the most popular film of the war, *This Is the Army* (1943). Made in cooperation with the War Department, and featuring Reagan and a future U.S. senator, George Murphy, the film operated as a show-within-a-show musical that charts the story of a father and son, played by Murphy and Reagan. The father fought in World War I only to see his effort to "make the world safe for democracy" fail. But when the Japanese attack Pearl Harbor, his son relinquishes his father's pessimism and opposition.

Soon the Reagan character creates an Army show composed of all racial and ethnic groups, including the black hero Joe Louis and the famed black comedy team, Stump and Stumpy. In the face of the external threat, they put aside class and racial conflict and perform before President Roosevelt. As the soldiers march beneath a huge American eagle, the story identifies victory with the wartime goals of affluence and the home.[29]

By the postwar era these converging trends—Reagan's newfound success, his disengagement from New Deal radicalism, his promotion of class consensus in hierarchical organizations, and the identification of his star persona with the consumer democracy—led him easily to see the strikes of the war and postwar years as the acts of unpatriotic

The climactic scene in *This Is the Army* (1943). The film starred two future presidents of the Screen Actors Guild, Ronald Reagan and George Murphy. Played before President Roosevelt in Washington, D.C., this scene celebrates the transformation of diverse ethnic groups from citizens to soldiers. (Courtesy Academy of Motion Picture Arts and Sciences)

enemies. To solidify the alliance with the producers and the probusiness IA, Reagan wrote to a congressional investigator that the charge of conspiracy and collusion between producers and Guild leaders was "groundless and ridiculous." Yet despite claims of "neutrality," he avidly encouraged members to cross CSU picket lines, while Conference members responded by making film stars "a special object of their wrath." Besides launching a boycott of some stars' films, the CSU press portrayed Reagan as a capitalist puppet.[30]

Class war was back in force. Only Reagan and his allies within the Guild believed that the union had to shed its alliance with lower-class radicals and align itself with the interests and cultural authority of the state and business leadership. Commenting on that ideological change, Reagan recalled in later years that "I learned my lesson . . . the bulk of communist work is done by people who are sucked into carrying

Publications of the Conference of Studio Unions (*above*) dramatize the impact of the national boycott on the studios and (*opposite*) portray Ronald Reagan as a dummy manipulated by a fat capitalist.

out red policy without knowing what they are doing." Meanwhile he became an undercover agent for the FBI because

> coming out of the cage of the Army . . . a series of hardnosed happenings began to change my whole view of American dangers. Most of them tied indirectly within my own bailiwick of acting.

Far from being an active (though unconscious) partisan of what now and then turned out to be communist causes, I little by little became disillusioned or perhaps in my case, I should say reawakened . . . to bring about the regeneration of the world.[31]

To attain that goal, anticommunism in Reagan's hands took on a populist aura in which the struggles against insurgents coalesced with Johnston's call for the "regeneration of the world." Out of that conversion experience Reagan's career as an anticommunist crusader began when he gave a major speech opposing the views of fellow Guild members, particularly Katharine Hepburn and Edward G. Robinson, that the stars should not cross CSU picket lines. The Guild's executive secretary recognized at this moment that "Ronnie [was] one of the greatest speakers that ever lived" and that he also "disliked the extras tremendously." Soon he saw that Reagan committed himself to fighting his "own people, the pro-Russian Americans." To Reagan there was no doubt that allies of the CSU performed the work of agents of "foreign dictators" who had "enslaved people" and tried to control the film industry.[32]

Anticommunism and the Realignment of Politics and Culture

What elevated the local battle to national significance and ultimately made it successful was that the Hollywood anticommunists yoked their wagon to mass politics and governmental power. The agent of that fusion was the arrival of the House Un-American Activities Committee (HUAC) in 1947 and 1948, for it solidified alliances between government, big business, and conservative union leaders that first emerged in World War II. Exactly what internal issues led HUAC to investigate the movie capital will probably never be fully known. To gain perspective, it is well to remember that the committee had investigated Hollywood in the thirties. Expressing the views of small-town, Anglo-Saxon conservatives, committee members believed that the film capital embodied a hotbed of all that was wrong with "modern" culture: mass unions, urban pluralism, and moral experimentation. Yet with the New Deal in power and unionization at high tide in Hollywood, the charge that James Cagney and Shirley Temple aided the communist cause proved ineffective and HUAC had little effect on the industry.[33]

By the postwar era, however, the committee had the upper hand. The Japanese attack on Pearl Harbor had unleashed fears that in an age of technology hostile powers endangered the United States. By 1947, the Soviet Union filled the role of hostile power on the world scene as Stalin imposed tyranny over eastern Europe and encouraged spying in the United States. President Truman and his advisers asked Congress for aid for the military rearmament of western Europe to thwart the spread of communism. Concurrently a State Department officer, Alger Hiss, went to prison for spying, and the courts found Ethel and Julius Rosenberg guilty of giving atomic secrets to the Soviet Union. Though it appears that Julius did operate as a spy, and Ethel was innocent, the state executed them both.[34]

With the communist danger appearing abroad and at home, the psychology of total war that permeated the battle against the communists justified blatant calls for violation of civil liberties in all major institutions, ranging from the State Department to the military and the universities. Indicative of the impact of these events on Hollywood, the attorney for the IA, Mathew Levy, told Congress that in the battle against the CSU in Hollywood, the union had to "isolate the communists" just as "America isolated the Japanese when the war started, and just as I hope the FBI will isolate communists if we ever get into trouble again." Similarly, the Guild sponsored a play, *Thieves Paradise,* which was staged at a Los Angeles theater. Afterwards the writer, Myron Fagan, told the press that this story was a warning that

> we don't care whether an individual can be proved to be an outright Communist. As far as we are concerned any man or woman who is a fellow traveler, or belongs to a Red Front organization, or has supported Communism with financial or moral support, a la Charlie Chaplin . . . or associates with known Communists openly or in secret, is just as guilty of treason, and is just as much an enemy of America as any outright Communist. In fact, more so! I have no fear of the *known Communist!* It is the rat who masquerades as a good American citizen but who secretly nourishes the Communist slimy cause who is our greatest menace.[35]

The evocation of total war meant that the line blurred between communist and republican values, a process that deradicalized American myths and symbols. Eric Johnston accordingly told HUAC in 1947 that the "rhetoric of class conflict" remained "foreign to American Civilization." Its promoters were at best irrational "crackpots" suffering from a "delusion" or at worst "traitors." Congressional committees apparently listened, for the government now stripped Sorrell of his leadership of the CSU, and writers and directors known as the "Hollywood Ten" served jail terms for refusing to answer the committee's question, "Are you now or have you ever been a member of the Communist Party?"

Within the industry, Johnston and his allies used the anticommunist crusade to alter the structure of power and ideology permeating the film capital. The producers and Johnston gathered to pass the Waldorf Statement, declaring that no longer would the industry "knowingly employ a Communist or member of any party or group which advocates the overthrow of the government of the United States by force or illegal constitutional methods." At the same time all the Hollywood guilds enforced the Taft-Hartley Act provision that required union leaders to sign a loyalty oath. But, most important, the industry instituted blacklisting procedures and supported public rituals of "naming names" before the committee.[36]

The congressional ritual unfolded when HUAC demanded that former communists reveal who had served with them as their Party comrades. According to Victor Navasky, this served as a "degradation ritual" in which witnesses humbled themselves before the committee. While this is true, the ritual in the case of artists like Elia Kazan and others was also a civic conversion narrative, complete with a confession of past sins and testimony to a new faith. A prime example of

The members of the Hollywood Ten and their families protesting their incarceration for defying Congress. *Hollywood on Trial* (1993). (Courtesy Academy of Motion Picture Arts and Sciences)

that transformation emerged in the case of Edward Dmytryk, who had served part of a jail term as one of the Hollywood Ten. During his prison term, he changed his mind. Seeking to secure the opportunity to work again, he named his communist allies to HUAC. Shortly thereafter, he also wrote a confession in a national magazine. An accompanying photograph showed Dmytryk looking at a newspaper headline, "Trial Board Convicts Sorrell." In the article Dmytryk wrote that he joined the Communist Party to end world poverty. Yet when the Russians imposed tyranny in eastern Europe, he converted to the view that "democratic capitalism" in the United States provided the only solution for world problems.[37]

With the aid of the state and rituals of conversion, Johnston and his allies mobilized the power to make the film capital a model of the new class consensus. Structurally, Johnston formed the Motion Picture Council to adjudicate labor-capital disputes far removed from a more active public arena. The Council gained great power because it provided a site for clearing artists for work in the industry. Besides enforcing a blacklist that denied work to communists and fellow travelers, the Council and the Screen Actors Guild became more hierarchical and removed from popular participation. In sharp contrast to the past, the leaders cut off petitions from the floor at annual meetings. They passed new rules to ensure that more class "A" members (stars) than "B" members (extras and supporting players) had to sign a petition to call special meetings—a measure that effectively silenced popular debate. Similarly, they denied members the right to place in debate alternative contract proposals at open meetings. Above all, secret ballots became the criterion for voting, and the Guild publications became oriented toward technical procedures, devoid of concern for the relation of the union to national civic life.[38]

Meanwhile the leaders and rank and file got the message that the basis of cultural authority had been transferred from lower-class to upper-class leaders, armed with special expertise. One actor told a reporter that he was "afraid that the public might have received a wrong impression about [actors] because of having them portray, say, a legendary hero who stole from the rich to give to the poor, or an honest crusading district attorney, or a lonely, poetic, anti-social gangster." It followed that with the implementation of "loyalty oaths," Guild members no longer joined militant Labor Day parades or boycotted businesses hostile to unions. Nor did members fill their meetings with republican rhetoric that condemned business and inequality. As one player explained, the impact of these policies was clear, namely, that "we've got to resolve any conflicts between what we are and what the public has been led to believe we are. We can't afford to have people think we are a band of strong men or crusaders."[39]

The reason why members felt it best to remain on the apolitical side of the public spectrum was not hard to find. Take the case of Marsha Hunt. The actress had gained success in forties films and served as a member of the Guild's board. But when she joined other artists to protest the treatment of the Hollywood Ten, her agent phoned, asking her to sign a statement saying she was an "innocent dupe. I had been masterminded by Commies. I said, 'But it's not true.'" The protest had been organized by "Willie Wyler and John Huston and [screenwriter] Philip Dunne." Realizing her confession would be false, Hunt told her agent, "No, I can't sign such a thing." Nonetheless, she recalled that afterwards "offers stopped" coming in for screen roles and her career ended. Though no one ever found her to be a member of the Party, the problem was that she "was an articulate liberal. And we had to be silenced right along with anybody else who had ever joined the Communist Party."[40]

Once this process began, it took on the contours of a purification ritual where Hollywood insiders would constantly strive to prove themselves innocent by uncovering the real subversives. When we ask what spurred that drive, it is important to realize that almost all of the Guild members and their leaders had participated in the radical union activities of the thirties, and their memories of that era went deep. It was also possible that the past could entrap one. So the need to prove oneself innocent by destroying those who still retained the old faith animated the anticommunist fervor.

One striking example of this tendency can be found within the Guild files in a letter from an executive at Columbia Pictures to a young actress apologizing because a "mistake had been made." The Columbia executive explains that "you are aware that we make a check on all actors, writers, directors being considered for employment. This is just regular routine. This investigation is made by a highly reputable organization in New York City." Yet an error occurred that denied work to the actress—who soon became Mrs. Ronald Reagan—because she had the same maiden name as a known fellow traveler, Nancy Davis. Still the executive complained that "I question where your criticism of the organization that checks for us is justified. Of course we could have taken it for granted, that the wife of Ronald Reagan could not be of questionable legality, and we could have disregarded the report." Others were not so lucky. Looking back, Jack Dales, the executive secretary of the Guild, confessed:

> What I have debated since is that so many people were tarred by that brush who I don't think should have been now. . . . Even at the time my doubts came to the fore. . . . I was not Ronnie Reagan or Roy Brewer [president of the IA]. . . . I would argue about how far we were going, particularly when it got to be this clearing depot, you know, for work. I think of people who were terribly, unfairly treated like Larry Parks, Marsha Hunt, who had viewpoints that were different from the majority of the Board members, but they were far from communist agents. . . . They were just strong liberal people who took their lumps. . . . The producers also carried it to ridiculous extremes and we did not stand up fairly to call a fair line. A line should have been called.[41]

A line was so hard to draw because, like many a convert to a new faith, many of the anticommunists engaged in expurgating even the faintest reminders of their own radical past and forging a closed civic sphere around the film industry. One sees this process unfold in the

Guild's reaction to the production in 1953 of *Salt of the Earth*. Made by several blacklisted artists and a radical miners union, the film might have been encouraged by the Guild in the thirties. It focused on Mexican organizers who form a union among exploited miners. As the men falter, women assist them, entering public life in defiance of men's view that their place is in the domestic sphere.

Yet the Guild leaders cooperated with the press, the FBI, and the large studios to thwart its distribution. The president of the Guild, Walter Pidgeon, alerted "government authorities," namely, the FBI, and sent reports to an ally at the *New York Post*. Victor Reisel wrote a syndicated column stating that the film had to be banned. Why? The production was located only a few miles from the government laboratory that built the atomic bomb. Linking the film and espionage, Reisel wrote that this communist film was made near the "Los Alamos Atomic Proving Grounds. Those grounds prove one inexorable law of modern politics—that where you try to hide secret weapons, you will find the concentrations of communists . . . men and women who have been charged by Congressional witnesses with being part of the pro-Soviet secret apparatus in this country." Reisel further revealed that the film was sponsored by a union whose lawyer, Nat Witte, had gone to jail. There he was a "friend of his Communist cell mate . . . Alger Hiss . . . who spied for the Soviet Union." The IA and the Guild organized a national boycott because the film was

> deliberately designed to inflame racial hatreds and to depict the United States of America as the enemy of all colored peoples. If this picture is shown in Latin America, Asia and India, it will do incalculable harm not only to the US but to the cause of free peoples everywhere, and it will help Stalin and Russia. In effect this picture is a new weapon for Russia.[42]

Behind the attack on *Salt of the Earth* was an effort to expurgate themes of overt class conflict and unionization of minorities from American films. This effort, however, did not stop with films. It carried over into attacks on stars associated with dissidence. Charles Chaplin and John Garfield, for example, had made enemies by not crossing CSU picket lines, supporting the Progressive Party campaign of Henry Wallace, and making independent, socially critical films. The American Legion responded by picketing the premieres of Chaplin's *Monsieur Verdoux* (1947) and *Limelight* (1952). When HUAC summoned Garfield to testify, the "tough guy" hero died in mid-career from, as some called it, a "broken heart."

Meanwhile conservative columnists launched an inquiry into Chaplin's presumed sexual immorality and "red" beliefs. When Congress called on Chaplin to testify, he left the country for Switzerland. Some of the more acute reporters watching these events claimed that the Red Scare had gone too far, for it was killing the goose that lay the gold eggs. Roy Brewer of the IA answered these charges by claiming in effect that ideology surmounted the mere call for profits within the national media. As he saw it,

> Chaplin has shown nothing but contempt for America and her institutions. His most recent statements that Hollywood succumbed to thought control so far as I am concerned confirms the fact that his thinking is in the communist orbit of influence. This is strictly Party line. . . . Nothing he has said or done would justify our assuming that he is on our side in this fight. Until we get such assurances, we are justified in resisting any further efforts to add to his fortune or his influence.[43]

Roy Brewer's words had a major effect, as one might expect, on artists working in the studios. In 1948, for example, Frank Capra made *State of the Union* to celebrate the struggles of a corporate reformer who resembled Eric Johnston. Nonetheless, Capra confessed that filmmakers were engaged in a "delicate operation. . . . For if we run down the democratic processes, we play into the hands of our detractors. Our job will be to make all criticisms expressed add up to praise—and I say it's going to be tough." Things got even tougher when director Joseph Losey refused to make an anticommunist film as demanded by Howard Hughes. Soon the studio fired Losey and he joined a host of blacklisted artists working in Europe. After experiencing the new order, the writer Moss Hart told a reporter that the studios "were as tight as a military system. It is a very totalitarian town. Its people are the most frightened of those in any industry." The director Lewis Milestone wrote that in the wake of HUAC and the Waldorf Statement:

> A fear and psychosis pervades the town, engendered by the recent witch hunts on the national, state and community level. Producers are asking for and getting pictures without ideas. In the frantic effort to offend no one, to alienate no groups, to create no misgivings in Congressional minds, studios are for the most part obediently concentrating on vapidity. The public . . . did not ask that pictures be sterilized of ideas; the notion was self-imposed.[44]

"The Self-Imposition": Screening the Cold War Consensus

Though he obviously had what Johnston would see as a "biased" view, Milestone's perception was not far off the mark. Against the backdrop of the thirties when film stars drew on their screen image to promote unions and the New Deal, the new anticommunist crusade had transformed the structure of power and politics. The convergence of state interests, conservative populism, and the call of Eric Johnston to create a new era of labor-capital cooperation had borne fruit. Yet along with the elimination of radical unions and the destruction of the careers of dissenting artists, the Cold Warriors aimed not just to eliminate subversive themes from the screen but to promote a positive vision of the virtues of the new American Way of unity and consumer democracy.

Generally the Cold Warriors' quest to transform film content moved on two interdependent tracks. To ensure that subversive values did not return to filmmaking, Johnston altered industrywide censorship guidelines. Where in the past the Production Code focused primarily on moral "do's and don'ts," now several new social categories appeared to prohibit criticism of institutions. The fundamentals gained widespread visibility when Johnston, Roy Brewer, Ronald Reagan, King Vidor, John Wayne, and others formed a new Motion Picture Alliance for the Advancement of American Ideals. One of the Alliance's first acts was to create *A Screen Guide for Americans*. Written by the anticommunist Ayn Rand, each chapter opened with a bold caption such as "Don't Smear the Free Enterprise System," "Don't Deify the Common Man," "Don't Show That Poverty Is a Virtue and Failure Is Noble." One must learn that the "nobility" of "little people" reflected the "drooling of weaklings." Little wonder that a writer who once found it profitable to submit scripts whose protagonists' main "fortune and happiness were threatened by a banker holding a mortgage over their heads" now found these scripts and ideas unmarketable.[45]

It was also not accidental that in enforcing these guidelines the large studios formed a covert alliance with the Cold War state. This did not appear simply in Johnston's cooperation with HUAC or in his alliance with the State and Commerce Departments to promote favorable films abroad. On the contrary, it emerged in the form of the Central Intelligence Agency (CIA) placing agents within the industry to alter film content. The most persuasive evidence we have of this interaction is a series of letters written to the CIA by the head of censorship at Paramount, Luigi Luraschi. While Robert Vogel at Metro-Goldwyn-Mayer performed a similar task, Luraschi seems to have had more industrywide power. He wrote to the CIA that he worked on an Academy Awards committee where a "large number of pictures come under our influence," and under Eric Johnston's leadership the "production code administration" was now a "wonderful spot to keep check on independents both from the standpoint of eliminating troublesome material as of injecting stuff." It was possible to "kill" a "commie picture" by appealing to men like Darryl Zanuck, the head of 20th Century-Fox, who would not "consciously do anything to help the left." Conversely he saw that the Metro studio head, Dore Schary, "leaned to the left" but made "anti-commie" films of "fellow travelers" and "misguided persons."[46]

Concurrently, Paramount's CIA agent did a "lot of personal work with the various members of the Board of Governors" of the Academy of Motion Picture Arts and Sciences to make sure that he "lined up enough people" to prohibit or promote awards favorable to the United States' interests abroad. Along these lines he speculated that the Academy's best foreign film award might go to *The Small World of Don Camillo* (1951), a favorite of our "leftist friends" with its theme that "Communism and the rest of the world can get along." Since it had won a prize at the prestigious Venice Film Festival, Luraschi worried that it might also win the Oscar (it didn't) and further the leftist cause. Looking to our "interests" abroad, he also worked to ban a reissue of Frank Capra's *Why We Fight* in Asia because it promoted America's old wartime alliance with the Soviet Union in a favorable light. He also advised banning a film by Roberto Rossellini because it was critical of the Catholic Church. In "this battle of minds" an antireligious film favored the enemy, for "the first step the Commies must take is to debunk religion." The agent did recommend promoting a film made by General Motors, *American Harvest.* It showed how "under our system of free enterprise" America makes great cars, leading the agent to conclude that "what is good for G.M. is good for the U.S.A. and vice-versa!"[47]

Under the impact of these pressures in the Cold War, movies continued the affirmation of big business and classlessness that first permeated the screen in World War II. Our plot tabulations reveal that the majority of films perpetuated that revolutionary alteration in national identity. The incidence of depictions of big business as villainous or of the rich as a moral threat decreased from 20 and 50 percent, respectively, to less than 5 percent during the fifties (appendix 2, figs. 1, 2). Films focusing on social reform did not disappear, but reform now was less the agency of citizens operating in the autonomous civic sphere than of experts aligned with established institutions (fig. 4). Along with the elevation of experts and official leaders, fears of internal subversion accelerated from 10 percent of films during World War II to over

25 percent from 1945 to 1955, an unprecedented trend (fig. 10). As in the war period, moviemakers identified subversion with beliefs that harkened back to dissident values.

Intimately related to the celebration of consensus, heroes and heroines recognized that their older values and beliefs were subversive, a process that led to their conversion to the new consensus. Take *On the Waterfront*, Elia Kazan and Budd Schulberg's Academy-Award-winning film of 1954. Kazan wrote that he used the story of a working-class youth who informs on his older gangster friends as a metaphor for his own testimony before HUAC. Another ex-communist who cooperated with the committee, Robert Rossen, in 1949 adapted for the screen Robert Penn Warren's best-selling novel, *All the King's Men*. The story focused on Willie Stark, a populist politician modeled on Huey Long. But where Long gained success by calling for a dramatic redistribution of wealth in the thirties, Stark emerges as a corrupt populist who suggests fascism. Similarly, Edward Dmytryk directed *The Caine Mutiny* (1954) to atone for his own communist activities. Significantly the story evoked memories of the Depression-era classic, *Mutiny on the Bounty* (1935). Where the earlier film justified the revolt of oppressed sailors against injustice, *The Caine Mutiny* portrayed rebels as an irrational mob of "immature men." No doubt this was the reason, explained the producers, that the Navy cooperated in producing a war film that would "justify their system."[48]

As these productions reassigned the basis of cultural authority to official leaders, others related that shift to a recasting of American myths and symbols. A striking example occurred in 1949 with the release of an adaptation of Ayn Rand's novel, *The Fountainhead*. Directed by a former New Dealer, King Vidor, the story focused on a major architect who resembles Frank Lloyd Wright. Where in reality Wright envisaged architecture as a vehicle for modernizing a producers' democracy at odds with monopoly capitalism, the film turned these facts upside down. The Wright surrogate converts to the new ethos of the lone genius and capitalist entrepreneur when he finds that social reformers and the people are corrupt. Similarly, *The Yearling* (1946) portrays the story of a youth who lives in a forest evocative of the older democratic myth of the frontier. In the innocent agrarian paradise he befriends a wild deer. Yet when the deer eats the family crops, the boy kills the deer in order to "grow up" and validate institutions and social roles.

The assumption of these narratives is that the values and institutions of liberal capitalism and family life are to be preserved from false internal values and the external enemy. At a time of international tension, that defense also identified America with the protection of the eternal and sacred values of western civilization itself. Nowhere was that trend more evident than in the vogue for films that evoked a return to "tradition." In sharp contrast to the past, Hollywood studios made an unprecedented number of Biblical epics, westerns, and war stories. Typically the Bible films, including *Samson and Delilah* (1949), *The Land of the Pharaohs* (1955), and *The Ten Commandments* (1956), focused on a sacred people—all of whom spoke English and were portrayed by well-known stars to heighten audience identification—who overcome the lures of sex and pleasure to defend themselves against a pagan tyrant. Explaining the meaning of these stories, the author of *The Robe* (1953) commented that the epic of a Roman soldier who defends Christians from pagans brought home to him that the first century A.D. was marked by the same problems as the twentieth century. Then as now, "the weeping wounded countries of Eastern Europe" will "see Christ come to renew his promise to a bewildered world."[49]

Carried into the modern age, similar cautions informed films highlighting the central myth of the nation: the frontier. Formerly westerns composed less than 20 percent of plots in any one year, but by the postwar era the cowboy epic increased to half of all plots in our samples, an astounding shift from earlier times (appendix 2, fig. 17). Where westerns featured whites moving into a frontier and pitted against hostile Indians or bandits, films focusing on World War II highlighted patriotic heroes advancing civilization on another front, defending the nation against the Japanese, Germans, and communists. Previously combat films had declined in time of peace; the postwar films, including *Sands of Iwo Jima* (1949), *From Here to Eternity* (1953), and *Battle Cry* (1955), hearkened back to the "good war" as a symbol of unity against a savage enemy.[50]

The rise of war films, westerns, and biblical epics corresponded to an unprecedented increase in films where violence provided the means to resolve the central problems presented by the plot (appendix 2, fig. 18). Formerly films that utilized violence to resolve problems predominated only in time of war. So as one might expect, from 1914 to 1918 films that charted violent victory over Germans rose to 25 percent. As one might also expect, such films decreased to 5 percent in the peaceful twenties. Once World War II began, 15 percent of Hollywood productions in our sample celebrated violence as the means to conquer the enemy. Yet at the end of the war, the turn to violence in American films did not diminish, as it had after World War I. On the contrary, by the early fifties well over 30 percent of the plots in our samples focused on violence as a solution, generating a 10 percent rise in such films since the World War II years and charting a fresh trend where violence continued to rise in time of peace.[51]

Behind the revival of tradition and the turn to violence lay a common denominator. With the country still in a condition of war and the demand for unity informing politics, when conflict or problems arose the preferred solution was not through negotiation or compromise. Rather, the protagonists engaged in a demonic battle to destroy, cure, or incarcerate the enemy. An insight into that shift comes into high relief when we compare the two major stars, both linked to the myth of the West, of the thirties and fifties. During the Great Depression Will Rogers embodied the ideal of a hybrid, hyphenated American. In film after film he operated in an autonomous civic sphere with others to transform society and peacefully negotiate across barriers. By way of contrast, the western hero of the postwar era was John Wayne, who evoked the image of the pure Anglo-Saxon hero. He operated as an official lawman, military officer, or businessman who protected established institutions and used violence to conquer enemies.[52]

If John Wayne defended the classless community from external threats in war and western films, this theme gave rise on the home front to the consumer-oriented home as the model for the postwar American Way. Several trends that emerged in our plot sampling revealed that this pattern pervaded moviemaking as a whole. In the twenties and thirties, the incidence of "empowered women" who worked outside the home occurred in over 20 percent of all Hollywood films. The trend continued and increased in the fifties so that the emancipated heroine informed 30 percent of all films in our plot samples (appendix 2, fig. 13). Yet the heroine's emancipation focused ultimately on a home life that preserved traditional gender roles, symbolized in the rise of "patriotic domesticity." Not only did this new category increase from 15 percent in 1944 to 25 percent by 1948, but heroines cast as "wife only" rose from 5 to 20 percent, a significant trend (figs. 13, 14).

Within the new home, mainstream moviemakers also contained the dangers of mass culture and the new woman. By far the most striking example of the way that trend informed moviemaking as well as real life in the postwar era emerged in concert with the enormous success of Walt Disney as perhaps the most important symbol of the postwar American Way. As Steven Watts has shown, Disney identified in the thirties with the New Deal, and left-wing critics saw his cartoons as a metaphor for resistance to injustice. Yet strikes against his studio during the war spurred Disney to convert to anticommunism. Celebrating the new ethos of class and family harmony, Disney's films, ranging from *Swiss Family Robinson* (1960) to *Mary Poppins* (1964), elevated the family as the arena where playful youthful impulses could be realized. To make that dream real for his audiences, Disney built an amusement park in the suburbs of Los Angeles. Far removed from the city, Disneyland provided an environment that embodied the postwar "Utopia of Production" and the home-centered public life of play, youth, and security.[53]

If the postwar suburban ideal provided a classless dream that preserved the ideals of white America, it was also in this context that mainstream moviemakers attempted to deal with the most pressing issue of postwar public life—that is, the demands of racial minorities to participate in the affluent society. On some levels this was not voluntary. In the earlier strike-laden era, civil rights groups sought the assistance of the Screen Actors Guild in pressuring producers to alter the portrayal of blacks on the screen. But the Guild refused, claiming that their black members would suffer if the "Sambo" role disappeared from the screen.

Things became more serious, however, when a group of left-wing activists published a report critical of the portrayal of blacks in Hollywood films and studio employment practices. The Guild board then received a memo from Ronald Reagan stating that the State Department would like "our motion pictures to show the entire world the continuing gains that negroes are making in this country. . . . This is an important issue in the war against communist propaganda." A "Negro Committee" was formed by the Guild to pressure producers to give blacks more dignified roles and to hire African-American workers. To prove its patriotism, the Guild Negro Committee placed an ad in the trade journals stating that its members rejected all "communist" agitation. Finally the Guild circulated a report that Lena Horne—a Guild member—condemned Paul Robeson as a communist, establishing her right to work.[54]

The effort to present a more favorable portrayal of minorities within the parameters of the postwar classlessness also engaged the attention of Luigi Luraschi, the Paramount CIA agent. Operating in tandem with the State Department's request for the favorable portrayal of nonwhites, he received a script for a western called *Arrowhead* (1953). Despite its positive portrayal of Indians, the script presented "a story which the Commies could use to their advantage in Asia," for it served as an "indictment" of America's treatment of Apache Indians. The story told how whites who hated Indians expropriated their land, which compelled the natives to revolt. Luraschi asked the producers to rewrite the script to present favorable portrayals of Indians that would also fit the national interest.

At first the film's star Charlton Heston resisted, but after being told of the Cold War imperatives at work, he relented. The new script told of conflict, but the source of discontent was neither institutionalized racism nor class oppositions. Rather, the conflict now emanated from a clash of personalities. The Indians in the altered script follow the misguided advice of Toriano (Jack Palance), who has a personal feud with Bannon (Heston), a white man raised by the Apaches. All the "offending dialogue" disappeared in favor of a story where adherence to reason—as defined by whites—created racial harmony. Still the "commies will probably make use of it," admitted Luraschi.[55]

Amid this constrained political environment, more favorable views of minorities did occur on screens at home and abroad, despite the appearance of strikingly contradictory messages. Liberals, black writers, and civil rights leaders all approved of films like *Pinky* (1949), *Home of the Brave* (1949), *Intruder in the Dust* (1949), *Lost Boundaries* (1949), *Broken Arrow* (1950), and *Chief Crazy Horse* (1955). Each gained favor for portraying minorities with dignity and courage, a positive shift from the classic racist stereotypes of the past. Yet minorities' redress of grievances in film narratives came not as the result of mass movements or communal actions of self-help, such as that gracing the current civil rights movement. The solution to racist conflict came from upper-class officials who had ties to official judges and lawmen.[56]

Most surprising of all, a sharp dualism in the portrayal of minorities showed that it was difficult, in an industry that idealized the defense of a classless white society, to shed older racial stereotypes. It was true that the incidence of minorities cast as principal players or subordinate heroes rose from 10 percent during the war to over 25 percent in the fifties. Reformers and radicals could take heart that minorities gained acceptance. On the other hand, plots portraying minorities as villains rose even more than heroic portrayals to over 30 percent of the samplings (appendix 2, fig. 19). How does one explain this contradiction? One reason was that in the western, war, and biblical films, good minorities subordinated themselves to white authority to fight a war against pagans. More often than not, good minorities mobilized to fight against bad minority characters in westerns, World War II revival films, biblical epics, and anticommunist films set in Korea and other parts of Asia (fig. 19).[57]

The portrayal of minorities in relation to the new ideal of the suburban, classless home and romance was even more problematic. In the twenties and thirties a staple of Hollywood moviemaking was cross-class love affairs and marriage. Sometimes love even occurred across racial barriers. *Mutiny on the Bounty,* for example, celebrated romance and marriage between Caucasians and Polynesians, played by actresses from Tahiti. By the postwar era, the notion that class differences and hybridity informed national life decreased dramatically. The category of cross-class love and marriage declined from 25 percent of films in the thirties to less than 5 percent in the fifties (appendix 2, fig. 15). When love across racial boundaries occurred in films like *Pinky* or *Showboat,* the nonwhite lover—unlike in *Mutiny on the Bounty*—was played by a white actress.

The cumulative effect was that the experimentation with class and racial differences of the Depression era gave way to a backlash that reinforced Anglo-Saxons as ideals. Bette Davis, for one, did not like the trend. In the thirties she played empowered women and took an active role in the Guild. During the war she was one of the few white stars to play before black troops and promote more positive roles for minorities in the film industry. But once Eric Johnston arrived on the scene, Davis saw that the movies were far more conservative in their promotion of a "man's age." Increasingly, she believed that "deception" ruled moviemaking for "sex cannot be shown honestly on the screen and any woman's story concerns sex." Though Jennifer Jones played a mixed-race rebel in *Duel in the Sun* (1946), at the end the mulatto heroine had to pay for her defiance of racial boundaries with her death. Reflecting on the need to punish rebellious women who defied racial and sexual boundaries, Jones observed that "I like to play any woman who is interesting, but there have got to be SOME who solve their problems in more satisfying, less harmful ways than by the destruction of others. Yet writers don't seem to write about them any more, and I think it's kind of frightening that they don't."[58]

Just as heroines who crossed racial barriers had to die, so female stars who defied the real-world parameters of the white woman's role encountered the outrage of industry leaders. No doubt the most sensational example of that reality erupted in the Rita Hayworth scandal.[59] During the war Rita rose to fame by transforming herself from a Spanish woman into the ideal pin-up girl whose figure graced an atomic bomb. Yet in the postwar era she defied the code, complete with its racialized definitions, by leaving her husband and taking her child on a world tour with a "dark" Indian prince, Aly Khan. When church groups condemned her amorous affair with a "colored man," Johnston gathered producers in a meeting to discuss terminating Hayworth's contract. Explaining why it was necessary to threaten Hayworth for moral turpitude, the editor for the *Hollywood Reporter* wrote in his daily column that it had become abundantly clear that

> the doings of Rita Hayworth hurt the picture industry much more than it hurt Miss Hayworth. . . . the stench from her amorous display with the Indian Prince hurts all pictures, everyone making those pictures. . . . We all got wet and are still drenched from the commie uprising in our industry. . . . If the industry had acted and not waited, we would have escaped the downpour. But the storm was on us. . . . It was then too late, as it will be on other matters like this that drag us in the mud.[60]

Audiences and the Postwar Consumer Democracy

The effort to avoid the racial taint that dragged the industry into the "mud" would not have been so effective if it had not served to reinforce the general political and social patterns of the day. Between 1946 and 1960, the American gross national product doubled, and the baby boom spurred a vast demand for modern television sets, cars, and home appliances. The rise of the suburbs brought white ethnics into the American middle-class world of consumption. Concurrently public opinion polls revealed that the populace looked to employment as a means of securing better wages and leisure time rather than advancing class conflict or improving working conditions. Similarly, magazines praised women who worked to buttress family income rather than pursue an independent career. As domesticity emerged as the focus of women's attention, the suburban communities reinforced the ideal of a white consumer democracy. Even as late as 1993, 90 percent of the population in the suburbs were white, while people of color composed less than 1 percent of their neighbors, a result of conscious decisions by state agencies, real estate agents, and urban developers.[61]

Within the larger society, Hollywood thus set the tone for a dramatic reorientation of Americanism and politics. The anticommunist crusade promised to realize New Deal dreams without class conflict or a tumultuous public life. With the promises of economic growth coming true, the industry and Guild leaders encouraged film stars to become models of the new life both on and off the screen.[62] By the early fifties the master at articulating this return to traditional family values was Ronald Reagan. Not only did Reagan play lead roles in westerns, war, and family films, but he gave a series of standardized talks for the

Guild and for General Electric. With the trials of the past behind him—class conflict in Hollywood, the subversive activities of communists, and a failed marriage—Reagan had remarried and identified his politics with creating a perfect family and society. In so doing the star's élan and feel for the vernacular evoked ideals of a family life more stable than that of the population as a whole. A news reporter watching "Dutch" Reagan give his talk to an audience in the film star's hometown of Dixon, Illinois, observed that

> Dutch gave a stirring defense of his new home, Hollywood. He explained that it was a few years ago that some churches wouldn't even bury an actor. That attitude . . . has changed today, because the film actors, unlike the thespians of old, now settle in one place, build homes and raise their children, attend school and churches and become part of the community. You certainly couldn't expect an actor who lives out of a trunk to do that.[63]

Years later the crusading Guild leader would rise to become president of the United States. One of his first acts in office was to appoint the IA leader Roy Brewer to a high post in the Labor Department. Since postwar Hollywood gave both men their political baptisms, what conclusions can we draw from these events? By now it should be clear that the Red Scare in the film capital served as more than a reactionary, paranoid crusade led by small-town conservatives. Rather, anticommunism gained its power because of efforts by corporate reformers and state and union leaders to legitimate for the first time a homogenous American Way. Along the way the assault on communists provided the firepower to destroy the republican creed and to sanctify a consumer ethos where freedom was found less at work than in a private suburban home removed from the city and the world of racial minorities.

Precisely because alternative republican traditions existed to challenge this new order, Johnston and his allies needed the power of the state and the rhetoric of a national jeremiad to tame the guilds and by implication the New Deal inheritance. The reason was not hard to find. The stars attracted attention because in the thirties they advanced a union movement that revitalized a republican creed rooted in dreams of modern morals, affluence, and diversity. Merging their screen roles to public life, film performers helped realign the old middle class from the interests of the wealthy to the interests of workers. The result was that screen players joined a mass labor movement that interjected voting by class into the national two-party system, providing support for the welfare state and the inclusion of minorities and women in civic life.

Yet even as these reforms promised to realize an Americanism rooted in a producers' democracy, the attack on Pearl Harbor spurred calls for unity that created a major turning point. Under the apolitical process of defense mobilization, the divisions of class, race, sexuality, and ideology were seen as subversive. This patriotic fervor meant that leaders such as Ronald Reagan and Eric Johnston equated the doctrine of economic growth with realizing a new "utopia of production" and victory. Once the Cold War began, they evoked the World War II success story to justify the making of an unprecedented postwar consensus. Unlike World War II, however, this cohesion was not voluntary. To enforce unity they now used the power of the state and mass politics to condemn left-wingers who helped create the consensus in the battle against the fascists. So with the Cold War beginning in 1947, and with the FBI uncovering real Soviet spies, Johnston and his allies yoked anticommunism and the new ethos of economic growth to restore traditional values.

On the screen these revolutionary changes assumed the cultural clothing of traditional myths and symbols. In the mainstream the dream of equality emerged less in rearranging work relations than in the quest for freedom in the home presided over by the new woman. Yet exactly at this point of triumph, remnants of the Left began to find a new market for a dark "film noir" that challenged the consensus and set the stage for a youthful counterculture. Out of that confluence of events arose stars who restored a critical edge to mass art and relaunched the search for an alternative self and public sphere. Exactly what implications this had for the origins of the postwar counterculture and youth culture provides the topic of the last chapter.

Chapter 6
"Outside the Groove of History":
Film Noir and the Birth of
a Counterculture

> When I hear the current attacks on free education, when I read articles
> from all over the country pouncing on any remaining vestige of inde-
> pendent progressive thought . . . I realize I'm living in a strange,
> strange time. What only two years ago was virtue is now vice; what was
> a friend is now foe, what was then patriotic is now often subversive.
> That's not a very easy adjustment. We find ourselves trying to maintain
> our sanity—trying to stand mentally upright in a world that's turned
> upside down.
> —Howard Koch, Hollywood screenwriter, 1947

By the early fifties, Eric Johnston's vision of a regenerated liberal order gained success. Great prosperity spread at home, and Johnston's fear of the "nightmare of class conflict" receded before the
wonders of economic growth and the defense of the "free world," giving rise to the consumer democracy centered on the suburban home.
Yet at this point of triumph many artists began to see, in the words of
the novelist Ralph Ellison, that they and their generation had stepped
"outside the groove of history."[1] Within the film industry where politics
and art had intersected in a contest over the course of progress and
history, a clue to the nature of that groove occurred when Arthur
Miller called his autobiography *Timebends* to suggest the character of
that contorted history.

Miller recalled that for his generation the Depression was the "sub-
liminal point from which all that came afterward is measured." In the
New Deal era, politics and art worked along the same tracks. Art fused
vernacular and high cultures, seeking to restore a vivid life of feeling
to the psyche that suffered from excess of reason. Out of that combination artists pointed the way to a more vital community and public life
to juxtapose against the excesses of capitalism and repressive sexual
and social roles. Yet Miller saw that he "could not help thinking in
1953–1954 that time was running out, not only on me, but on the tradi-

tional American culture . . . the rules of social intercourse had quite suddenly changed. Attitudes that had merely been anti-capitalist, anti-establishment, were suddenly morally repulsive and if not actually treasonous then implicitly so." As former friends and radicals named names and converted to a new American Way, he understood that "without guilt the 1950's Red-hunt could never have generated such power. Once it was conceded that absolutely any idea remotely similar to a Marxist position was not only politically but morally illicit, the liberal, with his customary adaptations of Marxist theory and attitudes, was effectively paralysed."

In the wake of this transformation Miller saw that history had been ruptured from its roots as a "reassurance of a familiar past had been pulled out from under us." Caught in an identity crisis, Miller experienced an "anxiety that would not leave me, that something life menacing and mean was stirring in the American spirit—something that had to be outmaneuvered and thwarted by the strategies of art." Embarking on that strategy, he created his first masterpiece, *Death of a Salesman* (1949), concentrating on a father—the bearer of tradition—who finds that American dreams have turned hollow. Devoid of a democratic tradition to pass on to his sons, Willy Loman commits suicide. The author hoped that a play focusing on the psychic torment of the postwar world would "place a time bomb under capitalism," creating a "protest against the new American empire" emerging in the Cold War era.

Like many artists, Miller also hoped to continue that protest by coming to Hollywood. At first he thought the studios would be eager to make a film version of *Death of a Salesman*. But he found instead that "the political drift of the country had a direct bearing on the movies one could expect to make, so there was more than academic interest in what was really going on in the headlines." With the Hollywood Red Scare in full flower, producers insisted that the film of *Death of a Salesman* begin with a disclaimer by a Columbia professor, explaining that the conditions that destroyed Willy Loman were no longer in existence in modern business. The film producers also insisted that Fredric March play Willy Loman as a psychotic, spurring Miller to protest that "if he was nuts he could hardly stand as a comment on anything." Played as crazy, Willy's dark anger could be dismissed from "sane" society.

Next Miller developed a screenplay that told the story of gangsters and class conflicts on the docks of New York City, a project that would evolve into *On the Waterfront* (1954). But when he presented the script to the producer, he asked that Miller and his colleague Elia Kazan clear it with Roy Brewer of the IA and the Federal Bureau of Investigation.[2] Miller's refusal led him to work instead with John Huston on *The Misfits* (1961). In many ways this was a marriage of like-minded souls, for Huston had been deeply committed to the New Deal and the antifascist war. But to express their disillusion with the postwar era, Huston and Miller made a film that used the metaphor of the West as a symbol of crisis. As their cowboys realize that the ideal of citizens controlling their own public lives and work has been lost, the heroine, played by Miller's new wife Marilyn Monroe, represents the possibility of a new beginning. Miller recalled that, along with Marlon Brando and James Dean, Marilyn was a true rebel for

> she had accepted the role of the outcast years ago, even flaunted it, first as a casualty of puritanical rejection but then with victorious disorder; from her refusal to wear bras to her laughing acknowledgment of calendar photos, her bracing candor—so un-American now in the new empire preparing to lead the war crippled West—was health, the strength of one who has abandoned the illusions of a properly ordered life for herself. With all her concealed pain she was becoming enviable, the astonishing signal of liberation and its joys.[3]

Why would Arthur Miller believe that the American tradition as he "had known it" faltered in the postwar era, generating deep anxiety and despair? Why did Marilyn Monroe, dark films, and the rise of a postwar youth culture perpetuate into the modern era the cultural if not political utopianism of the New Deal? The reason we find this so hard to answer is that we have been taught that the turn to inner, psychic explorations in novels, paintings, and film noir reflected internal developments in each field. Artists' and intellectuals' perception that they lived in an "age of anxiety" reflected a mature response to the loss of innocence caused by the atomic bomb, fascist genocide, and a bloody war. Yet Miller's autobiography suggests that the beginnings of the anxiety pervading the arts and the search for new forms of cultural experimentation had their roots in what many saw as a deep and profound crisis of American identity. While men like Johnston and Ronald Reagan believed that they had revitalized "democratic capitalism," others tapped a widespread feeling that the new order was a rupture from the past, which demanded a new search for utopia in cultural if not political realms of power.[4]

The aim of this chapter is to build upon and to extend Miller's insight. First, I will demonstrate that Hollywood's Cold Warriors looked

The creative artists gathered on the set of *The Misfits* (1961), including Marilyn Monroe, John Huston, Arthur Miller, and Clark Gable. (Courtesy Academy of Motion Picture Arts and Sciences)

to crime films to dramatize the demonic quest for conformity and consensus by labeling identities that had once permeated public life deviant and criminal. In response, major artists on the left, particularly Billy Wilder and John Huston, reshaped the "dark" crime film, later known as film noir, to keep alive a critique of capitalism and repressive social roles. Lastly, I will explore how the remnants of the Hollywood left gave form to a new postwar youth culture that at onced critiqued the consensus culture and launched the search for a utopian alternative. While scholars tend to keep these genres—film noir and youth films—separate, I will show that they not only intertwined but set the stage for the counterculture during the fifties and sixties.[5]

Middle-Class Americanism and the Criminalization of Desire

To begin our inquiry, it is important to realize that the anticommunist crusade attempted to bring all parts of the society into a cohesive whole. There could be no place for popular art or public amusements as independent variables that challenged the quest for economic and cultural order. In effect this meant, as Orson Welles noted in an article for *Esquire* magazine, that Hollywood had been contained as well. When Welles came to the film capital in the Depression, he found that moviemakers were "city people" who interjected the "frenzy and a buccaneering hurly burly" of the "circus" into films. He joined the new Actors Guild and found no distinction between his art, unionization, civil rights, and antifascist crusades. After the anticommunist purge, however, he observed that Hollywood had transformed itself into a "rigidly standardized middle-class suburbia" free of "the raucous, circusy traditions of the recent past." There "used to be some thing spoken of as the influence of movies," but "what is most noticeable today is that the rest of America is influencing Hollywood."[6]

Welles's observation contained a key insight: A central goal of the anticommunist crusade was to transform the nature of middle-class life. In the postwar era, the ideal of the American citizen expanded to include minorities and the working class of immigrant ethnic origin. Yet what formerly marked these citizens as resisters had to be isolated and contained to give birth to the classless society and harmonious capitalist order. On the screen the unprecedented revival of westerns, biblical, and war films celebrated male heroes who are loyal to universal ideals and patriotic or sacred causes. These films celebrated tolerance and the inclusion of outsiders. But the new woman was relegated to either the good girl or temptress characters, while comics who expressed lowbrow sexual impulses and rebellion followed a similar trajectory. Where Will Rogers blended comedy with heroism, the tendency of postwar moviemakers was to revive the Victorian artistic canon that divided the raucousness of lowbrow humor from the virtues of the good citizen. Comics now appear in teams, with the two elements playing off against each other. Combos such as Bing Crosby and Bob Hope, Dean Martin and Jerry Lewis, Bud Abbott and Lou Costello represent this split between the two sides of the self.

The unfunny side of the effort to revive the Victorian artistic canon and construct a new white middle-class identity divorced from the past found expression in postwar crime films. These stories, which reviewers at the time called "realistic melodramas," and later French critics defined as "film noir," portray the dismal fate of characters who still yearn for an integrated self and society. However, their "dark," hybrid desires are associated with primitive traditions or inner repressions that drive them to heinous crimes. Only when they pay for their sins can they find redemption by adapting to the norms of "white civilization." To attain realism and dramatize the struggle over identity, the makers of film noir generated enduring stylistic innovations coupled to a continuation of the social criticism and exposé that permeated films of the New Deal period. Yet far more ambivalence creeps around the edges of these works. Now the audience cannot help but identify with the longings and desires of the flawed characters whose quest for redemption falls into two broad categories. In the new conservative version, the stories focus on authority figures who violently destroy the evildoers or act as therapists who cure the individual psychologically, allowing adaptation to the utopian dream of an affluent, classless America often centered on the suburban home and family.[7] In the version produced by the remnants of the left, moviemakers celebrate the nonconformist who criticizes the new order and steps outside history to perpetuate the ideal of the hybrid rebel in quest of wholeness against an alienating society. Let us look first at the more ideologically conservative version of film noir.

Whether the narrative took the form of *Lucky Jordan* (1942), *This Gun for Hire* (1942), *Saboteur* (1942), *Across the Pacific* (1942), or *The House on 92nd Street* (1945), the criminals and deviant heroines in World War II realistic melodramas initially resisted the patriotic call for class unity and conformity. To link them to instability and dark desires, the camera becomes mobile, focusing on dark, evanescent optical phenomena—crowds, smoke and steam, wind in the trees, rain splattering off streets, faces seen behind Venetian blinds and in mirrors, windows, and neon signs that are hard to fix. The total effect, as a cameraman explained of the technique, was to convey the atmosphere of horror. That is, "where there is no light, one cannot see and when one cannot see, his imagination runs wild. He begins to suspect that things are about to happen. In the dark there is mystery."[8]

Yet at the same time, these films enact conversion narratives where the dark visual images complement the protagonist's quest to expurgate guilt and destroy the memories of an oppositional past. Take *The House on 92nd Street*. Made in cooperation with the FBI in the last year of the war, the story charts the infiltration of the United States by fascist spies to steal information about a secret weapon. Throughout the film, dark, off-center scenes show that the spies fool the hero by masquerading as "ladies," but in fact they are transvestites. Only when the hero and heroine see the light can they cooperate with the FBI to destroy Nazi deviancy. Transferred into the postwar era, the "dark" conversion story informed major anticommunist films, including *My Son John* (1952), *Big Jim McLain* (1952), and *The Fearmakers* (1958). Generally these productions identify the characters' present false beliefs with the oppositional class, racial, and sexual conflicts of the thirties that have led to subversion. These films suggest that "Reds" could number among one's old friends and their ideas could be part of one's former identity; to purge the self and society of impurity will lead to a conflict-free corporate order and a home life centered on heterosexuality and children.[9]

Over the forties and fifties, this dark theme served as a cautionary tale that showed that one's former beliefs could be subversive or aid an enemy who operated in secret, at night, and under the cover of masquerades. In *Kiss of Death,* made in 1947, the film charts the adventures of a poor Italian Catholic criminal who converts and informs on his friend, the vicious criminal Tom Udo. In preparing to play Udo, Richard Widmark visited the sites of many police raids on jazz clubs and musicians in the early Cold War era. In order to capture his evil character's essence on screen, the actor "did make a tour of the swing joints on 52nd Street and Greenwich Village just to get that hopped-up feeling." The story reveals that under these influences Udo cannot contain his sexual appetites and love for black-derived jazz. Similarly, he throws crippled mothers down stairs, gets his "kicks" in jazz clubs, and enjoys violence. The destruction of Udo at once expurgates the hero's guilt for his own criminal past, and provides him with the love of a good wife and wholesome children in the new suburbs, far from the promiscuous "dangers" of city life.[10]

Within this narrative of conversion and redemption writers and directors stigmatized as alien what had once been legitimate. In this way, the realistic melodramas dramatized the need to either contain or destroy women who rebelled from the ideal home. Of films sampled, not only did the category of deviant "vamps" rise from zero in 1940 to over 20 percent by 1949 (appendix 2, fig. 16), but female melodramas operated as cautionary tales. *Where Danger Lives,* for example, was made in 1950 by artists aligned with anticommunist conservatives. A rebellious woman uses her sexual allure to goad men's fall into a world of greed and lower-class decadence. The solution in films like *Leave Her to Heaven* (1945), *The Dark Mirror* (1946), *The Blue Dahlia* (1946), *The Snake Pit* (1948), and *All About Eve* (1950), is for the hero to kill, convert, or "cure" the vampish heroine, restoring traditional family values in the process.[11]

Major films also showed that protagonists who defy these values lose caste and become similar to blacks. Nowhere was this pattern more evident than in *A Double Life* (1947). The story charts the downfall of a Broadway actor, Tony John, played by Ronald Colman. Tony's success has yielded boring, routine roles; moreover, his actress wife has left him for another man. Filled with despair, he accepts a role playing Shakespeare's Othello, the black Moor. Tony, however, fails to separate his feelings of impotence from those of the black he plays. He takes on black traits by moving down the class order in a quest for sex and then kills his working-class lover. And since he cannot divide his real self from the role of the black Othello, Tony tries to kill his wife, who is playing Desdemona. Afterwards Tony kills himself rather than confront that he has become no better than a black.[12]

Just as the dark cinematic style and current cultural wars dramatized the fear that to give in to one's dark desires was to become no better than nonwhites, so reason and experts armed with science and the law brought light and happiness. No doubt the master of this duality was Alfred Hitchcock. In productions like *Foreign Correspondent* (1940), *Saboteur* (1942), *Shadow of a Doubt* (1943), and *Lifeboat* (1944), Hitchcock showed that just beneath the surface of wartime patriotism lay danger, spies, and hidden enemies. By the postwar era Hitchcock made films like *Rope* (1948), *Strangers on a Train* (1951), *Rear Window* (1954), *North by Northwest* (1959), and *Psycho* (1960). Each production featured alienated, deranged characters. Throughout, however, the narrative assured viewers that an orderly universe prevailed. As Hitchcock noted, the director and his camera

> should tell an audience as much as you can; let them know more than the characters on the screen—or as I've said before, "play God." In *Rope* for example the audience knew all along the body was hidden in the chest; how long before it would be discovered? It's almost like a game, like anagrams.[13]

At a time when Hollywood leaders sought to convert the middle class from its romance with the radical side of republicanism, it was not accidental that in these realistic melodramas crime and the deviant woman took on a new face. Unlike in the past, the outlaws were not working-class outsiders and ethnics who rebelled against poverty and discrimination. They were often war heroes, businessmen, and lawyers rooted in an upwardly mobile middle class. Indicative of that trend, moviemaking as a whole saw a dramatic rise in the appearance of the antihero. It is true that in the first years of the Depression Hollywood narratives featured antiheroes, criminals, and vamps in over 15 percent of the films in our plot samples (appendix 2, figs. 16, 20). But the antihero declined dramatically in films after 1933. However, the representation of the deviant increased from less than 10 to over 40 percent from 1938 to 1950 (appendix 2, fig. 20). Alongside that trend, "vampish" women who resisted conformity to postwar family values increased from zero to 20 percent from 1940 to 1948 (appendix 2, fig. 16).

When we ask where this formula came from, and what desires it expressed, it is possible to see that the vampish woman and the anti-hero dramatized a deep anxiety and identity crisis within the heart of postwar culture. In the Cold War era, middle-class men and women were asked, and at times forced, to undergo a transformation in national identity.[14] As such their past class, sexual, and racial identities had to be discarded and pushed into the dark recesses of the mind or into what film noir terms the "night." That is, crime expressed the psychic cost and compulsion inherent in the cultural war and its ramifications through public life. Narratives that reinforced the consensus of the war years, to make a presumably smoothly functioning corporate order and self, celebrated the new hero of the postwar era—the experts and state officials who contained and excluded disorder.

There was, however, a central irony to postwar filmmaking. The transformation in power and culture in the film capital, along with the rise of violent crime, biblical, war and western films, converged with a sharp decline in attendance for the industry as a whole. Ever since the twenties, audiences and moviemakers identified mass art with a realm in opposition to official norms, and audience demand expanded accordingly. Starting in 1948, however, the trade papers became filled with comments on the "lost audience." As one reporter noted, the "guys and gals with the coins at the box office refused to lay them down with a very few exceptions . . . a surprisingly long list of floppolas or near floppolas testified to that." Soon the decline in attendance generated a panic that received national exposure in all the major magazines. Suddenly major firms declined and went into bankruptcy, and studios now canceled players' contracts. Reporters accurately perceived that "the tradition of the star system, on which all motion pictures incubated and grew, requires some revising."[15]

Unfortunately for those whose livelihood depended on moviemaking, hard statistics confirmed the bad news. Attendance declined at the rate of 10 percent yearly after 1947 for nearly a decade. With profits declining, the impregnable studio system, with its capacity, as many scholars have told us, to control the public, crumbled and unemployment spread. With chaos coming from all sides, reporters began to probe the unthinkable: Where had the "lost audience" gone? Was it something we did or said? To contemporary commentators, as well as later scholars, the problem clearly emanated from something outside the industry. A main culprit was the Paramount consent decree, the result of a government antitrust case that forced the studios to relinquish ownership of their theaters. Once government separated the studios from large downtown theaters, and the medium of television expanded, attendance decreased.[16]

Still others saw that neither of these developments would suffice to explain the lost audiences. The declines in audience began in 1948, a full three years before even 20 percent of the population owned a television. Similarly, when audience demand did return a decade later, the deadly Paramount decree was still in effect, and close to 100 percent of the nation's families now had a television. Something else was going on, and that trend was not confined to the film industry. Whether it was swing music, nightclubs, or filmmaking, all the amusements that had their roots in the thirties began a sharp decline. The one common denominator they all possessed was the impact of the domestic Cold War and vice crusading.[17]

The police raided bebop clubs where whites and blacks interacted; meanwhile, local governments launched drug crusades that jailed jazz artists like Billie Holiday and closed homosexual bars and gay amusements. In Hollywood, police noted that since film stars were "practically one of the family in thousands of households," one had to clear "the dope out of Hollywood," a process that led to the jailing of many, including Robert Mitchum.[18]

Out of these converging trends—the criticism of Hollywood by former radicals, the decline of audiences and the studio system, the cultural war on public amusements of all kinds, the making of realistic melodramas that justified the rampant fears—trade reporters recognized that the remaining audiences wanted a product that did not so much reinforce as undermine official values. That is, the Cold War era generated films that promoted a retreat from public life and an affirmation of domestic privacy.[19] Yet critics saw how in New York a theater owner defied censorship guidelines and re-released the antiwar classic of 1930, *All Quiet on the Western Front*. Though the Pentagon had banned the film in Europe, a critic related that the Lewis Milestone classic still generated "standing room only audiences." Inside, patrons responded with "enthusiasm . . . and strong applause for its anti-war sentiments." Such reactions seemed to another critic to be "downright unpatriotic" for the "applause . . . could be construed as a sign of softness with overtones of treason." It even indicated that "our involvement in Korea is not going to be an easy public relations job. . . . Do you suppose that any great numbers of our youth are actually eager to be shot at in Korea under the good housekeeping of the United Nations . . . looks to me as if we are working on a very negative customer."

Further to the west, another independent theater owner found a market existed for films that evoked the appeal of public life as represented by Will Rogers. The theater owner "made a killing" by showing several Will Rogers formula films. At a time when Rogers's Indian roots and calls for a redistribution of wealth were carefully repressed by guardians of the Cherokee comic's memory, the theater owner noted that the authentic Rogers still "packed in" the crowds. Basking in that glow, the exhibitor wrote that the enduring popularity of Rogers formula films proved that something had gone wrong, for "if a man who has been dead for seventeen years can give you the best business in months," the producers "better stand up and listen." The lesson to be learned was that if

> we gross more money with it than we can with some super colossal production, that in itself is good enough proof that the names and faces that once made this business are still in demand. . . . One would think that either producers were trying to kill off the stars intentionally or people we used to have as regular patrons feel that we have let them down.[20]

"Crime Is Only a Left-Handed Form of Human Endeavor"

To remnants of the artistic left and independent producers and studios in Hollywood, the message was all too clear. Provided one found a way to conform to political and industry censorship guidelines, while reinterpreting the crime film to suit one's own and the audiences' interests, it was possible to garner profits. Nor was this far from the minds of moviemakers who represented a left-wing tradition that had to go underground. Officials in John Huston's *The Asphalt Jungle* (1950) refer to the outlaws as "criminals," but the gangsters' activity is justified, as one character says, because crime is just a "left-handed form of human endeavor." These sentiments informed the thinking of an entire group of artists who represented the Hollywood left-wing. Take the case of Abraham Polonsky. Recalling the motivations that informed *Force of Evil* in 1948, Polonsky noted that because in "those days censorship was much stronger," the film ostensibly had to be about a corrupt Wall Street lawyer who pays for his sins. Yet Polonsky observed that the story "*completely* on the surface didn't mean it at all. What I really meant were all those words at the end and all those images of: 'Down, Down, Down.'"

By reworking the crime genre to suit their own interests, such film-makers found it possible to reverse the intended meaning of the mainstream realistic melodrama, using it to convey their perspective on politics and social conditions. Polonsky, for example, saw that there was "plenty of trouble in the United States in political matters. We were all more or less involved with certain radical ideas and a great sense of loss—who had really won that war." If the struggle against fascism had led to the domestic Cold War, the criminals provided a "parallel to Fascism. I mean, that's an ordinary metaphor you find in all economic writing and in the poetry of the left-wing journalism: gangsterism is capitalism or the other way around." *Force of Evil* served as a "destructive analysis of the system" in that it counterpointed law against crime. But "in fact you can't tell one from the other." To convey that emptiness Polonsky asked his cameraman to look at Edward Hopper paintings where "even when people are there, you don't see them; somehow the environments dominate the people." So when "you do a thing like that what you do is utilize the familiar as a way of calling attention to the fact that it's not so *familiar* after all."[21]

Polonsky was not the only one who felt that the crime film provided a way to perpetuate left-wing agendas in covert forms. Orson Welles, the director of what many critics regard as the first "film noir," *Citizen Kane* (1941), operated in the same tradition as Nicholas Ray, the director of *They Live by Night* (1949), *Knock on Any Door* (1949), and *Rebel Without a Cause* (1955). Merging modernism with the folk revival in the New Deal years, Ray began his career as an architectural student of Frank Lloyd Wright and joined with John Avery Lomax to recover black folk songs in the Federal Arts Project. Similarly, Joseph Losey worked in labor theater and then joined with record producer John Hammond to promote black swing musicians as the true creators of an "American" music in the Depression. Billy Wilder, Edgar Ulmer, and Robert Siodmak were European Jews who fled from the Nazi regimes. Edgar Ulmer then wrote and directed Yiddish and black gangster films critical of racism and monopoly capitalism. Anatole Litvak, the director of *Sorry, Wrong Number* (1948), participated in the Soviet film experiments with the great director Sergei Eisenstein. Abraham Polonsky carried into his films commitments forged as a lawyer for the Communist Party and writer for union theater. Lewis Milestone moved from *All Quiet on the Western Front* to creating in 1946 *The Strange Love of Martha Ivers* with the former Communist Party member Robert Rossen.[22]

These artists, with their roots in the radical politics of the thirties, saw their work in crime films as perpetuating in an altered form the wider intellectual life of the New Deal and war years. Polonsky found no contradiction between his directing and his sponsorship of a radical film journal, the *Hollywood Quarterly*. Organized at the University of California at Los Angeles, the quarterly provided from 1945 through 1947 a bridge between academics and left-wing filmmakers, publishing articles on relations between media and society. As Joseph Losey recalled, "I was very, very aware then and even more so now of the impact of film on public attitudes, morality and ethics and individuals."[23] Where Billy Wilder had associated with Bauhaus artists in Weimar Germany and collected modern art,[24] John Huston saw his moviemaking at one with the German Expressionists, the Irish-American documentarian Robert Flaherty, and the Italian neorealists. These influences fed his desire to create in movies a "patriotism that cannot be questioned." It is of "the deepest kind, which requires that it fulfill all the requirements of our admiring hearts." Here artists did not simply record events but served as the "world's dark champion," speaking in "prophetic terms" to "torment the race of men" away from complacency.[25]

Given the impact of the Cold War on the studios, these artists labored to find innovations that would transfer into film one of the central tendencies of modern art: the fusion of the popular to the avant-garde. In doing so, John Huston found that during the Depression his work came alive with "the shift in public attitudes" that accompanied the New Deal, for "overnight it seemed there was a new spirit in the air, a feeling of high confidence which persisted through the first two Roosevelt administrations, right into World War II."[26] Yet afterwards he and others perceived that, under the impact of the Cold War, the "high hopes and ideals of much of the Roosevelt years were slipping away," with the result that Huston contemplated "a complete break away from the standard Hollywood patterns."[27]

To "break" from Hollywood patterns, Huston and his colleagues all found it necessary to conform to censorship but subvert the intent of Production Code guidelines and established genres. In an industry faltering at the box office, directors' opportunity to make an alternative crime film rose in proportion to one's commercial success and the rise of independent producers. By the war Billy Wilder found that he wanted to combine writing with directing "in order to protect my own scripts" and break from "type casting." But when he made *Double Indemnity* in 1944, Wilder found that several studios turned it down, until his own studio, Paramount, finally consented to release it. Once the film garnered great profits, Wilder attained autonomy over his work.[28] Even then, his struggle ran up against the need to evade the studio and industrywide censorship operating to encourage the production of films acceptable for export.

An example of that struggle can be discerned in a series of letters that the CIA agent at Paramount, Luigi Luraschi, wrote to his superior after dealing with Billy Wilder. The agent wrote that one has "to handle Billy easy," but that he had to object when Wilder wanted to make a new film about an American soldier who goes to Japan to find a child he fathered in the war. The plot played into the hands of "commies." But "since this is a picture which would be made outside of the . . . major companies, it is difficult to keep track of it, and next to impossible to bring 'front office pressure' to bear on the points we are interested in." The "racial element" provides a "wonderful piece of propaganda for the commies" and could affront "Japanese sensitivity." Yet since Wilder was not to be "deterred," the agent was "sceptical of the whole matter." Of course, the CIA man knew that inside the studio the project could be "killed" by pressure from the front office, but Wilder could then turn to an independent production company where the CIA operatives had less control. In a pickle, the censor noted that if Wilder proceeded, he "must make a trip to Japan and will need passports, permits etc." In Japan, an occupied country, we "can keep track of him, so that the proper people higher up can make our point of view valid." Yet the agent saw that since this was one of Wilder's "personal projects" and the "spirit of contradiction in him may make him continue anyhow," it would be difficult in an era of independents to make all the operatives' "views prevail."[29]

One also did not have to look far to find why censors of all kinds feared the difficulty of controlling the independents. In a time of studio disintegration and the advent of the "lost audience," the remnants of the Hollywood artistic community found a home with producers like Sam Spiegel, a Nazi refugee.[30] Still another independent, Mark Hellinger, moved from writing a New York newspaper column to producing *High Sierra* (1941), *The Killers* (1946), and *Brute Force* (1947). By the postwar years one writer, Richard Brooks, recalled that Hellinger not only gave writers a share of the profits—a practice that major studios rejected—but also provided a site where artists could skirt the industry censorship demands within new dramatic forms.[31] While the major studios submitted their scripts to censors to attain export licenses for foreign distribution, independents aimed their productions solely at the domestic market relatively free of government strictures.[32]

Hence John Huston said that in making *Key Largo* in 1948 he aimed to show that "once again" the monopolists were on the "move and taking advantage of social apathy. We made this the theme of the film." But the occupation authorities banned it in Europe, though it scored a commercial success in the domestic market.[33]

The success of left-wing noir productions rested on their capacity to reorient cultural authority from officials to the antiheroes and heroines. Robert Siodmak observed that in making crime films like *The Killers* (1946), the aim was to formulate a type of character whereby "if you give him a good enough motive for the crime, the audience will want him to win."[34] Billy Wilder recalled that he learned how to say one thing and mean another by working with Ernst Lubitsch, who had the ability to "let you know what happened, and it could not be censored—you could not put your finger on it." Working in this mode, the new directors also utilized performers who could convey ambiguity in speech and gesture. No doubt Humphrey Bogart was the master. Ever since *Casablanca* Bogart portrayed characters whose great expectations had been defeated by events. Similarly, performers like Burt Lancaster, Dan Duryea, Robert Ryan, Robert Mitchum, Kirk Douglas, Veronica Lake, and Shelley Winters gained fame by using their expressions and voice to convey characters' vernacular speech coupled with their inner torment and anxiety.

Even a director's and writer's manner of conveying the narrative communicated a similar message. Instead of telling a story in linear fashion, or from the standpoint of an omniscient narrator, films such as Wilder's *Sunset Boulevard* (1950) and *Double Indemnity* featured overheard narrators who told their stories from the vantage point of a subjective and confused flashback. Robert Siodmak explained that the aim of a convoluted narrative and disjointed visual style in *The Killers* was to have the audience discover not how, but why, crime occurred. Once critics got the point that these films would criticize society rather than the outlaw, they observed that the new realistic melodramas were "not only unprogressive pictures, but they indicate a most disturbing bent . . . it bodes no particular good. For pictures of crime and violence, of vicious and lawless folks, are open to serious social questions when they are made for none but save mere sensation's sake." One observed that such stories were profitable because their "success is determined by the establishment of a feeling of loneliness against the backdrop of a bustling, busy city." Another critic noted that these films revealed, despite our best hopes, that "we live in a great vacuum, an interrelationship of emptiness." The inverted success tale told the viewer that the modern personality was of "wavering outlines. He has pulled down upon himself the heroes of the past: he also assumes for a while the color of these and then another—but the colors blur. His nature is a chameleon. He is no longer very sure of what he is, because he is no longer very sure of where he lives."[35]

At the same time that these moviemakers created characters who no longer were sure of where they live, they were not without hope. In fact, many saw in their work the folk wisdom of nonwhites that tragedy could be a necessary learning experience that pointed the way to regeneration. In *Ride a Pink Horse* (1947), for example, a war veteran finds in the Southwest a community where corruption and greed rule the establishment, but love and compassion for failure survive among the Indians and Mexicans who promise a more vital organic world. W. R. Burnett explained that in writing the script for *High Sierra* (1941), he tried to capture the mestizo culture of southwest life among the Mexicans and Spanish. Similarly, the author of *Out of the Past* (1947) recalled that the film's plot derived from "Build My Gallows High," a poem written by an anonymous black poet, which inspired the film's central theme of how to confront tragedy with a stoic dignity. Furthermore, Philip Jordan recalled that in drawing the moral of gangster films, he evoked the Yiddish wisdom of "fishren." That is, "I like the guy that's struggling against that doom. I don't like the guy that's passive and crushed." Abraham Polonsky noted as well that the protagonist's death in *Force of Evil* paradoxically showed that

> a kind of liberation and freedom comes from failure. What I tried to do there was to get the feeling that, having reached the absolute moral bottom of commitment there's nothing left to do but commit yourself. There is no longer a problem of identity when you have no identity at all. So your very next step, you must become something.[36]

Billy and John: From Political to Cultural Radicalism

Faced with the withering away of public life, what was that something to be? The answer that emerged after World War II was not simply to critique the new order but to move from political to cultural radicalism, to take the desires focused on the night back into the day. Nowhere was that quest more evident than in the careers of the two most popular moviemakers of the day—John Huston and Billy Wilder. Wilder, for one, was well prepared to live and innovate on the margins. Born in 1906 in the town of Sucha, a Polish town in the Austro-

Hungarian Empire, young Billy matured as part of the marginalized Jewish population. As anti-Semitic politicians came to prominence in Austria, he turned away from a potential career as a lawyer to work as a newspaper reporter interviewing artists and intellectuals, ranging from Sigmund Freud to Arthur Schnitzler. Moving to Berlin during the Weimar Republic, Wilder encountered the world of Bauhaus modernism and wrote and directed films. Once the Nazis launched state-wide repression, he saw that Hitler blamed the "communists" and Jews for everything. The regime removed his "Jewish name" from films, forcing him to flee to the United States.[37]

Well before the Hollywood Red Scare, Wilder thus felt the full effects of state repression and its tragic consequences. Leaving Germany, Wilder left behind relatives who died in concentration camps. He escaped through France to Mexico where a judge, who Wilder recalled "looked a little like Will Rogers," admired the movies and let him enter the country. Reflecting back, Wilder saw that "my dream all along was to get to Hollywood which would have happened without Hitler." In his dream city, Wilder worked first for independent studios, then moved over to Paramount. Politically he recalled that "I came to America because I loved Roosevelt," and once in Hollywood participated in the establishment of the Screen Writers Guild. Joining the left-wing causes of the day, he supported the Spanish Loyalists' resistance to fascism and then joined the Anti-Nazi Leagues and later the Committee for the First Amendment that protested the jailing of the Hollywood Ten. In the war he served as an Army officer charged with reeducating the Germans.[38]

Throughout, his career echoed the merging of politics and art that characterized the careers of many artists in New Deal Hollywood. He told one interviewer that while he "loved America," as a writer and director he was aware that people in this society could "become immunized, mechanized, air conditioned" into standard roles. To counter that potential, he drew on a double-voice persona that reflected his awareness that he was an "American, but I have European roots. I become a melange—a word in Vienna of a man who orders a half coffee, half milk." A common Wilder formula echoed that dualism by having two characters meet, then exchange roles and undergo a metamorphosis of personal and political identity. Take his script for *Ninotchka* (1939), which told the story of a young capitalist and a female communist agent, played by Greta Garbo. As they fall in love in Paris, they poke fun at their absolute faiths, leading to a union where they combine the spirit of Marxist ideas with that of business enterprise.[39] A heroine in Wilder's script for *Hold Back the Dawn* (1941) evokes the dream of a new pluralistic America fused to social reform, when she tells her disillusioned lover that

> this is America—for the Rockefellers and the Joneses, for the McGanagles and Frankfurters, for the Jeffersons and the Slovinskis. It's like a lake, clear and fresh that will never get stagnant while new streams are flowing in.[40]

The commitment to cultural and political reform that would make a more just and vital community also placed Wilder on the same track as the other major writer-director of the immediate postwar era. Born in 1906 in Nevada, Missouri, John Huston remembered that his parents and grandparents "knew all the well-known frontier figures" of the nineteenth century. Politically his family found their roots in a "federalist tradition" in which the citizens created a nation free from aristocracy. At home he learned as a youth that the nation's "founding fathers were sacred figures," and his grandfather served as a Union officer in the Civil War dedicated to saving a republic rooted in free labor and free men. After the Union victory, John's grandfather moved west "in search of fresh pastures," while his aunts taught him to recite the "Bill of Rights by heart."[41] Symbolic of that faith, his aunts placed their father's Civil War sword in a place of honor in the living room, recalling family struggles to realize a society grounded in freedom. In assessing the impact of this family background on his politics and moviemaking, he noted, "I come from a frontier background. I feel constrained in the presence of too many rules, severe rules they distress me. I like the sense of freedom. I don't particularly seek the ultimate freedom of the anarchist, but I'm impatient with rules that result from prejudice."[42]

Against this background, Huston saw that the rise of the new corporate order generated a crisis that demanded a rethinking of both politics and culture. To free himself from Anglo-Saxon, Victorian culture, young Huston roamed Mexico where he came to admire the red flags flying over peasant houses in the wake of the Mexican revolution. Coming home, he pursued a career as a modern painter with Stanton Macdonald-Wright. Working in a synchromist style, Macdonald-Wright taught his students to create color in receding planes of interaction. He also insisted that his students copy the contrapposto of Michelangelo and emulate the cubist compositions of Paul Cézanne. Moving into a world of avant-garde art, Huston said that reading James Joyce's *Ulysses* was "probably the greatest experience that any book has ever given me, doors fell open." Here he learned that liberation involved freeing the mind from inappropriate cultural forms imposed from the top down.[43]

In the twenties Huston also complemented artistic innovation with an admiration for the art of racial minorities and the promotion of art dedicated to cultural change. Joining his father Walter Huston at the Provincetown Players and watching the cast develop Eugene O'Neill plays, Huston recalled that what he "learned there during those weeks of rehearsals would serve me the rest of my life." O'Neill's work described how the task of modern men was to redefine themselves in relation to outsiders and minorities. Huston's most important innovation was his validation of characteristics that whites considered to be the inferior characteristics of racial minorities. On the stage performers portrayed white heroes as men who disciplined their body and emotions, while minorities who expressed their bodily impulses were deemed inferior. To shatter these illusions, Huston studied with a black tap dancer who taught him and other performers the latest Harlem dance steps and performing styles. Once official institutions collapsed in the Depression, Huston met Howard Koch—one of the screenwriters for *Casablanca*—who cast Huston in a play of his that was being produced by the Federal Theatre Arts Company. *The Lonely Man* had a "CIO labor theme" with the "fantastic premise," as Koch saw it, "of the return of young Lincoln to our contemporary world to find that slavery still existed," leading the "great emancipator . . . to extend the concept of freedom to all races and segments of our society." Not long after, Huston joined Koch in Hollywood where they combined moviemaking with radical union politics.[44]

By the late thirties and war years, Huston participated in antifascist crusades and joined in intellectual circles that included emigrés from fascism, such as Thomas Mann, Bertolt Brecht, and Albert Einstein. Working as a screenwriter, Huston and his friend William Wyler wrote a script based on Oliver La Farge's novel of a young Navajo involved in race mixing, *Laughing Boy*. When the studios turned it down, Huston wrote a script that portrayed P. T. Barnum as a prime example of the "American dream of conquest and Manifest Destiny." But when producers altered the original idea, he worked on *Juarez* (1939) to dramatize a "contest of ideologies" in the Mexican revolution. Huston called himself "a Jeffersonian Democrat espousing ideals similar to those of Benito Juarez," such as a need to secure a republican democracy by redistributing land and ending prejudice across the races.[45]

From writing scripts he graduated to both writing and directing his own films, the pattern that characterized his best work for the remainder of his life. His first production was an adaptation of Dashiell Hammett's *The Maltese Falcon* in 1941. It told the story of a detective, Sam Spade, played by Humphrey Bogart, who embodied, in a society corrupted by greed, the virtuous, if cynical, citizen. The coming of the war, however, saw Huston subsuming criticism of domestic arrangements in favor of the ideal of unity. Working to convert the country, he helped write *Sergeant York* and *Across the Pacific*. Each dramatized a shift from isolation to internationalism, from class conflict to the making of a wartime consensus across races to defeat the enemy.

If Huston assisted in building the wartime consensus, he soon began to regret the consequences of that effort. The first indication that he had helped to create a monster occurred when Huston enlisted in the United States Army Signal Corps. On the Italian front, he made *The Battle of San Pietro* (1945), a documentary that told the story of "democracy's soldiers" advancing up a hill. On the way, German heavy artillery kills hundreds of infantrymen. Soon the Army banned the film. Though Huston claimed "I wanted in the war to kill as many Germans as possible," the film was not seen in public during the war years. A similar dilemma occurred when he directed another documentary, *Let There Be Light* (1946), about soldiers suffering psychological effects from combat. Many commended the film for its dignified and realistic portrayal of black soldiers who had been damaged in combat. Throughout the film Huston showed psychiatry as a miracle cure. Yet the Army banned this film as well because, as Huston saw it, the officers did not want to alter the "warrior myth" that men returned healthy from battle.[46]

His disillusion with the military paled before his awareness that the anticommunist crusade assaulted republican values. Coming home from the war, he supported strikes in Hollywood and the nation. When Congress called the Hollywood Ten to testify, he helped mobilize the Committee for the Defense of the First Amendment to protest. Next he became the political manager in southern California of Henry Wallace's Progressive campaign for president. Speaking before a Wallace rally, Huston argued that with anticommunism riding high, this was "not the atomic age, but the age of fear," for "international monopolists that were behind Hitler and Goering didn't die with either of them." Rather, the German trusts and their American counterparts and collaborators resurfaced as "greedy men who put property rights above human rights."[47]

Along with other progressives, Huston felt the full effects of the cultural side of the anticommunist crusade. While he believed that communists were "tedious and boring," he believed that they too had a "right to express their views." It was the anticommunists who created the new "atmosphere of fear" that prevented citizens from "coming to the aid of a few people who were fighting to save democracy." The effect was the Red Scare, which destroyed "one of the great democratic waves of this country, which has never really gotten over it." The "accusers" he saw as those who caused a great deal of "harm to themselves" and the industry. He also believed that the anticommunists wished to create a polity wherein "our beliefs are the only right ones in an otherwise wrong world." In fact, he experienced the full brunt of their effort to control the screen when the Cold Warriors condemned his film *We Were Strangers* (1949) as "a cleverly disguised piece of propaganda that advances the communist line." The story concentrated on an American hero, played by John Garfield, who supports black and Spanish revolutionaries in Cuba. To convey the democratic roots of the revolutionary cause, the film opened with a quotation from Thomas Jefferson to the effect that rebellion against tyrants was "obedience to God."[48]

Despite the evocation of a founding father's republican faith, the film earned the ire of a women's group that complained that the "objectives of the independent company responsible for this production invite public disapproval and official investigation. It is a very shocking, depressing and evil film." Next the *Hollywood Reporter* chimed in, seeing it as "a shameful book of Marxian Dialectics, and the heaviest dish of Red Theory ever served up to audiences outside the Soviet Union." Its aim, the editor wrote, was to undermine "today's governments that are friendly to the United States." Huston's producers responded, noting that a people whose own ancestors created a revolution should have no trouble supporting revolution in Latin America.[49]

The assault on dissenters did not stop with condemning their work. In the wake of congressional investigations, the militant Republican stalwart Cecil B. De Mille demanded that the Directors Guild conform to the Taft-Hartley Act provisions that members swear a loyalty oath. The board asked for a show of hands of all directors who supported the resolution. Later Huston wrote that the vote changed his life, since "it was stupid and the sole purpose it served was to take the liberals' voices away. . . . The rumor was circulated that all those who were against a show of hands were pro-communist. And everyone there supported the hand vote, except for me and Billy Wilder who was seated next to me. There were two of us against one hundred and there were

whispers in the room. We were communists. That was the last Directors Guild meeting I ever attended. The sad part of the story is that
the accusers . . . dirtied the soul of America."[50]

The Medium Is the Message

The cumulative impact of the Cold War meant that Wilder and Huston
devised cinematic forms that undermined official values. In the process
both learned how to evade what Huston called the "cannibals" who
owned the large studios and Cold War censorship demands. Describing the key to success as a filmmaker, Huston explained that a "successful director must have a part in the formation of the script. The
blueprint and the building are parts of the same process, and the mural
on the wall must carry out the architect's design."[51]

Besides seeking control over the story and its execution, Huston and
Wilder found that freedom came by working on location rather than
in the studio. Liberated from what he saw as the "tyranny" of the corporate art and publicity departments, Huston created on location an
atmosphere dedicated to group improvisation. Like the abstract expressionist painters and beat novelists of the day, Huston believed that
in the making of a film "improvisation is necessary." Location filming
thus allowed one to "take advantage of the terrain, of the things that
the settings can give you." In making *The Treasure of the Sierra Madre*
(1948), he took the crew to Mexican villages where they found a place
"to improvise from the imagination rather than the script." Here the
goal was neither to "impose" roles nor ask players to "duplicate me."
Rather, as the performers learned their lines, Huston encouraged them
to improvise and experiment with their roles.

Huston believed that through improvisation and spontaneity the
personality could reconnect with the body and recover the spirit of
play. As Huston explained, "I guess what I am trying to do with this
constant changing, is to try to put to work more my imagination, or
at least allow my imagination the liberty of play, which is me, my body
. . . to live and flower."[52] The daytime world of work subordinated
bodily desires, but the film medium itself carried the capacity to shatter
that division. Motion pictures, Huston said, "have a great deal in common with our physiological and psychological processes—more so
than any other medium. It is almost as if there was a reel of film behind
our eyes. As though our thoughts were projected onto the screen." To
convey visual images that resembled the way the mind worked, Huston
would eliminate sharp cuts that differentiated individuals from one another and create long scenes that tied things and people into a rhythm.

Here he saw that the "work of tl.c camera with the actors . . . amounts to a dance—panning, dollying, following the movement of the actors with grace not cutting. There's a choreography to it."[53]

If Huston developed an interdependent choreography, the effect was to reveal the interrelation of things in a dynamic relationship. By breaking down all sharp moral dichotomies, Huston and Wilder were in effect following the modernist strategy of developing forms that transcend the capacity of reason to isolate people and objects into set categories distinct from one another. Instead, they developed a style that visually undermined all fixed roles and symbols of cultural author-ity, creating a world that was more in flux than fixed in eternal forms and structures. Nowhere was this more evident than in Huston's and Wilder's casting "against type." Both realized that producers cast play-ers in formulaic roles because, as Huston explained, the stars radiated a clear "symbol of something" to the audience.[54] Yet they also saw that a star's predictable persona in the postwar era failed to provide a guide for behavior or for attaining inner satisfaction.

To encourage the viewer to rethink inherited and prescribed social roles, both artists followed the modernist strategy of confusing the im-age of a thing with its intrinsic meaning. Only in films the "thing" was a star's expected formulaic role. So Wilder convinced Barbara Stan-wyck against her will to shed her image of the noble heroine and play instead the adulterous killer in *Double Indemnity*. Similarly, Huston cast Humphrey Bogart against his normal type of the stoic hero in favor of a character whose lust for money turns him into an irrational killer in *The Treasure of the Sierra Madre*. Conversely, when Huston adapted Stephan Crane's novel *The Red Badge of Courage* for the screen in 1951, he cast the most decorated soldier of World War II, Audie Murphy, as a cowardly infantryman. When making Arthur Mill-er's *The Misfits*, Huston cast Clark Gable against his type of the heroic man in favor of an alienated cowboy who has to learn that the "good guys" are the problem rather than the solution. Both Wilder and Hus-ton also used popular music as a counterpoint to audiences' standard expectations. The victorious Union soldiers in *The Red Badge of Cour-age* thus conquer the enemy while the musical score evokes sadness. The result was, according to the composer,

> I come along and tell the audience, with sad music, what is so good about this? I make a little ridiculous the whole idea of one American killing another American.[55]

These converging forms—the baroque style that linked all things together, the casting of stars against type, the linkage of film style to bodily feelings—all combined to make viewers active rather than passive spectators. In contrast to the style of balanced compositions and concentration on one focal point typical of the biblical epics of Cecil B. De Mille, both Wilder and Huston often shot scenes off-center or at eye level, or they moved the camera inside the frame so that the images appeared as an extension of the viewer's eyes. In *The Treasure of the Sierra Madre* Huston staged a bloody fistfight between three men, taking each one's point of view. Or he emphasized multiple viewpoints where the players' speech, images, and actions overlapped, while shadows cut across objects and bodies, ensuring that viewers saw and felt the ambiguity of modern life. In order to heighten instability and flux, the background and foreground often remained opaque to suggest, as Huston saw it, that life was a "process" rather than a static entity.[56] Finally, he avoided standard closures by ending a scene before performers finished their lines, leaving the viewers' imaginations to fill in the void. After watching *We Were Strangers,* a critic observed that "again and again, thanks to perspective and dramatic use of depth, one finds oneself not so much looking at the scene but exploring inside of it."[57]

None of these aesthetic innovations were new, but in a period when mainstream studio directors like De Mille evoked a closed, classical style, the works of Huston and Wilder showed that the dialogical techniques that had informed moviemaking in the thirties remained a way to undermine the closed worldview informing public and personal life in the Cold War. Huston explained that he wanted his films to show "broad social conditions" so that viewers would "reflect upon the significant ideas about place and time. . . . Then I make every effort to enliven the dialogue . . . contrasting different actions, different voices, different colors. You actualize choreography and you move the eye of the audience with your camera until you reveal a second group and something beyond this to more movement."[58] The total effect asked viewers to interject play and passion into set social roles, thereby revitalizing daily life.

At a time when mainstream moviemakers reassigned cultural and social authority to the wealthy, complete with English accents and proper diction, it was not accidental that Huston and Wilder both continued to celebrate the beauty of vernacular speech and play, even in the most tragic and deadly situations. Wilder's *Double Indemnity* (1944), for example, depicts the first contact of two potential lovers. What ensues is a romantic competition between two people who will eventually commit adultery and murder. Yet Wilder makes the two scoundrels lovable through their vernacular speech and play. In one classic scene Phyllis (Barbara Stanwyck's character) asks Neff, an insurance salesman (played by Fred MacMurray), if he likes her name. Neff answers "may be . . . after driving it around the block a few times." When Neff asks if he can see Phyllis later, the answer yields one of the great scenes of competitive dialogue in film noir:

> Phyllis: There's a speed limit in this town, Mr. Neff, forty-five miles an hour.
> Neff: How fast was I going, officer?
> Phyllis: I'd say around ninety.
> Neff: Suppose you get down off your motorcycle and give me a ticket?
> Phyllis: Suppose I let you off with a warning this time?
> Neff: Suppose it doesn't take?
> Phyllis: Suppose I have to whack you over the knuckles?
> Neff: Suppose I bust out crying and put my head on your shoulder?
> Phyllis: Suppose you try putting it on my husband's shoulder?
> Neff: That tears it.[59]

The celebration of vernacular slang similarly asks viewers to sympathize not with the law but with the criminals and, in doing so, to question prescribed codes of success and social roles. The characters in *Double Indemnity,* for example, have already attained what would pass for a happy ending in most other films. The hero is a well-paid insurance agent; the heroine possesses a lavish Los Angeles home and a spouse who is a prosperous provider. Though they live the good life in the sun, however, they are deeply discontent. The pervasive feeling of meaninglessness and anxiety leads them to kill Phyllis's husband for the insurance money that will allow them to escape to Mexico. When their best-laid plans fail, the lovers' quest ends in death. Critics observed that this was more than a normal crime film. They recognized that Barbara Stanwyck and Fred MacMurray were cast in "completely different roles." Symbolic of that reversal, Stanwyck played a blonde-haired killer. Given that conventional icons identified blondes with virtue, Stanwyck noted that "I had always visualized murderesses as brunettes, but apparently blondes are considered harder and more unscrupulous, this season at least."

Besides reversing casting types and visual icons, the film begins the tale at the end. Wilder commented on this technique when he explained that "by identifying the criminals right off and by identifying ourselves with them we can concentrate on what follows—their effort to escape the net. . . . I think that the key to the film's success is what happens to MacMurray happens to us simultaneously." Critics at the time saw that by identifying the viewer with the outlaws, the director "broke the taboos of the industry." Wilder reinforced the message by showing that the criminals were not psychotic or even "immature" but "as grown up as you or I." Casting them as ordinary people allowed the viewer to see them as "ourselves." The result was, as one trade journalist observed, that Wilder "broke open a door closed to all those connected with the motion pictures. He has made the hero and heroine of his stark drama a pair of murderers. There is no gloss to their wrongdoing, no sugar frosting to make palatable their dark deeds. It is a drama which no other in recent memory brings to mind."[60]

Wilder used various strategies to compel viewers to identify with this "pair of murderers." To begin with, the story is told from Neff's perspective. As he will do again in *Sunset Boulevard* (1950), Wilder opens *Double Indemnity* as the hero slowly dies. While the dying man tells his story, the film unfolds as a flashback that explores why a respectable man came to such grief. Walter Neff gathers sympathy because he is a new man, the white-collar worker confined in a corporate business world of straight lines and rational structures. Inside the boxes Walter represses his instincts to conform to business routine, while Neff's lover, a young and beautiful woman, remains confined to the new privatized home. All around them social roles demand that non-Caucasians and immigrants remain subordinate. Young Phyllis's husband does not allow his daughter to date an Italian named "Zaccati," Neff's boss delights in catching a poor southern European immigrant who cheats on his insurance, and the servants and maids are all African Americans.[61]

Within a world where set social roles have been restored, the central characters have the status that comes with success and white skin. Yet in spite of having "everything," they feel confined and trapped in "tradition." While Neff's boss and father figure, Keyes, an insurance investigator, promotes rational egoism, the protagonists exalt the claims of the libido and erotic passion. Throughout Wilder uses visual styles and incidents to ask audiences to identify with their rebellion. As Neff and Phyllis murder her husband, the getaway car will not start. After repeated turnings of the ignition key, the motor finally turns over, and both the killers and the audience breathe easy. Another scene shows Phyllis hiding behind a half-opened door as Neff speaks to the insurance investigator. The viewer sees Phyllis, Neff, and Keyes in the same frame, but the composition and multiple viewpoints compel viewers to hope the outlaws will evade detection.[62]

Double Indemnity (1944). The shot exemplifies Billy Wilder's strategy to have the audience identify with the killers. One murderer, played by Barbara Stanwyck, hides behind the door, while the other, played by Fred MacMurray, tries to convince the insurance investigator, played by Edward G. Robinson, that he has nothing to hide. (Courtesy Academy of Motion Picture Arts and Sciences)

Ironically, Wilder reveals how the characters' internalization of the consumer dreams of the forties leads to their tragic defeat. Both Phyllis and Neff can imagine no other alternative than to kill for money and escape into a private world of romance, but that dream brings instead death and tragedy. In this self-referential world, such films appear to serve as a form of self-criticism. Both Wilder and Huston helped create the American myths of class consensus and the consumer democracy that Cold Warriors manipulated to repress dissent. In response, several of their films feature characters whose rational plans end in entrapment. In Wilder's *Ace in the Hole* (1951), *Sunset Boulevard,* and *Double Indemnity,* the antiheroes and vamps build their own self-imposed cages. In *Ace in the Hole* a young journalist exploits an accident in which a Mexican-American war hero lies trapped under a landslide. His desire for money inspires the journalist to create a bogus rescue operation so that he can sell the story. Wilder claimed that he put "news in every picture . . . to open up a problem" and to show the quest for the "'quick buck' and the American mania for making it even if it has to be made on someone's personal tragedy."[63]

Just as the journalist's quest for the "quick buck" leads to defeat, so too the protagonist in Wilder's masterpiece, *Sunset Boulevard,* lives with an older has-been film star, Norma Desmond, who has dreams of a comeback. The young man, as Lois Banner has shown, feels alienated from postwar Hollywood, and his budding romance with a pristine sweetheart encourages him to find happiness in the ideal of marriage and suburban homemaking. Instead, he becomes Norma's gigolo. Suggestive of Wilder's awareness that the consumer culture of the twenties has been revived in the fifties, Norma yearns to work again with Cecil B. De Mille, a major director of the twenties and now again in the fifties. Like De Mille, Norma emulates the styles of the very rich, but it leads to entrapment. In the end the star and the gigolo destroy each other because neither can imagine a viable alternative to the suburban home or highbrow ethos of the rich, a conflict that leads to their self-destruction.[64]

In their work both Wilder and Huston launched the search for such a viable alternative, one that would recover the visions that animated their politics and art in the thirties. One does not have to look further than a film that Huston helped write, *High Sierra* (1941), to find that quest informing his work. The film opens on a newspaper headline and a radio announcer describing the release from prison of "Mad Dog Earle," played by Humphrey Bogart. Soon viewers find that, in contrast to his public portrayal, Earle originally came from a farm, "cultivated, very fertile and rich." As such, Earle stands for the producer and virtuous citizen of the old republic whose land was seized by banks. Confronted with the rise of the new order, a friend says that "times have changed," and Earle responds, "Yeah, sometimes I feel like I don't know what it's about any more." Earle incarnates the spirit of the "last of the A-I guys" in a world of "jitterbugs." In contrast to the country club set and greedy youth, he honors his friends and assists the poor. When corrupt officials and friends betray him, Earle's death evokes sympathy for a displaced but far more virtuous democracy. One critic got the point, noting that the central character was clearly a crimnal, but in the end "it's a wonder the American flag wasn't wrapped around his corpse."[65]

Another film directed and cowritten by Huston, *The Asphalt Jungle* (1950), evoked memories of republican virtue to critique the ethos of liberal capitalism in postwar society. Like the Popular Front itself, the gang includes an intellectual German professor, a poor Italian working-class safecracker who wishes to save his home and family, and an Anglo-Saxon farmer who uses his money to recover his rural homestead lost in the Depression. One critic saw that none of the characters is the hero. Rather, "all of a dozen or so are allotted equal prominence." In contrast to the communal spirit of the gang, the good citizens and police take payoffs from gamblers and corrupt capitalists. A rich lawyer betrays his friends, while the criminals embody virtuous family and pluralistic communal values. One observer commented that in this reversal of expectations, Huston "broke through the iron-bound formula of the gangster picture to basic consideration of the human being. These are living, hopeful people, not sullen, inhumanly distant criminal types." Some found that by asking the audience to side with the outlaws, the production "hypnotized the audience to hobnob with a bunch of crooks and actually sympathize with their personal griefs." But others took a very different tack:

> What strikes this critic as most remarkable about the impact of this extraordinary film is the reality it lends to a cliche subject. The story has been told a thousand times. It conforms to all the precepts of the code by defeating and killing off the criminal protagonists. Yet there is no hint here of the "crime does not pay" homily. Their defeat and death is ours as well.[66]

What was "ours" in "their defeat and death" was the populist communitarianism and resistance to a corrupt society that informed the work and politics of so many in the New Deal years. Nor was that continuity lost on contemporaries. The final scenes of *The Asphalt Jungle* portray a police captain telling the press that only one criminal remains on the loose, but he is "the most dangerous of all, a hardened criminal, a hooligan, a man without human feeling." The captain is referring to Dix Handley. But the audience knows that Dix turned to crime only to recover the rural Eden of a farm lost in the Depression. Dix's quest to recover the heart of the republican land and tradition led Huston to observe that Dix embodied "the Everyman of the movie, the pilgrim lost in the maze of the asphalt jungle trying to get home." To convey that theme, Huston cuts from the police chief's moralizing to Dix bleeding to death and running "home." Here one critic saw that the "screen overflows with compassion and a technique that transcends the boundaries of time." Dix comes home, only to die at the feet of a mare and her colt. Watching these final scenes, James Agee— the celebrated left-wing writer who gained fame describing the dignity

The final scene of John Huston's *The Asphalt Jungle* (1950). As a police captain ensures the public that the savage criminal will be captured, the wounded Dix Handley drives home to recover the family farm lost in the Depression. He dies beneath the feet of a mare and her colt, with the implication that the republican dream has also been destroyed. (Courtesy Academy of Motion Picture Arts and Sciences)

of the folk in the Depression—wrote to Huston to ignore critics of the film. In fact, he went on:

> If anyone tells you that the end is "mawkish" as the *Time* guy did, shit on them for me. I was in uncontrollable tears from the moment the camera pulls away from the two horses through the crowd to the end.[67]

The distinctiveness of Huston's work lay in keeping alive the vision of republican virtue to counter the corrosive cultural authority of liberal capitalists. The heart of that counternarrative of American culture culminated in what was probably his masterpiece, *The Treasure of the Sierra Madre.* Winner of the Academy Awards for both the best direction and screenplay of 1948, Huston adapted a novel written by a German anarchist, B. Traven. The story opens in Tampico, an oil town in Mexico, that has been a battleground between Mexicans and American oil companies. Here a working-class "stiff" named Dobbs has internalized the values of the very rich, complete with a belief in white superiority. Though he has no money, Dobbs refuses to shine shoes, claiming that if he ever stoops to the degraded labor of Mexicans, no "American" will ever hire him. So Dobbs and a friend, Curtin, sell their labor to the builder of an oil rig. But when the owner refuses to pay for their work, they fight him and win their wages.[68]

Although these scenes provide a metaphor for labor-capital conflict, Dobbs's values of white superiority and admiration for the rich signal the downfall of the working class. That tragedy begins when an old prospector, Howard, played by the director's father, Walter Huston, leads the two workers to search for gold in the hinterland. Their journey provides an analogy to the white imperialists who invaded and exploited the Indians. When asked what he will do with his money, Dobbs ignores the natives and says he wants to have the comforts of the rich: their women, luxurious baths, and brown servants. The others are tempted, but Howard and Curtin validate beliefs similar to those of the Indians where a holistic community works together and where equality and play interact in a continuous but vital tradition. Curtin recalls the memories of home that evoke this populist paradise, noting that

> one summer when I was a kid I worked in the San Joaquin Valley. It was something. Hundreds of people—old and young—whole families working together. After the day's work we used to build big bonfires and sit around 'em and sing to guitar music, 'til morning sometimes. You'd go to sleep, wake up and sing, and go to sleep again. Everybody had a wonderful time. . . . Ever since, I've had a hankering to be a fruit grower. Must be grand watching your own trees put on leaves, come into blossom, and bear . . . watching the fruit get big and ripe on the bough, ready for picking.

Again and again these visions of owning one's own labor in a cooperative commonwealth come into conflict with Dobbs's growing and often violent resistance to cooperation with others. Despite Dobbs's objections, Curtin and Howard insist that after they dig mines in the earth, they, like the Indians, must restore nature back to its original state. At the same time Howard demands that all share equally in the fruits of their labor, again like the Indians. Mixing humor and work, Howard rescues an Indian child from disease. The natives take Howard

John Huston's *The Treasure of the Sierra Madre* (1948). Humphrey Bogart portrays the prospector crazed with greed for gold but temporarily confined by his companions, played by Walter Huston and Tim Holt. (Courtesy Academy of Motion Picture Arts and Sciences)

into their community as a wise man and elder. Highlighting the viability of similar dreams at "home," Curtin reads a letter written by a dead prospector's wife:

> Dear Jim . . . Little Jimmy misses his daddy. Almost as much as I. He keeps asking, "When is Daddy coming home?" You say if you do not make a real find this time you'll never go again. I cannot begin to tell you how much my heart rejoices at these words. Now I feel free to tell you I have never thought any material treasure, no matter how great, is worth these long separations. . . . I do hope you are back for the harvest. Of course, I'm hoping that you will at last strike it rich. It is high time for luck to start smiling upon you, but just in case she doesn't remember we've already found life's treasures. Forever yours, Helen.

Not long after, the clash between communal virtues and Dobb's acquisitive individualism leads to disaster. Vowing to share and share alike, Curtin and Dobbs depart for the city to cash in the gold they have discovered. On the way Dobbs's greed takes over his mind and renders him insane. He knocks out Curtin and wanders across the desert to a waterhole. There Dobbs encounters Mexican bandits whom he earlier disdained as foolish dolts that a white man could trick at will. Dobbs fails to take the Mexican outlaws seriously and they kill him. Ironically, the bandits mistakenly think Dobbs's saddlebags contain sand and empty them, unaware of the gold; later, both Howard and Curtin arrive to find gold blowing in the wind. The old man laughs hysterically in the face of fate. Undefeated, he will return to the Indians, but before departing he tells Curtin to find the dead prospector's wife and hopefully recover life's true "treasure": a republic of love, community, and independence.[69]

The Children of Noir

Paradoxically *The Treasure of the Sierra Madre* also revealed the manner in which the recovery of a holistic republic lost its hold on many moviemakers on the left. Despite the hidden dreams that surface in the daylight world, Howard stays in Mexico and Curtin returns to the United States in a vague quest to find the "real treasure" of a populist community in a society permeated with militant anticommunism and conformity. But the effort to assert the continuity of republican dreams and vernacular instincts continued to grow, spreading into the fresh realm of an autonomous postwar youth culture. As Arthur Miller recalled in his autobiography, *Timebends,* the film stars who arose in that period—James Dean, Marilyn Monroe, and Marlon Brando—carried on the search for an alternative culture within society.[70] Describing the contours of that shift, the wife of the director Nicholas Ray explained what led her husband to move from New Deal radicalism to film noir and then into directing the most famous youth culture film of the day, *Rebel Without a Cause:*

> Nick did not like his generation. He thought them betrayers whose acts of betrayal were in his words like asking your kid to jump into your arms and then pulling your arms away. He was more at ease with my generation [the youth of the fifties and sixties] and he seemed to know more about them than I did.[71]

To artists like Ray, youth replaced the insurgent middle and working classes as a viable alternative to postwar culture. In so doing it was not accidental that the youth stars who would embody the counterculture ethos manifested many of the same anxieties and discontent that permeated the outsiders in film noir. Marlon Brando and Marilyn Monroe, for example, started their careers playing tormented, alienated outsiders. In *The Men* (1950) Brando portrayed a disabled veteran trying to adjust to postwar society. Monroe, in turn, gained attention playing tormented "vamps" in *Niagara* (1953) and *Don't Bother to Knock* (1952). In the first, Monroe portrays a demonic wife who schemes with a lover to kill her husband, and in the second, Monroe plays an insane baby-sitter who tries to kill the children in her care and herself. At the end of these films the Brando and Monroe characters are either "cured" or killed, thus restoring normative social values.

What made them and James Dean so successful was that they moved on to portraying characters who took their alienation from the private into the public realm, using the spontaneous self as an ideal to challenge postwar American culture from inside the heart of the fifties. In films like *Rebel Without a Cause* (1955), *East of Eden* (1955), *The Wild One* (1954), *A Streetcar Named Desire* (1951), and *On the Waterfront* (1954), the Dean and Brando characters criticized a generation that asked youth to adjust to the values of acquisitiveness and normative family life. Over and over the protagonists resist what a critic called the "social killing and specialized life that awaits" youth as they mature to adulthood. James Dean in *Rebel Without a Cause* "interrogated all values," while Marlon Brando in *On the Waterfront* played a young man betrayed by his brother and surrogate father. His wounded personality erupts in a taxicab scene where Terry Malloy, played by Brando, tells his brother that their alliance with gangsters has prevented Terry from becoming a "contender," a "somebody," instead of a "bum," which "is what I am."[72]

Marilyn Monroe's career underwent a similar journey. In major films made with Billy Wilder, John Huston, and her husband Arthur Miller, she moved from the vamp to a critic of official gender roles. Wilder, for example, cast her in *The Seven Year Itch* in 1955 where she plays a single woman who has little if any guilt about sex. Since she refuses to conform to men's perception of her as a vamp because she likes sex, she evades men's efforts to control her. Similarly in *The Misfits,* written by Miller and directed by Huston, Monroe emerges as a woman who challenges masculine ideals of power among a group of cowboys who seek to master nature and women. In contrast, Monroe's heroine conceives of the cosmos and male-female relations as indicating nature's diversity and freedom. In the end, she convinces her lover to shed his quest to control nature and to rethink western manhood.

In both Wilder's and Huston's films Marilyn played women who challenge the repression of instincts at the heart of family and public life. Yet now she need not die but converts those around her. Taking this questioning of sex roles one step further in Wilder's *Some Like It Hot* (1959), Monroe plays a jazz singer who compels men to reevaluate their dream of heterosexual love and control over women. To accomplish that task Wilder moved from film noir to comedy by focusing on two male jazz musicians who seduce women to prop up their weak masculinity. After they witness a gangland killing, they disguise themselves as women in a jazz band to escape the mobsters. Moving south, they meet "Sugar," played by Monroe, who, believing they are women, exposes them to women's view of things. Surprise, surprise, the men like this reversal of roles, becoming by the end hybrid figures who break taboos against homosexuality and reversals of normative patterns of male-female relations.[73]

What made Dean, Monroe, and Brando so important was their capacity to bridge the screen and society, restoring mass art and the film star as focal points for a counternarrative of identity. In so doing, each projected a personality style that was not haphazard, for all three studied with Lee Strasberg in the school of Method acting. The Method first developed in European left-wing theater and entered the United States with the rise of the radical Group Theatre in New York in the thirties. All the new youth stars' teachers—Stella Adler, Strasberg, Elia Kazan—began their careers in the Group where artists "felt a need to believe . . . that they were working towards some valuable artistic, social and humanly significant goal." Under the impact of anticommunist politics, however, the civic élan withered and gave way to an effort to challenge society in the realms of culture. Strasberg and Adler sought to attain that goal by linking acting to creating a language for the "unknown" instincts and wishes. By shattering the "psychic chains," as Strasberg called them, that tie artists to "already existing patterns," the actor eroded the divisions between mind and body, generating a road map to a holistic identity.[74]

Transferred onto the screen and into real life, the validation of the instincts placed the new stars in direct opposition to many of the cultural precepts of the new middle-class consensus. All three players embodied a generation maturing in a presumed postwar paradise, which they did not like. Official cultural spokesmen, commented one admirer, thought Marlon Brando odd, but he offered an alternative to the "neurotic patterns of the society." Before we ask, the admirer noted, if "Marlon Brando can be tamed," we need to ask "can Society" change. That is, Brando's craziness provided a refreshing alternative to the repressed craziness of the new organization man and the suburban homemaker.

The importance of the neurotic personality as a viable counter-weight to middle-class family life emerged in an interview James Dean gave in 1955 on the set of *East of Eden*. The director, Elia Kazan, had been a member of the Communist Party and the Group Theatre. In the postwar era, however, Kazan cooperated with Congress to condemn what he saw as communist tyranny. He then turned from political to cultural radicalism as the way to liberate the self. On the way, Kazan saw that Dean and Brando were perfect vessels for expressing his own alien-ation and questioning. In adapting John Steinbeck's novel, Kazan cast Dean as a tormented son rebelling from a father who stood for the religious, patriotic, and Victorian ideals of Anglo-Saxon America.

Taking the lessons of Method acting to heart, Dean told an inter-viewer that his tormented character "is one I warmed up to very quickly, I felt sympathetic associations, felt very close. I considered it a challenge to reveal honestly the things in this part that were part of myself." Dean noted the character was "humanly demonic," like "my-self in that he was filled with a duality, that of evil and goodness." Yet he only learned to achieve goodness through the "sins of the Satanic rather than Puritanic." To a "neurotic person like me acting the role provided a way to express oneself . . . my neuroticism manifests itself in the dramatic. Why do most actors act? To express the fantasies with which they have involved themselves. . . . I hate anything that limits progress or growth. I hate institutions that do this: a way of acting that sets limits, a way of acting that limits a way of thinking. I hope this doesn't make me sound like a communist."[75]

To young people and others who wished to rebel but did not want to "sound like a communist," the turn to the Method and depth psy-chology provided a way to critique the core elements of the postwar consensus, particularly the family. Reporters also saw that the new stars were well prepared for that role. At a time when officials claimed that affluence and the stable home created well-balanced citizens, Dean's father was a poor itinerant laborer who left his young son with relatives on a farm in Indiana. Brando rebelled as an adolescent from what he saw as a confining Midwestern family. His attitude led his fa-ther to enroll his wayward son in a military school. There administra-tors soon expelled Brando for his unwillingness to conform to the masculine discipline appropriate for a young soldier.

Growing up in a poverty-stricken working-class world, Monroe en-dured an especially nightmarish family life: her father deserted the

James Dean wearing his red jacket in Nicholas Ray's *Rebel Without a Cause* (1955). Notice the intense but fragile look that Dean conveyed as the tormented teenager in the postwar era. (Courtesy Academy of Motion Picture Arts and Sciences)

home, her mother went insane, and Monroe was placed in an orphanage. Released, she then grew up under the care of strict aunts in poverty conditions. Little wonder that Monroe and the other youth stars spurred writers to comment that they evoked on screen and off the vulnerable identity of the new generation. Praising Dean's intense performance in *Rebel Without a Cause,* a critic saw that he had a "capacity to get into the skin of youthful pain, torment and bewilderment that is not often to be encountered." Critics, in turn, saw that Monroe's "beauty and inferiority complex gave her a great mystery" that explained her appeal to millions. Others saw that Brando evoked the torment of the lost generation.[76]

In a highly personal way, each of the new stars embodied the fragile identities and sense of loss permeating film noir. But in films as in real life, they took that rebellion directly into public life, refusing to be repressed. Though that stance often led to self-destructive behavior and a disturbing unwillingness to remember lines and arrive at work on time, they were distinct among film stars in that they rebelled from Hollywood itself. Unlike in the past when stars praised Hollywood as the summit of their dreams, the postwar youth rebels labeled it a middle-class prison. Reporters described how Brando refused to pose for fan pictures or conform to dress codes; instead, he wore working-class blue jeans and t-shirts. When questioned about his attire, Brando observed that the "marvellous thing about Hollywood is that these people are recognized as sort of the norm, while I am the flip. . . . I'm not slick. It's all so artificial." The result was that reporters saw Brando as a star who "has never adhered to convention, he will always be a puzzle."[77]

James Dean provided an even greater puzzle. A critic noted that in making *East of Eden,* "Dean was an enigma in Hollywood . . . he avoided publicity, wore the clothes he thought most comfortable and refused to conform to the public idea of what a star should be and do." Another saw that "there is no telling how he will react to any situation. Sometimes he jumps up and down, sometimes he giggles like a lunatic and sometimes he is surly and offended."[78] How then was one to react? If Dean and Brando refused to be conventional men, Monroe refused to conform to proper femininity.

With a modernized Victorian ethic reinfusing Hollywood, females were either "vamps" or "good girls." But Monroe refused to fit either. Photographers in the war had turned her into a "pin-up" who embodied the "girl back home." By the fifties, however, she rebelled. Monroe admitted that she rejected bras, did not wear nightgowns to bed, and did not feel ashamed for posing in the nude. Inquiring about her ideal home, reporters discovered that Monroe delighted in disorder and let her yard plants grow wild rather than have them tamed and manicured. And, of course, she liked rather than tolerated men's sexuality. Indicative of the confusion she had sparked, articles appeared with titles like "Hollywood Against Marilyn Monroe," and when she spoke of her nonmarital sexuality, Joan Crawford attacked her brazenness as subversive. But Monroe told interviewers that sex was "wholly natural . . . and I'd rather go along with nature for there is nothing to be ashamed of." A producer reprimanded her for wearing a red, low-cut dress. "You're a star and you should choose your clothes carefully. The dress you're wearing—well it's—er—not quite right." She innocently answered, "Why, don't you like red?"[79]

Producers and reporters uncomfortable with women's humor and rebellion from personal decorum tried to dismiss this behavior as the antics of youth who would in time "grow up." Yet the problem was

The Wild One (1954). Brando played a motorcycle gang leader who spoke in the black bop style of the "hipsters," popularizing in the process the teenage dress of t-shirts, leather boots, and black leather jackets for the youth of the United States and the world. (Courtesy Academy of Motion Picture Arts and Sciences)

that the youth stars never seemed to want to be "mature." In fact, they bent the racial and gender categories that defined the core of normal life. Magazine and newspaper reporters registered surprise that Brando, Dean, and Monroe read Shakespeare, loved classical music, and admired modern painters, yet each enjoyed the rough world of the city streets.[80] Each wore blue jeans and white t-shirts that linked them with the working class. They also crossed racialized cultural barriers as Brando and Dean played the bongo drums associated with Latin-American and Afro-Cubano musicians. All three enjoyed black jazz and bebop clubs and admired the "beatniks." When Marlon Brando made *The Wild One,* fans around the globe emulated his black leather jacket, boots, and slang dialect. On the set interviewers found that Brando enjoyed his new role as a "cool bebopper" who called them "Daddy-o." If he grew restless, he would take his leave by saying, "I'm a cool hipster, Cornball, I just gotta go."[81]

This style countered the middle-class whiteness permeating respectable Hollywood. By validating vernacular working-class and black culture, Brando, Dean, and Monroe restored the image of the hybrid star. Critics of *The Wild One* likened Brando's role as the leader of a motorcycle gang that terrorizes a small town to that of the inhabitants of a "nut house," or "ape men," or "zombies." Others observed that when Brando spoke like a "white Negro," "English subtitles under the jive talk would have benefitted such squares as this reviewer." Similarly, Brando's portrayal of a Polish-American worker in Elia Kazan's adaptation of Tennessee Williams's *A Streetcar Named Desire* spurred a critic to call Brando a "sullen, likeable 'Pollack'—a big hunk of man, rough, crude, and primitively passionate."[82]

Still others observed that Monroe was loved in proportion to her capacity to reveal that women were also "primitively passionate" and her refusal to conform to the ideal of the postwar home. At a time when moralists prescribed that a sexually attractive woman contain her emancipation in the home, Monroe did marry and hope to have children. But she refused to become either Mrs. Miller or Mrs. Joe Di Maggio and kept her self-created name, Marilyn Monroe, as well as her thriving career. Like the other two rebels, she also saw that money served less to enhance one's status than provide the basis for self-expression and the flowering of a generous egalitarianism. She shocked studio heads when she recalled that one day she "was walking down the street when this soldier looked at me and gasped. I could tell he was lonely, so I invited him to come and watch us work. He showed up every day and we had long talks about his hometown." Her ideals carried over into race relations. She told a nightclub owner reluctant to hire blacks that if he employed Ella Fitzgerald, she would sit in the first row to attract audiences. Crowds came, Ella broke the color line, and Marilyn applauded.[83]

Throughout the fifties, the new stars helped to reassert the identification of mass culture with resistance, gaining their support from the rise of a new autonomous youth culture. Trade reporters and fan magazines saw that what made the films of Dean, Brando, and Monroe so successful was that they appealed to a fresh sociological group: postwar adolescents. Not only did teenagers constitute a "new" audience, they also reversed the decline in audience numbers that began in 1948.[84]

The work of these three stars gained popularity by giving form and meaning to the new youth culture. Together they restored a critical edge to mass art and celebrated once again the hybrid personality.

Since they were also creating a language for what did not yet exist, critics observed that their work was "hard to pin down" and did not "fit any of the old categories." Assessing the Brando character in *The Wild One,* a trade critic commented that his and his gang's life "proves to be annoyingly pointless. There is no rhyme or reason given for their actions other than 'hotheads are hotheads.'" In fact, they "talk in a peculiar jive lingo. . . . It was a film that stands in no particular direction."[85] The result of this apparent chaos was that plots that linked popular art with youth and cultural renewal had risen from zero to over 10 percent from the forties through the fifties (appendix 2, fig. 24).

At this point it is useful to consider the question with which we began: Why was it that Arthur Miller believed that under the impact of the Cold War, Americanism had been transformed? A crisis in national identity and politics had emerged as the Cold War legitimized big business and destroyed the utopian dreams of the New Deal years. A conservative crime film mirrored the cultural war against the expectations of the New Deal era. But with film attendance in decline, John Huston and Billy Wilder kept alive the cultural critique of liberal capitalism and the privatized home. By the fifties, left-wing moviemakers lifted these hopes from the underground of film noir into the light of day. Helping to create a new rebellious youth culture, they recovered a counterculture that came to focus on the development of youth stars who in effect replaced the proletariat and insurgent middle class as a focal point for cultural radicalism. Even the tragic death of Dean in a car crash and the suicide of Monroe added to the sensibility of a generation whose dreams had died young, but whose memory lived on to inspire the future.

Two events suggest how that dynamic operated in the fifties. When James Dean died in a car crash, a young admirer wrote to a fan magazine that the youthful rebel gave voice to a discontent that as yet had no name: "To us teenagers Dean was a symbol of the fight to make a niche for ourselves in the world of adults. Something in us that is being sat upon by convention and held down was in Dean free for all the world to see."[86] Still later Arthur Miller would recall that during the period he was writing the script for *The Misfits,* his wife Marilyn lived in a world of narcissistic isolation, assaulted on the outside by scolding guardians of morality and on the inside by desires and emotions that had no name. Yet even after Monroe's suicide Miller clearly saw that in a society where the course of history and utopian dreams went wrong, she held out a vision of hope, for

> Marilyn lived in the belief that she was precisely what had to be denied and covered up in the conventional world. . . . She relied on the most ordinary layer of the audience, the working people, the guys in the bars, the housewives in the trailers bedevilled by unpaid bills, the high school kids mystified by explanations they could not understand, the ignorant—as she saw them—tricked and manipulated masses. She wanted them to feel they'd gotten their money's worth when they saw a picture of hers.[87]

With that, one can see that a postwar counterculture challenging the consumer paradise had been born, setting the stage for the unique quality of the political and cultural wars of the sixties and beyond—a development that will be briefly outlined in the epilogue.

Epilogue
Reimagining Postwar America

The goal of this study has been to build upon, but also advance, the work of my fellow cultural and film historians. Throughout I have found that we need to understand the popular arts generally, and the movies in particular, as a new institution that altered the boundaries of public life and national identity. To grasp the meaning of our current battles over culture and media images, we have to see that moviemaking has been part of a competitive civic sphere where artists and audiences engaged in a contested terrain. Prior to the Depression, the United States possessed what Benedict Anderson has called a nationalism that was "incompletely imagined."[1] That is, the builders of modern nations had to dismantle the old rulers' house and replace it with a better one, using the materials that their masters utilized. In the most ethnically and racially divided society in the western world, Americanism in the nineteenth and early twentieth centuries revolved around concepts of a republican producers' democracy where citizens controlled their work and engaged in governing. The ideal of citizens capable of exercising control over their property in opposition to monopoly capital rested on white Anglo-Saxon norms from which the new immigrants from eastern and southern Europe and nonwhites were excluded. Until the advent of mass culture broke down these divisions, Anglo-Saxon opinion makers used the republican creed or liberal capitalist ideologies to exclude minorities, who were so divided among themselves as to pose virtually no threat to the rise of the new corporate order in the twenties.[2]

The movies contributed to making an art and public space that allowed the divided and excluded groups, particularly the new immigrants, to begin to express themselves through the voices and imaginations of artists who used the mechanism of the market to appeal to the taste of such groups. However, the eruption of new cultural and political styles from the bottom, particularly the rise of filmmakers catering to the class consciousness of workers, spurred the Anglo-Saxon bourgeoisie and corporate leaders to regain control over public symbols. In the aftermath ambitious showmen of Jewish stock made Hollywood in the twenties a place where a more consolidated industry unfolded, and film stars showed that in leisure one could find release from the routinization of work and a stratified class order. The answer was to uplift mass amusements and the home with the historicist symbols of high art derived from European aristocrats and the wealthy. At the grassroots, racial and ethnic groups could reinterpret mass-produced images to suit their own desires. But at the point of production, Hollywood films tended to serve the interests of corporate leaders, making a consumer culture that preserved rather than undermined their cultural authority.

The coming of the Great Depression, however, delegitimized the wealthy and the Hollywood dreams the upstart Jewish producers had done so much to promote. It soon became obvious to many that to make the wheels of industry run, purchasing power had to be spread among the masses.[3] The film industry became a primary institution for creating an alternative Americanism that justified the people's right to abundance to counter a corrupt capitalism. This alteration in values began as audiences rejected the highbrow film and theater styles of the wealthy. In response, moviemakers created sound films that accomplished two remarkable goals. First, they provided a mechanism where the dialects and vernacular arts of the lower class moved from local communities to gain a hearing in the national civic sphere. Second, stars like Will Rogers and productions featuring heroes like Nick Charles collapsed the barriers between the vernacular and high arts, comedy and drama, that informed the Victorian artistic canon. Well before the New Deal came to power, sound films thus created composite characters who did what seemed impossible: They made a public sphere that allowed artists and their audiences to reimagine the boundaries between the margins and the center.

Together, these findings suggest that we have to revise the analysis and theories of the functioning of the film industry that have guided scholars' previous formulations. Assuming that the American Way permeating the postwar era informed the twentieth century as a whole, film and cultural historians, ranging from Neal Gabler and Michael Rogin to Robert Sklar and Warren Susman, have taught us that the popular arts from the thirties to the fifties promoted the ideals of liberal capitalism and classlessness.[4] In his famed explorations of Depression-era popular art, Susman argued that the movies and radio forged a consumer culture rooted in the ethos of Anglo-Saxon individualism and backward-looking myths and symbols. Neal Gabler similarly observed in his study of Jewish film producers that studio owners assimilated to a "shadow America, one which idealized every old glorifying bromide about the country" and "colonized the American imagination." Michael Rogin incorporated that view into scholarship dealing with race, pointing out that Jewish moviemakers and other immigrants perpetuated stereotypes that allowed them to assimilate to a static nationality rooted in white superiority.

So when postwar scholars asked what impact the movies had, the answer was that corporate leaders and deluded audiences promoted a false consciousness that took spectators' attention away from issues of class inequality and cultural experimentation. The same analysis has informed the work of the most prominent school of film historians. To these scholars the singular "genius" of the Hollywood system revolved around producers' capacity to infuse plots and movie genres with uniform narratives and visual styles for five decades.[5] The most cited example for this reading has been *The Classical Hollywood Cinema: Film Style and Mode of Production to 1960* by David Bordwell, Janet Staiger, and Kristen Thompson. Using a theoretical paradigm derived from Karl Marx, they argue that the modes of production determine the ideological content of a universal type of story. They state in their introduction that "we cannot presuppose that the periods used to write political or social history will demarcate the history of an art. That is, there is no immediate compulsion to define a 'cinema of the 1930's' as drastically different from that of 'the 1940's,' or to distinguish pre–World War II Hollywood style from postwar Hollywood style." To prove this hypothesis, they viewed over a hundred films covering a fifty-year period, which they admit is "not strictly a random sample," and from that material concluded that "from 1917 on, the classical model became dominant, in that since that moment American fiction films employed fundamentally similar narrative, temporal, and spatial systems." Within these systems existed a universal film type that unfolded in a linear fashion, focused on self-contained characters, evoked a transparent visual style, and ended with clear closures of all narrative problems that affirmed heterosexual love and the values of liberal individualism.[6]

The importance of this analysis cannot be denied. It alerted film scholars that the type of production system can determine the formal properties of mass art. It also taught us that studios, artists, and businessmen all tried to standardize their product to garner predictable profits and to infuse films with ideological content. Along similar lines it is also true that racist imagery, themes of liberal individualism, and backward-looking symbols appeared in major films. The problem with this analysis, however, is that its ahistorical methodology cannot account for the power of audiences at key historical moments to disrupt the production system and compel studios to alter their films in response to market demand. If the large studios consistently dominated production, then why did the studios lose audiences, and new companies come to prominence, in the thirties and fifties? And if the studio system universally created films that advanced a classic narrative and backward-looking and racist symbols, how did Will Rogers, gangster, and fallen women films arise to challenge racial and sexual stereotypes, to promote not individualistic, but communal and public, solutions to social and personal problems confronted by the characters? And why did Eric Johnston evoke anticommunist rhetoric in the forties to destroy Depression-era film formulas, blacklist artists, and censor films, if moviemakers already popularized a uniform American Way to preserve the status quo?

Given these unresolved issues, it is not accidental that recently these views have been challenged by scholars examining the power of moviemakers to create films that resist dominant images of power and authority. Steven Ross has clearly demonstrated that prior to the rise of Hollywood, small producers made silent films permeated with themes of class conflict. Jonathan Munby has shown that gangster films from the thirties to the forties served as a vehicle to critique unjust class and race relations. Dana Polan has revealed in a fine study of World War II films that popular narratives exhibited less a seamless classical style than images of disruption. Criticizing those who believe that a monolithic Hollywood style pervaded the era, Polan tells us that we "need to theorize the possibility of slippage between the discourse and its actualization in specific historical moments." Finally, Fredric Jameson drew on postmodern literary theory to explain that to gather audiences producers must ensure that even the most "degraded forms" of mass art appeal to "our deepest fantasies about the nature of social life, both as we live it now and as we feel in our bones it ought to be lived." And despite their different points of view, feminist scholars have shown that cinematic representations of gender can embody tensions and contradictions that are left unresolved by normative prescriptions of femininity promoted by the classical style or normative values promoted in the narrative.[7]

The effect of these examinations of Hollywood moviemaking has created a dualistic view of the way mass art functions in modern America. One school uncritically assumes that because the Hollywood production system has been dominated by large corporations that needed a predictable film narrative, a uniform and unchanging American Way has permeated filmmaking. Rooted in codes of "whiteness" and liberal capitalism, these classic narratives reinforced repressive racist norms and conservative interests. A more recent group of scholars acknowledges that corporate leaders try to use mass-produced sounds and images to mystify power relations, but that popular artists and audiences can generate modes of resistance. While these two approaches have informed parts of this study, I have shown that the boundaries between the center and the margins are not static but open and fluid. At key historical moments modes of resistance can alter public culture and American dreams.

In so doing, I see my evidence reinforcing the views of the Marxist social philosopher Antonio Gramsci and the Russian literary critic Mikhail Bakhtin, and current scholars who draw on their insights, such as George Lipsitz, Lawrence Levine, and Stuart Hall, who see that popular art and culture compose part of a dialogic and contested terrain in which ideas emanating from the past and present and expectations for the future operate in a conversation with each other.[8] Both Gramsci and Bakhtin demonstrate that artists and groups maintain collective memories of cultural and political struggles that never completely die. In the context of the United States, one can see that it was the collective memory of a republican producers' democracy that spurred union, populist, abolition, and women suffrage crusades in the nineteenth century. But as the republican creed seemingly disappeared under the impact of racial and cultural divisions and the rise of the new corporate order, the delegitimization crisis of the Depression saw radicals revive that "American" tradition at the grassroots as well as in the popular arts.

Our plot samples derived from the major trade journals demonstrate the broad outlines of this contested and shifting terrain. In the twenties hostility to big business was small. The most common plot device centered on the effort of members of the Anglo-Saxon "old middle class"—professionals and businessmen—to save themselves from the dangers of "too much moral revolution" associated with the lures of the new woman and nonwhite races. If this encouraged protagonists to elevate their desires with the status symbols identified with the wealthy, this plot device reinforced the cultural authority of the new corporate order. During the Depression, however, characters aligned to big business and old-style professionals underwent a conversion. They shed the values of the wealthy and emerged as composite heroes who combined the forbidden qualities of gangsters, fallen women, and minorities with the virtues of the good republican citizen. Out of these interpenetrating opposites emerged a revival of middle-class life as modern protagonists—dancers and singers, radio performers and showmen, airplane pilots and comics—combined cultural and political reform. Shedding the codes of highbrow art and Victorian sexual roles, the new protagonists cooperated with the lower classes to create a new community rooted in reciprocal relations among the classes and a civic arena that began to include the new woman and minorities.

Implicit in this shift in public culture was a battle over the meaning of Americanism between Anglo-Saxon proponents of liberal individualism and hybrid protagonists of a populist republican ideal. The uniqueness of that battle was that it was not confined to the screen alone. As the new sound films expanded markets into the countryside, the South, and small towns, theater owners provided a public arena where diverse groups reinvented the contours of public space. Designers shed the lavish cathedral-style movie house modeled on the tastes of the rich in favor of an "American" streamlined theater, complete with egalitarian seating, modernist aesthetic forms, and murals that portrayed the common producers rebuilding their society. Within these theaters viewers made a Cherokee Indian, Will Rogers, the major film star of the day. Drawing on collective Cherokee memories of a pluralistic republic, Rogers promoted calls to reshape wealth and power to realize dreams of affluence and a more just community. In Hollywood itself, a similar élan drove Rogers and others to create a Hollywood labor movement. Drawing on modern republican images, the guilds made the film capital the most unionized industry in the country, bringing together workers, women, and minorities in a common effort.

The coming of World War II and the Cold War, however, generated a major transformation in national identity that has had lasting impact to this day: It displaced the modern republican ideology in favor of a homogeneous American Way rooted in liberal capitalism and universal, classless values. It was here rather than in the thirties that the liberal consensus that scholars see permeating twentieth-century moviemaking was born. And it did not happen by accident, for it mirrored the impact of wartime political demands on the industry. Best articulated by the leader of the producers' association, Eric Johnston, the function of wartime Hollywood lay in creating a mass culture that reinforced instead of challenged official institutions. Johnston saw that the making of class harmony would realize economic growth and overcome the fears of economic depression and national security that haunted modern life.

As Johnston, big businessmen, conservative union leaders, and proponents of an older national identity saw it, the task of the future was to root out the subversive "nightmare of class conflict" that informed working-class and middle-class life in the thirties. With filmmakers voluntarily acquiescing in the World War II consensus, our plot surveys show that unlike in the thirties, the main characters dramatized a top-down conversion narrative in which they joined hierarchical military organizations and patriotic businesses. A sharp decline occurred as well in the portrayal of big business and the rich as villains. Instead, the central characters discard republican values and class antagonism and envisage the internal enemy as villains who adhere to the disruptive class and cultural loyalties of the past. The result is the uncontested linkage of Americanism in these narratives not with men and women who operate as citizens in an autonomous civic sphere or who control their own work; rather the approved characters serve in official patriotic institutions as organization men dedicated to winning the war at home and abroad.

If World War II rather than the Depression era saw the rise of the consensus ideology in the popular arts that legitimized the corporate order, it also spurred a major change in the meaning of democracy. Previously republican dreams of freedom were focused on control over work and public life. But now that state goals and big business demanded unity, the quest for personal freedom and for a realm of stability focused on private life and mass abundance. This dichotomy bred an expression of alienation and disruption coupled with the faith that a domesticated consumer culture could supply the means to overcome the "anxiety" that attended the crisis in American identity. Symbolic of that process were the enormously popular "road films" of Bing Crosby and Bob Hope in which Crosby portrayed the heroic protagonist who identified with the pursuit of success. But because success in large organizations stifled the instincts and control over work, Crosby's double, Bob Hope, made fun of those who took their adult responsibilities too seriously. Hope expressed the deep anger against the new organization, but unlike his counterparts in the thirties, he was the heroic clown who focused play and dreams of freedom on the consumer home. The result was that America was no longer personified by "Uncle Sam" but by "Uncle Sugar," who linked victory with attaining a "Shangri La" of delights with white pin-ups on the "home" front.

Hope and Crosby also set the tone for a new female ideal of the "pin-up" who embodied the patriotic vision proposed by Uncle Sugar. This meant that through the war stars like June Allyson, Betty Grable, and Rita Hayworth incarnated on the screen the ideal pin-up whom the soldiers desired. To do their patriotic duty, heroines continued to work as the empowered women who had informed the thirties, but now they found their identity in a new category, that of "patriotic domesticity," where women sought employment but not for reasons of professional advancement or self-expression. To support the dream of the suburban home as a place to recover freedom and intimacy, women, like the men, would have to undergo a conversion experience. The heroine in Bing Crosby's *Holiday Inn* turns away from a career and divisive sexual identities. Shedding her previous lowbrow desires, she whitens her appearance to create the ideal female for a man who wishes to retreat from a meaningless work world. Indicative of that trend, the pin-up Rita Hayworth "whitened" her appearance and behavior. Shedding the image of the dark, Spanish female, she emerged as the ideal of a "classless" Caucasian girl who moved from a pluralistic public life toward a new identity as sexually attractive wife and mother. The result was that as public life became more pluralistic, the dream of suburban bliss focused on the ideals of white beauty and classlessness.

Taken together, these trends—the creation of a classless norm, the shedding of divisive sex and racial identities, the turn to the home for freedom—set the tone for postwar culture as well. It is possible that the displacement of republican ideals would have ended after World War II, if the demands for unity and authority had not once again been reinstated in response to the Cold War. As articulated by Eric Johnston, the new Cold War against the Soviet Union was not simply a negative doctrine. Rather he saw that the creation of domestic unity would restore cooperation between capital and labor and generate the politics of economic growth and prosperity. Yet because the Cold War happened in a time of peace, the anticommunist crusaders could not count on voluntary acquiescence. So to sanction their hegemony and a new historical bloc of groups, the new Hollywood leaders turned to the state, in the form of the House Un-American Activities Committee, to contain radical unions, blacklist artists, and impose censorship within the film capital.

Yet the contradictions embedded in the alteration of national identity soon became apparent. Once the anticommunist crusade institutionalized the cultural and political paradigm of consensus, moviemakers gave birth to the striking duality that came to inform postwar American culture as a whole. Our plot calculations show that the major studios created an unprecedented number of war, biblical, and western films where the heroes and heroines no longer operated as citizens in an autonomous civic sphere. Rather, the new postwar American heroes, best exemplified by John Wayne, were officials, military officers, and experts operating in professional and state organizations. Here disorder no longer stems from big business or corrupt institutions, but from below in the form of enemy aliens, lower-class delinquents, and psychotic deviants who fail to conform to updated Victorian sexual roles and hierarchical organizations. That Manichaean battle to destroy the subversive enemy corresponded to a striking rise in films where violence comes to the center. The ensuing battle demanded death or containment of adversaries rather than altering the society in order to accommodate competing views within a monolithic civic sphere.

The Manichaean struggle to construct a classless Americanism also bred a series of plots aimed at purifying the self of forbidden memories. Generally belonging to the new genre of "film noir," these films revealed that the desires of the modern republican creed were now anathema. Reflective of a battle permeated with images of personal guilt, the number of characters portrayed as nonconformist antiheroes and rebellious women rises dramatically. These female "vamps" are erotic women who reject the traditional ideal of wife and mother, while the alienated, subversive men dislike the rich and modern work. If in the past, these values would have made the protagonists heroes, they now force them to inhabit the criminal world of the night. At the same time minorities also come to embody this split. Nonwhites who put aside divisive traditions of race and class interests were portrayed positively in increasing numbers of films. But villains in the western and war films increasingly took the form of nonwhite Indians, Japanese, Chinese, and later the North Vietnamese. All in all, this suggests that the rise of deviant men and women protagonists expressed the "dark" desires forced to the margins of the self and society. In these narratives officials then destroy the outsiders or use force and science, particularly the field of psychology, to compel the outsiders to adapt.

Even as these dramas constructed the sharp duality resting at the core of the postwar American Way, dissent did not die. In fact, the counterpoint to the new liberal consensus reemerged in the striking popularity of the left-wing film noir and youth films that revived the critical edge to mass art. This alternative was possible because of the continuing power of the market and audience demand. Ironically, as the once-powerful film studios lost audiences and the Hollywood "system" dissolved, the remnants of the Hollywood left retained relative autonomy. They turned to independent firms or gained autonomy in large studios willing to experiment with innovations in narrative and film style in order to recover profits. Exemplifying the capacity of collective memory to survive repression, Billy Wilder and John Huston symbolized the move from political to cultural radicalism that informed the postwar trajectory of beat poets, abstract expressionist painters, bebop musicians, playwrights, and novelists. Their film noir productions drew on modernist techniques to evoke admiration for the antiheroes and vamps who rebelled. Wilder's *Double Indemnity* and Huston's *The Asphalt Jungle* and *The Treasure of the Sierra Madre* asked viewers to identify with outlaws' resistance to corrupt capitalism and revived Victorian family life.

To many viewers, this mode of resistance provided an artistic continuity between the innovations of the thirties and the confining atmosphere of the postwar period. Nowhere was that more evident than when the "beat" novelist John Clellon Holmes wrote in the mid-sixties about the impact of moviegoing on the mind of his generation for the readers of *Harper's* magazine. In the thirties he recalled that players like the Marx Brothers, W. C. Fields, and Jean Harlow liberated the American psyche from repressive sexual and class roles. Holmes also saw movies providing a political education, warning against the dangers of big business and war. Frank Capra's fat capitalist in *Meet John Doe* symbolized for Holmes the "desperate lust for power" that bred modern totalitarians, while at the same time *All Quiet on the Western Front* taught that all wars were frauds. Once he joined the Army in World War II, he regarded Humphrey Bogart as the new existential knight, for "Bogey" remained, like Holmes, "suspicious of sentiment, verbosity and cheap idealism that came from our leaders." In this context, Holmes joined postwar beat writers' efforts to keep alive the cultural if not political side of thirties' dreams. Recalling how moviemakers influenced his politics in the thirties and postwar alienation, he told readers:

> It has been said that if you would understand the mind of my generation you must start with World War II. The war seems a likely enough starting place, and yet in a subtler sense everyone who is now between the ages of thirty-odd and forty-odd had already a common experience by the time they entered the armed services. It was the experience of moviegoing in the 1930's and early forties and it gave us a common fantasy life from which we are still dragging up the baggage that obsessed us.[9]

At a time when films from the thirties provided the "fantasy life" that still "obsessed" Holmes and his colleagues, remnants of the Hollywood left found in the rebellious youth stars a vehicle to bring their quest for an alternative to Cold War culture into the light of day. By tapping a new audience composed of an unprecedented number of adolescents, these filmmakers—those who resisted as well as cooperated with the anticommunist investigations of Hollywood—found a way to challenge the monolithic civic sphere. They adapted the voices of resistance to create characters who found a new freedom in exploring the boundaries of instinct that subverted the personal if not political prescriptions of official norms. Their films, featuring James Dean, Marlon Brando, and Marilyn Monroe, recovered the capacity of mass art to serve as a counterculture to official values. Whether it emerged in *Rebel Without a Cause, The Wild One, Some Like It Hot,* or *The Misfits,* that counterculture celebrated the capacity of youth to renew a vernacular art rooted in the promise of the hybrid protagonists. As these characters merged images linked to white and black culture, drama and comedy, and male and female, each restored the vitality of a composite personality capable of reinventing itself. In essence, Brando, Dean, and Monroe were cultural radicals who reshaped the dichotomy between work and play that had split apart under the shadow of war.

The youth stars were thus the start of something new but also reflected the move from political to cultural radicalism of the writers and directors of their best films. Yet the youth stars also remained trapped in the highly individualistic nature of that rebellion. Increasingly manufacturers capitalized on their appeal by mediating the personas of Dean, Brando, and Monroe through a perspective that labeled them as emblematic of childlike or "adolescent" impulses that had to be controlled or shed with the advent of "adult" responsibility. Yet this quality sold products, since it appealed to linkage of the consumer culture and leisure with adolescent rebellion removed from the adult realm of responsibility in the daylight world of work and politics. Along these lines *Entertainment Weekly* reported in 1993 that a mammoth commercial "machinery spews out Marilyn tee shirts, collectors' plates, calendars, clocks, ash trays, address books, shower curtains and hundreds of other items worth over 30 million in sales *every* year." The tragedy of Monroe's suicide and Dean's death contributed to the impulse to keep this rebellious spirit apart from public life by allowing one to dismiss their work as either self-destructive or lacking seriousness. The result was that mass art created by the remnants of the Hollywood left generated resisting images. But in the hands of advertisers the youth rebels also advanced the interests of big business in search of markets.[10]

The recovery of utopian expectations flowing from the thirties to the fifties could not be contained indefinitely. On the contrary, they reemerged directly into the political arena of the sixties. The stimulus emerged from the civil rights movement led by African Americans, who had been excluded from the consensus. Not only did the civil rights movement revitalize public life, but it spurred social criticism and reform of mainstream middle-class life. Once the political movements of the sixties spread, often admirers of Dean, Brando, and Monroe looked to them as models of dissent against prescribed gender and racial roles. The prominent feminist Gloria Steinem combined the editorship of *Ms.* with writing a serious biography of Marilyn Monroe. Steinem titled the first chapter of *Norma Jean* "The Woman Who Will Not Die" and linked Monroe's life to the quest for female liberation. In addition, the rock singer Madonna, though recognizing the limits of Monroe's dependency, portrayed her in song and on stage as a model for women like herself who refused to remain subordinate and confine their sexuality to the privatized home.

The male youth rebels also had a similar influence. Brando participated in the civil rights, antiwar, and American Indian movements of the sixties and seventies. In explaining the roots of the radical beliefs of the sixties, Tom Hayden, one of the founders of Students for a Democratic Society, recalled that he "was a college editor, very influenced by the Beat Generation. My thing was to hitchhike all over the country. I was always very divided between what now you would call a radical and what then didn't have a name . . . it was mainly like trying to mimic the life of James Dean or something like that."[11] Little wonder that John Huston, speaking in the sixties from his self-imposed exile in Ireland from Cold War politics praised Arthur Penn's *Bonnie and Clyde* (1967) as a recovery of forgotten memories. As Huston saw it, the film linked the sentiments expressed in his work to the new art and political experimentation of the sixties, for it was, as he explained, simply

> an extraordinary work, steeped in the unknown and adventure. . . . An adventurer is somebody who begins by leaving behind his house and who then abandons all conventions and rules to seek something for its intrinsic values. . . . This search then becomes their reason for being. . . . *Bonnie and Clyde* fit in to that category: They had taken a funny way, a strange way, all those murders, robberies, assassinations—but they were succeeding in creating their own world. They were recreating their own life![12]

It was also not accidental that when Huston expressed the continuity between the spirit of the thirties and that of the sixties that those who had cut their spurs in containing that élan should also operate on a larger scale. For when the politics of economic growth and anticommunism faltered under the impact of civil rights and the war in Vietnam, the promoters of a counterculture politics celebrated the arts of collective resistance and individualism. Yet the loss of a republican tradition with which to criticize capitalism and activate political skills to solve common problems was an Achilles' heel.

The challenge to Cold War policies and racial and sexual roles institutionalized in the Cold War stimulated Ronald Reagan to leave Hollywood to defend the liberal consensus he had done so much to build. Along the way the former Actors Guild leader turned away from the party of Roosevelt to the Republicans to revitalize the ideology of traditional family values, economic growth, and anticommunism. Indicative of how much Reagan saw this battle in terms of his memories of the anticommunist crusade of the forties, a young reporter interviewed Reagan as he ran for the presidency in 1980. Afterwards the journalist wrote that it was simply remarkable that

> Reagan, with no prompting from me, in what seems in fact to be a compulsive non-sequitur, had resurrected events that took place some thirty years earlier, his wounds still raw and his hatred of the enemy unyielding. Most curious of all is that his view of the Soviet menace today is so deeply colored by events that took place in Hollywood more than a generation ago, as if today's Soviet government were simply the Hollywood communists projected on a larger screen.[13]

Strong testimony indeed to the way that the rise of the making of Cold War America in Hollywood between 1930 and 1960 influenced events well into the 1980s. And if the cultural wars of our own day—the desire of conservatives to restore the ideal home and polity of the fifties as the national norm—are any indication, the residue of the battle over the content of the media and culture continues to influence our current politics and may engage the American people well into the new millennium.

Appendix 1
Sampling Methods and Research Data

T he battle over the contours of Americanism gained visibility throughout the nation and informed a major trend in moviemaking. Where this was most in evidence was in the broad shift in values informing the plot samples evaluated in this study. Generally I have assumed that audience gratification is gained psychologically by identification with main characters. In the context of this study, this provides ways to define the boundaries of public life and national identity—who is to be included or excluded within these boundaries. Since viewers identify with a particular character, protagonists exemplify ideological positions and debates. By ideology I mean a worldview that allows one to organize facts into a set of beliefs that guide one's view of the past, present, and future. Though we cannot gauge other aspects of moviemaking—subplots, stylistic devices, performances—a longitudinal study allows us to assess how ideological values are modified in relation to new social conditions from the New Deal years through the Cold War years.

These conclusions were derived by my research assistants and me from a systematic sampling technique that draws on hundreds of film plots. The primary source was the *Motion Picture Herald* (*MPH*)— the film industry's major trade journal of the period studied. *MPH* offered exhibitors (i.e., theater managers) a variety of services, one of which was weekly digests of recent film releases in the form of plot synopses. These film-plot synopses served as the basis for our sample and its broad categories. To ensure consistent coverage of the time period, film synopses were drawn from every even-numbered year, and two film plots per month were collated. That is, we applied twenty-four films per year to the sample's categories.

To ensure that both A- and B-class films—films geared for first-run feature exhibition and films made for double bills, respectively—were included in the sample, we used the following methods: We chose the first film review of every month and also the last film reviewed in the penultimate week of every month. This ensured that there was consistent spacing of the product over time and that both A and B films would be represented. Each synopsis was then submitted to evaluation according to a list of categories that covered various aspects of the narrative. Every time a prime feature of the plot under scrutiny filled any of our categories, this was noted. We then collated categories gathered for each year and put them in a "totals" chart. They were compared with others in the sample across time. This material was then converted into percentages that appear in visual form on our figures in appendix 2. Lastly, each figure has been calculated on four-year intervals in order to clearly discern long-term alterations over time.

Appendix 2
Trends in Film Plots and the Changing Face of American Ideology

Figure 1. Films Portraying Wealthy Decadence as a Danger to Individuals or Society 1920–1960

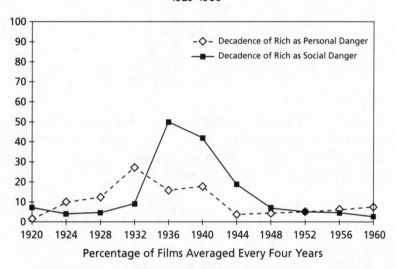

Percentage of Films Averaged Every Four Years

These are plots where the central protagonists perceive that the life-style of the rich endangers themselves or society. Typically in these narratives, the rich will commit crimes, but then blame them on the poor or the hero or heroine. This theme of the dangers of the decadent rich emerges in Will Rogers, "Thin Man," and Frank Capra films.

Figure 2. Films Featuring Big Business Villains
1914–1958

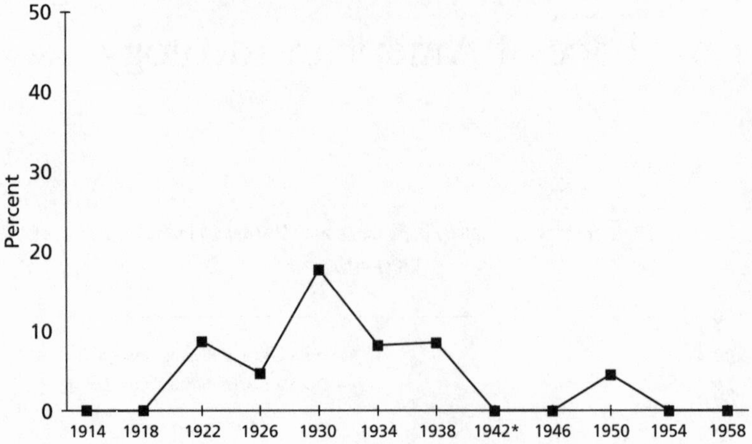

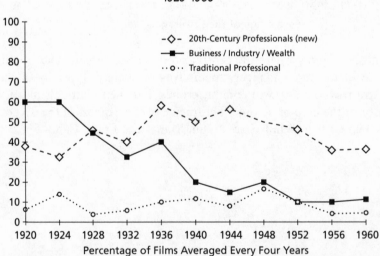

*Estimated percentage.

The category of big business villain appears when local bankers, manufacturers, or merchants falsely accuse the hero of a crime, threaten to
foreclose on a mortgage, or align with a corrupt politician to advance
their interests against the public good.

Figure 3. Alterations in the Occupations of the Protagonists
1920–1960

We calculated this category by simply noting which class or group heroes or heroines found themselves situated in. By the thirties the mod-

ern, twentieth-century professional would be manifest in a Will Rogers film or in the "Thin Man" or "Hardy Family" series.

Figure 4. Films Featuring Progressive Reform of Society
1914–1958

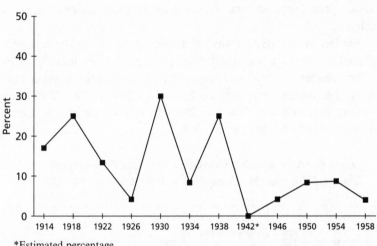

*Estimated percentage.

These are films in which the actions of the hero or heroine are clearly linked to public activities that serve to reform society, overcome prejudice, or achieve justice.

Figure 5. Independent Companies, Holdovers, and Films Released
Total Indy Companies, Foreign Indy Companies, Holdovers,
& Indy Films as % Total Film Releases, 1916–1964

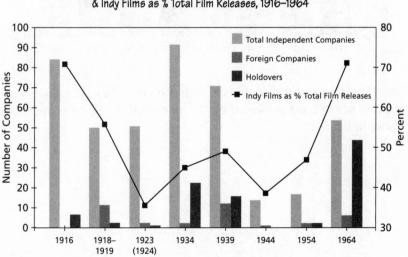

This figure illustrates the number of independent companies in film production, as well as the number of foreign companies importing films to the United States. Holdovers represent the companies from the previous four years that were still in business. Generally the figure shows that turnover was rapid and consistent. The line graph illustrates the overall percentage of films released by an independent company or producer.

The number of companies was calculated by counting the independents listed in the section entitled "Independents" in *Film Daily Yearbook*. The number of films produced yearly, as well as the number produced by the majors, was derived from Joel Finler, *The Hollywood Story* (New York: Crown, 1988), p. 280. His figures are drawn from a survey of the major trade journals.

Figure 6. Total Independent Films Compared to Total Films Released
Total Indy Films, Total Films, & Indy Films as % of Total Films, 1916–1964

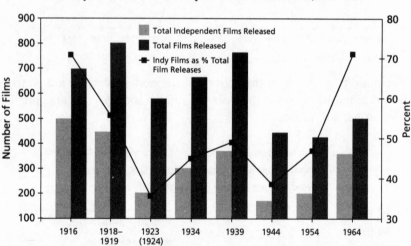

This figure compares the number of films produced by the majors with the number of films produced by the independents. Sources are listed above in figure 5.

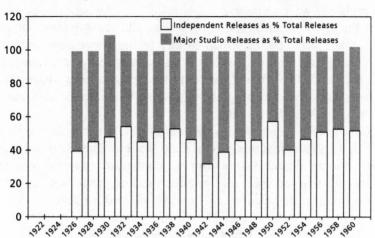

Figure 7. Independents versus Majors: A Detailed Look
Percentage of Total Films Released in United States, 1922–1960

This more precise chart allows us to see that in some years the number of films made by independents exceeded that of the majors as a percentage of total releases. The sources are listed in figure 5.

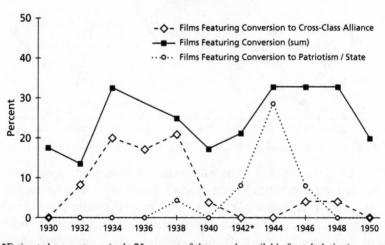

Figure 8. Conversion Narratives
1930–1950

*Estimated percentages (only 75 percent of the sample available for tabulation).

These films feature a character who changes loyalty from a key person, community, or nation to another entity. There are three kinds of conversions: individual, group, and object lesson. The latter takes the form of a rereading of history. Here, the implication is that if the conversion had in fact taken place, then "we"—the audience—would not have the problems we have today.

In the thirties, narratives of cross-class alliance dominate. In such films, characters renounce their loyalty to the upper class and align with the common people. Such conversions often involve the marriage of a hero or heroine to a character of the opposite class, suggesting a shift in cultural authority and alignment. Examples of this can be found in the Will Rogers films.

Narratives of conversion to the patriotic state occur during World War II, with repercussions into the Cold War era. They involve conversions from an alliance with an oppositional group to an alliance with institutions that represent national interests and patriotism. Examples of this occur in *The Fighting Sullivans* (1944) and *Air Force* (1943).

Figure 9. Patriot Heroes and Savior Institutions
1930–1950

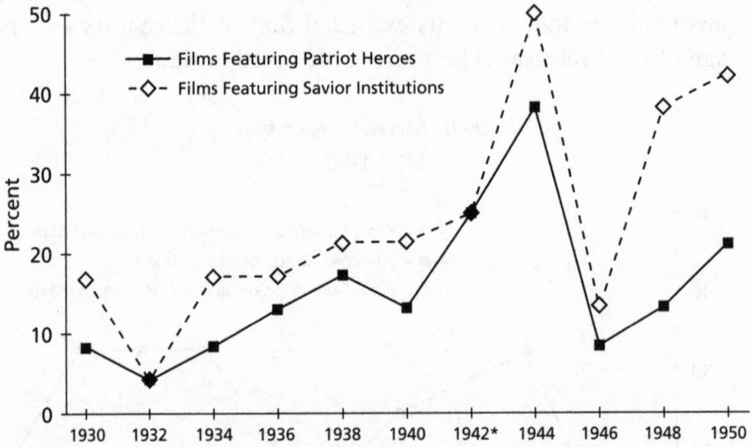

*Estimated percentages (only 75 percent of the sample available for tabulation).

These films feature characters whose individual interests converge with those of state institutions, such as the Federal Bureau of Investigation or the armed services, dedicated to protecting the nation from foreign or domestic enemies. Since such characters give their loyalty to institutions that "save" the people, we have also called these entities "savior" institutions.

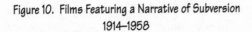

Figure 10. Films Featuring a Narrative of Subversion
1914–1958

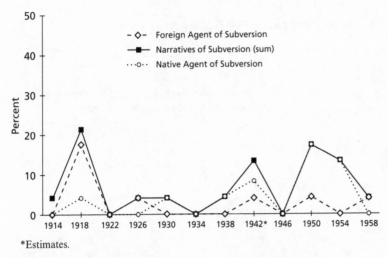

*Estimates.

These plots feature an agent who intends harm to the social order, the state, or the dominant ideology of unity identified with the national interest. Subversion can involve deception or adherence to an ideology that runs counter to patriotism, such as fascism in *The House on 92nd Street* (1945) or communism as in *The Fearmakers* (1958) or *My Son John* (1952). A foreign agent of subversion is someone who resides outside the United States; a native agent resides inside the country.

Figure 11. Films Portraying Foreign Elements as a Danger to Hero/Heroine
1920–1960

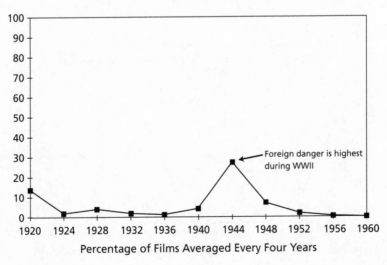

These are films in which, say, the Germans or the Japanese are seen as a threat, such as in war films.

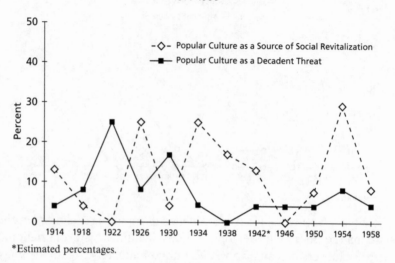

Figure 12. Films Featuring Popular Culture
1914–1958

*Estimated percentages.

Here the characters perceive that the institutions and values associated with the "new" popular culture—nightclubs, popular dance, the new woman, "youth," cross-cultural exchange, jazz, or rock and roll—are either a threat or a means to social renewal.

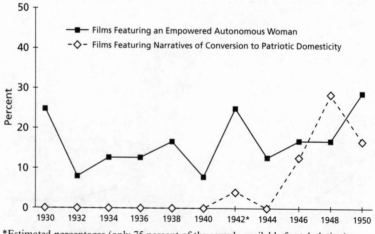

Figure 13. Empowered Woman and Conversion to Patriotic Domesticity
1930–1950

*Estimated percentages (only 75 percent of the sample available for tabulation).

A female lead who participates in public life is an "empowered woman." She competes with males. The ideal of patriotic domesticity informs the actions of women in films like *Since You Went Away* (1944) or *Hollywood Canteen* (1944). Here, the woman works, but her identity is found in supporting the home to which her husband or lover—who serves a patriotic cause in a savior institution—looks to find freedom.

Figure 14. Films Featuring Female Occupation as Wife Only
1914–1958

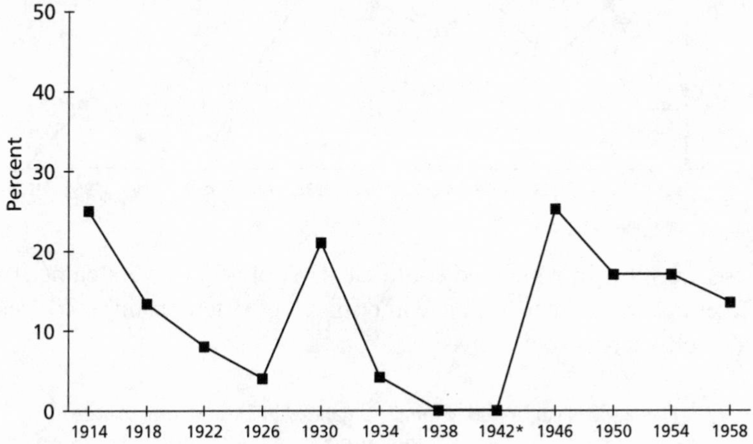

*Estimated percentage.

In these films the heroine has no career outside of being a wife or mother.

Figure 15. Films Featuring Marriage/Romance Across Class Lines
1914–1958

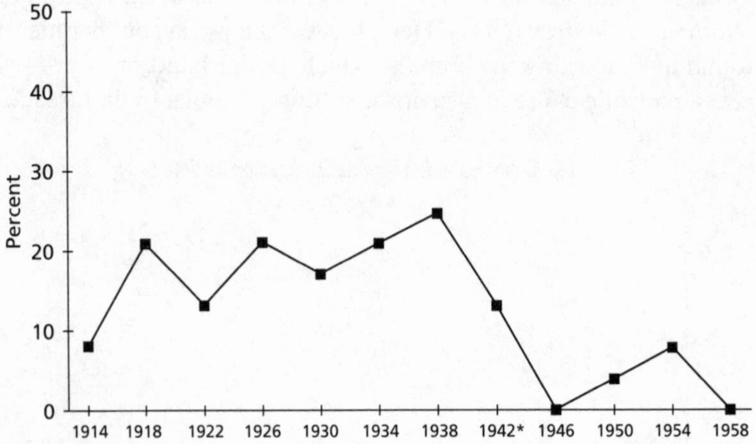

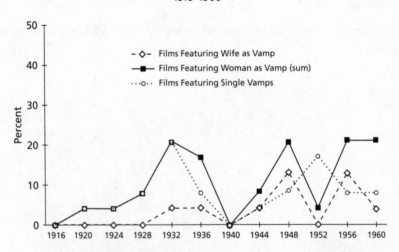

*Estimated percentage.

These are films in which we could clearly note that lovers came from different classes. Their romance and marriage often promises to create reciprocity across social divisions.

Figure 16. Films Featuring Vamps, Organized by Their Marital Status
1916–1960

This category features a sexually empowered woman who has the power to seduce and manipulate men to her advantage, creating a threat to the social order.

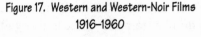

Figure 17. Western and Western-Noir Films
1916–1960

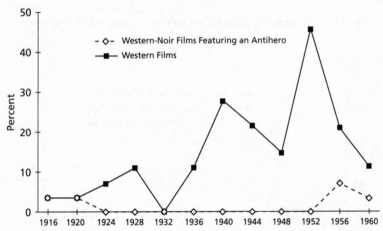

These are films taking place in the American frontier. Western noir, which appears in the fifties, indicates a film where the central character is alienated from the ideals of the West and masculinity, as in *The Misfits* (1961).

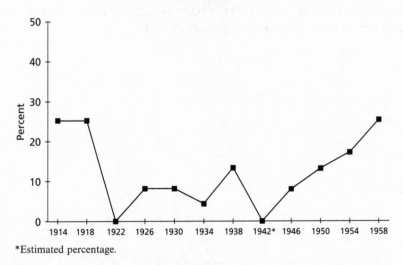

Figure 18. Films Ending in Violence
1914–1958

*Estimated percentage.

The central plot tension involves the clash of two individuals, groups, or countries. The resolution to that problem lies in the violent destruction of the adversary. Most war, biblical, and western films illustrate this theme, but so do film noir and crime and spy films.

Figure 19. Films Featuring Racial Heroes/Heroines, Villains, and Principal Actors
1916–1960

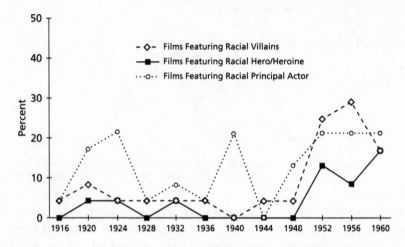

These are films that feature clearly identified racial minorities as either heroes or heroines, villains, or principal actors.

It is interesting to note that the category of villain in the Depression was class-based—represented by the rich and big business. But in the forties and fifties, usually the villain is racially rather than class-marked. See and compare with figures 1 and 2.

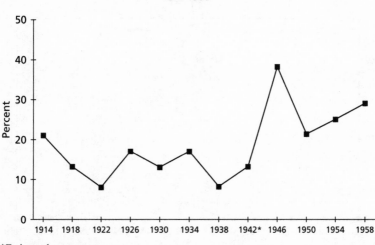

Figure 20. Films Featuring Antiheroes
1914–1958

*Estimated percentage.

This category indicates a male lead who can be weak or strong, but whose ethical motives are also ambivalent. His confusion is often highlighted against an empowered, seductive woman. The antihero is often deluded into the idea that he can master a situation, only to find himself a pawn in someone else's game. Often his masculinity is under duress, as his male agency becomes intertwined with sex.

At the same time the antihero can be more virtuous than the guardians of official institutions, as in *High Sierra* (1941).

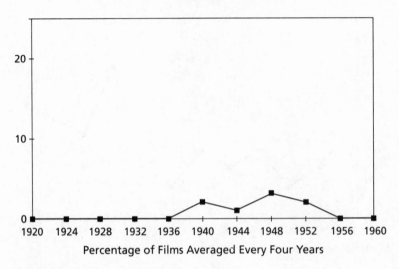

Figure 21. Noir Endings
1920–1960

Percentage of Films Averaged Every Four Years

These are films in which a happy ending is not realized. In most cases the central character, often the antihero, is defeated or meets an unhappy end. This corresponds to a world out of control that the characters cannot master.

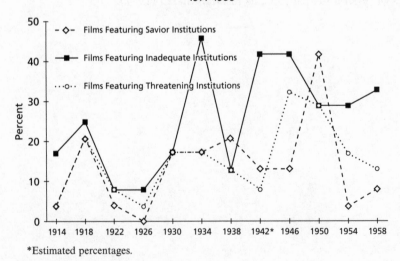

Figure 22. Films Featuring Institutions
1914–1958

*Estimated percentages.

Inadequate Institutions (world out of control). This category bears a correlation to the rise of antiheroes, noir endings, and reform agents. The inadequate institutions correspond to plots where the main characters have a fatalistic view of authority and official institutions.

Threatening Institutions. This category covers films where legitimate authority actively prosecutes innocent or morally good individuals. Classic examples occur in war films, which pit the evil enemy institutions against good domestic ones. Both, in this case, are legitimate, but they threaten the protagonists.

Savior Institutions. Savior institutions are powerful and gain their legitimacy by their capacity to advance national goals and patriotism.

Figure 23. Films Where Main Character Is Endangered by Personal Weakness 1920–1960

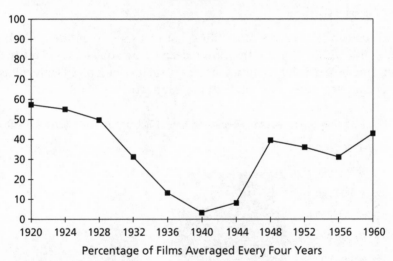

Percentage of Films Averaged Every Four Years

Weak character traits are associated normally with the dangers presented by the new woman, nightclubs, Chinatown, dance halls, jazz, and modern morals. Since in the thirties, the new, modern culture is Americanized, the danger falls dramatically. Yet with the arrival of film noir, pessimism and vamp characters appear once again.

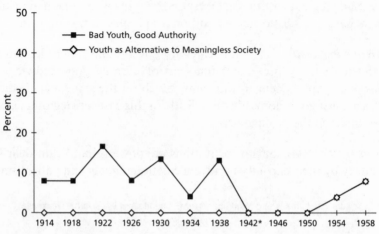

Figure 24. Films Featuring Youth
1914–1958

*Estimated percentage.

This category measures those films that focus solely on the problems of youth. In the thirties, they are redeemed by adults and adapt to a reformed society. By the fifties, however, such as in James Dean's films, they are seen as an alternative to the adult world.

Figure 25. Two Estimates of the Average Number of Tickets Purchased Weekly in 1940

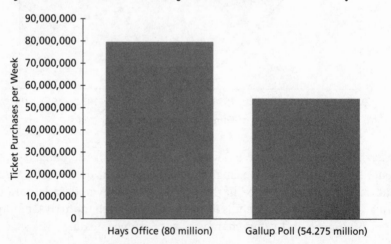

This comparison demonstrates that the Hays Office overestimated the weekly audience by about 25 million filmgoers. A contemporary Gallup Poll accurately estimated the audience to be 54.275 million weekly.

This independent evidence corresponded exactly to our calculations cited in figure 27, leading to the firm conclusion that our revised figures more accurately reflect rising weekly patronage.

SOURCE: This was compiled from data supplied by the American Institute of Public Opinion, *Increasing Profits with Audience Research* (Princeton, New Jersey, 1940), p. 140.

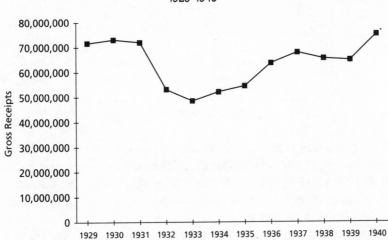

Figure 26. Gross Receipts in Motion Picture Industry
1929–1940

This figure demonstrates that receipts in the film industry during the thirties surpassed the total amount accrued in the last year of prosperity in 1929. In addition, given that deflation was about one quarter over the decade, the real income of the film industry rose rather than declined in the thirties.

SOURCES: Gross receipts are derived from the U.S. Department of Commerce, *Survey of Current Business,* June 1944, p. 151; *National Income Supplement to Current Business,* 1959, pp. 206–208; *Historical Statistics of the United States from Colonial Times to the Present,* Series H 506.

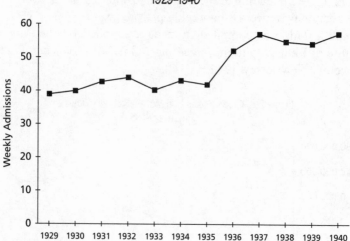

Figure 27. Weekly Admissions to Movies in the United States
1929–1940

This figure reveals that admissions did not decline, as statistics derived from the Hays Office claim. Rather, admissions rose by almost a third from 1929 to 1940, increasing from 40 million to almost 60 million filmgoers, and revealing that in the thirties a new mass culture spread to the people in all regions.

SOURCES: Average ticket prices are derived from *Film Daily Yearbook of Motion Pictures,* 1934; "Box Office Receipts," *Motion Picture Herald,* January and June of each year from 1931–1938; for 1940–1945, see Michael Conant, *Monopoly and the Motion Picture Industry* (Berkeley: University of California Press, 1960). The average prices for each year were added to total receipts (see figure 26) to get attendance.

Figure 28. Theater Expansion in Three Major Regional Cities 1930–1941

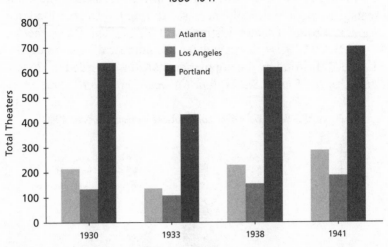

This figure shows that the number of theaters expanded dramatically in the thirties. When coupled with the spread of radio in the same decade, this figure reveals that it was in the thirties that a "mass" American culture spread across regions and classes.

SOURCES: "Theater Listing, Outstate, Non-Metro, 1930–1941," *Film Daily Yearbook, 1930, 1933, 1938, 1941*

Figure 29. Audience Expansion in Three Major Regional Cities 1930–1941

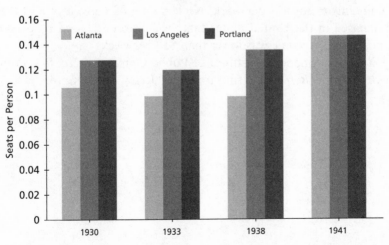

This figure illustrates how in three representative regional cities, one in the South, one in the West, and one in the Northwest, the number of seats per person gradually increased during the Depression era.

SOURCE: From "Theater Listing" section of *Film Daily Yearbook, 1930, 1933, 1938, 1941,* we calculated the number of seats in each city and divided the total by the population statistics recorded in *Historical Statistics of the United States from Colonial Times to the Present.*

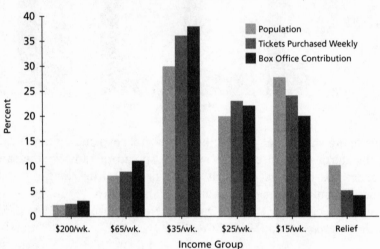

Figure 30. Weekly Box-Office Contributions by Income Groups, 1940

This figure demonstrates that the typical theatergoer in 1940 had a family income of $28 per week. No less than 88 percent of all tickets purchased in the United States that year were purchased by persons whose family income was lower than $50 per week.

SOURCES: American Institute of Public Opinion, *Increasing Profits with Audience Research* (Princeton, New Jersey, 1940), p. 145.

Figure 31. Location of Film Plot
1920–1960

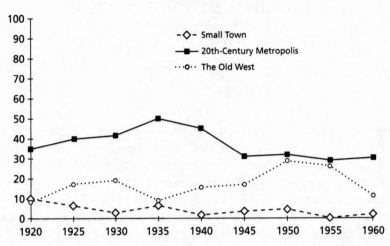

This category measures the locations that provide the setting for the film narrative.

Appendix 3
Examples of Film Reviews
from *Motion Picture Herald*

This appendix provides four examples of the film synopses that appeared in the trade journal *Motion Picture Herald* and are representative of the many plot summaries that became the basis for the figures in appendix 2. As noted in appendix 1, each synopsis was evaluated according to a list of categories covering various aspects of the representation of authority. Each time a plot under scrutiny fitted any of the categories, this information was noted on spreadsheets. My research assistants and I collated the material for each year surveyed and converted the yearly totals into percentages, thereby arriving at the data that appear in appendix 2. Four of the sample synopses derive from the 1930s and one from the 1940s. Together they exemplify the major trends informing the ideological changes unfolding in American films from the Depression to World War II.

The first film, *An American Tragedy* (1931), displays several categories in high relief. First, it portrays an antihero endangered by personal weakness in a metropolitan locale where he works as a factory foreman, and is thus included in figures 20, 23, and 31. Since in this film a wealthy woman leads to the protagonist's downfall, it also belongs in figure 16, denoting women as sexual threats to men. Because the film also ends in violence and has a noir or tragic ending, we noted it in figure 21. Lastly, since the justice system fails the hero, the film displays inadequate institutions, calling for its notation in figure 22.

Washington Show, released in 1932, clearly delineates several political themes common in Depression moviemaking. The story revolves around the downfall of a United States senator who is destroyed by a successful businessman. The villain uses a seductive woman to undermine the "man of the people." As such, the film evokes the themes of figures 1 and 2: big business as a danger and big business as the central villain. Similarly, the occupation of the protagonist is that of a traditional professional of the nineteenth century and he operates in a metropolitan locale, both plot elements denoted in figures 3 and 31. Popular culture, in the form of the new woman and consumerism, poses a "decadent threat," as in figure 12, and the woman is a single "vamp," corresponding to plot characteristics treated in figure 16.

A reformist theme and bottom-up conversion narrative appear in *Mills of the Gods* (1935). Big businessmen, in the form of the board of directors of a large industry, endanger prosperity and the well-being of a town. The offspring of the rich, who are expected to act responsibly, succumb to the lures of Paris and the highbrow consumer ethos of the twenties and thirties. But the new generation of factory owners, the youth of the Depression, aligns not with the cultural values and interests of the corrupt rich but converts to alliances with the workers. To solidify bonds across the classes, the heroine falls in love with a worker. Together the lovers forge a cross-class coalition and validate the vernacular art of the people. So the narrative formula conforms to patterns represented in figures 1, 2, 22, and 23. In sum, there is a conversion narrative coupled to a theme of progressive reform. An empowered, autonomous woman helps the workers combat corrupt monopolists and restore a commonwealth where reciprocity exists across the classes, themes pertinent to figures 4, 9, 13, and 15.

The fourth review, *The Hour Before the Dawn* (1944), exemplifies the making of the top-down conversion narrative that permeated World War II Hollywood. It focuses on a pacifist who loves a foreign woman, who pretends to be an Austrian refugee. But the hero's lover is in fact a Nazi spy who assists foreign agents to sabotage a military airfield. Once the hero discovers his lover's subversive acts, he discards his pacifism, ultimately kills the vampish spy, and emerges a patriotic hero. Instead of internal class conflict and cultural reorientation pervading the story, narrative tension focuses on the hero's conversion to the cause of war and the containment of female vamps and subversives. The protagonist's commitment to patriotic causes and institutions demands the use of violence to destroy his former lover and the subversive agents, ensuring a patriotic, classless society. Together these various characteristics set the tone for the cultural consensus of World War II and the Cold War, and the film finds representation in figures 8, 9, 10, 11, 16, 18, and 22.

PASSING IN REVIEW

This department does not attempt to predict the public's reactions to pictures. It does, instead, present detailed and accurate information on product, together with the frank and honest opinion of the reporter.

An American Tragedy

(Paramount)
Drama

Conducting the case of Clyde Griffiths versus humanity, Paramount through Josef von Sternberg delineates in a few strokes the character which occupies two volumes of text in Theodore Dreiser's "An American Tragedy."

The audience is introduced to Clyde (as portrayed by Phillips Holmes) at the point of his career when he is a foreman in the collar factory of his uncle. His adolescent reactions to the awakening of sex are revealed. He is merely a normal boy interested and attracted by feminine charms, but the rules of the factory prohibit "department chiefs" from associating with the girls employed in their offices. This ruling, coupled with Clyde's innate shyness and inexperience, leaves him without social contacts. His own relatives barely tolerate him.

The inarticulate longing of Clyde for feminine companionship is conveyed to the audience by his covert glances at the legs of the shop girls, his interest in lingerie and bathing suit displays in department store windows. He is passing through the stage preliminary to maturity when all that occupies his mind is girls and more girls.

Then he finds THE girl, Bert, an untutored miss direct from the country, who comes to work in the factory. They meet after hours, despite the rules, and throughout the summer engage in a harmless, joyous affair. But with the arrival of cold weather, they are forced indoors and seek a private meeting place in her room.

Their romance has not run its course when Clyde meets Sandra, daughter of wealth. He is dazzled and flattered by her interest in him, and Bert suffers the consequences of his infatuation for another. She might have taken his desertion of her like a good sport but for the fact that she is to have a child.

Clyde sends Bert away while he seeks a solution of their tangled affairs. The solution seems to present itself in a newspaper headline which tells of a young couple drowning in the lake. That's it; he will drown Bert and cover his tracks so that it will appear to have been an accident.

He plans the crime in every minute detail. Decoying Bert to a strange locality, he is about to execute the murder when he has a change of heart. But Bert in her alarm upsets the boat herself, and drowns.

Clyde's plans have gone awry. He is arrested and is tried for murder, a trial scene aimed to expose a farce in American "justice." At the same time, no attempt has been made to glorify the character of Clyde or his plot. The spectacular never intrudes upon simplicity in the direction of this production. Repression high-lighted by dramatic scenes characterizes the playing of Phillips Holmes as Clyde. Individual applause was won from the preview audience by Sylvia Sidney, Frances Dee, Irving Pichel as the district attorney and Charles Middleton as the defense counsel.

From all sides, among the non-professional members of the audience, came expressions of enjoyment of the picture, and not one dissenting voice was heard. And the theme of the picture is tragedy.

Running time at preview, 95 minutes. Release date, August 29, 1931.
Produced and distributed by Paramount. Directed by Josef von Sternberg. Based on novel by Theodore Dreiser. Screen play by Samuel Hoffenstein. Photographed by Lee Garmes.

CAST

Clyde Griffiths.................Phillips Holmes
Roberta Alden.................Sylvia Sidney
Sondra Finchley.................Frances Dee
Orville Mason.................Irving Fichel
Samuel Griffiths.................Frederick Burton
Mrs. Samuel Griffiths.................Claire McDowell
Gilbert Griffiths.................Wallace Middleton
Myra Griffiths.................Vivian Winsten
Belknap.................Emmett Corrigan
Mrs. Asa Griffiths.................Bodil Rosing
Jephson.................Charles B. Middleton
Titus Alden.................Albert Hart
Mrs. Alden.................Fanny Midgley
Bella Griffiths.................Arline Judge

Newly Rich

(Paramount)
Comedy

Following the lines of "Skippy" in juvenile theme, but with gags and situations for adults, is "Newly Rich," seen in preview in Hollywood.

The original story was "Let's Play King," by Sinclair Lewis. It tells of the rivalry between the mothers of two child stars of the screen, Mitzi Green and Jackie Searl. The mothers, played by Edna May Oliver and Louise Fazenda, are formerly home town friends but now bitterly opposed in a battle for social and professional supremacy. This situation opens the way for much filmtown satire.

The rival mothers plan European trips so that Mitzi and Jackie may meet a child king and benefit by the publicity thus derived. Separately they seek a royal audience in the London hotel where the boy monarch is staying, and discover that their progeny, film stars or no film stars, mean nothing to royalty.

While the mothers are planning the next steps in their campaigns, Mitzi employs her own methods to meet the king. The children check stories and find that the restrictions placed upon young kings and young stars are much the same. They aren't permitted to play and have good times when they want them. So they decide to run away and Jackie, though not wanted, manages to join them. Dressed in old clothes, they set out for the big adventure.

Meeting a waterfront gang, they enroll after the king has pummeled the gang leader. With their new companions, they spend a happy, eventful day, but it ends with the kidnaping of Jackie by a pair of toughs. Then comes the rescue scene. The gang, led by Mitzi and the king, outwits the thugs and Jackie escapes.

A young newcomer, Bruce Line, plays the part of the king.

Miss Fazenda plays a straighter role than usual.

Running time in preview, 85 minutes. Release date, June 20.
Produced and distributed by Paramount Publix. From the story "Let's Play King" by Sinclair Lewis. Adaptation by Edward Paramore, Jr. Continuity and dialogue by Norman McLeod and Joseph L. Mankiewicz. Directed by Norman Taurog. Photography by Charles Lang.

CAST

Daisy Tait.................Mitzi Green
Bessie Tait.................Edna May Oliver
Maggie Tiffany.................Louise Fazenda
Tiny Tim Tiffany.................Jackie Searl
King Max.................Bruce Line
Queen Sidonia.................Virginia Hammond

The Five Year Plan—
Russia's Remaking

(Amkino)

Pictorial Record

Amkino, American distributor of Russian produced films, is showing at the Central Theatre in New York "The Five Year Plan— Russia's Remaking," a pictorial silent record of conditions in Russia today as the result of the Five Year Plan, now in its third year of operation.

In this country, dialogue, written by an American economist and rendered by Mark Hawley, was synchronized. The audience at the Central was noticeably composed of what might be termed the radical element of New York. They were unmistakably thrilled by the record of industrial progress shown them, and reacted with vigorous applause when Stalin and other well-known Soviet figures appeared on the screen.

The Union of Soviet Socialist Republics, composed, we are told, of 160,000,000 people of all races, is introduced with short sequences meant to be illustrative of the enormous size of the country, its highly varied geographical conditions, and its unusually diversified population, ranging from the Eskimo of Siberia to the peasant of the Tibetan steppes.

With the verbal description keeping rapid and uninterrupted pace with the moving cameras, the audience is presented with a picture of a vast industrial development, including in its scene the building of factories, for automobiles, tractors, farm implements, the production of steel, and so on down the line of the necessities of an industrial and agricultural economic effort.

Pictured also are the efforts being made in the direction of social betterment, including the building of schools and the attempts to bring the rudiments of education to the masses, the erection of workers' homes and apartment houses, the construction of sanitariums and workers' clubs, in the cities.

We are told by the economist, via the voice of the announcer, that Russia will reach its five-year objective before 1933, the time set. Dams are shown in the course of construction, and power plants are seen rising from the previously barren plains. American engineers are the backbone of the industrial development, we are informed, and American products, automobiles and tractors, farm machinery and similar commodities are shown being unloaded from ships, and in use on the so-called cooperative farms, of the Russian peasantry, which appears much the same to the American eye as it did before the revolution.

There is no attempt at drama, cohesion or the human struggle in the film, nor is there any semblance of continuity. Rather, it is a record, in newsreel style, of mechanical and industrial methods and the results of those methods up to the present.

The only credit lines appearing on the film are one noting the synchronization by Pathe News, Inc., and the other advising that the dialogue recording was done with RCA Photophone equipment.

Film Reviews from *Motion Picture Herald*

SHOWMEN'S REVIEWS

This department deals with new product
from the point of view of the exhibitor
who is to purvey it to his own public

Washington Show

(MGM)

Drama

A timely picture! Telling the story that will headline every paper in the land, be on the tip of everyone's tongue, from now until the fourth of March, 1933—Politics!

A semi-inside story, laying bare the trials and temptations that beset the paths of our Congressional representatives in Washington. Set against a fascinating background of intrigue, deception, romance, patriotism, the menace of invisible government; colorful and interesting as the characters and the capitol it portrays. Withal, packed with that element of human interest that is so necessary in every picture.

Graphically picturing the rise of a "man of the people," who shatters the powerful political machine of a great Midwestern state—who goes to Washington as a senator. Who fights on the floor of the Senate that the rights and properties of the people may be torn from the grasp of invisible government. The story of a man who succumbs to the temptations of the "power trust," falls victim to the charms of a voluptuous feminine lure. Deserting the cause of the people to crumble himself and their hopes and aspirations in ruin. Picturing his fall, with startling realism and in a way that is all too familiar to the body politic of every town, city and state in the union.

You will have no difficulty selling this one to your patrons. Everything is in your favor. The theme is more than adequate. The personalities are great. No one needs to tell you what to do with Lionel Barrymore. More dramatic, more real than he was in "A Free Soul." Nor is it necessary to pass out any suggestions in regard to Karen Morely, who plays the sexy lobbyist, eventually marrying and double crossing Barrymore as part of the game of super-politics.

Out of the headlines of the papers, from the time of the Teapot Dome scandals, right down to all the sensational developments of the current presidential campaign, you'll get all the catchlines you want to whip up interest. The story of "Washington Show" is today's news. You can approach your campaign from a crusader angle. Of what happens to the most sincere and high minded congressmen who become enmeshed in the glittering whirlpool of Washington social life. Who forget the "folks back home" when there's prestige to be built, careers to be carved out. The story of the grip that "big business" has on the government of this country. Of the ways in which it makes its power work to insure the accomplishment of its own purposes and the defeat of the will of the people.

Inside pictures of the Senate at work—vividly portraying machine politics on the floor. Dramatic speeches. Tense excitement of packed galleries. The deals, the trading, the bargaining for votes. The button-holing in the cloak rooms. The hectic hulabaloo of the news services and the special writers, all fighting for exclusive sensational inside stories. The drama of the investigating committee, where the super-lobbyist asks the nation "what are you going to do about it?" All these are dynamic catchlines.

Here is plenty of everything that intrigues

THE concept of this department is that the exhibitor is concerned not with any critic's idea of "how good?" or "how poor?" but rather with the question of precisely what the product is and what is to be done with it when and as it is played. The exhibitor, in general, is concerned with the special aspects of strength and of weakness in the product, its appeals and shortcomings, that he may adequately deal with it when he becomes its sponsor to his public. These "review" pages aim to aid the exhibitor as the retailer of the merchandise concerned.—THE EDITOR.

---

the interest of the people. A picture that tells the story of their power and their weakness. You can stir your town with interest if you play this picture up to the limit as a stark revelation of what's wrong in Washington and why. You don't have to worry about treading on anybody's toes. You can make this picture a part of every campaign speech that every candidate makes. Get them to talk about it. Get the newspapers to talk about it. Get the civic leaders in your town to endorse and recommend it. Get all the furore and excitement of the current political campaign into your film campaign. Use the same stunts that the politicians are using, with banners, trucks, meetings. If you can tie up with a radio station for a broadcast of Barrymore's speech on the floor of the Senate direct from your projection room—or shoot it out on the streets over a loud-speaker system, you'll be turning loose the best political speech of the year.

Get behind this one with every ounce of showmanship you possess and you should need the S.R.O. sign every time you show it.—McCARTHY, Hollywood.

Produced and distributed by M-G-M. Directed by Charles Brabin. From the play "The Claw," by Henry Bernstein. Continuity and dialogue by John Meehan in collaboration with Samuel Blythe. Photographed by Gregg Toland. Film editor, Ben Lewis. Release date, July 9, 1932. Running time, 74 minutes.

CAST

Jeff Keane	Lionel Barrymore
Consuela Fairbanks	Karen Morley
Ruth Keane	Diane Sinclair
Brenner	Nils Asther
Senator Withers	Reginald Barlow
Babcock	William Collier, Sr.
Senator Hodge	William Morris
Mona	Rafaela Ottiano
Hinsdale	C. Henry Gordon
Senator Bitler	Burton Churchill
Stapleton	Henry Kolker

Lucky Girl

(British International)

Musical Comedy

If Hollywood had given this to Lubitsch he might have enjoyed himself, for it is a story of the kind dear to his democratic heart. Stephan Gregorovitch suddenly finds himself crowned king of Karaslavia, a territory of

---

small dimensions and smaller exchequer. What can he do but call in his efficiency expert and right-hand pal, Mr. Hudson Greener of Boston, U. S. A., who, having an eye for the money's worth of the crown jewels, arranges forthwith a visit to London there to realize.

Once in London, our king assumes incognito as "Mr. Abdulla," and with his friend Greener mixes with the best company in order to sell the jewels. At one house party, the two are mistaken for a couple of crooks known to be planning a raid on the jewel cases of several well placed ladies there. Complications further overtake "Mr. Abdulla" when he falls heavily for a Lady Moira Somebody-or-other. The whole party sings, dances and complicates its way through the usual string of adventures, and finally the real identity of "Mr. Abdulla" is revealed and a hint of personal happiness and greater financial stability for the king of Karaslavia is conveyed via a match between the rich Lady Moira and her modest "Mr. Abdulla."

It is all good fun, and moves with fair speed. There is more comedy than real music, but the acting of Gene Gerrard as the king and Molly Lamont as the Lady Moira make up for musical shortcomings. Gus MacNaughton as Greener gives a performance very suggestive of Woolsey of the Wheeler and Woolsey duo. Direction is smooth enough, and the motif provides a change from the long run of domestic farces which have lately come from British studios. Gene Gerrard shows well not only as the star, but as the director, and with his assistant, Frank Miller, takes credit for a nice little job—MOORING, London.

Produced by British International. Distributed in U. S. A. by Powers. Adapted from the musical comedy by Douglas Furber, R. P. Weston and Bert Lee, and from the play "Mr. Abdulla" by Reginald Berkeley. Running time, 75 minutes.

CAST

King Stephan	Gene Gerrard
Lady Moira	Molly Lamont
Hudson E. Greener	Gus McNaughton
The Duke	Spencer Trevor
The Duchess	Tonie Bruce

New Morals for Old

(MGM)

Drama

Here is a picture almost completely lacking in money names for your marquee and newspaper ads, yet, by reason of the very humanness of its characters it deserves a niche in the gallery of fine pictures.

There may be nothing new in a plot where a doting mother and father are so fond of their children that they become absolutely selfish, but there is something decidedly different when that mother, father and children are played by Laura Hope Crewes, Lewis Stone, Margaret Perry and Robert Young.

Without attempting a synopsis of the story we need only point out that the children disagree with the old fashioned ideas of their parents, yet, before the final fadeout, are thinking and talking exactly as did their parents before them.

The title can be played around with quite a bit. In some spots it may be immediately taken as another "sex" proposition, which is not entirely so. True, the daughter does go to live with a married man, but this seems to fade out of the audience's mind by reason of the

had been in love with Keith, that Miss Furness and Wadsworth had not been the dovelike couple they appeared, that she had gone to Douglas for sympathy and understanding, that Douglas had actually stolen the money to save Miss Furness from a financial debt of which she feared to tell her husband, that Miss Bruce really was in love with Nagel, and that she had shot Keith in self-defense on a visit to his home, all of which Douglas had guessed. Nagel, in a final washup, kills himself. That's what might have happened.

Then what *did* happen. Wadsworth finds another tube, replaces the burned one, the group dances and chats, and in the moonlight Miss Bruce says yes to Douglas.

Typical stage material, it is effectively done on the screen, but it is still a stage play, except that it is in celluloid.—AARONSON, New York.

Produced and distributed by RKO Radio. From the play by J. B. Priestley. Directed by Phil Rosen. Associate director, Arthur Sircom. Screen play by Anne Morrison Chapin and Madelein Ruthven. Musical director, Max Steiner. Photographed by J. Roy Hunt. Art directors, Van Nest Polglase and Perry Ferguson. Recorded by John L. Cass. Edited by Archie Marshek. P. C. A. Certificate No. 237. Running time, 67 minutes. Release date, Oct. 5, 1934. Adult audience classification.

CAST

Olwen	Virginia Bruce
Robert	Conrad Nagel
Charles	Melvyn Douglas
Freda	Erin O'Brien-Moore
Martin	Ian Keith
Betty	Betty Furness
Gordon	Henry Wadsworth
Miss Mockridge	Doris Lloyd

The Wandering Jew

(Olympic Pictures)

Drama

From the famed play of the same title by E. Temple Thurston, Julius Hagen in England has produced a powerful motion picture, but one which would appear to have a definitely limited appeal. In its basic significance it stirs a deeplying religious question, and for that reason the exhibitor is rather under the necessity of treading warily.

This film some time ago was purchased by MGM for distribution here, but subsequently was dropped at the firm protest of the rabbinical interests of New York, as being of too highly controversial a nature.

From the standpoint of the production as a motion picture, however, it has been excellently presented, and throughout the outstanding highlight is the brilliance of the performance of Conrad Veidt as the Wandering Jew, who spat upon Jesus and was cursed to wander through the ages, thus doing penance for his wrathful act. At all times, the work has been elaborately and authentically produced, with all the fanfare and pageantry of the periods of which it tells. The support, quite completely unknown in this country, is none the less capable.

The story is divided into four phases, the first the scene of the original act of the Jew, the others the following chapters in his life, until at last it is given to him to find the rest and peace which comes with death, his eternal wandering at an end. Breaking waves on a sandy shore separate phase from phase, effectively, and it may be mentioned that there is an outstanding technical excellence in the film.

First in Jerusalem, as Veidt's wife, dying, calls for Jesus, Veidt becomes enraged, rushes to the street, and as Christ carries the cross toward Calvary, spits upon him. The curse, that Veidt shall wait upon the earth until Christ shall return, comes to him, and as he attempts to stab himself to join his dead wife, the blade snaps.

Then he appears in the guise of a strange and fearless knight in armor, in the days of the Crusades, where he, winning at the jousts, stealing the wives of others, lives utterly without fear of death. In the third phase, Veidt is seen as a merchant in Sicily, generations later, loving dearly his wife and their son. When the son, bitten by an adder, dies, Veidt sees his wife taken from him by the spirit of

the church, personified by a kindly neighboring monk. When she leaves, he cannot kill her, is completely beaten, seeing yet his fate to continue his wandering.

Finally, in the city of Seville, in Spain, he is a kindly and able doctor, who treats the poor for no return. It is at that time that the cruel and tortuously oppressive Spanish Inquisition holds its fearsome sway, seeking out, torturing and burning heretics, especially Jews. When Veidt treats a street walker, and innocently makes a damaging remark to her, the weight of the Inquisitors turns upon him, and he is haled before the council. He refuses to speak, but finally does to save the girl. About to be burned at the stake, he falls dead, finally granted the death he had sought so long.

Powerful, dramatic material, brilliantly performed, the film is nevertheless limited for audiences.—AARONSON, New York.

A Julius Hagen-Twickenham production. Distributed by Olympic Pictures. Directed by Maurice Elvey. Musical score by Hugo Reisenfeld. Adapted from the play by E. Temple Thurston. Running time, 83 minutes. Release date, not yet set. Adult audience classification.

CAST

The Wandering Jew	Conrad Veidt
Judith	Marie Ney
Rachel (Mathias' sister)	Cicely Oates
Pontius Pilate	Basil Gill
Joanne de Beaudricourt	Anne Gorey
Joemund, Prince of Tarentum	Bertram Wallis
Issachar	Hechtor Abbas
De Beaudricourt	Dennis Holy
Godfrey, Duke of Normandy	Jack Livesey
Phirous	Takase
Gianella	Joan Maude
Pietro Morelli (the Priest)	John Stuart
Andrea Michelotti	Arnold Lucy
Olalla Quintano	Peggy Ashcroft
Juan de Texedo (Inquisitor General)	F. L. Sullivan
Ferera	Felix Aylmer
Castro	Ivor Barnard
Zapporitas	Abraham Sofaer
Juan	Stafford Hilliard
First Monk	Robert Gilbert

Mills of the Gods

(Columbia)

Drama

A dramatic story of the strength and courage of an elderly woman of wealth, whose own straightforwardness is in direct contrast to the worthlessness of her offspring and grandchildren, this picture appears entertaining material, developing an almost secondary romantic theme as it progresses, and concluding on a note of the character rejuvenation of at least one member of the wholly unnecessary family.

The best name in all probability will be that of May Robson, from the selling standpoint, supported in particular by Fay Wray and Victor Jory. The others are inconsequential from an exploitation angle. There is a current note in the thematic situation of a great factory in danger of complete shutdown as a result of the depression, which would result in throwing out of work thousands of workers. As the elderly woman would step into the breach, the young granddaughter, with romance with one of the workers' leaders as the mainspring, stands beside the grandmother to bring order and renewed hope out of approaching labor chaos.

There is a touch of unnecessary tragedy at the conclusion as the weak-spined brother meets death attempting to aid his stronger willed sister.

For many years, following the death of her husband, Miss Robson has carried on the major business which her husband founded. Seeking retirement, she turns the business over to a board of directors of old employees, not daring to trust her worthless family. There are Miss Wray and James Blakely, the grandchildren; Raymond Walburn and Josephine Whitell, the son and daughter. All are wasters and prefer living in the smart resorts of Europe to staying at home. Three years after Miss Robson's retirement, the depression hits, payrolls are cut, departments close and the town, dependent on the plant, is in danger of ruin.

When Miss Robson learns the plant is in danger she summons the family from their pleasures, and they refuse to put up their money to keep the plant open. Reluctantly Miss

Robson steps out, leaving Walburn in charge. He decides to close the mills and leave with the family for Paris. Agitators, led by Jory, stir trouble. Jory accidentally meets and falls in love with Miss Wray. When a committee demands action Walburn promises a meeting, but plans to flee. The workers plot to stop him when he's to board his private car. Miss Robson, meanwhile, has raised all available cash, but before she can prevent a riot, young Blakely is killed. Miss Robson promises to reopen the plant, and keep it open. Jory and Miss Wray part, with the understanding that they will soon be together again.—AARONSON, New York.

Produced and distributed by Columbia. Directed by Roy William Neill. Story by Melville Baker and John S. Kirkland. Screen play by Garret Fort. Assistant director, Art Black. Cameraman, Al Seigler. Sound engineer, Edward L. Bernds. Film editor, Jack Rawlins. P. C. A. Certificate No. 465. Running time, 67 minutes. Release date, Dec. 15, 1934. General audience classification.

CAST

Mary Hastings	May Robson
Jean	Fay Wray
Jim Devlin	Victor Jory
Willard	Raymond Walburn
Alex	James Blakely
Henrietta	Josephine Whitell
Sarah	Mayo Methot
Filippi	Albert Conti
Burroughs	Samuel S. Hinds
Thomas	Willard Robertson
Morgan	Edward Keane
Komeoski	Edward Van Sloan
Barrett	Frank Reicher
Nordstown	Fredrik Vogeding
Kennedy	Guy Usher

Isle of Bermuda

(Fox)

Interesting

In this number of the Magic Carpet series, the camera has ably pictured the beauty and tranquility which characterizes England's quiet island in the south Atlantic. Seen are the natural beauties of the island, the crystal caves, the unexcelled view from the famous Gibbs' Lighthouse, the coast line and the festivities which mark the celebration of St. George's Day by the British military garrison. The fact that many of the film's patrons have been in Bermuda should heighten the interest in scenes which for many will be familiar.—Running time, 11 minutes.

So You Won't T-T-T-Talk

(Vitaphone)

Good Comedy

An unusually good comedy, chiefly that by reason of the appearance of two ace comedians, Roscoe Ates of the unstable tongue, and Shemp Howard of the canopy of hair. The two, much beset by respective wives and the small brother of Ates' wife, go on a picnic in the woods, after many a mishap in the home. One of the neatest comedy touches in many a day is the manner in which Howard plays solitaire with innumerable sandwiches he is supposed to be making. At the picnic grounds, with the boy chiefly at fault, the two move from one mishap to another, ending in a wild flight for home, pursued by a polecat. Ates is well known and amusing, Howard is less known, but if anything even more amusing.—Running time, 20 minutes.

Toyland Premiere

(Universal)

Good

Highly entertaining and in Technicolor, this number of the Cartune Classics series is a shade late for the Christmas material it offers, but it still should be found enjoyable, especially by the youngsters, and is appearing closely enough to the holiday season to reduce that factor to a negligible obstacle. Santa Claus visits the big city on the invitation of Oswald, and at the toyland bazaar he is the guest at a dinner, where various film stars, in caricature, perform. Most of the fun is supplied by the characters of Laurel and Hardy.—Running time, 9 minutes.

Film Reviews from *Motion Picture Herald*

PRODUCT DIGEST

The Hour Before the Dawn

(Paramount)

Drama of Ideals

This is not a war picture but a picture with a wartime setting. It is one of a number of films dealing in the drama of ideas and ideals, the ideas and ideals of democracy in conflict with fascism. And it is the story of an integrity that transcends faith. As such, it is a superb picture, one of the best in its category. William Dozier, the producer, and Frank Tuttle, the director, have caused to be brought forth a smooth, highly polished and well contrived adaptation of the Somerset Maugham novel.

In a brief prologue young Jim Hetherton accidentally shoots and kills his pet dog. As a result, he grows into manhood pathologically hating guns and killing. Franchot Tone plays the role of Jim Hetherton as a young man and gives a poignantly realistic and understandable portrayal of a conscientious objector when England goes to war with Germany upon the invasion of Poland.

Jim is in love with a Dora Bruckmann, ostensibly an Austrian refugee, and the only weak note in the picture with Veronica Lake in the role, making it all too obvious to the English family, into which she has ingratiated herself, that she is a Nazi espionage agent. Nearby the Hetherton estate is a secret airfield, the headquarters of Jim's brother, an RAF commander. The while Dora endeavors to guide the Luftwaffe to the secret airport, one of her confederates works on Jim's pacifism in an effort to involve him in a scheme for a negotiated peace. Jim's small nephew Tommy, comes upon Dora in the act of firing a haystack during an air raid. He tells his Uncle Jim who thereupon experiences a metamorphosis in the knowledge that perfidy is even more at odds with his ideals than is killing. He kills Dora.

Exhibitors can exploit this film as drama, a tale of intrigue and espionage. Miss Lake, throughout the footage in which she appears, makes a beautiful, albeit a rather obvious, spy. The cast in every other respect is uniformly good, especially John Sutton, Binnie Barnes, Henry Stephenson and young David Leland.

Seen in the home office projection room. Reviewer's Rating: Excellent.—BERT HICKS.

Release date, Block 4. Running time, 75 min. PCA No. 9371. General audience classification.
Jim Hetherton........................Franchot Tone
Dora Bruckmann........................Veronica Lake
Roger Hetherton........................John Sutton
Binnie Barnes, Henry Stephenson, Philip Merivale, Nils Asther, Edmond Breon, David Leland.

Knickerbocker Holiday

(PCA - United Artists)

Fun in Old New York

The initial release of Producers Corporation of America is unique among current screen offerings, although it is, in the truest sense, musical comedy. The film is costume farce of the

Reviews

This department deals with new product from the point of view of the exhibitor who is to purvey it to his own public.

(Running times in all instances are the official times given by the distributors.)

1650's, without being more than broadly historical, and it is operetta, fitted to the voice and style of Nelson Eddy, with no time out for arias or staged production numbers.

The accent is on comedy in song and story. Charles Coburn, taking a part in both as Peter Stuyvesant, is its mainstay, while Ernest Cossart, Johnny "Scat" Davis and Percy Kilbride lend capable assistance. When the comedy clicks, whether slapstick or satire, Harry Joe Brown, who produced and directed it, has a highly amusing film.

At all times the music, including four songs from the original stage show by Maxwell Anderson and Kurt Weill, is delightful and well-sung by the principals and chorus. The lyrics of "September Song" are still fresh enough to promise a revival of the musical hit of the show. Five songs, of which two are by Eddy himself, have been added to keep the splendid baritone at the trade in which he has few rivals.

The story, adapted from the Anderson-Weill play by Thomas Lennon, David Boehm and Rowland Leigh, mixes politics and romance in merry and tuneful fashion, pitting a crusading printer against the future of New Amsterdam and the hand of pretty Constance Dowling. The situation is resolved with the two men joining forces for democratic rule.

If this sounds like unnatural history, there is enough reference to trafficking with the Indians in fire-arms and fire-water as well as a Councilman named Roosevelt—a man of some honor among thieves—to give it the proper farcical flavor.

Carmen Amaya and her company of dancers are introduced at two points for their vivid specialties, but are under a disadvantage in the stylized colonial setting.

Seen in the home office projection room. Reviewer's Rating: Good.—E. A. CUNNINGHAM.

Release date, not set. Running time, 85 min. PCA No. 9830. General audience classification.
Brom Broeck........................Nelson Eddy
Peter Stuyvesant........................Charles Coburn.
Tina Tienhoven........................Constance Dowling
Ernest Cossart, Shelley Winter, Johnny "Scat" Davis, Percy Kilbride, Otto Kruger, Richard Hale, Fritz Feld, Chester Conklin.

You Can't Ration Love

(Paramount)

Teen-Age Musical

Two timely topics are combined to create the plot of this entertaining musical—the current devotion to crooners among the younger set and the present shortage of manpower, with or without vocal talent. The result has novelty, light hearted high-jinks, a handful of good songs by Lester Lee and Jerry Seelen and engaging performances by Betty Rhodes and Johnnie Johnston. Audiences in and out of the "bobby-sock" age should find the film diverting.

The principals are students in a small college, and very "hep." The few remaining males are rationed on a point value system according to their desirability for dates. A not-so-lucky girl whose steady boy friend costs too many points finds herself falling back on "Two Point Simpson" for solace. Turning him into a modish crooner, she stimulates overwhelming competition and must resort to an ancient female deception to win him back.

Several attractive young performers, including Marjorie Weaver, Marie Wilson, Bill Edwards and Johnnie "Scat" Davis, add zest to the story, while D'Artega and his All-Girl Orchestra contribute swing music, very much in the groove.

Lester Fuller and Michel Kraika, director and associate producer, rate praise for a well-paced and nicely varied production. Val Burton and Hal Fimberg wrote the screenplay from a story by Muriel Roy Bolton.

Seen in a New York projection room. Reviewer's Rating: Good.—E. A. C.

Release date, Block 4. Running time, 79 min. PCA No. 9837. General audience classification.
Betty........................Betty Rhodes
John Simpson........................Johnnie Johnston
Bill Edwards, Marjorie Weaver, Marie Wilson, Johnnie "Scat" Davis, Mabel Paige, Jean Wallace, Roland Dupree, Christine Forsythe, D'Artega and his All-Girl Orchestra.

The Halfway House

(Ealing Studios)

Flesh and Fantasy from Britain

Michael Balcon's second contribution to the year's offerings is a characteristic adventure into the twin worlds of flesh and fantasy.

Tormented by the strain of continued war, allowing their private troubles to overcome them, is a knot of people, each unassociated with the others, all seeking the sanctuary of the quiet peace of a wayside inn set in the remote valleys of North Wales. There is a flying officer and his wife, bickering their way to the tragedy of a divorce; an embittered ex-officer just released from a prison sentence; a ship's captain wrongfully accused of cowardice and his wife inveterately mourning their dead son; three or four other victims, as each imagines, of the cruel circumstance of war. All of them, at dif-

Product Digest Section   1781.

Notes

The following abbreviations are used in the notes:

AMPAS	Academy of Motion Picture Arts and Sciences
FDY	*Film Daily Yearbook*
HUAC	House Un-American Activities Committee
MOMA	Museum of Modern Art Library
MPH	*Motion Picture Herald*
SA	*Screen Actor*
SAG	Screen Actors Guild
UCLASC	University of California at Los Angeles Special Collection
V	*Variety*
WRM	Will Rogers Memorial, Santa Monica, California
WRMA	Will Rogers Memorial Archive, Claremore, Oklahoma
WRML	Will Rogers Memorial Library, Claremore, Oklahoma

Prologue

1. Bernard Weinraub, "Senator Moves to Control Party's Moral Agenda," *New York Times*, June 1, 1995, p. 1. See also "Dan Quayle vs. Murphy Brown," *Time*, June 1, 1992, pp. 20, 29, 33. For the conservative critique of current movies, complete with the uncritical assertion that to experience the "dull ache over what we have lost" is only to recall that once Hollywood reinforced the "fundamental" values of the people, see Michael Medved, *Hollywood vs. America: Popular Culture and the War on Traditional Values* (New York: Harper Collins, 1992), 316–318. For a far more positive account of current moviemakers, see Peter Biskind, *Easy Riders, Raging Bulls: How the Sex-Drugs-and-Rock'n'Roll Generation Saved Hollywood* (New York: Simon and Schuster, 1998).

2. For the contours of this debate, see Lary May, ed., *Recasting America: Culture and Politics in the Age of Cold War* (Chicago: University of Chicago Press, 1989).

3. On nationalism in the arts, see Benedict Anderson, *Imagined Communities: Reflections on the Origin and Spread of Nationalism* (New York: Verso, 1991); Andrew Higson, "The Concept of National Cinema," *Screen* 30, no. 4 (Autumn 1989): 36–46.

4. Lary May, *Screening Out the Past: The Birth of Mass Culture and the Motion Picture Industry* (Chicago: University of Chicago Press, 1983).

5. This story constitutes chapters 1 and 4. For an earlier version based on the description presented here, see Lary May, "Movie Star Politics: The Screen Actors Guild, Cultural Conversion and the Hollywood Red Scare," in May, ed., *Recasting America*, pp. 125–153.

6. For a discussion of republicanism, see David Noble, *The End of American History: Democracy, Capitalism and the Metaphor of Two Worlds in Anglo American Historical Writing, 1880–1980* (Minneapolis: The University of Minnesota Press, 1985), and Sara Evans and Harry Boyte, *Free Spaces: The Sources of Democratic Change in America* (New York: Harper and Row, 1986), pp. 1–25.

7. On Benton in Hollywood, see Erika Doss, *Benton, Pollock and the Politics of Modernism: From Regionalism to Abstract Expressionism* (Chicago: University of Chicago Press, 1991), pp. 147–229.

8. See Warren Susman, *Culture as History: The Transformation of American Society in the Twentieth Century* (New York: Pantheon, 1984). See also Robert Sklar, *Movie-Made America: A Cultural History of American Movies* (New York: Vintage Books, 1975), ch. 12. A recent and important book adds the politics of the New Deal to the story, but still argues that the films and politics of the day served the conservative function of saving capitalism. See Giuliana Muscio, *Hollywood's New Deal* (Philadelphia: Temple University Press, 1997). For a similar view, see Alan Trachtenberg, *Reading American Photographs: Images as History—Mathew Brady to Walker Evans* (New York: Hill and Wang, 1989); Andrew Bergman, *We're in the Money: Depression America and Its Films* (New York: Harper and Row, 1971); Richard Pells, *Radical Visions and American Dreams* (New York: Harper and Row, 1977). A welcome exception to these trends can be found in two books. See Brian Neve, *Film and Politics in America: A Social Tradition* (London: Routledge, 1992), pp. 1–56; Robert S. McElvaine, *The Great Depression in America, 1929–1941* (New York: Times Books, 1984), pp. 196–221.

9. See David Bordwell, Janet Staiger, and Kristen Thompson, *The Classical Hollywood Cinema: Film Style and Mode of Production* (New York: Columbia University Press, 1985); Thomas Schatz, *The Genius of the System: Hollywood Film Making in the Studio Era* (New York: Pantheon Books, 1988); Robert B. Ray, *Certain Tendency of the Hollywood Cinema 1930–1980* (Princeton: Princeton University Press, 1985). For the dialogical approach, see Mikhail Bakhtin, *The Dialogical Imagination* (Austin, Tex.: University of Texas Press, 1981); Horace M. Newcombe, "On the Dialogical Aspects of Mass Communications," *Cultural Studies in Mass Communications* 1 (1984): 34–50.

10. The hegemonic approach is best advanced by T. J. Jackson Lears, "Making Fun of Popular Culture," *American Historical Review* 97 (1992): 1418, and Jean Christophe Agnew, "Coming Up for Air: Consumer Culture in Historical Perspective," *Intellectual History Newsletter* 12 (1990): 3–12. The fact that the studios dominated production and created a "classical American cinema" formula that was capable of being repeated to guarantee profits is the subject of Tino Ballo, ed., *Grand Design: Hollywood as a Modern Business Enterprise, 1930–1939* (New York: Scribners, 1993). See also the similar thesis advanced by Douglas Gomery, *The Hollywood Studio System, 1930–1949* (New York: St. Martin's Press, 1986).

For the capacity of Hollywood to promote a uniform Americanism for immigrants, much like the moviemakers themselves, see Neal Gabler, *An Empire of Their Own: How the Jews Invented Hollywood* (New York: Crown, 1988). Michael Rogin builds on Gabler's work to argue that the Americanism was racist or permeated with codes of white superiority. See Rogin, *Blackface, White Noise: Jewish Immigrants in the Hollywood Melting Pot* (Berkeley: University of California Press, 1996).

That audiences reinterpreted mass-produced images in the thirties is the subject of Lawrence Levine, "The Folklore of Industrial Society: Popular Culture and Its Audience" in Levine, ed., *The Unpredictable Past* (New York: Oxford University Press, 1993), 291–319. See also Janice Radway, *Reading the Romance: Women, Patriarchy and Popular Literature* (Chapel Hill: University of North Carolina Press, 1993).

11. For the New Left view, see Barton Bernstein, "The New Deal: The Conservative Achievements of Liberal Reform," in Bernstein, ed., *Towards a New Past* (New York: Pantheon, 1968). For the classic liberal views, see Arthur Schlesinger, Jr., *The Age of Roosevelt,* 3 vols. (Boston: Houghton Mifflin, 1957–1960), and Erik Goldman, *Rendezvous with Destiny: A History of Modern Reform* (New York: Knopf, 1952).

12. Those interested in the dynamics of this family, see my sister's Emmy-Award-winning documentary, *Secret Daughter,* produced and directed by June Cross, *Frontline* (WGBH, Public Broadcasting Co., November 1996). On Chaplin and Epstein, see Jerry Epstein, *Remembering Charlie: A Pictorial Biography* (New York: Doubleday, 1989).

13. Lizabeth Cohen, *Making a New Deal: Industrial Workers in Chicago, 1919–1939* (New York: Cambridge University Press, 1990); Gary Gerstle, *Working Class Americanism: The Politics of Labor in an Industrial City, 1914–1960* (New York: Cambridge University Press, 1989); Alan Brinkley, *Voices of Protest: Huey Long, Father Coughlin, and the General Depression* (New York: Alfred A. Knopf, 1982). On the manner in which voting by class entered the two-party system, see Richard Oestreicher, "Urban Working Class Political Behavior and Theories of Electoral Politics, 1879–1940," *Journal of American History* 74 (1988): 1257–86.

14. On regionalist painting and the writing of progressive history, see Erika Doss, "The Art of Cultural Politics: From Regionalism to Abstract Expressionism," and David Noble, "The Reconstruction of Progress: Charles Beard, Richard Hofstadter and Postwar Historical Thought," in May, *Recasting America,* pp. 195–220, 61–75. On swing music, see Lewis Erenberg, *Swingin' the Dream: Big Band Jazz and the Rebirth of American Culture* (Chicago: University of Chicago Press, 1998). On film, see Steven Watts, *The Magic Kingdom: Walt Disney and the American Way of Life* (Boston: Houghton Mifflin, 1997), 63–203. See also Michael Denning, *The Cultural Front: The Laboring of American Culture in the Twentieth Century* (New York: Verso, 1996).

15. See appendix 1 for a longer discussion of the methods used to gather this data and collate the conclusions for the figures that can be found in appendix 2. I wish to thank my research assistants at the University of Minnesota—Chris Lewis, Michael Willard, Jonathan Munby, and Scott Zimmerman—for their invaluable aid in this task. They helped devise the categories, collate the material for the computer, and create the figures that illustrate the themes.

Chapter One

1. The accounts of Rogers's funeral were gleaned from the Will Rogers Obituary File, Academy of Motion Picture Arts and Sciences (hereafter known as AMPAS), Los Angeles, California. All the accounts derive from the *Los Angeles Times,* the *Los Angeles Examiner,* and *Variety* from August 16 to 20, 1935. Many of the same accounts can be found in Reba Collins, *Will Rogers and Wiley Post in Alaska: The Crash Heard 'Round the World* (Claremore, Okla.: Will Rogers Heritage Press, 1984), pp. 60–80. The quotation comes from the *Chicago American,* August 19, 1935, unpaginated clipping in Will Rogers Memorial Library, Claremore, Oklahoma (hereafter known as WRML).

2. Most of these broadcasts are in Steven K. Gragert, ed., *Radio Broadcasts of Will Rogers* (Stillwater, Okla: Oklahoma State University Press, 1983). The quotations are taken from Will Rogers, Columbia Network, November 11, 1934, in P. J. O'Brien, *Will Rogers: Ambassador of Good Will and Prince of Wit and Wisdom* (Philadelphia: John C. Winston, 1935), pp. 147–150.

3. Robert S. Lynd and Helen Merrell Lynd, *Middletown in Transition: A Study in Cultural Conflicts* (New York: Harcourt Brace Jovanovich, 1937), p. 481; Editorial, *New York Times,* November 28, 1932; Letter of Harry Chandler to Will Rogers, September 26, 1932, in Will Rogers Memorial, Claremore, Oklahoma (discussion of controversy). See *The Autobiography of Will Rogers,* ed. Donald Day (New York: Avon Books, 1975), pp. 268–269, for Rogers's answer to a hostile *Wall Street Journal* editorial. See also Will Rogers, "The Pilgrims," in Gragert, *Radio Broadcasts,* April 14, 1935, p. 119.

4. The classic statement of this view appeared in Warren Susman's essays reprinted in *Culture as History: The Transformation of American Culture in the Twentieth Century* (New York: Pantheon Books, 1984), pp. 150–211. For one among many current statements of the same view, see Alan Trachtenberg, *Reading American Photographs: Images as History: Mathew Brady to Walker Evans* (New York: Hill and Wang, 1989), p. 247; T. J. Jackson Lears, "Making Fun of Popular Culture," *American Historical Review* 97, no. 5 (December 1992): 1418; Jean Christophe Agnew, "Coming Up for Air: Consumer Culture in Historical Perspective," *Intellectual History Newsletter* 12 (1990): 3–12. An exception to this trend is Brian Neve, *Film and Politics in America: A Social Tradition* (London: Routledge, 1992), pp. 1–56.

On Depression-era audiences' capacity to make their own choices and reinterpret images at the point of reception, see Lawrence Levine, "The Folklore of Industrial Society: Popular Culture and Its Audiences," in Levine, ed., *The Unpredictable Past* (New York: Oxford University Press, 1993), pp. 291–319. The emphasis here is on the creativity of audiences, but divorced from their capacity as consumers to influence overall film content.

5. Andrew Bergman, *We're in the Money: Depression America and Its Films* (New York: Harper and Row, 1971), xvi, 71. The thrust of most scholarship is to treat Rogers as a backward-looking mythmaker. See Peter C. Rollins, *Will Rogers: A Bio-Bibliography* (Westport, Conn.: Greenwood Press, 1984); William R. Brown, *Imagemaker: Will Rogers and the American Dream* (Columbia: University of Missouri Press, 1970); E. Paul Alworth, *Will Rogers* (New York: Twayne Publishers, 1974). Outside the scholarship, the trend has been to write hagiography. See Richard M. Ketchum, *Will Rogers, His Life and Times* (New York: McGraw Hill, 1973); David Randolph Milsten, *Will Rogers the Cherokee Kid* (Chicago: Glenheath, 1987). Earlier biographers, closer to the scene, were far more conscious of Rogers's radical politics. See Donald Day, *Will Rogers: A Biography* (New York: David McKay, 1962). The most recent biographer again sees Rogers as a backward-looking icon. See Ben Yagoda, *Will Rogers* (New York: Alfred A. Knopf, 1993).

6. Craig Calhoun, "The Radicalism of Tradition," *American Journal of Sociology* 88, no. 5 (March 1983): 886–913.

7. William E. Leuchtenberg, *Franklin Roosevelt and the New Deal* (New York: Harper & Row, 1963), p. 102; Eric Foner, *The Story of American Freedom* (New York: W. W. Norton and Co., 1998), pp. 195–196.

8. Foner, *American Freedom,* pp. 195–199.

9. See Lary May, *Screening Out the Past: The Birth of Mass Culture and the Motion Picture Industry* (Chicago: University of Chicago Press, 1983); Lewis Erenberg, *Steppin' Out: New York Nightlife and the Transformation of American Culture* (Chicago: University of Chicago Press, 1984).

10. May, *Screening Out the Past,* pp. 147–236; Steven Ross, *Working Class Hollywood* (Princeton: Princeton University Press, 1998).

11. Bergman, *We're In the Money,* pp. xx–xxii.

12. *Film Daily Yearbook,* 1930, pp. 997–1003 (hereafter cited as *FDY*); *FDY,* 1931, p. 39; *FDY,* 1932, pp. 963–965; and *FDY,* 1933, p. 957.

13. *Variety,* January 8, 1930, pp. 78, 80–88 (hereafter cited as *V*); *V,* January 7, 1931, p. 5; *V,* January 5, 1932; *FDY,* 1932, pp. 1–7; R. W. Sexton, "Changing Values in Theater Design," *Motion Picture Herald,* March 14, 1931, pp. 25–68 (hereafter cited as *MPH*); Tom Waller, "The Year in Pictures," *V,* December 29, 1931, p. 4; Martin Quigley, "Less Heat and More Light from Hollywood," *MPH* (December 5, 1931, pp. 9–12.

14. Bergman, *We're In the Money,* p. xxii.

15. For one of many accounts of Rogers's statement that his ancestors met the boat, see Collins, *Will Rogers and Wiley Post,* p. 83, or the very insightful biography by his wife, Betty Rogers, *Will Rogers: His Wife's Story* (Norman, Okla.: University of Oklahoma Press, 1941), p. 33. The best account of early Cherokee history is Tom Hatley, *The Dividing Paths: Cherokees and South Carolinians Through the Era of Revolution* (New York: Oxford University Press, 1994). A superb overview of their culture and politics can be found in Theda Perdue, *The Cherokee* (New York: Chelsea House, 1989). The place of Clem and Mary Rogers in that larger story can be gleaned from Ellsworth Collings, *The Old Home Ranch: Birthplace of Will Rogers* (Claremore, Okla.: Will Rogers Heritage Press, 1964), especially pp. 97–109.

16. See James H. Merrell, *The Indians' New World: Catawbas and Their Neighbors from European Contact Through the Era of Removal* (Chapel Hill: University of North Carolina Press, 1989).

17. See Perdue, *The Cherokee.*

18. On land in common and sharing, see Perdue, *The Cherokee,* pp. 24–25, 46–47. On the response of Will Rogers's wife when he gave her land and money so she would be indepen-

dent, thus carrying on Indian ideals, see Betty Rogers, *Will Rogers*, p. 36. And on redistributive economics among tribes in the area, see Daniel Richter, *The Ordeal of the Long House: The Peoples of the Iroquois League in the Era of European Civilization* (Chapel Hill: University of North Carolina Press, 1993), pp. 21–22.

19. Alan Kilpatrick, "Going to the Water: A Structural Analysis of Cherokee Purification Rituals," *American Indian Culture and Research Journal* 15, no. 4 (1991): 49–58; Barbara Babcock, "Arrange Me in Disorder: Fragments and Reflections on Ritual Clowning," in *Rite, Drama, Festival, Spectacle: Rehearsals Towards Theory of Cultural Performance*, ed. John J. MacAloon (Philadelphia: Institute for the Study of Human Issues, 1984), pp. 102–128.

20. For one among many accounts of cultural exchange in the Indian frontier in the eighteenth century, the period when the Cherokee nation adapted to western ways, see Richter, *The Ordeal of the Long House.*

21. Perdue, *The Cherokee,* pp. 13–47. For the Rogers family tree and his ancestors, see Reba Collins, *Climbing the Will Rogers Family Tree,* vol. I (Claremore, Okla.: Will Rogers Heritage Press, 1982), pp. 10–12.

22. See Perdue, *The Cherokee,* pp. 49–81, and Anthony F. C. Wallace, *The Long Bitter Trial: Andrew Jackson and the Indians* (New York: Hill and Wang, 1993). A graphic account of Rogers's dislike of Andrew Jackson can be found in Ben Dixon MacNeil, "Recollection," in William Payne and Jake G. Lyons, eds., *Folks Say of Will Rogers: A Memorial Anecdotage* (New York: J. P. Putnam and Sons, 1936), pp. 114–120; Will Rogers, "A Jackson Day Dinner," in *A Will Rogers Treasury: Reflections and Observations,* ed. Bryan B. Sterling and Frances N. Sterling (New York: Bonanza Books, 1982), pp. 128–132.

23. On Clem Rogers's career, see Harold Keith, "Clem Rogers and His Influence in Oklahoma History," Master's thesis, University of Oklahoma, 1938. For historical context, see Hanna R. Warren, "Reconstruction in the Cherokee Nation" and "Freedmen in Indian Territory," *The Chronicles of Oklahoma* 49, no. 2 (Summer 1971). Clem Rogers's letter is in Collings, *The Old Home Ranch,* p. 57. For a classic misunderstanding of Clem Rogers, none beats the statement that "Clem followed the ways of the white man in all respects," in Ketchum, *Will Rogers,* p. 58. The quotation is from editor C. V. Rogers, *The Daily Progress,* October 1911, in Will Rogers Memorial Archive, Claremore, Oklahoma (hereafter cited as WRMA).

24. The best account of his loyalty and communal spirit to the "folks" in Claremore is Betty Rogers, *Will Rogers,* pp. 118, 175–179, 209. See also Payne and Lyons, *Folks Say,* pp. 9–15; Fred Roach, Jr., "Will Rogers' Youthful Relationship with His Father, Clem Rogers: A Story of Love and Tension," *Chronicles of Oklahoma* 58 (1980): 325–342. On money sent home to buy back the ranch, see letters of Will Rogers to Clem Rogers, June 11, 1904; April 30, 1909, in Will Rogers Memorial, Claremore, Oklahoma (hereafter known as WRM). For an account of the lawyer whom Rogers hired in the twenties and thirties to buy land to restore the ranch, see Collings, *The Old Home Ranch,* pp. 112–114.

25. Accounts of the migration frenzy among Cherokees can be found in *The Brooklyn Citizen,* July 12, 1897; *Tahlequah Arrow,* April 1898; *St. Louis Globe Democrat* April–May 1898. I owe this information to my former colleague and expert on Cherokee politics, Professor Alan Kilpatrick, who is currently working on this subject. For Will Rogers's letters home, see Reba Collins, *Will Rogers: Courtship and Correspondence, 1900–1915* (Oklahoma City: Neighbors and Quaid, 1992), pp. 37–56. Rogers's South American letters are from April to October 1902. For his sisters' letter on allotment, see Collins, p. 57. For "don't know how good your country is" letter, see Will Rogers to C. V. Rogers, June 17, 1902, and August 1, 1902 in WRML. On "I was always proud," see Will Rogers to family, September 28, 1903, in WRML and Collins, p. 82.

26. See Richard Slotkin, "Buffalo Bill's Wild West and the Mythologization of the American Empire," in Amy Kaplan and Donald E. Pease, eds., *Cultures of United States Imperialism* (Durham, N.C.: Duke University Press, 1993), pp. 164–184.

27. "Cowboys Carnival," 1905, in WRML. On letters to his father about playing blacks

and Indian savages, see Collins, *Correspondence,* pp. 61–66. All the letters are dated from November 1902 to February 1903.

28. For instances of Rogers's despair and labeling of himself as a "bum" who "ain't got no regular place to call my home," and on living a "lie," see Collins, *Correspondence,* pp. 59, 172–176. The accounts of white girls rejecting Rogers and of the desire of Betty Rogers to live like a white are in Collins, *Correspondence,* p. 98. The account of the woman who was "strong for me" derives from the recollection of a coworker on the Wild West circuit, Tom Mix. One reason for Rogers's rejection was the parts he was given to play: A review in 1907 noted "Mr. Rogers" came through "the Indian massacre without a scratch." Collins, *Correspondence,* p. 148.

29. For the merger of concepts of "white" superiority and nationality to popular entertainment like the Wild West and minstrel shows, see David Roediger, *The Wages of Whiteness: Race and the Making of the American Working Class* (Verso: London, 1991), pp. 115–133; Alexander Saxton, "Blackface Minstrelsy and Jacksonian Ideology," *American Quarterly* 27 (March 1975): 1–26; and *The Rise and Fall of the White Republic: Class Politics and Mass Culture in Nineteenth-Century America* (London: Verso, 1990).

30. On Rogers's ability to communicate across cultures, see Eddie Cantor with Jane Kesner Ardmore, *Take My Life* (New York: Doubleday and Co., 1957), pp. 104–115. For his enjoyment of nightclubs, sports, and city pleasures, see Betty Rogers, *Will Rogers,* pp. 105, 261. For a typical observation of audiences' admiration for Rogers's capacity to say "what everybody thought," see "All Claremore Sobs over Death of Will," *Los Angeles Times,* August 17, 1935, in Rogers File, AMPAS. The Indian perspective and "other person's angle" quotations come from Day, *The Autobiography,* pp. 114, 286. For one among many examples of Rogers pointing out to audiences that he was a Cherokee, see Gragert, *Radio Broadcasts,* p. 17.

31. The classic statement of the double voice informing minority humor can be found in Ralph Ellison, *Going to the Territory* (New York: Vintage Books, 1986), pp. 138–139. See also Peggy Wood interview, in Bryan Sterling, *The Will Rogers Scrapbook* (New York: Grosset and Dunlap, 1976), pp. 125–126. Rogers's hostility to western imperialism and Americanization drives permeates his writing, see Day, *The Autobiography,* pp. 109–110, 153–158, 301–304, 343, 367, 377–378. See also Betty Rogers, *Will Rogers,* pp. 286–291. On classes in America, see Day, *Autobiography,* p. 92. For Indians and nature, see Gragert, *Radio Broadcasts,* p. 121. The understanding of culture as the means by which dominant classes reinforce their rule is explained best in T. J. Jackson Lears, "The Concept of Cultural Hegemony: Problems and Possibilities," *American Historical Review* 92 (December 1985): 567–593.

32. Day, *The Autobiography,* pp. 173, 190, 193, 213, 219–220, 348.

33. Bryan B. Sterling and Frances N. Sterling, *Will Rogers in Hollywood* (New York: Crown Publishers, 1984); Hal Roach interview, in Sterling, *Scrapbook,* p. 141. On Rogers's early career in silent film, see "Rogers Flopped as an Actor, but Starred Sensationally by Playing Himself," unpaginated and undated clipping, probably 1935, in WRMA. See also Betty Rogers, *Will Rogers,* p. 150; Will Rogers, "I'm Not a Movie Actor, I'm a Writer," *Boston Globe,* November 20, 1927, WRMA.

34. Irvin S. Cobb interview, in Payne and Lyons, *Folks Say,* pp. 77–83. A good account of how Rogers worked with writers can be found in Homer Croy, *Our Will Rogers* (New York: Duell, Sloan and Pierec, 1953), pp. 235–274. Croy was one of Rogers's first writers in talking films. See also Henry King, John Ford, Irene Rich, Sterling Holloway, and Lew Ayres interviews, in Sterling, *Scrapbook,* pp. 136, 147, 162–164, 169, 174–175; Will Rogers, "Hollywood, The Galloping Pictures," in Sterling, *Scrapbook,* p. 80. See also "Will Rogers: The Only Stage, Movie, Radio and Literary Star Tells How He Works at Fun," unpaginated and undated clipping from a Kansas newspaper, about 1933. This is perhaps the best description by Rogers himself of his artistic control in Hollywood. Other firsthand accounts come from an interview with a Hollywood producer, Charles W. Dwyer, in Payne and Lyons, *Folks Say,* pp. 69–75, and an interview with Lew Ayres in Sterling and Sterling, *Rogers in Hollywood,* pp. 128–129.

35. The analogies and symbolic references to Will Rogers can be seen in the advertisements for his talking films contained in WRMA. For a glimpse of the troubled courtship, compounded, one can surmise, by racial and class divisions, of Betty and Will, see the letters in Collins, *Courtship and Correspondence,* pp. 173–198.

36. All of Rogers's talking films can be found in WRMA. A brief summary of each, with sample reviews, is in Sterling and Sterling, *Rogers in Hollywood.*

37. *Handy Andy* (1934), in WRMA. A brief description of the film is in Sterling and Sterling, *Rogers in Hollywood,* pp. 143–145.

38. Comments on the "Rogers formula film" appear in "Screen Loses Star at Peak of Influence," *Dallas Texas News,* August 17, 1935, unpaginated clipping, WRMA.

39. *Ambassador Bill* (1931), in WRMA. For a sampling of Rogers's criticism of imperialism from a left-wing isolationist stance, see Day, *The Autobiography,* pp. 256–264, 293, 377; Will Rogers, *There's Not a Bathing Suit in Russia and Other Bare Facts* (New York: Albert and Charles Bori, 1927).

40. The film *Young As You Feel* (1931) and its production notes and script can be seen at WRMA.

41. *State Fair* (1933) can be seen at WRMA. A plot summary is in Sterling and Sterling, *Rogers in Hollywood,* p. 125. Mikhail Bakhtin contrasts the epic character with the modern personality rooted in metamorphosis. See "Discourse in the Novel," in *The Dialogical Imagination: Four Essays by M. M. Bakhtin,* ed. Michael Holquist, trans. Cayl Emerson and Michael Holquist (Austin, Tex.: University of Texas Press, 1981), pp. 259–422.

42. See, for example, Donald Bogle, *Toms, Coons, Mulattoes, Mammies and Bucks: An Interpretive History of Blacks in American Films* (New York: Continuum Books, 1991), pp. 35–53, and Michael Rogin, *Blackface, White Noise: Jewish American Immigrants in the Hollywood Melting Pot* (Berkeley: University of California Press, 1996).

43. *In Old Kentucky* (1935), in WRMA.

44. *Judge Priest* (1934), in WRMA.

45. Will Rogers, Syndicated Column, November 11, 1934, in Sterling and Sterling, *Rogers in Hollywood,* pp. 150–151.

46. Will Rogers, "Stars' Salaries 1933," in ibid., p. 130.

47. "The County Chairman," *New York World Telegram,* January 19, 1935, unpaginated clipping, WRMA; "Life Begins at Forty," *New York Sun,* April 5, 1935, unpaginated clipping, WRMA.

48. M. A. McConnell, Emerson Theater, Hartford, Arkansas, *MPH,* February 25, 1933, p. 58; *MPH,* March 3, 1934, p. 35.

49. Photos of the Will Rogers Theater and murals are in the Chicago Historical Society Library and can be seen in Lary May, "Designing Multicultural America: Modern Movie Theaters and the Politics of Public Space," in *Movies and Politics: The Dynamic Relationship,* ed. James Combs (New York: Garland, 1993), pp. 221–222. See also Ted Malone interview, in Payne and Lyons, *Folks Say,* pp. 193–195; "The County Chairman," *New York Telegram,* January 19, 1935, unpaginated clipping, WRMA, and Chapter 3.

50. The quotation is from the Frank Borzage interview in Payne and Lyons, *Folks Say,* pp. 60–62.

51. *Steamboat 'Round the Bend* (1935), in WRMA. An excellent discussion of Rogers's work with the director John Ford can be found in Martin Rubin, "Mr. Ford and Mr. Rogers: The Rogers Trilogy," *Film Comment,* January–February, 1974, pp. 54–57. Rubin emphasizes Ford as the central artistic force behind these films. While some of this is true, the film is permeated with Rogers's Cherokee values and traditions, updated with political implications for modern times in the Depression.

52. Will Rogers, *There's Not a Bathing Suit in Russia.* For his admiration of Mussolini in the twenties, see Will Rogers, *Letters of a Self-Made Diplomat to His President* (Claremore, Okla.: Will Rogers Heritage Press, 1988), pp. 55–80. For Rogers's condemnation of Mussolini, see Day, *The Autobiography,* pp. 377–378.

53. Most of these broadcasts are in Gragert, *Radio Broadcasts.* The quotations are taken

from Will Rogers, Columbia Network, November 11, 1934, in O Brien, *Will Rogers: Ambassador of Good Will,* pp. 147–150.

54. A file containing letters from Theodore and Franklin Roosevelt and many other politicians seeking to gain Rogers's favor can be found in WRMA.

55. Will Rogers, "Bacon, Beans and Limousines," October 18, 1931, in Gragert, *Radio Broadcasts,* pp. 65–67; Day, *The Autobiography,* pp. 296, 304–305.

56. Day, *The Autobiography,* pp. 247, 252, 263–269, 282–284, 292–296, 304, 367, 377–388; Will Rogers, "Bacon, Beans and Limousines" and "Good Gulf Shows," in Gragert, *Radio Broadcasts,* pp. 65–66, 117–122, 123–128, 156–160. The quote on redistributing wealth can be found in Day, *Will Rogers: A Biography,* p. 265.

57. James A. Farley interview, October 30, 1974, in Sterling, *Scrapbook,* pp. 181–182. Farley said that "Mr. Roosevelt did like him, he liked him very much, and everything that was ever said by Will about Mr. Roosevelt, whether it was good or not, he appreciated. No doubt about that."

58. Day, *Will Rogers,* pp. 263–268; Will Rogers, "Bacon, Beans and Limousines" and "Good Gulf Shows," in Gragert, *Radio Broadcasts,* pp. 65–66, 117–122, 123–128, 156–160; Day, *The Autobiography,* pp. 247, 252, 267, 269, 282–284, 292–296, 304, 367, 377–378. For Rogers's early trips to the Soviet Union and his complicated response, see Rogers, *There's Not a Bathing Suit in Russia.* For Mussolini, see Will Rogers, *Letters of a Self-Made Diplomat,* pp. 55–80. And for his later criticism, see Day, *The Autobiography,* pp. 377–378.

59. Lew Ayres interview, December 31, 1970, in Sterling, *Scrapbook,* p. 137; Joel McCrea interview, May 24, 1970, in ibid., *Scrapbook,* p. 117; Evelyn Venable Mohr and Hal Mohr interview, January 4, 1971, in ibid., pp. 151–155. Rogers's financial generosity with crews and friends was well known. See Peggy Wood interview, September 10, 1970, in Sterling, *Scrapbook,* p. 125; see also Mohr and Sterling Holloway interviews, ibid., pp. 153 and 164. Rogers also served as an informal bargainer for labor with management. See Charles Dwyer interview, in Payne and Lyons, *Folks Say,* pp. 74–76.

60. Pictures and description of the house can be found in Ketchum, *Will Rogers,* pp. 317–320. These descriptions are also based on several journeys to the estate, now a state park, by Lary May, July 1990. On Rogers's polo game, see Henry King interview, January 14, 1972, in Sterling, *Scrapbook,* p. 171. Robinson's interview and Rogers's comments about Fetchit can be found in Day, *Will Rogers,* p. 340.

61. Full accounts of the funeral and the host of monuments built in Rogers's name can be found in Collins, *Will Rogers and Wiley Post in Alaska,* pp. 61–115. See also *Increasing Profits with Audience Research* (Princeton: American Institute of Public Opinion, 1941), p. 54.

62. Herbert Hoover, *Los Angeles Times,* August 17, 1935; Cecil B. De Mille, "Will Rogers Memorial Speech," in Payne and Lyons, *Folks Say,* pp. 4–5. See also *Will Rogers—Shrine of the Sun,* memorial pamphlet, p. 3 (sold at the shrine, no publisher or date listed). The murals can be seen in *The Will Rogers' Shrine of the Sun* (Colorado Springs, Colorado, 1937), in WRMA.

63. Yagoda, *Will Rogers,* pp. 285–332, and especially pp. 333–335.

64. "Will Rogers, 'Congressman at Large for a Day,'" in Payne and Lyons, *Folks Say,* p. 176.

65. I am using the concept of the civic sphere as developed in Jürgen Habermas, *The Structural Transformation of the Civic Sphere: An Inquiry into a Category of Bourgeois Society* (New York: G. P. Putnam's Sons, 1936), especially pp. 222–236.

Chapter Two

1. On Orson Welles's life, art, and politics, see Welles and Peter Bogdanovich, *This Is Orson Welles* (New York: Harper Perennial, 1993), pp. xxvi, 13, 33, 80, 93–98 (the lost Eden informing work and relation to family), 102, 168, 183–185 (his political activities), 258. The quotation on *Kane* comes from Juan Cobs, Miguel Rubio, and J. A. Pruneda, "A Trip to

Don Quixote-land: Conversations with Orson Welles," *Cahiers du Cinema* (English), No. 5 (1966): 34–47. A full exposition of Welles's political activities and their relation to his art can be found in Michael Denning, *The Cultural Front: The Laboring of American Culture in the Twentieth Century* (New York: Verso, 1996), pp. 362–394. Denning stresses that Welles's politics grow out of the communist-inspired "Popular Front." This ignores the fact that his key beliefs derive from republican roots that were modernized during the thirties. The quotation evoking the republic and denying Marxism derives from Orson Welles, "Moral Indebtedness," *Free World Magazine* (October 1943), p. 375.

2. The view that thirties culture was backward-looking is best presented in Warren Susman, *Culture as History: The Transformation of American Society in the Twentieth Century* (New York: Pantheon, 1984). An exception to this view can be found in two books. Robert McElvaine in *The Great Depression, American, 1929–1941* (New York: Times Books, 1984), pp. 196–224, stresses that the popular arts expressed a "moral economy" at odds with the new modern consumer culture. Giuliana Muscio, *Hollywood's New Deal* (Philadelphia: Temple University Press, 1997), is more in tune with the theme of this chapter. Yet even as Muscio sees that Hollywood included new groups, she still believes that it served to "stabilize" the new order of capitalism. This view is one that formed after 1948, as we shall see, in the first years of the Cold War. In the Depression, many Hollywood moviemakers and radicals regarded their work as advancing a republican ideal, as did Welles, at odds with unjust class arrangements, inequality of power, and acquisitive individualism. That form of radicalism was not seen by conservatives in the thirties as a force for stabilizing the new order. Recently Denning, in *The Cultural Front*, has revised the Susman view that a monolithic Americanism pervaded the era. Yet he pays little attention to Hollywood, assuming apparently that it remained a bastion of conservative politics and art. For the labor radicalism of the decade, see Lizabeth Cohen, *Making a New Deal: Industrial Workers in Chicago, 1919–1939* (New York: Cambridge University Press, 1990) and Gary Gerstle, *Working Class Americanism: The Politics of Labor in an Industrial City, 1914–1960* (New York: Cambridge University Press, 1989).

3. Neal Gabler, *An Empire of Their Own: How the Jews Invented Hollywood* (New York: Crown Publishers, 1988); Michael Rogin, *Blackface, White Noise: Jewish American Immigrants in the Hollywood Melting Pot* (Berkeley: University of California, 1996).

4. For the creation of a cross-racial intellectual community in New York, see Ann Douglas, *Terrible Honesty: Mongrel Manhattan in the 1920's* (New York: Farrar, Straus and Giroux, 1995). On labor filmmaking, see Steven Ross, *Working Class Hollywood* (Princeton: Princeton University Press, 1998).

5. A generous sampling of documents created by moralists promoting censorship in the states and the industry's response, the creation of censorship codes centered in the Hays office, can be found in *The Movies in Our Midst: Documents in the Cultural History of Film in America,* ed. Gerald Mast (Chicago: University of Chicago Press, 1982), pp. 176–213. The comments about "foreign-born" domination of Hollywood are from an article entitled "News from Hollywood" in *St. Louis Mo. Post Dispatch,* August 7, 1927, p. 1D.

6. My view of the Jews in Hollywood differs from that of Gabler, *Empire of Their Own.* Where Gabler sees the Jews adapting to a fixed and unchanging Americanism, they were in fact major participants in the transformation of the culture to make it more pluralistic. See Lary May, *Screening Out the Past: The Birth of Mass Culture and the Motion Picture Industry* (Chicago: University of Chicago Press, 1983). On pariah capitalism, see *From Max Weber: Essays in Sociology,* ed. and trans. H. H. Gerth and C. Wright Mills (New York: Oxford University Press, 1946), pp. 66, 96, 114, 189–190, 399.

7. Dudley Nichols, "Speaking from Personal Experience," *New York Times,* November 9, 1947, Screen Section, p. 4.

8. Thorstein Veblen, "The Intellectual Pre-Eminence of the Jews in Modern Europe," in *Essays in Our Changing Social Order* (originally published in 1919; New York: The Viking Press, 1934), pp. 220–235.

9. Gabler, *Empire of Their Own,* p. 225; Andrew Sinclair, *Spiegel: The Man Behind the Pictures* (Boston: Little Brown and Co., 1987), pp. 8, 14.

10. See May, *Screening Out the Past,* ch. 5.

11. Ibid. Fred Niblo, "Americanizing American Pictures," from *Theatre Magazine,* May 1928, in *Hollywood Directors, 1914–1940,* ed. Richard Koszarski (New York: Oxford University Press, 1976), p. 194. Our plot samples are derived from the film industry's major trade journal, *Motion Picture Herald* (*MPH*) and its weekly summaries of recent film releases. This source provided the basis for the sample and its categories. To ensure consistency over time and to ensure that major and second-run films were included, two plots were drawn each month from even-numbered years. The first film review of each month and the last film reviewed in the penultimate week of each month provided the basis for our tabulations, generating 24 films per year for study and 120 per decade. See the appendixes for a fuller exposition of our methods in calculating these narrative categories over time.

12. "Phoney Splurges Weakens Sex Lure," *V,* December 10, 1930, p. 1.

13. For the collapse of box-office stars' popularity in the twenties and the changing nature of audience demand, see *V,* January 8, 1930, pp. 7–80. See also "If Hoke Is Passed Out of Pictures, Peasants Won't Go—and That's That," *V,* December 24, 1930, p. 2; "Stars of 1931," *V,* December 29, 1931, p. 7; *V,* January 7, 1931, pp. 3–5; Roy Chartier, "Year in Pictures," *V,* December 29, 1931, p. 6; Tom Waler, "The Year in Pictures," *V,* December 29, 1931, p. 4; *V,* January 3, 1933, p. 2; *FDY,* 1932, pp. 1–7. For "not a hoot about tradition," and throwing items at the screen, see *MPH,* October 8, 1931.

14. *V,* December 29, 1931, p. 4.

15. Upton Sinclair, *Upton Sinclair Presents William Fox* (Los Angeles: by the author, 1933).

16. This was calculated by comparing the listings of the major firms in the *FDY,* 1924, with the listings of the major companies in *FDY,* 1934. See also Douglas Gomery, "Rethinking US Film History: The Depression Decade and Monopoly Control," *Film and History* 10, no. 2 (1980): 32–38, for a different view.

17. "Audits of Marquee Values," *Gallup Looks at the Movies, 1941* (Princeton: AIOPO, 1979). The Warner stars who were most popular with the lower classes were James Cagney, George Raft, Humphrey Bogart, Mickey Rooney, William Powell, and John Garfield. The major writers who came from the penny press were such screenwriters as Dudley Nichols, Ben Hecht, Robert Riskin, Nunnally Johnson, and Philip Dunne. On the turnover in the industry and the characteristics of the writers in the thirties, see Leo C. Rosten, *Hollywood: The Movie Colony and the Movie Makers* (New York: Harcourt Brace and Company, 1941), pp. 290, 306–327.

18. A fine summary of the arguments of scholars who stress the monopolistic control of Hollywood in this era can be found in Giuliana Muscio, *Hollywood's New Deal,* ch. 4. The materials that allowed us to calculate the number of independent companies and the number of films they made were derived from several interrelated sources: *Wids Yearbook 1916, 1918, 1919* (New York: Wids Films and Film Folks, Inc.) had listings for all companies making films for the teens; the *Film Daily Yearbooks* for 1923 to 1964 (New York: Quigley Publications) listed all production companies for those years; Joel W. Finler, *The Hollywood Story* (New York: Crown, 1988), lists the total number of films made by both independents and majors. We counted the number of independent firms every five years from 1916 to 1964. I wish to thank Michael Willard and Daniel May for their invaluable help in this research.

19. "Independents See '32 as Big Opportunity," *V,* December 22, 1931, pp. 5, 7, 41; Walter Green, "The Indies' Big Year" *V,* January 1, 1935, p. 1; "The Indies' Bull Season," *V,* January 1, 1936, p. 1. For a comprehensive view of the advent of talking films, see Scott Eyman, *The Speed of Sound: Hollywood and the Talkie Revolution, 1926–1930* (New York: Simon & Schuster, 1997).

20. Susman, *Culture as History,* p. 159. For the view of middle-class contemporaries that sound challenged rather than reinforced standard values, see Mast, *The Movies in Our Midst,* pp. 282–294.

21. Martin Quigley, "Warners and Jolson," *Exhibitors' Herald and Movie Picture World,* November 17, 1928, p. 24.

22. See Robert Sherwood, "*Don Juan* and the Vitaphone," *Life,* August 26, 1926, in Mast, *Movies in Our Midst,* pp. 257–258. The quotation is from Ralph L. Henry, "The Cultural Influence of the 'Talkies,'" *School and Society,* February 1929, in ibid., pp. 292–293.

23. The film is on video. See Leonard Maltin, *TV Movies and Video Guide,* (New York: New American Library, 1998), p. 500. The original script and the quotation of the father concerning "nigger music" can be found in *The Jazz Singer,* ed. Robert L. Carringer (Madison: University of Wisconsin Press, 1979), p. 61.

24. Samson Raphaelson, *The Jazz Singer* (New York: Brandon's, 1925), pp. 9–10; Herbert G. Goldman, *The Jolson Journal* (International Al Jolson Society) no. 51 (1978): 7–8, in Carringer, *The Jazz Singer,* pp. 12, 23. On the difference between audiences in the small towns and cities, see the section called "What This Film Did for Me," *MPH,* October–November 1927. This is a column of letters from theater owners across the country commenting on how films were received by audiences in their communities. For *The Jazz Singer,* the theater owners in small towns complained that it failed to draw audiences; the reverse was the case for the big northern cities.

25. Fitzhugh Green, *The Film Finds Its Tongue* (G. P. Putnam and Sons, 1929), in Mast, *Movies in Our Midst,* p. 266. The condemnation from critics oriented to high culture who perceived "black young Hebrews" degrading the arts derives from Aldous Huxley, "Silence Is Golden," *Golden Book Magazine,* April 1930, in Mast, ibid., pp. 284–285. The response of black critics is derived from Thomas Cripps, *Slow Fade to Black: The Negro in American Film, 1900–1942,* 2d ed. (New York: Oxford University Press, 1993), pp. 106, 222.

26. W. R. Burnett interview, in *Backstory: Interviews with Screenwriters of the Golden Age,* ed. Pat McGilligan (Berkeley: University of California Press, 1986), pp. 56–58; Alan Scott interview, in ibid., pp. 315–333; Norman Krasna interview, in ibid., pp. 212–241; Edna Ferber, *A Peculiar Treasure* (New York: Doubleday, Doran and Co., 1939), p. 10.

27. Rosten, *Hollywood,* p. 290. In responses to questionnaires submitted to all the directors in Hollywood, Rosten found that over half the directors started their film careers after the advent of talking pictures. Since directing was among the most conservative of trades, one can assume that the turnover for writers and players was even higher.

28. The ethnic backgrounds of these directors can be gleaned from interviews or biographies. See Lewis Milestone interview, AMPAS; Edgar Ulmer interview, AMPAS; William Dieterle interview, AMPAS; Busby Berkeley file, AMPAS; Joseph McBride, *Frank Capra, The Catastrophe of Success* (New York: Simon and Schuster, 1992); Andrew Sinclair, *John Ford* (New York: Dial Press, 1979); Madsen, *William Wyler: The Authorized Biography* (New York: Thomas Crowell, 1973); Mervyn LeRoy, as told to Dick Kleiner, *Take One* (New York: Hawthorne Books, 1955).

29. "Hollywood Stops Making Films for Hollywood," *V,* December 29, 1931, p. 7; Cecelia Agar, "Ways and Means to the Screen," *V,* December 29, 1931, p. 18; Ruth Morris, "Screen's Best Liked Men," *V,* December 29, 1931, p. 163, all testify to the rise of a new type of star and formula film.

30. *Cavalcade* and *All Quiet on the Western Front* can be found on video. See Maltin, *Video Guide.* See also Lewis Milestone, Special Collections, Kevin Brownlow interview, AMPAS.

31. All these films are on video. See Maltin, *Video Guide;* "Frankenstein," *The Hollywood Reporter,* November 3, 1931. See also Thomas Doherty, *Pre-Code Hollywood: Sex, Immorality, and Insurrection in American Cinema, 1930–1934* (New York: Columbia University Press, 1999).

32. The studio most identified with topical films was Warner Brothers. For its move to social realist films based on current news headlines, see Jack Warner with Dean Jennings, *My First Fifty Years in Hollywood* (New York: Random House, 1964), pp. 210–222. The rise of the journalism film in the thirties is brilliantly analyzed by Pauline Kael in "Raising Kane," in *The Citizen Kane Book* (New York: Limelight, 1984), p. 17. The comment about journalistic productions comes from "Showmen's Reviews" of *Washington Show,* in *MPH,* July 2,

1932, p. 1. These reviews were geared solely toward theater owners and express the reviewers' assessment of why a film would appeal to audiences. At the end of this review, for example, the writer comments, "Get behind this one with every ounce of showmanship you possess and you should need the S.R.O. sign every time you show it." See Appendix 3; see also Dudley Nichols, "Theatre, Society, Education," *Educational Theatre Journal* (November 1956), p. 183. Nichols was a major screenwriter for John Ford.

33. For an excellent discussion of the place of the gangster genre in the patterns of American ethnicity and working-class life, see Jonathan Munby, "*Manhattan Melodrama*'s 'Art of the Weak': Telling History from the Other Side in the 1930s' Talking Gangster Film," *Journal of American Studies* 30, pt. 1 (1996): 101–118 and *Public Enemies, Public Heroes: Screening the Gangster from* Little Caesar *to* Touch of Evil (Chicago: University of Chicago Press, 1999), chs. 1 and 2.

34. See David E. Ruth, *Inventing the Public Enemy: The Gangster in American Culture, 1918–1934* (Chicago: University of Chicago Press, 1996), for a fine discussion of the way the gangster was seen as the embodiment of the dangers of the modern city prior to the thirties. See also "Little Caesar," *V,* January 14, 1931; W. R. Burnett, "The Outsider," interview by Ken Mate and Pat McGilligan, in McGilligan, *Backstory,* pp. 56–59; Edward G. Robinson, *All My Yesterdays* (New York: Hawthorn, 1974). All these gangster films can be seen on video. See Maltin, *Video Guide.*

35. Data on the origins of the Fu Manchu films and their release can be found in the Fu Manchu file, AMPAS. The quotation is from DuBose Heyward, "Key to Study Guide for the Screen Production of *Emperor Jones,*" unpaginated and undated clipping, in *Emperor Jones* file, AMPAS. See also Norman Kagan, "The Return of Emperor Jones," *Negro History Bulletin* 34, no. 7 (November 1971): 162, for a fine description of the film's production and distribution.

36. The quotations are from "Sinful Girls Lead," *V,* December 29, 1931, pp. 5, 37; Cecilia Agar, "Ways and Means to the Screen," *V,* December 29, 1931, p. 18; *V,* December 31, 1931, pp. 7, 10.

37. All these "fallen woman" films are on video. See Maltin, *Video Guide.* The best and most comprehensive analysis of these films can be found in Lea Jacobs, *The Wages of Sin: Censorship and the Fallen Woman Film, 1928–1942* (Madison: University of Wisconsin Press, 1991).

38. For one among many accounts, see Alexander Saxton, *The Rise and Fall of the White Republic: Class Politics and Mass Culture in Nineteenth Century America* (New York and London: Verso, 1990), pp. 165–183.

39. See Thomas Cripps, "Stepin Fetchit and the Politics of Performance," in Paul Loadas and Linda K. Fuller, eds., *Beyond the Stars: Stock Characters in American Popular Fiction* (Bowling Green, Ohio: Bowling Green Press, 1990), pp. 35–48. For Fetchit's origins, work in black vaudeville, and activism in the NAACP, see Joseph McBride, "Stepin Fetchit Talks Back," *Film Quarterly* (Summer 1971). On his black utopia, see "Black Heaven," *Illustrated Daily News,* July 29, 1936; "Stepin Fetchit Planning Dark Utopia, Harlemwood," *The Pittsburgh Press,* March 24, 1933, unpaginated clippings, Stepin Fetchit file, AMPAS. See also *Pittsburgh Courier,* April 4, 1936, and May 23, 1936, unpaginated clippings, Fetchit file, AMPAS.

40. The best single analysis of these films is Henry Jenkins, *What Made Pistachio Nuts? Early Sound Comedy and the Vaudeville Aesthetic* (New York: Columbia University Press, 1992).

41. See Bruce Jenkins, *What Made Pistachio Nuts?* All the cited films are on video. See Maltin, *Video Guide.* The quotations derive from two sources: Marybeth Hamilton, "'A Little Bit Spicy, but Not Too Raw': Mae West and Urban Performance," *The Gateway to Hays* (Venice, Italy: Biennale di Venezia, 1991), pp. 183–187, and Jeanine Basinger, *A Woman's View: How Hollywood Spoke to Women, 1930–1960* (Hanover and London: Wesleyan University Press, 1993), pp. 17–183.

42. All of Chaplin's features, including *City Lights,* can be found on video. See Maltin, *Video Guide.*

43. On censorship, see Richard Malty, "The Production Code and the Hays Office," in Tino Balio, ed., *Grand Design: Hollywood as a Modern Business Enterprise, 1930–1939* (New York: Scribners, 1993), pp. 37–72; Jacobs, *The Wages of Sin;* Leonard Leff and Jerold Simmons, *The Dame in the Kimono: Hollywood Censorship and the Production Code from the 1920s to the 1960s* (New York: Grove Weidenfeld, 1990). Stephan Vaughan, "Film Censorship in America, The Motion Picture Code of 1930," in *Gateway to Hays,* pp. 81–93, presents evidence that the producers saw the market as more powerful than the censors. Gregory Black, *Hollywood Censored: Morality Codes, Catholics and the Movies* (Cambridge: Cambridge University Press, 1994). See also John Huston, *An Open Book* (New York: Ballantine Books, 1980), pp. 94–95.

44. This process of altering a colonial artistic canon to create a new self and national ideal is similar to the analysis that informs Declan Kiberd, *Inventing Ireland* (London: Jonathan Cape, 1995), pp. 1–29, 327–359.

45. *Cimarron* is on video. See Maltin, *Video Guide.* See also Ferber, *A Peculiar Treasure,* pp. 8–12; Julie Goldsmith Gilbert, *Ferber: A Biography of Edna Ferber and Her Circle* (Garden City, New York: Doubleday and Co., 1978), pp. 3, 209.

46. Ferber, *A Peculiar Treasure,* p. 10.

47. *Grand Hotel* can be seen on video. See Maltin, *Video Guide.*

48. *42nd Street* is on video. See Maltin, *Video Guide.* The original script and a discussion of the film's production and reception can be found in *42nd Street,* ed. Rocco Fumento (Madison: University of Wisconsin Press, 1980). A superb analysis of the show-within-a-show musicals and their implications for public life can be found in Mark Roth, "Some Warners Musicals and the Spirit of the New Deal," *The Velvet Light Trap,* no. 17 (Winter 1977): 1–8. The musical, of course, is often seen as the ultimate example of popular escapism. For an alternative view that is close to my interpretation, see Richard Dyer, "Entertainment as Utopia," *Movie,* no. 24 (Spring 1977): 2–13.

49. Reviews, *Motion Picture Herald,* May 19, 1934, and *New York News,* June 30, 1934, unpaginated clippings in *The Thin Man* file, AMPAS. Most of the films are on video. See Maltin, *Video Guide.* For a fine article dealing with the cross-pollination of genres, see Mark Winokur, "Improbable Ethnic Hero: William Powell and the Transformation of Ethnic Hollywood," *Cinema Journal* 27, no. 1 (Fall 1987): 5–22.

50. *A Family Affair* (1937) launched the series. It featured the judge in battle against a corrupt newspaper editor, the richest man in town and a promoter of a water project that threatens to aggrandize public land. The film is on video. See Maltin, *Video Guide.* For a listing of this production and the others in the series, see ibid. The *Variety* review, complete with plot, appeared on March 6, 1937. A brief, accurate, and contemporary analysis of the films' central themes, though avoiding their political side, was written by Bosley Crowther, "So Long Andy," *New York Times,* February 21, 1943.

51. King Vidor interview with Kay Mills, *Los Angeles Times,* September 13, 1981, pt. IV, p. 2. See also Milestone, American Film Institute oral interview, about 1980, in Milestone Collection, AMPAS.

52. On De Mille's and Griffith's visual styles, see May, *Screening Out the Past,* chs. II and V.

53. See McBride, *Frank Capra,* pp. 280–300.

54. Milestone interview, American Film Institute, in Milestone Collection, AMPAS.

55. Frank Capra, *The Name Above the Title* (New York: Macmillan, 1971), pp. 140–160; Edmund Goulding interview, Metro-Goldwyn-Mayer publicity release, scrapbook for *Grand Hotel,* in AMPAS.

56. William Wyler, "No Magic Wand," *Screenwriter,* February 1947, reprinted in *Hollywood Directors, 1941–1976,* compiled by Richard Koszarski (New York: Oxford University Press, 1977), p. 112. The cameraman on many of Wyler's and John Ford's films, as well as on Welles's *Citizen Kane,* was one of the central innovators in this style. *Kane* simply brought

it to fruition. See Gregg Toland, "Realism for *Citizen Kane*," *American Cinematographer* (February 1941; reprinted, April 1991), pp. 37–42. The Welles quotation is in this article as well.

57. All the cited films are on video. See Maltin, *Video Guide*. Fine reproductions of key scenes in gangster films that illustrate these themes can be found in Ruth, *Public Enemy*. The critical reactions to *42nd Street* can be found in *42nd Street* scrapbooks, AMPAS. See also Milestone interview, American Film Institute, in Milestone Collection, AMPAS.

58. Ruth Morris, "Capra Foresees Satirical Cycle: Many Subjects 'Ripe for Ridicule,'" *V,* February 2, 1932, p. 2; Krasna interview, in McGilligan, ed., *Backstory,* p. 221; Scott interview, ibid., p. 322.

59. Gilbert Seldes, "The Movies in Peril," first appeared in *Scribners Magazine,* February 1935, reprinted in Mast, *The Movies in Our Midst,* pp. 427–438. The quotation is on pp. 431–432. See also Lincoln Kirstein, "James Cagney and the American Hero," *The Hound and Horn* (April–June 1932), in Stanley Kauffmann with Bruce Henstell, *American Film Criticism: From the Beginnings to Citizen Kane* (New York: Liveright, 1972), pp. 262–264. On Powell, see Winokur, "Improbable Ethnic Hero," pp. 18–22. The Gable quotation is from Ruth Morris, "Screen's Best Liked Men," *V,* December 29, 1931, p. 163. See Robert Sklar, *City Boys: Cagney, Bogart, Garfield* (Princeton: Princeton University Press, 1992).

60. "Dream Wife of a Million Men," *Look* (November 1937); "Myrna Loy in Colorado," unidentified clipping, Loy file, AMPAS.

61. Basinger, *A Woman's View;* Elizabeth Kendall, *The Runaway Bride: Hollywood Romantic Comedy in the 1930's* (New York: Alfred A. Knopf, 1990); Hart Seymore, "Carole Lombard Tells 'How I Live by a Man's Code,'" *Photoplay,* June 1937, p. 17. See also James Harvey, *Romantic Comedy in Hollywood: From Lubitsch to Sturges* (New York: Alfred A. Knopf, 1987); Myrna Loy interview, *Good Housekeeping,* unpaginated and undated clipping in Loy file, AMPAS.

62. Jay Leyda, "Eisenstein on Disney," in Steven Watts, *The Magic Kingdom: Walt Disney and the American Way of Life* (New York: Houghton Mifflin Co., 1997), pp. 127–128. Most Shirley Temple and Deanna Durbin films are on video. See Maltin, *Video Guide*. For Gene Autry and by implication Roy Rogers, see Douglas B. Green, "Gene Autry, the Singing Cowboy," *The Journal of Country Music* (May 1978), pp. 10–20.

63. The films in Capra's populist trilogy are all on video. See Maltin, *Video Guide*. The quotation is from *V,* March 13, 1941, p. 2. The scholarly literature on Capra is vast. Most scholars see his work as backward-looking populism, or if they focus on the humor that undermines authority, they see it as a form of postmodern discourse, divorced from social meaning. In the first vein, see the superb biography by McBride, *Frank Capra,* and Charles Maland, *Frank Capra* (Boston: Twayne Publishers, 1989). In the second, see Raymond Carney, *American Vision: The Films of Frank Capra* (New York: Cambridge University Press, 1986). Carney sees that Capra's films are "anti-ideological" because the characters try to transcend all "social categories." The key to their appeal, however, is not one or the other category, but rather the fusion of both. For a splendid article that focuses on Capra's critique of a privatized society and the quest to create a new public life, see Glenn Alan Phelps, "The Populist Films of Frank Capra," *American Studies* 13, no. 3 (1979): 377–392. Of course, Capra's own account of his life and art is indispensable. See Capra, *The Name Above the Title*.

64. All the cited films can be seen on video. See Maltin, *Video Guide*. See also Sergei Eisenstein, "Mr. Lincoln by Mr. Ford," in Jay Leyda, ed., *Film Essays* (London: Dennis Dobson, 1968), pp. 139–149. For a different reading of *Young Mr. Lincoln,* see the seminal postwar French Marxist view that places the film in the context of corporate control and middle-class values of individualism that subvert reform. See Collective Text by the Editors of *Cahiers du Cinema,* "John Ford's *Young Mr. Lincoln,*" in Gerald Mast and Marshall Cohen, *Film Theory and Criticism, Introductory Readings,* 2d ed. (New York: Oxford University Press, 1979), pp. 779–831.

65. On black and swing bands in urban theaters, see Lewis Erenberg, *Swingin' the Dream: Big Band Jazz and the Rebirth of American Culture* (Chicago: University of Chicago Press,

1998), pp. 150–178. For women and minorities reinterpreting mass-produced sounds and images to suit their own purposes, see Mary Carbine, "The Finest Outside the Loop: Motion Picture Exhibition in Chicago's Black Metropolis, 1905–1928," *Camera Obscura* 23 (May 1990): 16. See also Junkio Ogihara, "The Exhibition of Films for Japanese Americans in Los Angeles During the Silent Film Era," *Film History* 4, no. 2 (1990): 83; Lizabeth Cohen, *Making a New Deal,* pp. 99–158. On women, see Miriam Hansen, *Babel and Babylon: Spectatorship in American Silent Film* (Cambridge: Harvard University Press, 1991).

66. Nettie Zimmerman, "Making an Asset of an Accent . . . Talkies Point the Way," *Jewish Daily Forward,* August 13, 1930, p. 10.

67. *V,* July 24, 1929, describes the first Fu Manchu film, including Fu Manchu's family being destroyed by the British and his quest for revenge on the "white foreign devils." Biographical material on Oland is derived from Warner Oland obituary, *V,* August 10, 1938. He was then replaced as Chan by Sidney Toler.

68. The quotations are from reviews in *V,* January 26, 1932; "*Chan at Circus:* Nice B.O.; Story Stacks Up with Predecessors," *The Hollywood Reporter,* March 12, 1936; "Charlie Chan Carries On," *Film Daily,* March 22, 1936. On audiences among the "oriental trade," see "Charlie Chan Carries On," Charles Chan file, AMPAS. For all the facts on the making of the films and the characters, see Ken Hanke, *Charlie Chan at the Movies: History, Filmography, and Criticism* (Jefferson, N.C.: McFarland and Co., 1989). Many of the Charlie Chan films are on video. See Maltin, *Video Guide.*

69. Cripps, *Slow Fade to Black,* pp. 106, 222.

70. Ibid.

71. Rex Ingram interview, unpaginated and unidentified clipping in Ingram file, AMPAS.

72. See Paul Robeson file, AMPAS. This scene can be viewed on video. See *Showboat* listing in Maltin, *Video Guide,* p. 897. See also Rex Ingram interview, *Hollywood Citizen News,* February 22, 1967, unpaginated clipping in Ingram file, AMPAS.

73. The best discussion of cross-group romance serving as the foundational myth for national building projects can be found in Doris Summer, "Irresistible Romance: The Foundational Fictions of Latin America," in Homi K. Bhabha, ed., *Nation and Narration* (London: Routledge, 1990), pp. 71–99.

74. Barbara Stanwyck interview, in McBride, *Frank Capra,* p. 281. All the cited films are on video. See Maltin, *Video Guide.*

75. Unsigned, "I Am an Individual," *Screen Actor,* January 1936, p. 5 (hereafter *SA*); Eddie Cantor, "What the Guild Stands For," *SA,* March 1934, p. 2; "The Wire to President Roosevelt and the Executive Order," *SA,* May 15, 1933, pp. 4, 16; "Text of Eddie Cantor's Speech at the Annual Meeting," *SA,* May 15, 1934, pp. 1, 12; Editors, "The Menace of the Academy," *SA,* April 15, 1934. For a summary of the scholarly work on republicanism, see Sara M. Evans and Harry C. Boyte, *Free Spaces: The Source of Democratic Change in America* (New York: Harper and Row, 1986), pp. 1–25. See also Lester Cole, *Hollywood Red: The Autobiography of Lester Cole* (Palo Alto, Calif.: Ramparts Press, 1981), pp. 143–151.

76. See Hadley Cantril and Mildred Struck, eds., *Public Opinion, 1935–1946* (Princeton University Press, 1951), pp. 116–117, 755–757, for support for President Roosevelt by age and class; for faith in the future, middle-class identification, Americanism, and science, see pp. 337 and 829. See also *Public Opinion Quarterly* (April 1938), pp. 262–264, 382, for beliefs cited about business, security, and inequality.

77. John Clellon Holmes, "15 Cents Before 6 PM: The Wonderful Movies of the Thirties," *Harper's* (December 1965), pp. 51–55.

78. See Lewis Milestone Special Collections, AMPAS, which contain a series of oral interviews, one done by the American Film Institute, the other by Kevin Brownlow in the sixties. See also *San Francisco Examiner,* August 8, 1930, unpaginated clipping, *All Quiet on the Western Front* scrapbook, AMPAS. Lew Ayres' letter to Lewis Milestone, December 17, 1975, can be found in Milestone Special Collections. On Ayres' lifelong commitment to pacifism, see Obituary, "A Quiet Refusal to Kill," *The Manchester Guardian,* January 1, 1997,

p. 12. For Hitler's ban of the film, see interview with Sam Spiegel, in Sinclair, *Spiegel*, pp. 19–20. The film is on video. See Maltin, *Video Guide*.

79. See the "Progressive Educational Association Study Guides for *Fury*, 1939," in *Fury* file, AMPAS. The study guide also contains newspaper articles recording the lynching of blacks in Florida and Georgia. Though the film focused on a white man who is almost lynched, thereby avoiding the main issue of lynching of blacks, it was clear that the designers of the study guide were aware that lynching most concerned blacks. See also the "Progressive Educational Association Study Guides for *How Green Was My Valley*, 1941," in *How Green Was My Valley* file, AMPAS, and "Progressive Educational Association Study Guide for *A Family Affair*, 1937," in *A Family Affair* file, AMPAS.

80. *42nd Street* press book, in AMPAS, has numerous contemporary pictures and articles recording the tour of the "42nd Street Special" across the country to Roosevelt's inaugural. Warner Brothers, of course, was a major New Deal studio and promoted Roosevelt's campaign in southern California. The quotation comes from an unidentified clipping in the AMPAS file. Roosevelt also was a figure in such Warners films as *Footlight Parade*. For Warners and Roosevelt, see Jack Warner, *My First Hundred Years in Hollywood* (New York: Random House, 1964), pp. 216–239; Nick Roddick, *A New Deal in Entertainment: Warner Brothers in the 1930's* (London: The British Film Institute, 1983).

Chapter Three

1. Terry Ramsaye, "New Deal—Superman and Today," *MPH*, March 18, 1933, pp. 9–10.

2. Jürgen Habermas, *Legitimation Crisis* (Boston: Beacon Press, 1975), pp. 71–75. For an early criticism of the lavish theater as inappropriate for the modern age, see "Deluxe Theater Palace," *The New Republic*, March 27, 1929, p. 176; "Why Remodel?" *MPH*, April 11, 1931, p. 5. For the housing act, see "$30,000,000 in Government Loans Now Available to Reopen and Modernize Theaters," *MPH*, September 22, 1934, pp. 1–5, and October 22, 1934; John Eberson, "Theater Trends," *FDY*, 1930, pp. 943–960.

3. For a comprehensive examination of movie theaters before 1930, see Charlotte Herzog, "The Motion Picture Theater and Film Exhibition, 1896–1930" (Ph.D. dissertation, Northwestern University, 1980). For a look at theater design in the modern style, see Herbert Scherer, *Marquee on Mainstreet: Jack Leibenberg's Movie Theaters* (Minneapolis: University Gallery, University of Minnesota, 1982). See also Terry Ramsaye, "Westward Bound Editor Finds Double Billing Even on Ferry," *MPH*, November 9, 1935, p. 17; November 16, 1935, pp. 21–23; "New Sante Fe Gibraltar Is One Man Epic of Southwest," *MPH*, November 30, 1935; "A Typical Theater in an Average Town, Beaver Dam, Wisconsin," *MPH*, January 8, 1938, pp. 6–9.

4. For the rise of mass culture and the architecture of historicism that surrounded it, see Lewis A. Erenberg, *Steppin' Out: New York Nightlife and the Transformation of American Culture, 1890–1930* (Chicago: University of Chicago, 1984); Lary May, *Screening Out the Past: The Birth of Mass Culture and the Motion Picture Industry* (Chicago: University of Chicago Press, 1983); David Nasaw, *Going Out: The Rise and Fall of Public Amusements* (New York: Basic Books, 1993).

5. On the uplift and refinement of the Capitol Theater, see *Architectural Forum* 42 (June 1925): 360–390 and *American Architect* 131 (May 20, 1927): 681–690. For a firsthand account of the effort to remove movie theaters from their disreputable origins in the working class, see Carrie Balaban, *Continuous Performance: The Story of A. J. Balaban as Told to His Wife* (New York: G. P. Putnam and Sons, 1950).

6. The quotation is from Harold Rambusch, "Decorations," in R. W. Sexton, *American Theaters of Today* (New York: Architectural Book Publishing, 1927), pp. 1, 24. For the national trend, see Herzog, "Motion Picture Theater."

7. On the placement of the box office, see Emil Milner, "Motion Picture Theater Data," *Pencil Points* 3 (July 1922). On advertisements and seating, see David Naylor, *American Picture Palaces: The Architecture of Fantasy* (New York: Van Nostrand and Reinhold, 1981);

Sexton, *American Theaters of Today,* p. 14; Ben Hall, *The Best Remaining Seats* (New York: Clarkson N. Potter, Inc., 1961); William Fox, "Possibilities of the Modern Picture Unlimited," *Fox Exhibitors' Bulletin* (June 1914), p. 31, in Fox file, Museum of Modern Art Film Library (hereafter cited as MOMA).

8. See Thomas Talmadge, "The Screen, a New Art, Should Pave Road to a New Architecture," and R. E. Hall, "Today's Jazzy Interiors of Theaters Short-Lived, Declare American Architects," both in *Exhibitors Herald* (Better Theaters Section), March 17, 1928, pp. 9–10 and 17–18. See also John F. Berry, "The Times Square Paramount," *Theatrical Historical Society Annual* 3 (1976): 3; Samuel Katz, "Theater Management," in *The Story of the Films,* ed. Joseph P. Kennedy (Chicago: A. W. Shaw Co., 1927), p. 273.

9. *V,* January 8, 1930, pp. 78, 80–88; *V,* January 7, 1931, p. 5; *V,* January 5, 1932; *FDY,* 1932, pp. 1–7; R. W. Sexton, "Changing Values in Theater Design," *MPH,* March 14, 1931, pp. 26, 28; Tom Waller, "The Year in Pictures," *V,* December 29, 1931, p. 4; Martin Quigley, "Less Heat and More Light from Hollywood," *MPH,* December 5, 1931, pp. 9–12.

10. For three statements, all germane to our topic, of the common view that modernism in the United States was devoid of ideology, see Robert A. M. Stern, Gregory Gilmartin, and Thomas Mellins, *New York 1930: Architecture and Urbanism Between the Two World Wars* (New York: Rizzoli, 1987), pp. 575–581; Alan Balfour, *24 Rockefeller Center: Architecture as Theater* (New York: McGraw Hill, 1978); Carol H. Krinksy, *Rockefeller Center* (New York: Oxford University Press, 1970), pp. 81–82. A brilliant outline of the distinct European trends and their ideological underpinnings is Carl Schorske, "An International Style," *New York Times,* March 25, 1979, pp. 13, 36. A discussion of the historical roots of the modern style in Germany, France, and Russia can be found in John Willett, *Art and Politics in the Weimar Period: The New Sobriety, 1917–1933* (New York: Pantheon Books, 1970).

11. Paul T. Frankl, *Machine-Made Leisure* (New York: Harper and Brothers, 1932), pp. 5, 13, 136, 173–180.

12. "Observations," *MPH,* April 7, 1934, p. 7. For the integration of art deco into playhouse designs in the late twenties and thirties, see *Exhibitors' Herald,* October 27, 1928, p. 14. See also "The Warner Theater in Morgantown," *MPH,* August 1, 1931), p. 10. For the influence of Paris theaters, see Georges Clarriere, "Three Smart Cinema Styles from Paris," *MPH,* September 17, 1931, pp. 12–16. For Europe and the art-deco mode, see David Atwell, *Cathedrals of the Movies: A History of British Cinemas and Their Audiences* (London: The Architectural Press, 1980), pp. 139–159; Morton P. Shand, *Modern Picture Houses and Theaters* (Philadelphia: Lippincott, 1930).

13. Raymond B. Fosdick, *John D. Rockefeller, Jr.: A Portrait* (New York: Harper Brothers, 1956).

14. For Hood's reformist vision and training, see S. J. Woolf, "An Architect Hails the Rule of Reason," *New York Times Magazine,* November 1, 1931, p. 6; Raymond M. Hood, "The Spirit of Modern Art," *Architectural Forum* 51 (November 1932): 445–449. H. B. Alexander, *Liberty and Democracy* (Boston: Marshall Jones Co., 1930), pp. 124–175, reveals Alexander's deep fears for the nation, fears not too different from those of his class. The quotations come from Alexander Hartley, "Rockefeller City: Thematic Synopsis," January 25, 1932 (Business Interests, Rockefeller Archive Center, North Tarrytown, New York). I wish to thank the archivist, Harold Oakhill, for making this material available to me. See also Merle Crowell (director of Center's public relations), "The Story of Rockefeller Center," *The Architectural Forum* (May 1932), pp. 428–430; Eugene Clute, "The Story of Rockefeller Center, The Allied Arts," *The Architectural Forum* (February 1933), pp. 128–132; Louise Cross, "The Sculpture for Rockefeller Center," *Parnassus* 5 (October 1932): 1–3. A shrewd assessment of the vision of corporate renewal embodied in the design can be found in Frederick Lewis Allen, "Radio City: Cultural Center?" *Harper's,* April 2, 1932, pp. 535–545.

15. Initially hopes were high for the theater. See "Observations," *MPH,* December 17,

1932, p. 7. On opening night, see "Gorgeous Theatrics Mark Roxy's Radio City Debut," *MPH,* January 14, 1933, p. 11; $100,000 Cut Off Radio City's Overheads, May Be Chance for Profits," *V,* January 24, 1933, pp. 23, 54. See also Anita Brenner, "Art and Big Business," *The Nation,* January 4, 1933, p. 136; Ben Schlanger, "Two Late Theater Forms: A Criticism," *MPH,* February 11, 1933, p. 8; "Roxy Lets Fly at the 'Wolves of Broadway,'" *New York Herald Tribune,* February 15, 1932.

16. O. A. Shvidkovsky, ed., *Buildings in the USSR, 1917–1932* (New York: Praeger Publishers, 1971); Shand, *Modern Picture Houses,* pp. 20–25; Atwell, *Cathedrals of the Movies,* pp. 139–159; Robert O. Boller, "Modernism: Its Meaning in Practical Remodeling," *MPH,* March 9, 1935, pp. 14, 35–37.

17. Douglas Fox, "The Film Guild Cinema, an Experiment in Theater Design," *MPH,* March 16, 1929. For a precursor in the same vein, see "Carnegie Theater: The Spirit of Today in Cinema Designing," *MPH,* November 24, 1928.

18. For the overall context of modernism in the decade, see Jeffrey L. Meikle, *Twentieth Century Limited: Industrial Design in America* (Philadelphia: Temple University Press, 1979); Robert Boller, "What Style of Theater Design Fits the Variety of the American Scene?" *MPH,* July 25, 1936, pp. 8, 9. For Wright's linkage of his design with the republican principles of the producers, see Frank Lloyd Wright, "In the Cause of Architecture," *Essays of Frank Lloyd Wright for the Architectural Record* (New York: Architectural Record Books, 1975), pp. 131–151. For the fusion of modernism to the vision of "America," see Joseph Urban, *Theaters* (New York: Theater Arts, Inc., 1930), pp. 15–16. The quotation is from George Schultz, "Modernistic Art: Its Significance to America and the Photoplay," *Exhibitors Herald,* October 27, 1928, p. 38.

19. Ben Schlanger, "Theaters of Tomorrow," in *American Theaters of Today* (1930), pp. 3–9, 51–59; "Looking Towards a Better Theater," *MPH,* November 19, 1932, pp. 8–9; "Planning Today's Simplified Cinema: A Practical Consideration of a New Theater Design," *MPH,* September 21, 1935, pp. 7–8, 30, 35. For the success of theaters based on Schlanger's ideas, see "Trend to Smaller Capacity Continues," *MPH,* February 6, 1937, p. 5; "The New Rialto at Forty Second Street 'n' Broadway," *MPH,* February 8, 1936, pp. 5, 10–12.

20. Ben Schlanger, "Planning Low Cost Theaters," *MPH,* April 7, 1934, pp. 14–16; "Motion Picture Theaters of Tomorrow," *MPH,* February 14, 1932, pp. 12–14, 56–57; "Motion Picture Theaters," *Architectural Record* 81 (February 1937): 17–24. See also Schlanger, "Planning Today's Simplified Cinema."

21. Urban, *Theaters,* pp. 15–16; Boller, "Modernism," p. 14; Ben Schlanger, "The Architect and the Engineer," *MPH,* 120–121; "Observations," *MPH,* June 3, 1933, p. 5; Irving Bowman, "Modern Theater Construction," *MPH,* August 1, 1931, pp. 19, 82.

22. Ben Schlanger, "New Theaters for the Cinema," *Architectural Forum* 57 (September 1932): 253–260; "Vision in the Motion Picture Theater," *MPH,* July 30, 1932, pp. 8–12; "Use of the Full Screen Today," *MPH,* June 3, 1933, pp. 11–13; "Applying the 'Continental Plan' to American Theater Seating," *MPH,* May 30, 1936, pp. 8–12; "Two Versions of the Reversed Floor," *MPH,* October 22, 1932, pp. 12–14; Douglas Fox, "The Film Guild Cinema," pp. 15–19. For the dynamic fusion of the individual and the group within swing music, see Lewis Erenberg, *Swingin' the Dream: Big Band Jazz and the Rebirth of American Culture* (Chicago: University of Chicago Press, 1998), pp. 65–119. For regionalism, see Erika Doss, *Benton, Pollock and the Politics of Modernism from Regionalism to Abstract Expressionism* (Chicago: University of Chicago Press, 1993). For film, see ibid., ch. 2.

23. Ben Schlanger, "Remodeling to Welcome Today's Patrons," *MPH,* October 20, 1934, pp. 24, 62; "Theaters of Tomorrow"; "Planning Low Cost Theaters"; "Planning Today's Simplified Cinema"; Eugene Clute, "New Schemes in Modern Remodeling," *MPH,* October 20, 1934, pp. 11–14; "The Studio Theater: A Machine Age Cinema," *MPH,* September 26, 1931, pp. 14–28; Boller, "Modernism." The quotation is from Ben Schlanger, "Vision in the Motion Picture Theater."

24. Frankl, *Machine-Made Leisure,* pp. 136–140. A similar view is expressed by Robert

Boller, "Modernism," pp. 14, 34. See also Boller, "What Style Fits?" The quotation is from Urban, *Theatres*, pp. 15–16.

25. In 1929 the theaters listed in *FDY* totaled almost 23,000, while in 1939 the total was 19,032, a fall of almost 4,000. See *FDY*, 1930, pp. 947–988, and *FDY*, 1940, p. 41. The industry's tallies can be found in Garth Jowett, *Film: The Democratic Art* (Boston: Little, Brown, 1976), p. 475; *FDY*, 1936, p. 39; U.S. Bureau of the Census, *Historical Statistics of the United States from Colonial Times to 1957* (1957), pp. 221–225.

26. The confusion caused by the inaccuracy of the Hays Commission is vast. A fine scholar such as Garth Jowett sees that movies never had a greater influence than in the thirties, but then quotes the Hays statistics and comments that movies never recovered their popularity of the twenties (Jowett, *Democratic Art*, pp. 260–261, 286). Yet there exist plenty of commonsense reasons to doubt the numbers. To have weekly attendance figures ranging from 90 to 110 million is highly unlikely. In a country with a little over 110 million people in the twenties, this would mean that either everyone went weekly, or large amounts went three and four times a week, an unlikely scenario. For criticism of the Hays Commission statistics, see Richard E. Chaplin, *Mass Communications: A Statistical Analysis* (East Lansing: Michigan State University Press, 1957), p. 125; Bruce Austin, *The Film Audience* (Metuchen, N.J.: Scarecrow Press, 1983); Robert W. Chambers, "Need for Statistical Research," *Annals of the American Academy of Political and Social Science* (November 1947), pp. 169–172. Still these questions did not prevent the census bureau from publishing the faulty Hays tallies. See Bureau of the Census, *Historical Statistics*, pp. 221, 225. For Robbins's quotation, see Charles Champlin, "Robbins Readers Feast on Fantasy, Ignore the Critics," *Minneapolis Star and Tribune*, December 30, 1985, sec. C10. For the Gallup Poll, see *Hollywood Reporter*, June 19, 1941. The head of a sociological study sponsored by the Carnegie Foundation in 1941 observed that "Dr. Gallup figures are the most reliable known to this writer; they are the only figures based on an empirical and systematic survey." See Leo C. Rosten, *Hollywood: The Movie Colony and Moviemakers* (New York: Harcourt, Brace and Co., 1941), p. 415.

27. Gross receipts for any given year from 1929 to 1945 are derived from Commerce Department figures. See Will H. Shaw of the National Income Unit, Bureau of Foreign and Domestic Commerce, "Consumption Expenditures, 1929–1943," *Survey of Current Business* (June 1944), pp. 6–13. For subsequent years, see U.S. Department of Commerce, *U.S. Income and Output, 1958*, p. 151, and *National Income Supplement to Current Survey of Business* (1958), pp. 206–208. Average ticket prices come from the "Box Office Receipts" section of *MPH* in January and June for every year from 1931 to 1938, and are corroborated by another independent source, "Admissions Price Index, U.S. Bureau of Census," cited in Michael Conant, *Antitrust and the Motion Picture Industry* (Berkeley: University of California Press, 1960), and *Historical Statistics*, p. 224. See the Gallup Poll, "Two Estimates of Average Number of Tickets Purchased Weekly in 1940," in American Institute of Public Opinion, *Increasing Profits with Audience Research* (Princeton: American Institute of Public Opinion, 1941), p. 140. Money spent on all amusements in the thirties went up, not down. See Julius Weinberger, "Money Spent on Play: An Index of Opinion," *Public Opinion Quarterly* (April 1938), pp. 1–15.

28. For a synthesis of this scholarship and a listing of all the relevant publications on the "studio system," see Tino Balio, *Grand Design: Hollywood as a Modern Business Enterprise, 1930–1939* (New York: Charles Scribner and Sons, 1993); I. C. Jarvie, "Explorations in the Social Career of Movies: Business and Religion," in *Thinking About Society: Theory and Practice* (Boston: D. Reidel, 1986) and "The Social Experience of Movies," in S. Thomas, ed., *Film/Culture* (Metuchen, N.J.: Scarecrow), pp. 247–268; see also Jack Jungmeyer, "Film Production Trends," *V*, January 4, 1939.

29. "Reduction of Admission Price Adopted in Most Large Cities," *MPH*, October 24, 1931; Fred Ayer, "Neighborhood Theaters Are Getting Most of the New Business," *MPH*, June 16, 1934, pp. 9–10.

30. On the split in small-town and urban markets in the early thirties, see "New York

Hits, Home Town Flops," *V,* December 6, 1932, pp. 5, 21. On the rise of neighborhood theaters at the expense of the lavish theater palaces, see Abel Green, "Changing Downtown Theater Map," *V,* December 29, 1931, p. 18. For the lifting of blue laws and the start of Sunday and weekday showings in rural locations, see "Sunday Show Legislation," in *FDY,* 1937–1938. The *Film Daily Yearbook* supplied the data on theaters and their locales. The regional statistics were derived from counting the numbers of theaters listed for five selected cities. Each was a main urban center in key regions of the nation for 1931, 1934, and 1942. We counted seats per capita by dividing the total seats in a city or state by its population. *FDY,* 1940, p. 45, reported that the 25 percent rise in all weekly receipts came from Sunday showings. The quotation is from *MPH,* November 16, 1935, p. 23.

31. For the suburban, middle-class orientation of Hollywood in the twenties, see Douglas Gomery, "Movie Audiences, Urban Geography and the History of American Film," *The Velvet Light Trap,* no. 19 (Spring 1982), pp. 23–30. A prime example of vice investigators' condemnation of the working-class theater compared to the "quality" infusing movie houses downtown or in middle-class areas can be seen in *Better Theater Movement* (Minneapolis: The Women's Cooperative Alliance, 1921), pp. 2–44, in the Gilman papers, Box 34, Minnesota Historical Society. On the rise of double bills and game nights as a means to undercut the downtown theaters that were aligned to the large studios, see "Premium Policy Spreads to 100 Chicago Theaters," *MPH,* February 2, 1935, p. 9; "Prize Night in 4,400 Theaters as Fight to Control Practice Grows," *MPH,* February 29, 1936. See also Walter Green, "The Indies' Big Year," *V,* January 1, 1935, p. 6; "The Indies' Bull Season," *V,* January 1, 1936.

32. Douglas Monroy, "'Our Children Get So Different Here': Film, Fashion, Popular Culture and the Process of Cultural Syncretization in Mexican Los Angeles," *Aztlan* 19, no. 1 (1990): 79–108. I wish to thank Michael Willard for bringing this important article to my attention.

33. For the difference in quality between first- and second-run theaters in the twenties, see Women's Cooperative Alliance, *Better Theater Movement,* pp. 42–44, 53–56. For the increase of moviegoing among ethnic communities in the Northeast, and the spread of first-class theaters into workers' areas in the thirties, see W. Lloyd Warner, *The Social Life of a Modern Community* (New Haven: Yale University Press, 1941), pp. 412–419, and Caroline Ware, *Greenwich Village 1920–1930* (Boston: Houghton Mifflin, 1935), pp. 330–338, 350–351, 366–369. For the number of modern theaters built nationally after 1933, see Ben Schlanger, "Cinemas," *Architectural Record* 84 (July 1938): 113–115. The calculations for the Twin Cities were done by comparing the listings of new modern theaters in the trade journals with a study done in the thirties that outlined the different classes in every area of the city. See Calvin F. Schmid, *Social Saga of Two Cities: An Ecological and Statistical Study of Social Trends in Minneapolis and St. Paul* (Minneapolis: Minneapolis Council of Social Agencies, 1937). On black swing musicians and the streamline style, see Lewis Erenberg, *Swingin' the Dream,* pp. 94–119. For black theaters, see "800 Negro Theaters in 32 States Point to Growing Demand," *MPH,* August 15, 1936, p. 27, and *FDY,* 1936, pp. 45–47.

34. On ethnic radio stations, entertainments, and the capacity of groups to reinterpret films to suit their interests in the twenties, see Lizabeth Cohen, *Making a New Deal: Industrial Workers in Chicago, 1919–1939* (New York: Cambridge University Press, 1990), pp. 99–159. See also William Ackerman, "The Dimensions of American Broadcasting," *The Public Opinion Quarterly* (Spring 1945), p. 4. Ackerman was director of the Reference Department of the Columbia Broadcasting System. On blue laws and limited showings in rural settings, see *FDY,* 1928, p. 7, and "Sunday Show Legislation," in *FDY,* 1937–1938, pp. 56–103, 1032–33.

35. For the number of patrons in Europe and the United States, see Paul Monaco, *Cinema and Society: France and Germany During the Twenties* (New York: Elsevier, 1976), pp. 18–31; *FDY,* 1930, p. 304; May, *Screening Out the Past,* pp. 165–166. That the regimes in various European countries saw the American film as radically different in style and content, and thus a threat to their own social projects, see Victoria De Grazia, "Mass Culture and Sover-

eignty: The American Challenge to European Cinemas, 1920–1960," *Journal of Modern History* 61 (March 1989): 53–87. For studies that show that the audience was divided by class in Germany, from which one can probably surmise, in the absence of other comparable investigations, that the case was not different elsewhere, see Bruce Arthur Murray, "Film and the German Left in the Weimar Republic" (unpublished Ph.D. dissertation, University of Minnesota, 1985); Anton Kes, "Mass Culture and Modernity: Notes Towards a Social History of Early American and German Cinemas," *America and the Germans,* vol. II, ed. Fran Trommler and Joseph McVeigh (Philadelphia: University of Pennsylvania Press, 1985), pp. 317–332; George Huaco, *The Sociology of Film Art* (New York: Basic Books, 1965), pp. 146–151. The historical style and its continuing dominance in Europe can be seen in Dennis Sharp, *The Picture Palace* (New York: Frederick Praeger, 1969); Atwell, *Cathedrals of the Movies.*

36. George Mosse, *The Nationalization of the Masses: Political Symbolism and Mass Movements from the Napoleonic Wars Through the Third Reich* (New York: H. Fertig, 1975); Carl Schorske, *Fin de Siecle Vienna* (Princeton: Princeton University Press, 1985); Jeffrey Brooks, *When Russia Learned to Read: Literacy and Popular Literature, 1861–1917* (Princeton: Princeton University Press, 1985), especially pp. 295–396. On Russia, see Richard Taylor, "The Birth of Soviet Cinema," in Abbott Gleason and Richard Stites, eds., *Bolshevik Culture* (Bloomington: Indiana University Press, 1985), pp. 190–205. See also Eric Hobsbawm, *The Age of Extremes* (New York: Pantheon Books, 1994), pp. 142–178, 178–199.

37. See for example, Robert Boller, "Designing to Fit the Local Scene," *MPH,* April 3, 1937, pp. 8–10; "The Community Theater Idea," *MPH,* February 5, 1938, pp. 9–10; Ben Schlanger, "Planning Low Cost Theaters." See also "Kirkendale Urges Cooperation with Community," *Exhibitors Herald,* February 1, 1930, p. 22. The comparison of names is derived from the titles listed in the theater directory of *Film Daily Yearbook* from 1925 to 1940. Romantic names, of course, were retained by some of the older theaters, but the trend was toward communal and patriotic naming by the early thirties.

38. See Boller, "Designing to Fit the Local Scene." For Duluth and Minneapolis, see Scherer, *Marquee on Mainstreet;* Robert Boller, "The Ute: A Design Exploiting Native Western Culture," *MPH,* April 4, 1936, pp. 9–12. See also Stern, *New York 1930,* pp. 260–261; "Modernized Colonial Theaters," *MPH,* February 5, 1938. For the South, see "Redesigned in Newer Materials," *MPH,* October 15, 1938, pp. 63–65. For black theaters, see "800 Negro Theaters," *MPH,* p. 27. The murals in most cases follow the regionalist style common in post offices and other public buildings in the New Deal era. See Marlene Park and Gerald E. Markowitz, *Democratic Vistas: Post Offices and Public Art in the New Deal* (Philadelphia: Temple University Press, 1984).

39. Interview with Larry Storch, July 6, 1988, and my discussions with James Cross in the fifties. For civic groups, see "Kirkendale Urges Cooperation with Community," *Exhibitors Herald,* February 1, 1930; "100% Representation Needed for Success of Theater," *MPH,* March 28, 1931, pp. 19, 95. See also "The Little Fellow," *MPH,* July 4, 1931, p. 8; "A Typical Theater in an Average Town," *MPH,* January 8, 1938, p. 7. The primary material on bank nights, lotteries, and giveaways is vast, and its importance warrants a book. In the meantime, see "Conflict on Bank Nights Widens: Iowa Exhibitor Wins in Test Case," *MPH,* January 12, 1935, p. 15; "Premium Thriller," *Business Week,* December 8, 1934, p. 24; "Bank Night," *Time,* February 3, 1936, p. 57; "The Audience at Play: Games and Premiums Rival Hollywood's Stars as Box Office Attractions," *New York Times,* April 24, 1938, sec. X, p. 4; Forbes Parkhill, "Bank Night Tonight," *Saturday Evening Post,* December 4, 1937, pp. 20–22.

40. "Fox Orders All Ad Reels Out of Circuit Theaters," *MPH,* June 6, 1931, p. 19.

41. Ibid. Press books for all the cited premieres are in Warner Brothers Collections, University of Southern California Film Archives Library. See also *FDY,* 1940, pp. 802–809. For Santa Claus Lane, see "Hollywood's Big Parade," *Los Angeles Examiner,* November 25, 1970, sec. A6; *V,* January 2, 1934, p. 5.

42. On the industry mobilizing as an arm of the wartime state, see *FDY,* 1941, p. 773; *V,* October 9, 1940, and December 11, 1940, p. 4; "43 Features and 84 Short Subjects on Americanism from the Studios," *MPH,* February 25, 1939, p. 17, and April 15, 1939, p. 135. For pictures of the Uptown and its friezes in Minneapolis, see Lary May, "Making the American Way: Modern Theaters, Audiences and the Film Industry, 1929–1945," *Prospects* 12 (1987): 118.

43. On the premiere, see *Knute Rockne* film file, AMPAS, and *South Bend Tribune,* October 1, 1940.

44. *South Bend Tribune,* October 4, 1940, p. 10; Franklin D. Roosevelt to Mrs. Rockne, October 1, 1940, PPF. No. 6899, Franklin D. Roosevelt Library, Hyde Park, New York.

Chapter Four

1. Philip Dunne, *Take Two: A Life in the Movies and Politics* (New York: Limelight Editions, 1980), pp. 21, 109, 118–122, 335–340.

2. See, for example, John Morton Blum, *V Was for Victory: Politics and American Culture During World War II* (New York: Harcourt Brace Jovanovich, 1976), and Jean Christophe Agnew, "Coming Up for Air: Consumer Culture in Historical Perspective," *Intellectual History Newsletter* 12 (1990): 3–21.

3. See Blum, *V Was for Victory.* On labor's cooperation with management and the state and the pledge of the communists to avoid strikes, see Nelson Lichtenstein, *Labor's War at Home: The C.I.O. in World War II* (New York: Cambridge University Press, 1983) and George Lipsitz, *Rainbow at Midnight: Labor and Culture in the 1940s* (Urbana: University of Illinois Press, 1994).

4. See Dorothy Jones, "The Hollywood War Film: 1942–1944," *Hollywood Quarterly* 6 (1945–1946): 1–19; Clayton R. Koppes and Gregory Black, "What to Show the World: The Office of War Information and Hollywood, 1942–1945," *Journal of American History* 64 (1977): 88, and *Hollywood Goes to War: How Politics, Profits and Propaganda Shaped World War II Movies* (Berkeley: University of California Press, 1990).

5. On the shifting face of national identity, see Philip Gleason, "American Identity and Americanization," in *The Harvard Encyclopedia of American Ethnic Groups* (Cambridge: Harvard University Press, 1980), pp. 38–57. See also John Higham, *Strangers in the Land: Patterns of American Nativism* (New Brunswick, N.J.: Rutgers University Press, 1955) and *Send These to Me* (Baltimore: Johns Hopkins University Press, 1984). Chapters 8, 9, and 10 of the latter are critical for cultural pluralism. The fact that the war was fought in the name of realizing the dream of general abundance is the central theme of Blum, *V Was for Victory.*

6. K. R. M. Short, "Washington's Information Manual for Hollywood, 1942," *Historical Journal of Film, Radio and Television* 3 (1983): 171–180.

7. See editors of *Look* magazine, *Movie Lot to Beachhead: The Motion Picture Goes to War and Prepares for the Future* (Garden City, New York: Doubleday, Doran and Co., 1945), pp. 58–69, 82–96, 148–158, 204–215; Colin Shindler, *Hollywood Goes to War: Films and American Society, 1939–1952* (London: Routledge & K. Paul, 1979). On the film industry and Jews, see Lary May, *Screening Out the Past: The Birth of Mass Culture and the Motion Picture Industry* (Chicago: University of Chicago Press, 1983), ch. 6. The death of Kauffmann is recounted in Otto Friedrich, *City of Nets: A Portrait of Hollywood in the 1940s* (New York: Harper and Row, 1976), p. 49.

8. Howard Koch, "The Making of Casablanca," in Howard Koch, *Casablanca: Script and Legend* (New York: Overlook Press, 1992), p. 19. See also *Movie Lot to Beachhead.* "Hollywood Victory Caravan" file, in AMPAS, has newspaper articles from around the country reporting the stars' victory parades.

9. Photographs of battleships named in honor of Will Rogers are on display in the Will Rogers Memorial, Claremore, Okla. For the amount of war bonds sold in movie houses, see *Movie Lot to Beachhead,* pp. 58–69. On Lena Horne, see Horne file, AMPAS.

10. On Davis, see *Los Angeles Daily News,* November 11, 1941, and *Hollywood Citizen News,* July 27, 1942, unpaginated clippings in the Bette Davis file, AMPAS.

11. See Sleepy Lagoon file, University of California at Los Angeles Special Collections Library (hereafter UCLASC); Orson Welles, "Race Hate Must Be Outlawed," *Free World Magazine* (July 1944), pp. 9–11.

12. Robert Rossen, "New Characters for the Screen," *New Masses,* January 18, 1944, in *Hollywood Directors,* ed. Richard Koszarski (New York: Oxford University Press, 1976), pp. 190–194.

13. All the cited films are on video. See Leonard Maltin, *TV Movies and Video Guide* (New York: Signet Books, 1999). The quotation can be found in Thomas Cripps, *Making Movies Black: The Hollywood Message Movie from World War II to the Civil Rights Era* (New York: Oxford University Press, 1993), p. 207.

14. This quotation derives from an OWI script review of *For Whom the Bell Tolls,* as cited in Koppes and Black, "What to Show the World," p. 92.

15. See Lew Bergen, "Lew Ayres Obituary," *The Manchester Guardian,* January 1, 1997, p. 12; James Naremore, "The Trial: The FBI versus Orson Welles," *Film Comment* (January–February 1991), pp. 22–27; Dunne, *Take Two,* p. 160.

16. Joseph McBride, *Frank Capra: The Catastrophe of Success* (New York: Simon and Schuster, 1992), pp. 356, 451–501. For the revisions of *Why We Fight,* especially the Japanese sections, see John Dower, *War Without Mercy: Race and Power in the Pacific War* (New York: Pantheon Books, 1986), ch. 1.

17. John Huston, "The Courage of the Men: An Interview with John Huston," in *Film: Book 2,* ed. Robert Hughes (New York: Grove Press, 1962), pp. 22–35; K. R. M. Short, "Hollywood Fights Anti-Semitism," in Short, ed., *Film and Radio Propaganda in World War II* (London: Croom Helm, 1983), pp. 147–151. The *Mr. Skeffington* censorship story is recounted in ibid., pp. 160–162.

18. These collations and data derive from *Film Daily Yearbook* for 1916, 1918–1919, 1924, 1934, 1939, 1944, and 1954. I wish to thank my research assistant Michael Willard for tabulating and collating this complicated data. For a fine examination of the independents in the thirties, see Brian Taves, "The B Film: Hollywood's Other Half," in Tino Balio, ed., *Grand Design: Hollywood as a Modern Business Enterprise, 1930–1939* (New York: Charles Scribner and Sons, 1993). There is some irony in having Taves's article in a book that basically argues that there was a monopolistic, closed Hollywood system in the Depression, since the independents often successfully challenged and competed with all the majors.

19. See May, *Screening Out the Past,* chs. 2 and 5, for censorship and the movies. See also Richard Maltby, *Reforming the Movies: Hollywood, the Hays Office and the Campaign for Film Censorship, 1908–1938* (New York: Oxford University Press, 1995).

20. Lester Koenig, "Back from the Wars," *The Screenwriter* 1 (1945): 23–25. On a larger scale this is also one of the central themes of Thomas P. Doherty, *Projections of War: Hollywood, American Culture and World War II* (New York: Columbia University Press, 1993).

21. John Huston, World Brotherhood Speech, in Huston Collections, *AMPAS;* Robert Andrews interview by Philip Scheur, *Los Angeles Times,* December 5, 1943.

22. See Irving Pichel, "Seeing with the Camera," *Hollywood Quarterly* 1 (1945–1946): 138–145; Irving Pichel, "Areas of Silence," *Film Quarterly* 3 (1947): 51–55.

23. *New York Times,* January 13, 1944, in Shindler, *Hollywood Goes to War,* p. 76.

24. Examples of this tendency can be found in *Back to Bataan, Bataan, Casablanca, The House on 92nd Street, Americans All, December 7th,* and almost all the war films cited in the chapter.

25. The original screenplay can be found in Howard Koch, *Casablanca, Script and Legend* (Woodstock, New York: The Overlook Press, 1992). It is also on video. See Maltin, *Video Guide.*

26. Howard Koch, *Casablanca,* p. 29.

27. Ibid., pp. 51, 65, 76, 108, 163–170, 185, 204–205.

28. Ibid., pp. 100–127.

29. Ibid., pp. 218–228.

30. Richard Slotkin, *Gunfighter Nation: The Myth of the Frontier in Twentieth Century*

America (New York: Harper Perennial, 1992), pp. 318–326. All the films cited are on video. See Maltin, *Video Guide.* The quotation comes from Dudley Nichols, *Air Force,* ed. Lawrence Suid (Madison: University of Wisconsin Press, 1983), p. 73.

31. *Americans All* can be viewed at the Immigration History Research Archive, University of Minnesota.

32. See Maltin, *Video Guide.* All the cited films are on video and listed in this guide.

33. The film is on video. See Maltin, *Video Guide;* "World War Hero Makes Its Appearance at the Astor," *New York Times,* July 3, 1941. The account of York's visit to the White House is from "President Praises 'Sergeant York' to the Living Hero of the Picture," *News and Feature Service of Warner Brothers Studio,* in Sergeant York file, AMPAS.

34. See Maltin, *Video Guide.* This film and interpretation first came to my attention in the work of Jennifer Delton, "Sundered by Memory: Cold War Internationalism and the Problem of American Identity," senior thesis in the program in American Studies, University of Minnesota, Spring 1989.

35. Ibid.

36. A print of this film is in the United States National Archives, and the library of the American Studies program, University of Minnesota, has a copy. Jones, "Hollywood War Film," shows that the overwhelming majority of films focusing on the foreign enemy took place on the home front rather than in combat.

37. All of the cited films of Preston Sturges are on video. See Maltin, *Video Guide.*

38. *Going My Way* is available on video. See Maltin, *Video Guide.*

39. *Holiday Inn* is available on video. See Maltin, *Video Guide.*

40. All the "road films" are on video. See Maltin, *Video Guide.*

41. Bob Hope, *I Never Left Home* (New York: Simon and Schuster, 1944), pp. 84–86; Leo Rosten, "Bob Hope, Gags and Riches," *Look* magazine, February 24, 1952, p. 102–104; Bob Hope, "Take It from Me," *Coronet* (October 1945) and "Christmas Island," *Hollywood Citizen News,* September 9, 1944. All in Hope file, AMPAS.

42. The best descriptions of his tours can be found in Bob Hope, *I Never Left Home,* pp. 80–140. See also Hope, "Take It from Me" and "Back from the Pacific," *Los Angeles Times,* November 12, 1944; unpaginated clippings in Hope file, AMPAS. A fine analysis of Hope's humor and its appeal can be found in Rosten, "Gags and Riches," pp. 102–104. The quotation comes from Hope, "Tomorrow Is a New Day," *The American Magazine,* March 4, 1949, p. 135.

43. "The Singing Padre," *New York Times,* October 9, 1943; "We Can't Go Wrong with McCarey, Bing, Fitzgerald," *Hollywood Reporter,* February 28, 1944; Ray Le Strange, "Dr. Bing Crosby, Wartime Therapist," *Motion Picture Magazine* (October 1944), pp. 44–45; Father Victor Follen, "With a Song in His Heart," *Photoplay* (May 1945); Victor Boesen, "There's Only One Bing," *Liberty,* July 21, 1945, pp. 49–50. All in Bing Crosby file, AMPAS.

44. For the theme of the pin-up girl in wartime popular art, see Robert Westbrook, "I Want a Girl Just Like the Girl That Married Harry James: American Women and the Problem of Political Obligation in World War II," *American Quarterly* 42 (1990): 587–614. See also Lewis A. Erenberg, "Swing Goes to War: Glen Miller and the Popular Music of World War II," in *The War in American Culture: Society and Consciousness in World War II,* ed. Erenberg and Susan E. Hirsch (Chicago: University of Chicago Press, 1996), pp. 144–165.

45. See Jeanine Basinger, *A Woman's View: How Hollywood Spoke to Women, 1940–1960* (Hanover and London: Wesleyan University Press, 1993).

46. For examples of how stars' imagery changed to meet this demand, see Bette Davis, "Code for American Girls in Wartime," *Photoplay* 54 (September 1940): 17; Ann Sothern, "What Kind of Woman Will Your Man Come Home To?" *Photoplay* 25 (November 1944): 85–86. See also Elaine Tyler May, *Homeward Bound: American Families in the Cold War Era* (New York: Basic Books, 1988), pp. 58–91; Westbrook, "I Want a Girl Just Like the Girl." All the cited films are on video. See Maltin, *Video Guide.*

47. For the larger implications of the new home and women in war, see Joyce M. Baker,

Images of Women in Film: The War Years, 1941–1945 (Ann Arbor, Mich.: Unit Research Press, 1980). *Since You Went Away* (1944) is available on video. See Maltin, *Video Guide.*

48. On Hayworth's first husband, see *The San Diego Union,* August 10, 1941. For her face and figure on the atomic bomb, see "Bombed and Buried," *Motion Picture Herald,* April 12, 1947. The complete saga of her career can be found in the Rita Hayworth file, AMPAS.

49. Lena Horne interview, *Ebony* (July 1968), pp. 130–134. See also Lena Horne file, AMPAS.

50. See "World Organization Polls from 1937 to 1945," *Public Opinion Quarterly* (Summer 1945), p. 253.

51. See Godfrey Hodgson, *America in Our Time: From World War II to Nixon, What Happened and Why* (New York: Doubleday, 1976), p. 77.

52. See May, *Homeward Bound,* especially pp. 3–15.

53. Dellie Hahn, "Interview," in Studs Terkel, *The Good War: An Oral History of World War II* (New York: Pantheon Books, 1984), pp. 117–118.

54. Paul Pisciano, "Interview," in Terkel, *The Good War,* pp. 141–142.

55. The trade journals are filled with these new designs, but for a representative sample, see "Theater of the Americas," *Better Theaters Section of MPH,* May 31, 1947, pp. 22–25; "Headquarters Showplace," *Better Theaters Section of MPH,* August 23, 1947, pp. 18–22; "Integrating the Movies into Daily Community Life," *Better Theaters Section of MPH,* March 3, 1951, pp. 14–16; "American Theater, 16 East Lake Street, Minneapolis" (1940), in Liebenberg Collections, North West Architectural Archives, Minneapolis, Minn.; "The 2500 Seat Calderon," *Better Theaters Section of MPH,* July 2, 1949, pp. 24–26; "Luminous Murals," *Better Theaters Section of MPH,* April 5, 1947, pp. 18–20.

56. On drive-ins, see "Vending at the Drive-In," *MPH,* October 9, 1948, pp. 54–56; "Drive-Ins Are Show Business—But That Ain't All," *Better Theaters Section of MPH,* February 4, 1950, pp. 26–29; and Rodney Luther, "The Drive-In Theater," *MPH* (Summer 1951), pp. 400–421.

57. The many areas in which that "anxiety" surfaced are explored by Warren Susman, "Did Success Spoil the United States?: Dual Representations in Postwar America," in Lary May, *Recasting America* (Chicago: University of Chicago Press, 1983), pp. 19–38. Susman has a different explanation for what caused that anxiety than will be found in this investigation.

58. See McBride, *Frank Capra,* pp. 504–505, 536–531, 562, 590–595.

59. For her wartime image as the pin-up, see "Stay As Sweet As You Are," *Motion Picture Magazine* (October 1944); *Los Angeles Times,* December 24, 1944; "GI's Glorify June as Fan Mail Tops," *Los Angeles Times,* February 18, 1945; "June Is a Radiant Personality—Marriage Accounts for That," *Los Angeles Times,* September 30, 1945; "Cover Story," *Life,* October 1, 1945; *Look,* July 4, 1950; "June Allyson, Paradox Among Pin-Up Girls," *MGM News,* July 9, 1945. For her relation with Powell, see "The Original Miss Goody Two Shoes," *V,* June 25, 1957; "The Big Lie About June Allyson," *Movieland* (July 1956). On her advice to women on how to be good wives, see *Women's Home Companion* (July 1955). On the crackup and her little girl persona, see *People,* June 21, 1982, and *Harpers Bazaar* (September 1983). All of the above articles can be found in June Allyson file, AMPAS.

60. Lena Horne interview, *Ebony* (July 1968), pp. 130–134; *Hollywood Citizen News,* June 22, 1950; *New York Times,* October 27, 1957; *Los Angeles Daily News,* June 3, 1948; Lena Horne interview, *Vogue* (June 1972); *Women's Wear Daily,* October 24, 1974. On her capacity to "compete on an Aryan level," see Robert Rourke, *Esquire* (1953). All are unpaginated clippings in Lena Horne file, AMP.

Chapter Five

1. Eric Johnston, "Utopia Is Production," *Screen Actor* 14 (April 1946): 7 (hereafter cited as *SA*).

2. See Charles Maier, "The Politics of Productivity," *International Organization* 31, no. 4

(1977): 607–632. On theories of nationality see Benedict Anderson, *Imagined Communities* (London: Verso, 1983).

3. Godfrey Hodgson, *America in Our Time: From World War II to Nixon, What Happened and Why* (New York: Doubleday, 1978); Charles Maier, "The Politics of Productivity"; John Morton Blum, *V Was for Victory: Politics and American Culture During World War II* (New York: Harcourt, Brace, Jovanovich, 1976); Michael S. Sherry, *In the Shadow of War: The United States Since the 1930's* (New Haven: Yale University Press, 1995). For the family, see Elaine Tyler May, *Homeward Bound: American Families in the Cold War Era* (New York: Basic Books, 1988).

4. Eric Johnston, *America Unlimited* (Garden City, N.J.: Doubleday, Doran and Co., 1944), pp. 12–13, 235–245 and *We're All in It* (New York: Dutton, 1948), p. 69. See also "Utopia Is Production." For Johnston's involvement in business communities outside Hollywood, see Karl Schriftgiesser, *Business Comes of Age: The Story of the Committee for Economic Development and Its Impact on the Economic Policies of the United States, 1942–1960* (New York: Harper, 1960).

5. Ibid.

6. Johnston, "Utopia Is Production," p. 7.

7. Johnston, *America Unlimited*, pp. 12–13, 235–245 and *We're All in It*, p. 69.

8. For a full exposition of the "New Century" context, see Johnston, *America Unlimited*, and Schriftgiesser, *Business Comes of Age*, pp. 13, 23, 73–75. On postwar strikes, see George Lipsitz, *Rainbow at Midnight: Labor and Culture in the 1940s* (Urbana: University of Illinois Press, 1994); Anthony Dawson, "Hollywood's Labor Troubles," *Industrial Relations Review* 1 (July 1948); *Life*, October 14, 1946, pp. 29–33. See also Michael Nielson and Gene Mailes, *Hollywood's Other Blacklist: Union Struggle in the Studio System* (London: British Film Institute, 1995). The quotation from the office worker on strike comes from Herbert Sorrell, "You Don't Choose Your Friends: The Memoir of Herbert Knott Sorrell," Oral History Project, UCLA, 1963, p. 153.

9. Murray Schumach, *The Face on the Cutting Room Floor: The Story of Movie and Television Censorship* (New York: Morrow, 1964), p. 129.

10. Johnston, *America Unlimited*. For the new censorship code, see Jonathan Munby, *Public Enemies, Public Heroes: Screening the Gangster from* Little Caesar *to* Touch of Evil (Chicago: University of Chicago Press, 1999), pp. 144–185. On the drive for censorship and its earlier institutionalization, see the fine study by Richard Maltby, *Reforming the Movies: Hollywood, the Hays Office and the Campaign for Film Censorship, 1908–1938* (New York: Oxford University Press, 1995). For attempts to ban *All Quiet*, see the *Hollywood Reporter*, September 22, 1950, and *V*, April 9, 1952, unpaginated clippings, in *All Quiet on the Western Front* production file, AMPAS. See also *Grapes of Wrath* production file, AMPAS. Johnston's quotation is from Schumach, *The Face on the Cutting Room Floor*, p. 129.

11. Bob Hope, "Tomorrow Is a New Day," *The American Magazine*, March 4, 1949, pp. 21, 134–136; Hope news column, *Hollywood Citizen News*, December 11, 1947, unpaginated clipping, in Hope file, AMPAS.

12. See note 3.

13. A comprehensive exposition of these two views—anticommunism was a real response to a real danger, and yet was carried away by paranoid excesses—informs a fine overview of the key events and images of the era that can be found in Stephen J. Whitfield, *The Culture of the Cold War* (Baltimore: The Johns Hopkins University Press, 1991). The literature focusing on the escapist and hegemonic view of popular art is vast. A good summary and introduction can be found in Patrick Brantlinger, *Bread and Circuses: Theories of Mass Culture as Social Decay* (Ithaca: Cornell University Press, 1984). For a view of anticommunism as the province of small-town conservatives, see Jane De Hart Matthews, "Art and Politics in Cold War America," *American Historical Review* 81 (October 1976): 762–787. This view is not wrong, but it ignores that small-town anticommunism had existed in the past. What makes it effective in the postwar era is the culture of war and the rise of the new corporate

liberals and Cold War state. For a welcome corrective to the general account of the Red Scare in the film capital, see Thom Andersen, "Red Hollywood," in *Literature and the Visual Arts in Contemporary Society,* ed. Suzanne Ferguson and Barbara Grossclose (Columbus: Ohio State University Press, 1986), pp. 141–96.

14. See Lary May, *Screening Out the Past: The Birth of Mass Culture and the Motion Picture Industry* (Chicago: University of Chicago Press, 1983); Steven J. Ross, *Working Class Hollywood: Silent Film and the Shaping of Class in America* (Princeton: Princeton University Press, 1998).

15. For New Deal voting in Hollywood, see *Hollywood Reporter,* October 8, 1936. On the industry workforce and unionization, see Leo C. Rosten, *Hollywood: The Movie Colony, the Movie Makers* (New York: Harcourt and Brace, 1941), pp. 373, 381–394; Murray Ross, *Stars and Strikes: The Unionization of Hollywood* (New York: Columbia University Press, 1963); "The Guild and the Labor Movement," *SA* (July 1936). For voting by class entering the two-party system via the New Deal, see Richard Ostreicher, "Urban Working Class Political Behavior and Theories of Electoral Politics, 1879–1940," *Journal of American History* 74 (1988): 1257–86.

16. Ross, *Stars and Strikes;* Louis B. Perry, *A History of the Los Angeles Labor Movement, 1911–1941* (Berkeley: University of California Press, 1963); Sorrell, "You Don't Choose Your Friends." For the CIO, see David Brody, *Workers in Industrial America* (New York: Oxford University Press, 1980), pp. 82–173.

17. Sorrell, "You Don't Choose Your Friends": on "no communist," p. 208; on strikes at Warners, pp. 152–153; on "John L. Lewis," p. 146; on backing left-wing politicians such as Upton Sinclair, p. 88; on organizing minorities and shedding racism, pp. 80–86; on the producers' demanding sexual favors from their secretaries and the producers' opposition to organizing office workers, pp. 76–79; on sending Joe Schenck, a major producer, to jail for giving payoffs to unions, p. 80. See also Father George Dunne, "Christian Advocacy and Labor Strife in Hollywood," UCLA Oral History Project, 1981.

18. On the CSU, SAG, and their common alliance and tolerance for the few communists in their midst, see Sorrell, "You Don't Choose Your Friends," pp. 50–51, 77–78, 86–87, 134, 143–150; Testimony of Herbert Sorrell, Hearings before a Special Committee on Education and Labor, House of Representatives, *Jurisdictional Disputes in the Motion Picture Industry,* 80th Cong., 1st sess., 1948, pp. 784–805, 1860–1903 (hereafter known as *Jurisdictional Disputes*); Testimony of Father George Dunne, *Jurisdictional Disputes,* pp. 403–433, 443–456, and "Christian Advocacy," p. 52. For SAG, see Robert Montgomery, SAG Oral History Project, 1979, SAG files, Los Angeles. For Guild and dissident union alliances, see Board of Directors Minutes, SAG files, April 15, 1937; February 21, 1938, pp. 683, 714; June 13, 1938, p. 802; October 1938 (hereafter known as *Minutes*). For the letter to the longshoremen, see *Minutes,* March 1, 1937, p. 483.

19. Rosten, *Hollywood,* pp. 301–394; Editorial, "The Guild and the Labor Movement," *SA* (July 1936), pp. 4–5.

20. For a recent account that repeats the mistaken view that the Actors Guild was simply geared to protecting the stars' salaries, see Garry Wills, *Reagan's America: Innocents at Home* (Garden City, N.Y.: Doubleday, 1987), pp. 215–223. Roy Brewer, the president of IA, told the author in an interview that the Hollywood guilds were a communist plot hatched in the thirties. Roy Brewer, July 7, 1985, tape in author's possession. See Frank Scully, "Is the Middle Class in the Middle?" *SA* (December 1936), pp. 8–9; Nunnally Johnson, "American Epic," *SA* (August 1934), p. 4; Fred Keating, "Are We Really Laborers? Under Conditions of Modern Economic Society Motion Picture Actors Are Laborers Whether They Admit It or Not," *SA* (August 1934), pp. 2, 18–21.

21. Unsigned, "I Am an Individual," *SA* (January 1936), p. 5; Eddie Cantor, "What the Guild Stands For," *SA* (March 1934), p. 2; "The Wire to President Roosevelt and the Executive Order," *SA,* May 15, 1933, pp. 4, 16; "Text of Eddie Cantor's Speech at the Annual Meeting," *SA,* May 15, 1934, pp. 1, 12; Editors, "The Menace of the Academy," *SA,* April

15, 1934. For a summary of the scholarly work on republicanism, see Sara M. Evans and Harry C. Boyte, *Free Spaces: The Source of Democratic Change in America* (New York: Harper and Row, 1986), pp. 1–25. See also Lester Cole, *Hollywood Red: The Autobiography of Lester Cole* (Palo Alto, Calif.: Ramparts Press, 1981), pp. 143–151.

22. Rosten, *Hollywood,* p. 335. For Guild leaders' recollection of their cultural break from their middle-class Victorian racial and sexual roles, see Jack Dales, Gale Sondergaard, Robert Montgomery, Leon Ames, SAG Oral History interviews, 1979, SAG files, Public Relations, Los Angeles, California. On racial intolerance, see "Guild Combats Danger of Minority Baiting," *SA* (April 1946), pp. 7, 8; *Minutes,* November 9, 1939, p. 1307.

23. See almost any issue of *SA* from 1935 to 1945 for examples of the merging of labor and popular art and consumer desires. For boycotts, fairs, and radio shows, see *Minutes,* February 21, 1938, p. 714; August 23, 1937; January 3, 1938, p. 657; May 15, 1939, p. 1162; and February 19, 1940, p. 1454. See also "Screen Guild Theater over CBS," *SA* (April 1941), p. 6. On FDR's hat, see *SA* (April 1941), p. 6. For consumerism, mass production, and higher wages as central to the Guild's and Hollywood union rhetoric, see *Los Angeles Citizen* (September 1936), pp. 3, 10; September 1937, pp. 3, 11. On strikes and beauty queens, see *Hollywood Sun,* July 25, 1945. For the comment on happy kids, see Sorrell memoir, "You Don't Choose Your Friends," Special Collections, UCLA Research Library. For the Montgomery letter to the Guild on birth of his son, see *Minutes,* March 2, 1936, p. 77.

24. "Labor Day Parade," *Los Angeles Citizen* (September 1936), pp. 3, 10; September 1937, pp. 3, 11; "Brother Eddie Cantor," *Los Angeles Citizen* (September 1936), p. 10; "Guild Joins Labor Day Parade," *SA* (August 1936), p. 3.

25. On war and postwar strikes, see Lipsitz, *Rainbow at Midnight.* For the implications of wartime wild-cat strikes, inflation, and the conflict with labor leaders that created a more conservative union hierarchy across the nation, see Nelson Liechtenstein, *Labor's War at Home: The CIO in World War II* (New York: Cambridge University Press, 1982). For the conflict between the extras' strikes, the CSU, and SAG leadership, see *Minutes,* December 30, 1942; January 5, 1943; February 21, 1943; March 1, 1943; April 12, 1943; May 24, 1943; December 18, 1943, p. 2704; October 17, 1945. See Jack Dales, SAG Oral History interview; Sorrell, "You Don't Choose Your Friends," pp. 70–77; Kenneth Thomson, "Report on Extras," *Minutes,* March 14, 1943.

26. See Johnston, *America Unlimited,* pp. 34–60, and *We're All in It,* pp. 1–60; Johnston, Testimony, House Committee on Un-American Activities, *Hearings Regarding the Communist Infiltration of the Motion Picture Industry,* 80th Cong., 1st sess., 1947, pp. 305–310 (hereafter cited as *HUAC 1947*). For the larger wartime and postwar context of this new ideology of consensus and internationalism, see Maier, "The Politics of Productivity." To contrast this positive anticommunism with the negative brand after World War I, see John Higham, *Strangers in the Land: Patterns of American Nativism, 1860–1925* (New York: Atheneum, 1971).

27. A fine analysis of postwar strikes in the context of the emerging Cold War can be found in Lipsitz, *Rainbow at Midnight.* For the recognition that Reagan was the most important Hollywood anticommunist, see Testimony of Roy Brewer, House Committee on Un-American Activities, 82nd Cong., 1st sess., 1951, p. 517 (hereafter cited as *HUAC 1951*); Ronald Reagan and Richard C. Hubler, *Where's the Rest of Me?* (New York: Doubleday, Doran and Co., 1965), pp. 1–65, 147–230; Wills, *Reagan's America,* pp. 247–250. For an analysis of his life, his films, and their relation to his Hollywood politics, see Stephen Vaughn, *Ronald Reagan in Hollywood: Movies and Politics* (New York: Cambridge University Press, 1994). On Reagan's divorce settlement, see Reagan vs. Reagan, 1948, in Los Angeles County Archives, Los Angeles, California, no. D360058m.

28. For the rise of working-class patriotism in the war and its implications, see Gary Gerstle, "The Working Class Goes to War," in Lewis Erenberg and Susan Hirsch, eds., *The War in American Culture: Society and Consciousness During World War II* (Chicago: University of Chicago Press, 1996). There simply is no comment on the deportation of the Japanese in

Minutes or *SA*. The FBI forms for proving one's citizenship and their promotion by the Guild as policy by Ronald Reagan are in *Minutes,* February 9, 1942, p. 2014.

29. On the linkage of mass consumption and wartime goals and nationalism, see Blum, *V Was for Victory,* pp. 31–54, 90–117. For the Guild's and the industry's role, see "Radio," *SA* (July 1942), p. 4; "Mobilization," *SA* (June 1943), p. 4; "Marching Men," *SA* (June 1942), p. 13; "SAG Cited by Army and Navy," *SA* (April 1946), p. 4; James Cagney, "Spirit of '42," *SA* (June 1942), p. 9. *This Is the Army* is on video. See Leonard Maltin, *TV Movies and Video Guide* (New York: Signet Books, 1999). See also *This Is the Army* file in MOMA.

30. As late as 1945, the Guild leadership proclaimed its neutrality. See *Minutes,* October 16, 1945, pp. 2884–92, 2915. But then the *Minutes* of February 18, 1946, say the IA will lock out CSU members but must have the support of the Guild. *Minutes* of August 20, 1946, pp. 2853–54, record the Guild's support. See Ronald Reagan to Honorable Ralph W. Gwinning, March 2, 1948, SAG files. On the CSU pickets' hatred of the actors, see *CSU News* (June–August 1943), Hollywood Strike file, University of California Special Collections (hereafter known as Strike Folder).

31. Reagan and Hubler, *Where's the Rest of Me?,* p. 245.

32. Ibid. The quotation comes from "Ronald Reagan Testifies He Didn't Know Jeffers," *Los Angeles Times,* unpaginated clipping, probably January 1951, in Ronald Reagan file, *Los Angeles Times Library,* Los Angeles, California.

33. See Andersen, "Red Hollywood," for a fine survey of the vast literature on the Hollywood HUAC hearings. For an account of HUAC's hearings in the thirties and the public response, see Rosten, *Hollywood,* pp. 140–153.

34. The general political and social events informing anticommunist crusading can be found in Sherry, *Shadow of War,* pp. 123–187. For an account of these events from the standpoint of a liberal anticommunist, see Whitfield, *The Culture of the Cold War.* On the details of the crusade in Hollywood, see Larry Ceplair and Steven Englund, *The Inquisition in Hollywood: Politics in the Film Community, 1930–1960* (Garden City, N.Y.: Doubleday, 1980). On the Soviet's requirement of American Communist Party members to spy in the United States during World War II, see John Earl Haynes and Harvey Klehr, *Venona: Decoding Soviet Espionage in America* (New Haven: Yale University Press, 1999).

35. On the universities and the Red Scare, see Ellen Schrecker, *No Ivory Tower: McCarthyism and the Universities* (New York: Oxford University Press, 1986). See Mathew Levy testimony, *Jurisdictional Disputes,* p. 2428. Levy also served in the American Socialist Party and was elected a supreme court judge in New York in 1950. See Mathew Levy obituary, *New York Times,* September 5, 1971, p. 41. See also Myron Fagan speech, April 12, 1948, SAG files.

36. Ceplair and Englund, *Inquisition in Hollywood;* Wills, *Reagan's America,* pp. 231–261; Johnston, *America Unlimited,* pp. 152–160; Victor Navasky, *Naming Names* (New York: Viking Press, 1980); Eric Johnston, *The Hollywood Hearings* (Washington, D.C.: Motion Picture Association of America, 1947), pp. 1–10.

37. Elia Kazan, *A Life* (New York: Anchor Books, 1989), pp. 448–460. For the Dmytryk confession, see Richard English, "What Makes a Hollywood Communist?" *Saturday Evening Post,* May 19, 1951, pp. 30–31, 147–148.

38. Reagan and Hubler, *Where's the Rest of Me?,* pp. 160–161; Dales, SAG Oral History Project, p. 38, SAG files; Dales, Oral History Project, UCLA, pp. 34, 51; *Minutes,* Annual Meeting, October 2, 1946, p. 3092; "Special Membership Meeting," *SA* (January 1947), pp. 4–12; *Screen Actor's Guild Intelligence Report,* May 15 and June 16, 1947.

39. The elimination of public activities on the part of the Guild is based on a survey conducted from 1946 to 1955 by the *Screen Actors Intelligence Report,* the journal that replaced *Screen Actor* for several years after 1946. (*Screen Actor* was later revived.) On the Guild's new arbitration boards, see Eric Johnston, "Motion Picture Industry Council," *New York Daily News,* unpaginated, undated article, probably about 1948, in Motion Picture Industry Council file, AMPAS, Los Angeles, California (hereafter cited as *MPIC*); Lillian

Ross, "Onward and Upward with the Arts," *New Yorker,* February 21, 1948, pp. 32–48. For loyalty oaths, see SAG Press Release, April 10, 1951. For their clear implementation in SAG, see Board of Directors to Gale Sondergaard, March 20, 1951, SAG files.

40. Marsha Hunt interview, *SA* (January 1998), pp. 10–15.

41. Wills, *Reagan's America,* pp. 251–261; B. B. Kahane to Mrs. Ronald Reagan, January 7, 1952, SAG files; Jack Dales, SAG Oral History Project, 1979, pp. 12–13, SAG files. For an insightful view of the wider political implications of the Hollywood anticommunist crusade from the standpoint of one of those blacklisted, see Abraham Polonsky, "How the Blacklist Worked in Hollywood," *Film Culture* (Fall 1970), pp. 50–51.

42. *Salt of the Earth* file, SAG files. The quotation is from "Statement of Facts and Some Conclusions RE Motion Picture Being Made in Silver City, New Mexico" (February 1953), SAG files. See Victor Reisel, "Inside Labor," Post-Hall Syndicate, February 9, 1953, SAG files.

43. For Garfield, see Andersen, "Red Hollywood," pp. 177–191. For stories and pictures of Chaplin supporting the CSU rallies in favor of the Progressive party and Wallace, see *CSU News,* May 24, 1947. See also Eric Johnston, "Mr. Wallace Proposes Appeasement," unpaginated and undated clipping, *MPIC. Los Angeles Times,* January 16, 1948, and October 5, 1948, noted that Ronald Reagan's first act as chairman of the Film Council of the American Federation of Labor (AFL) was to "denounce Wallace." On the CSU, Garfield, and Chaplin in the Wallace campaigns, see *Hollywood Citizen* (January 1948). On Chaplin and the FBI, see Timothy J. Lyons, "The United States versus Charlie Chaplin," *American Film* (September 1984), pp. 29–34. See also "Roy Brewer Blasts Lessing for Branding IA 'Selfish,' Takes New Jab at Chaplin," *V,* undated clipping, about 1952, *MPIC.*

44. Philip K. Scheur, "Moss Hart Hits Hollywood as Totalitarian, Frightened," *Los Angeles Times,* March 2, 1947, and *"State of the Union* to Pace Election," *Los Angeles Times,* September 28, 1947; Joseph Losey interview, in Michael Ciment, *Conversations with Losey* (New York and London: Methene, 1983), pp. 81–82. See Lewis Milestone, *All Quiet on the Western Front* speech, about 1948, in Milestone Special Collections, AMPAS.

45. For Johnston's concern that the correct view of the nation inform films, see Testimony of Eric Johnston, *HUAC 1947,* pp. 305–310. See also Johnston, *The Hollywood Hearings,* pp. 1–10. Details and exact reproductions of the new Code can be found in Munby, *Public Enemies, Public Heroes,* pp. 227–240. See *A Screen Guide for Americans* (Beverly Hills: Motion Picture Alliance for the Preservation of American Ideals, 1948), pp. 1–12; Ross, "Onward and Upward," pp. 32–48.

46. I am indebted to David Eldrige and Nick Cull for showing me this material based on their research. The declassified letters to the CIA can be found in C. D. Jackson Records, 1953–1954, Box 5, Movies File, Case File, "Dear Owen," January 24, January 27, and February 6, 1953, Dwight D. Eisenhower Library, Abeline, Kansas.

47. Ibid., January 27, 1953; March 9, 1953.

48. All these films are on video. See Maltin, *Video Guide.*

49. All these films are on video. See Maltin, *Video Guide.* The quotation comes from a program for *The Robe* created for the opening night premiere. See *The Robe* file, AMPAS. See also Thomas P. Doherty, *Projections of War: Hollywood, American Culture, and World War II* (New York: Columbia University Press, 1993), pp. 260–275, who also sees that World War II provided the reference point for many westerns and war films after 1945. A fine exploration of postwar westerns can be found in John H. Lenihan, *Showdown: Confronting Modern America in the Western Film* (Urbana: University of Illinois Press, 1980).

50. Doherty, *Projections of War;* Lenihan, *Showdown.*

51. Ultimately the rise in violence also suggests that beneath the culture of classlessness that scholars see informing the fifties was a threat of violence to enforce conformity. See Roland Marchand, "Visions of Classlessness, Quests for Dominion: American Popular Culture, 1845–1960," in Robert H. Bremner and Gary W. Reichard, eds., *Reshaping America: Society and Institutions, 1945–1960* (Columbus: Ohio State University Press, 1982), pp. 163–196. Though Marchand does not relate classlessness to the ethos of war and the threat of

violence, a recent scholar does make some of the connections that I do. See Sherry, *In the Shadow of War.*

52. See Gary Wills, *John Wayne: The Politics of Celebrity* (New York: Simon and Schuster, 1998). The limitation of Wills's view is that he sees Wayne as emblematic of the essentialized western hero. This view ignores that Will Rogers had a much different view of the cowboy, the West, and the frontier hero during the thirties.

53. See Steven Watts, *The Magic Kingdom: Walt Disney and the American Way of Life* (New York: Houghton Mifflin, 1997), pp. 63–183, 283–455.

54. On the rejection of the NAACP request and the desire to protect members' "Sambo" roles, see *Minutes,* May 24, 1943, p. 2355, and October 20, 1947. "The Negro Question" and "Negro Employment Committee" box in SAG archives has this material. See especially Statement by Lena Horne; "Even Negro Stars Can't Crack Hollywood's Jim Crow Policy," *Daily People's World,* August 4, 1952; and Report of the Meeting of Negro Employment Committee, March 18, 1952.

55. C. D. Jackson Records, Letter, January 24, 1953.

56. For a full analysis of these films and their impact, see Thomas Cripps, *Making Movies Black: The Hollywood Message Movie from World War II to the Civil Rights Era* (New York: Oxford University Press, 1993), pp. 215–250.

57. In many ways this racial dynamic of good and bad minority continues earlier patterns. See Alexander Saxton, "The Racial Trajectory of the Western Hero," *Amerasia* 11, no. 2 (1984): 67–79.

58. Philip Scheur, "Jennifer Jones Due for Film Boom After a Long Absence," *Los Angeles Times,* July 27, 1952. For Davis in the war, see *Los Angeles Times,* July 25, 1942. On her performing for black troops, see *Hollywood Citizen News,* July 27, 1942. See also "Bette Davis Deplores the Man's Age in Films," *Los Angeles Times,* May 22, 1945, and "Bette Tells What's Wrong with Movies," *Los Angeles Times,* June 8, 1948. All the articles are in Bette Davis file, AMPAS.

59. For the war on amusements, see Lewis Erenberg, *Swingin' the Dream: Big Band Jazz and the Rebirth of American Culture* (Chicago: University of Chicago Press, 1998), pp. 241–253. On the pressures to restore traditional sexual and family roles, see May, *Homeward Bound.*

60. On Hayworth's transformation of herself from Spanish to white under the aegis of her first husband, see *San Diego Union,* August 10, 1941. On her face and figure on the atomic bomb, see "Bombed and Buried," *Motion Picture Herald,* April 12, 1947. See "Club Women Plan Boycott on Hayworth Pix," *V,* January 13, 1949; "Rita's Conduct Flayed by British Newspapers," *Los Angeles Times,* January 9, 1949. On liaison with a "colored man," see Robert Ruark, *New York Daily News,* January 17, 1949; "Film Chieftains Study Hayworth Situation in Florida," *V,* January 19, 1949. The quotation is from W. R. Wilkerson, "Trade News," *Hollywood Reporter,* January 13, 1949. All articles are in Rita Hayworth file, AMPAS.

61. On the culture of consumerism in the Cold War era, see Eric Foner, *The Story of Freedom* (New York: W. W. Norton, 1988), pp. 264–266. See also May, *Homeward Bound.*

62. Reagan and Hubler, *Where's the Rest of Me?,* pp. 160–161; Dales, Oral History Project, p. 38, SAG files; Dales, Oral History Project, UCLA, pp. 34, 51; *Minutes,* Annual Meeting, October 2, 1946, p. 3092; "Special Membership Meeting," *SA* (January 1947), pp. 4–12; *Screen Actor's Guild Intelligence Report,* May 15 and June 16, 1947.

63. "Speakers Kit," 1948, SAG file; Ronald Reagan, "Special Editorial to the *Hartford Times,*" October 8, 1951, SAG files. The quotation is from *Dixon Evening Telegraph,* August 22, 1950, cited in Wills, *Reagan's America,* p. 144.

Chapter Six

1. Ralph Ellison, *The Invisible Man* (New York: Random House, 1947), pp. 441–444.

2. Arthur Miller, *Timebends: A Life* (New York: Grove Press, 1987), pp. 149, 302, 320, 341, 350.

3. Ibid., pp. 180–200, 305–360.

4. For the debate over the causes of postwar culture, see Lary May, ed., *Recasting America: Culture and Politics in the Age of Cold War* (Chicago: University of Chicago Press, 1989). For a fine book that explores the work of left-wing filmmakers in Hollywood, though the crisis of identity and the new culture of anxiety are not his main concerns, see Brian Neve, *Film and Politics in America: A Social Tradition* (London: Routledge, 1992).

5. Humanists' analysis of film noir is vast and often highly sophisticated. A listing of all the films, with accurate plot descriptions and complete bibliography, can be found in Alain Silver and Elizabeth Ward, *Film Noir: An Encyclopaedic Reference to the American Style* (Woodstock, New York: The Overlook Press, 1979). A quick point of entry to the scholarly analysis is in Alain Silver and James Ursini, eds., *Film Noir Reader* (New York: Limelight Editions, 1996). The application of Foucault theories to the genre is the subject of J. P. Telotte, *Voices in the Dark: The Narrative Patterns of Film Noir* (Urbana: University of Illinois Press, 1989). Film noir's place within the classic genres promoted by the studios is the subject of Frank Krutnik, *In a Lonely Street: Film Noir, Genre and Masculinity* (London: Routledge, 1991). Dana Polan, *Power and Paranoia: History, Narrative and the American Cinema* (New York: Columbia University Press, 1986), accurately places the disrupted narratives of film noir in the context of new power constellations. Two recent books see film noir in some of the terms evident in this chapter: Jonathan Munby, *Public Enemies, Public Heroes: Screening the Gangster from* Little Caesar *to* Touch of Evil (Chicago: University of Chicago Press, 1999), pp. 186–221, and James Naremore, *More Than Night: Film Noir and Its Contexts* (Berkeley: University of California Press, 1998).

The best single book on the development of youth culture in film and the new consumer culture is James Gilbert, *A Cycle of Outrage: America's Reaction to the Juvenile Delinquent in the 1950's* (New York: Oxford University Press, 1986). A tentative outline of the continuity in several key areas between the left-wing artists of the thirties and forties and the counterculture of the sixties informs Michael Denning, *The Cultural Front: The Laboring of American Culture in the Twentieth Century* (New York: Verso, 1996), pp. 463–473. My point will be that the continuity is even more overt in the move from film noir to youth culture films and that all represented a response to the crisis of Americanism and the closing down of an alternative public life.

6. Orson Welles, "Twilight in the Smog," *Esquire* (March 1959), pp. 53–54.

7. Generally the ideologically conservative politics of film noir have been slighted. For the start of a corrective, see the splendid article by Philip Kemp, "From the Nightmare Factory: HUAC and the Politics of Noir," *Sight and Sound* 55, no. 1 (Autumn 1986): 266–270.

8. John Alton, *Painting with Light* (Berkeley: University of California Press, 1995), pp. 44–45.

9. All these films are on video. See Leonard Maltin, *TV Movies and Video Guide* (New York: New American Library, 1998). On FBI cooperation and collaboration in making *The House on 92nd Street,* see Philip K. Scheur, "Cameras Use F.B.I. Haunts for Adventure in Reality," *Los Angeles Times,* July 22, 1945.

10. Philip Scheur, "Interview with Richard Widmark on the Set of *Kiss of Death,*" *Los Angeles Times,* 1947, undated clipping in *Kiss of Death* file, AMPAS. The film is on video. See Maltin, *Video Guide.*

11. All these films are on video. For particular selections, see Maltin, *Video Guide.*

12. *A Double Life* is on video. See Maltin, *Video Guide.* See also Eric Lott, "The Whiteness of Film Noir," in *Whiteness: A Critical Reader,* ed. Mike Hill (New York: New York University Press, 1997), pp. 81–101.

13. For the war on drugs and vice that pervaded the postwar era, especially as it affected jazz musicians, see Lewis Erenberg, *Swingin' the Dream: Big Band Jazz and the Rebirth of American Culture* (Chicago: University of Chicago Press, 1998), pp. 240–255. See also Scheur, Widmark interview, *Kiss of Death* file, AMPAS; Philip Scheur, "Hitch Your Mystery to a Star, but Let Your Audience in on It, Says Hitch," *Los Angeles Times,* February 15, 1953.

14. For a prime example of historians' desire to ignore the Cold War in explaining the

dynamics of popular art and politics over the century that both summarizes and advances this position as the common wisdom, see Jean Christophe Agnew, "Coming Up for Air: Consumer Culture in Historical Perspective," *Intellectual History Newsletter* 12 (1990): 3–22. For the rise of the new sensibility, that of optimism and despair in the postwar era, see May, *Recasting America.*

15. The problem of the "movies" and the declining audience was the subject of several discussions. See Eric Hodgins, "A Roundtable on the Movies," *Life,* (June 1949), pp. 90–110. "Floppolas" quotation comes from "Stars Not Main Draw," *V,* January 7, 1948, p. 2. A good look at the internal industry discussion can be found in "Top Execs Accept Quality Film as Sole Antidote for That So-Called Lost Audience," *V,* January 4, 1950, pp. 5–6. See also "Flop of Pix with High Voltage Names Makes Rating of Top Stars Dubious," *V,* January 5, 1949, p. 1. On the penetration of television, year by year, into percentages of the population, see Irving Bernstein, "The Economics of Television Film Production and Distribution," (Hollywood: Motion Picture Industry Council, 1959), p. 4. For falling profits and the fracturing of the studio system, see Irving Bernstein, *Hollywood at the Crossroads: An Economic Study of the Motion Picture Industry* (Hollywood: American Federation of Labor Film Council, 1957).

16. Bernstein, *Hollywood at the Crossroads.* See Douglas Gomery, "The Coming of Television and the 'Lost' Motion Picture Audience," *Journal of Film and Video* 37, no. 3 (1985), pp. 5–12, and Thomas Schutz, *Boom and Bust: American Cinema in the 1940s* (Berkeley: University of California Press, 1998).

17. For the decline of amusements, particularly in relation to some of the major entertainments of the era—swing music, dance halls, and nightclubs—see Erenberg, *Swingin' the Dream,* pp. 211–218.

18. The postwar war on drugs that affected many stars in music and film is outlined in Erenberg, *Swingin' the Dream,* pp. 241–253. On Robert Mitchum, drug raids, and the police and film industry response, see "Dope Arrests," *Los Angeles Herald Examiner,* September 2, 1948.

19. For the war on amusements, see Erenberg, *Swingin' the Dream,* pp. 241–253. On the pressures to restore traditional sexual and family roles, see Elaine Tyler May, *Homeward Bound: American Families in the Cold War Era* (New York: Basic Books, 1988).

20. On the industry's cooperation with the Pentagon in banning *All Quiet on the Western Front* in Europe and discouraging its reissue, since it was in "bad taste to reissue the film at this time" in the United States, see the *Hollywood Reporter,* September 22, 1950. See also "All Quiet on the Western Front," *New York Daily News,* September 22, 1950, unpaginated clippings, *All Quiet on the Western Front* file, AMPAS. On Rogers, see "What This Picture Did for Me," *MPH,* January 19, 1952.

21. Abraham Polonsky interview, in Eric Sherman and Martin Rubin, *The Director's Event: Interviews with Five American Film Makers* (New York: Athenaeum, 1970), pp. 3–38.

22. A fine survey of Orson Welles's left-wing activities can be found in Denning, *The Cultural Front,* pp. 362–403. See also John Francis Kreidl, *Nicholas Ray* (Boston: Twayne, 1977); Michael Goodwin and Naomi Wise, "Nicholas Ray, Rebel!" *Take One* (January 1977); Michel Ciment, *Conversations with Losey* (London: Methuen, 1985); Peter Bogdanovich, "Edgar Ulmer: An Interview," *Film Culture,* nos. 58–60 (1974), pp. 189–238. On Polonsky, see Christine Noll Brinckmann, "The Politics of *Force of Evil:* An Analysis of Abraham Polonsky's Pre-blacklist Film," *Prospects: The Annual of American Culture Studies* 16 (1981): 357–386. See also Philip Scheur, "Anatole Litvak—A Movie Career on Two Continents," *Los Angeles Times,* February 19, 1967; "Anatole Litvak, 72, Dies in Paris," *V,* December 12, 1974.

23. Ciment, *Conversations with Losey,* p. 98.

24. "Billy Wilder," *Architectural Digest* (April 1994).

25. Gerald Pratley, *The Cinema of John Huston* (South Brunswick: A. S. Barnes, 1977); John Huston, "World Brotherhood Speech," 1955, in John Huston Special Collections, AMPAS; Gideon Bachman, "Interview with John Huston," *Film Culture* 2, no. 28 (1956);

"How I Make Films: An Interview with John Huston," *Film Quarterly* (Fall 1965), pp. 3–13; John Huston, "Do Movies Tend to Raise or Lower Moral Standards?" radio speech, 1947, in John Huston, Special Collections, AMPAS. The engagement of film noir moviemakers with left-wing causes and modernism is also the subject of Naremore, *More Than Night,* pp. 96–136.

26. John Huston, *An Open Book* (New York: Ballantine Books, 1980), pp. 67–68.

27. Ibid., p. 171. For a brilliant examination of these developments, see Thomas Crow, "Modernism and Mass Culture in the Visual Arts," in Benjamin H. D. Buchloh, Serge Guilbaut, and David Solkin, eds., *Modernism and Modernity* (Halifax, Nova Scotia: The Press of Nova Scotia College of Art and Design, 1981), pp. 215–264.

28. "Billy Wilder Interview," *Los Angeles Reader,* March 21, 1986, unpaginated clippings in Wilder file, AMPAS.

29. "Movies File," C. D. Jackson Records, 1953–1954, Box 5, Letter 7, January 24, 1953, Eisenhower Library, Abilene, Kansas.

30. Andrew Sinclair, *Spiegel: The Man Behind the Pictures* (Boston: Little Brown, 1987), pp. 24–70. Spiegel was Huston's independent producer for several films. Spiegel, like the Hollywood salon culture that he helped galvanize, was also an Austrian Jewish refugee who fled the Nazis before he came to Hollywood. The outlines of this refugee community and its relation to many left-wing moviemakers can be teased out of Otto Friedrich, *City of Nets: A Portrait of Hollywood in the 1940's* (New York: Harper and Row, 1986), pp. 270–277.

31. "Richard Brooks: The Professional," in Pat McGilligan, ed., *Backstory: Interviews with Screenwriters of the 1940's and 1950's* (hereafter cited as *Backstory 2*) (Berkeley: University of California Press, 1991), p. 44. Brooks worked for Hellinger as a writer and until his death in 1992 still received a yearly check for the films he wrote with Hellinger.

32. See James J. Parker, "The Organizational Environment of the Motion Picture Sector," in Sandra J. Ball-Rokeach and Muriel G. Cantor, eds., *Media, Audience and Social Structure* (London: Sage Publications, 1986), pp. 143–161.

33. Huston, *An Open Book,* p. 171. On films banned in occupied Europe, see Reinhold Wagnleitner, "The Irony of American Culture Abroad: Austria and the Cold War," in May, *Recasting America,* pp. 285–301.

34. Robert Siodmak, "Hoodlums: The Myth," in Richard Koszarski, ed., *Hollywood Directors, 1941–1976* (New York: Oxford University Press, 1977), pp. 283–289.

35. All the cited films are on video. See Maltin, *Video Guide.* The single best description and analysis of the film noir style can be found in Paul Schrader, "Notes on Film Noir," in Silver and Ursini, *Film Noir Reader,* pp. 53–65. See also Siodmak, "Hoodlums." The quotes are from Bosley Crowther, "Violence Erupts Again," *New York Times,* October 1, 1946; John Houseman, "Today's Hero: A Review," *Hollywood Quarterly* 4 (July 1947): 161–163; Abraham Polonsky, "'Odd Man Out' and 'Monsieur Verdoux,'" *Hollywood Quarterly* 2 (December 1946): 401–407.

36. W. R. Burnett, "The Outsider," interview by Ken Mate and Pat McGilligan, in McGilligan, ed., *Backstory: Interviews with Screenwriters of Hollywood's Golden Age* (Berkeley: University of California Press, 1986), p. 63; Daniel Mainwaring, "Americana," interview by Tom Flinn, in McGilligan, *Backstory 2,* p. 196; Philip Jordan, "The Chameleon," interview by Pat McGilligan, in McGilligan, *Backstory 2,* pp. 331–381. The Polonsky quotation comes from an interview in Brinckmann, "The Politics of *Force of Evil,*" p. 386.

37. Kevin Lally, *Wilder Times: The Life of Billy Wilder* (New York: Henry Holt and Co., 1996), pp. 1–53.

38. Ibid., pp. 63–168, 220–221.

39. Philip Scheur, "Wilder Seeks Films with 'Bite' to Satisfy a 'Nation of Hecklers,'" *Los Angeles Times,* August 20, 1950; "Interview with Billy Wilder," Screen Writers Guild Oral History Project, February 1993, in Wilder file, AMPAS; Aljean Harmetz, "Seven Years Without Directing and Billy Wilder Is Feeling Itchy," *New York Times,* October 3, 1988. On his early career in the Writers Guild, see "Billy Wilder Writes Some Words for Striking Scribes," *V,* July 25, 1988. For his love and fear for "America," see Michiko Kakutani, "Ready for His Close Up," *New York Times,* July 28, 1996.

40. For a description of the film *Hold Back the Dawn* and the quotation, see Lally, *Wilder Times*, pp. 98–104.

41. Huston recounts his family's past and patriotic commitments in Lillian Ross, *Picture* (New York: Reinhard, 1950), pp. 50–70.

42. Huston, "How I Make Films."

43. Huston, *An Open Book,* pp. 29–40.

44. Huston, *An Open Book,* pp. 56–58; Pratley, *John Huston;* Howard Koch, *As Time Goes By: Memoirs of a Writer* (New York and London: Harcourt Brace Jovanovich, 1979), pp. 65–68; Rui Nogueira and Bertrand Tavernier, "Interview with John Huston," in Gaylyn Studlar and David Desser, eds., *Reflections in a Male Eye: John Huston and the American Experience* (Washington: Smithsonian Institution Press, 1993), pp. 212–220.

45. Huston, *An Open Book,* pp. 81–83. See Axel Madsen, *William Wyler* (New York: Thomes C. Crowell Co., 1973), pp. 73–90.

46. A complete description, along with photos and some reviews, of Huston's films can be found in John McCarty, *The Complete Films of John Huston* (Secaucus, N.J.: Citadel Press, 1987). All of Huston's films are on video. See Maltin, *Video Guide.* Huston's recounting of the making of his war documentaries can be found in John Huston, "The Courage of the Men: An Interview with John Huston," in *Film Book 2,* ed. Robert Hughes (New York: Grove Press, 1962), pp. 22–35. See also Gary Edgerton, "Revisiting the Recordings of Wars Past: Remembering the Documentary Trilogy of John Huston," in Studlar and Desser, *Reflections,* pp. 33–61. On the portrayal of black soldiers, see letter from Ernestine Evans to John Huston, March 6, 1946, *Let There Be Light* file, John Huston Collection, AMPAS. See also Huston, *An Open Book,* pp. 138–142. On Huston's queries as to why *Let There Be Light* was banned from distribution, see letter, April 15, 1945, to G. Menninger, *Let There Be Light* file, John Huston Collection, AMPAS.

47. Huston's support of progressive political causes and resistance to HUAC can be garnered from two sources. The first is Nogueira and Tavernier, "Interview with John Huston," pp. 223–225. The second source is the letters and speeches during the period of 1946–1948 in John Huston Collection, AMPAS. The quotations come from John Huston, "Speech Before Progressive Citizens of America," July 9, 1949, and "Speech Before Henry Wallace Rally," 1948, in John Huston Collection, AMPAS.

48. Huston, *An Open Book,* pp. 15–153; Nogueira and Tavernier, "Interview with John Huston," pp. 222–224.

49. W. H. M., *The Tidings,* May 6, 1949, clipping in *We Were Strangers* file, Production Code Administration Papers, AMPAS; "Los Angeles Federation of Women's Clubs," *Los Angeles Times,* May 13, 1949. *MPH,* May 28, 1949, repeats the charge. See *Hollywood Reporter,* April 22, 1949; Robert Sklar, "The Havana Episode: The Revolutionary Situation of *We Were Strangers,*" in Studlar and Desser, *Reflections,* pp. 63–78.

50. Nogueira and Tavernier, "Interview with John Huston," p. 224.

51. See Huston, "How I Make Films," p. 6. The quotation comes from Otis L. Guernsey, Jr., "The Playbill: John Huston, the 'Sierra Madre' Man," *New York Herald Tribune,* January 30, 1949.

52. Huston, "How I Make Films," p. 6.

53. Huston best articulated the aesthetic principles and philosophy that guided his work at the end of his autobiography. See Huston, *An Open Book,* pp. 407–413.

54. Huston articulates this view in his speech, "Do Movies Tend to Raise or Lower Our Moral Standards," in John Huston file, Special Collections, AMPAS. See also Ross, *Picture,* p. 150.

55. Ross, *Picture,* p. 144.

56. The best contemporary analysis of Huston's film style can be found in a reprint of an article that first appeared in *Life* magazine in 1950. See James Agee, "Undirectable Director," in Studlar and Desser, *Reflections,* pp. 255–267.

57. See Huston, "How I Make Films," pp. 12–13; "Interview with John Huston," *Movie*

World Weekly, undated and unpaginated article, probably from the 1970s, in John Huston file, Special Collections, AMPAS.

58. "Interview with John Huston," *Movie World Weekly.*

59. *Double Indemnity* is available on video. See Maltin, *Video Guide.*

60. For the Wilder quotation, and comments about blondes and the characters as "grown up as you and I," see "Interview with Billy Wilder," *Los Angeles Times,* August 6, 1944, "Double Indemnity," *The Hollywood Reporter,* April 24, 1944, and "Barbara Stanwyck Interview," *Paramount News* (March 1944), all in *Double Indemnity* Production file, AMPAS.

61. An excellent analysis of *Double Indemnity* and its production can be found in Naremore, *More Than Night,* pp. 81–95.

62. Ibid.

63. Scheur, "Wilder Seeks Films with 'Bite' to Satisfy a 'Nation of Hecklers'"; "Interview with Billy Wilder," Screen Writers Guild Oral History Project, in Wilder file, AMPAS.

64. An excellent description and analysis of *Sunset Boulevard* can be found in Lois Banner, *In Full Flower: Aging Women, Power and Sexuality* (New York: Alfred Knopf, 1992), pp. 25–57. All the cited films are on video. See Maltin, *Video Guide.* The argument that the alienated characters in film noir cannot psychologically escape the ideals and motivations determined by established institutions is fully developed in Telotte, *Voices in the Dark.* The theory guiding Tellote's analysis derives from the French theorist Michel Foucault.

65. *High Sierra* (1941) is on video. See Maltin, *Video Guide.* The script, from which I derive the quotations, has been published. See Douglas Gomery, ed., *High Sierra* (Madison: University of Wisconsin Press, 1979), pp. 42–43, 74, 80.

66. Ezra Goodman, "The Asphalt Jungle," *Los Angeles Daily News,* June 22, 1950; Bosley Crowther, "The Asphalt Jungle," *New York Times,* June 23, 1950; "The Asphalt Jungle," *Independent Film Journal,* September 6, 1950; "The Asphalt Jungle," *Los Angeles Times,* June 21, 1950.

67. "The Asphalt Jungle," *Los Angeles Times,* June 21, 1950. For Huston on criminals, see Ezra Goodman, *Los Angeles Daily News,* March 13, 1950. See also James Agee to John Huston, letter, September 13, 1950, John Huston Collection, AMPAS.

68. *Treasure of the Sierra Madre* is on video. See Maltin, *Video Guide.*

69. An excellent article on the relation between B. Traven's book and the film is John Engell, "Traven, Huston and the Textual Treasures of *The Treasure of the Sierre Madre,*" in Studlar and Desser, *Reflections,* pp. 79–95. Engell is far too dismissive, as are most film and cultural historians, of the "Jeffersonian" tradition, which he rightly sees as central to the film. For the screenplay and an introduction by James Naremore, see John Huston, *The Treasure of the Sierra Madre* (Madison: University of Wisconsin Press, 1979). All of the quotations are from this publication. See also the extraordinary series of letters written between B. Traven and John Huston while Huston wrote the script. They are in Huston Special Collections, AMPAS.

70. Miller, *Timebends,* p. 366.

71. Susan Ray, introduction, *I Was Interrupted: Nicholas Ray on Making Movies* (Berkeley: University of California Press, 1993), p. xxii.

72. All of these films are on video. See Maltin, *Video Guide.* The quotation comes from Edgar Moran, "The Case of James Dean," *Evergreen Review,* no. 5 (1958).

73. *Some Like It Hot* is on video. See Maltin, *Video Guide.*

74. For the heart of what Strasberg called the "ideology" behind the "method," see Lee Strasberg, *A Dream of Passion: The Development of the Method* (Boston: Little, Brown and Co., 1987), pp. 198–201. See also Harold Clurman, *The Fervent Years: The Group Theatre and the 30's* (New York: Harcourt Brace Jovanovich, 1975), pp. 281–313. On Kazan's involvement, see Thomas H. Pauly, *An American Odyssey: Elia Kazan and American Culture* (Philadelphia: Temple University Press, 1983), pp. 13–56.

75. Michael Sheridan, "Why Brando Baffles Hollywood," *Movieland* (June 1952). The

quotation on society as neurotic comes from John V. Buffin, Jr., "Can Marlon Brando Be Tamed?" unidentified clipping in Marlon Brando file, AMPAS. See also Philip Scheur, "James Dean: I Have My Own Personal Revolts," *Los Angeles Times,* April 3, 1954.

76. The horrors of Monroe's childhood are one of the central themes in Gloria Steinem, *Marilyn: Norma Jean* (New York: H. Holt, 1986), pp. 54–79. This was also so important to her appeal that the publicity department gave reporters outlines of her early life for their stories. See Harry Brand, "Marilyn Monroe Biography," February 7, 1951, in Monroe file, AMPAS. The quotation is from Robert Cahn, "The 1951 Model Blonde," *Colliers,* September 8, 1951. On Dean, see Elia Kazan, *A Life* (New York: Doubleday, 1989), pp. 534–535; Evelyn Washburn Nielson, "The Truth About James Dean," *Chicago Sunday Tribune Magazine,* September 9, 1956. See also Sheridan, "Why Brando Baffles Hollywood."

77. Sheridan, "Why Brando Baffles Hollywood"; "The Enigma of Marlon Brando," *Silver Screen* (May 1962).

78. "Moody New Star: Hoosier James Dean Excites Hollywood," *Life,* March 7, 1955; "The Current Cinema," *New Yorker,* March 19, 1955.

79. Three contemporary writers, despite their otherwise different views of Marilyn, see her as a woman who challenged before her time, in a prefeminist form, set female roles. See Norman Mailer, *Marilyn: A Biography* (New York: Grosset and Dunlap, 1973); Richard Dyer, *Heavenly Bodies: Film Stars and Society* (Houndmills, Basingstoke: Macmillan, 1986), pp. 19–66; Gloria Steinem, *Marilyn.* The most insightful reading, however, is that by one of her three husbands, Arthur Miller, in *Timebends,* pp. 360–400. For the contemporary accounts that I draw on, see "Hollywood Topic A-Plus, Whole Town Talking About Marilyn Monroe," *Life* magazine, April 7, 1952, pp. 101–104; "Marilyn," *Movieland* (January 1952); Cahn, "The 1951 Model Blonde."

80. Miller, *Timebends,* pp. 320–400. For contemporary accounts, with amazed incredulity, of Monroe's intellectual interests, see Hedda Hopper, "They Call Her the Blowtorch Blonde," *Chicago Sunday Tribune,* May 4, 1952. On Dean, see the publicity material used by writers across the land to describe the new star, in "Biography of James Dean," Warner Brothers Biography, July 28, 1954, James Dean file, AMPAS. See also Sheridan, "Why Brando Baffles Hollywood"; "Marlon's New York," *Screen Guide* (August 1950). Both are in Marlon Brando file, AMPAS.

81. Arthur Miller clearly saw that their quest for authenticity and defiance of bourgeois norms aligned him and Marilyn with the ideas of the youthful male delinquents and their "life style." See Miller, *Timebends,* pp. 355–370. See also "Marlon's New York"; "Marlon Brando Interview: The Wild One," unidentified clipping, Marlon Brando file, AMPAS; Scheur, "I Have My Own Personal Revolts"; "Studio Ban on Racing, Broken Romance Told," *Herald Express,* October 1, 1955. A truly brilliant article detailing the impact of the youth films on German youth, particularly their association with black and working-class style that challenged the postwar consensus on sexual and racial roles in a way similar to that in the United States, is the subject of Uta Pager, "Rebels with a Cause? American Popular Culture, the 1956 Youth Riots and the New Conceptions of Masculinity in East and West Germany," in Reiner Pommerin, ed., *The American Impact on Postwar Germany* (Providence, Rhode Island: Berghahn Books, 1995), pp. 93–124. On Indonesian youth's attraction to these new stars, complete with emulating their blue jeans and t-shirts, see "Culture Note," *New York Times,* September 15, 1957.

82. "'Wild One' Craftsmanlike Film of Unpleasant Topic," *Hollywood Reporter* (December 23, 1953), p. 4; "The Wild One," *MPH,* December 26, 1953; "'Desire' Powerful Drama," *Hollywood Reporter,* June 14, 1951, p. 4. For the concept of the "white Negro," as described by Norman Mailer, see Jay Stevens, *Storming Heaven: LSD and the American Dream* (New York: Perennial Library, 1988), p. 117.

83. Bob Thomas, "Cheesecake Is No Deterrent to Marilyn's Acting Career," *Long Beach Press Telegram,* November 19, 1951. On the Ella Fitzgerald incident, see George Lipsitz,

Rainbow at Midnight: Class and Culture in Postwar America, (Urbana: University of Illinois Press, 1994). Chapter 1 has a fine portrait of Monroe's past and her place in the personal politics of postwar America. See also Steinem, *Marilyn,* pp. 81–105.

84. On the rise of the postwar youth culture, see James Gilbert, *A Cycle of Outrage.*

85. "The Wild One," *MPH,* December 26, 1953.

86. Letters to the Editor, *Life* (October 1956).

87. Miller, *Timebends,* pp. 366–367.

Epilogue

1. Benedict Anderson, *Imagined Communities: Reflections on the Origin and Spread of Nationalism* (London: Verso, 1983), pp. 127–146.

2. See Alexander Saxton, *The Rise and Fall of the White Republic: Class Politics and Mass Culture in Nineteenth Century America* (New York: Verso, 1990); Eric Foner, *The Story of Freedom* (New York: W. W. Norton and Co., 1998), pp. 3–195.

3. For a summary of contemporary purchasing power arguments, see Robert S. McElvaine, *The Great Depression in America, 1929–1941* (New York: Times Books, 1984), pp. 25–51.

4. See Warren Susman, *Culture as History: The Transformation of American Society in the Twentieth Century* (New York: Pantheon, 1984); Robert Sklar, *Movie Made America: A Cultural History of American Movies* (New York: Vintage Books, 1975), ch. 12; Neal Gabler, *An Empire of Their Own: How the Jews Invented Hollywood* (New York: Crown Publishers, 1988); Michael Rogin, *Blackface, White Noise: Jewish Immigrants in the Hollywood Melting Pot* (Berkeley: University of California Press, 1996).

5. See, for example, Thomas Schatz, *The Genius of the System: Hollywood Film Making in the Studio Era* (New York: Pantheon Books, 1988).

6. See David Bordwell, Janet Staiger, and Kristen Thompson, *The Classical Hollywood Cinema: Film Style and Mode of Production* (New York: Columbia University Press, 1985). On Marxist theory as the foundation for this approach, see pp. xiv–xv, 88–89. For their sampling technique, see pp. 388–389. For the view that the formal Hollywood style related intimately to a static, unchanging ideology of Americanism, see David Bordwell, "Happily Ever After, Part Two," *Velvet Light Trap,* no. 19 (Spring 1982), pp. 2–7. Still, for all its insight, the theory cannot account for the fact that in the late 1920s and 1930s, independent companies and upstart moviemakers challenged the dominance of the large studios; moreover, audiences were not passive but capable of forcing moviemakers to innovate in style, narration, and ideology. So while the theory of the "classic cinema" assumes that formal style reinforces a static "American" ideology of an "optimistic democracy," it also follows that when that ideology was contested, as it was in the thirties, major moviemakers like Lewis Milestone and others innovated on filmmaking they inherited from artists like D. W. Griffith and Cecil B. De Mille. World War II saw the studios consolidate their power over competitors, and during the Cold War they fired dissenting artists and imposed an official ideology and uniform style on moviemakers. Ironically, when the studios did try to impose a uniformity on the public, Hollywood began to lose audiences. In response, film noir productions made by remnants of the Hollywood left once again disrupted the inherited narrative and visual patterns. These artists drew on modernist techniques to alter form and content and portray characters who were not fixed but open to development. Here the camera moved inside the frame to explore a world that was not transparent but filled with heterogeneity, multiple focal points, and ambiguous lighting. Plots often disrupted clear cause-and-effect, and their closures, even happy ones, were capable of leaving viewers questioning official values of integration and heterosexual gender relations, particularly the ideal of the nuclear, suburban home.

7. Steven Ross, *Working Class Hollywood* (Princeton: Princeton University Press, 1998); Dana Polan, *Power and Paranoia: History, Narrative and the American Cinema, 1940–1950* (New York: Columbia University Press, 1986), pp. 17–18, 311; Fredric Jameson, "Reification

and Utopian Mass Culture," in *Signatures of the Visible* (New York: Routledge, 1992), pp. 9–34; Teresa De Lauretis, *Technologies of Gender: Essays on Theory, Film and Fiction* (Bloomington: Indiana University, 1987), p. 2. See also Jonathan Munby, *Public Enemies, Public Heroes: Screening the Gangster from* Little Caesar *to* Touch of Evil (Chicago: University of Chicago Press, 1999).

8. Mikhail Bakhtin, *The Dialogical Imagination* (Austin: University of Texas Press, 1981); Antonio Gramsci, *Selections from Prison Notebooks,* ed. Quintin Hoare and Geoffrey Smith (New York: International Publishers, 1971); George Lipsitz, *Time Passages: Collective Memory and American Popular Culture* (Minneapolis: University of Minnesota Press, 1990); Stuart Hall, "Notes on Deconstructing the Popular," in Raphael Samuel, ed., *People's History and Socialist Theory* (London: Routledge, Kegan Paul, 1981), p. 228; Lawrence Levine, *The Unpredictable Past* (New York: Oxford University Press, 1993).

9. John Clellon Holmes, "15 Cents Before 6 PM: The Wonderful Movies of the Thirties," *Harper's* (December 1965), pp. 51–55.

10. See S. Paige Baty, *American Monroe: The Making of a Body Politic* (Berkeley: University of California Press, 1995), p. 62.

11. Tom Hayden, "Memoirs," *Rolling Stone* (1972), in Godfrey Hodgson, *America in Our Time* (New York: Vintage Books, 1978), p. 280.

12. Rui Nogueira and Bertrand Tavernier, "Interview with John Huston," in Gaylyn Studlar and David Desser, eds., *Reflections in a Male Eye: John Huston and the American Experience* (Washington: Smithsonian Institution Press, 1993), p. 237.

13. Robert Scheer, *With Enough Shovels: Reagan, Bush and Nuclear War* (New York: Random House, 1982), pp. 42–43.

Film Index

Page numbers in italics refer to illustrations.

Subject Index

Page numbers in italics refer to illustrations.